The *Riddling* between Oedipus and the Sphinx

Ontology, Hauntology, and Heterologies of the Grotesque

Yuan Yuan

University Press of America,® Inc.
Lanham • Boulder • New York • Toronto • Plymouth, UK

4501 Forbes Boulevard, Suite 200, Lanham, Maryland 20706
UPA Acquisitions Department (301) 459-3366

Unit A, Whitacre Mews, 26-34 Stannary Street,
London SE11 4AB, United Kingdom

Printed in the United States of America
British Library Cataloguing in Publication Information Available

Library of Congress Control Number: 2015948939
ISBN: 978-0-7618-6662-6 (cloth : alk. paper)—ISBN: 978-0-7618-6663-3 (electronic)

∞™ The paper used in this publication meets the minimum requirements of American National Standard for Information Sciences Permanence of Paper for Printed Library Materials, ANSI/NISO Z39.48-1992.

Contents

Acknowledgments

Michel de Certeau in *The Practice of Everyday Life* reminds us that we never write on a blank page; instead, we always write on one that has already been written on. According to Bakhtin's *The Dialogic Imagination*, all texts are fraught with citations from other texts in terms of hybridizations, parodies, or dialogic exchanges. In this case, textual acknowledgements or inter-textual indebtedness to all scholars who inform this project are hardly possible. First, I would like to thank California State University San Marcos for granting me two sabbaticals as well as faculty research funds that help bring this project to fruition. Without all the institutional support, completion of the book would be extremely difficult. In particular, I am deeply indebted to two dear friends and respected colleagues, Prof. Martha Stoddard-Holmes and Prof. Salah Moukhlis, for their generous assistance to this project. Not only have they offered thorough reviews of the draft of the manuscript at various stages, but also provided insightful suggestions that helped clarify the focus of some critical issues. Also, I would also take this opportunity to express my gratitude to two brilliant scholars who initially introduced me to the enchanted fields of postmodernism and psychoanalysis: Prof. Ihab Hassan and Prof. Kathleen Woodward. In the realm of hauntology, I have traveled in good company with the awesome spirits of Nietzsche, Hegel, Freud, Lacan, Derrida, Bakhtin, and Anzaldúa as well as the inspiring minds of Butler, Kristeva, Irigaray, and Levinas besides various other theoretical ghosts or academic hosts whereof I am unaware.

Last but not least, I would like to thank my wife, Shan Shan and my daughters, Joanna and Erica, for their genuine support and enduring love.

Introduction

The Return of the Grotesque

All books start somewhere. This book on the grotesque evolves at the conjunction that interfaces with various textual, cultural, and theoretical spaces as well as responds to a number of invocations (past and present) via both provocative departures and evocative returns. According to Peter Brooks, the "masterplot" of repetition postulated in Freud's *Beyond the Pleasure Principle* involves both desiring for end and yeaning toward beginning. These repetitions of departure and return, in Brooks' words, "allow us to bind one textual moment to another" and link "different movements together as a middle which might turn forward or back."[1] In this case, the intricate *topos* of the grotesque, plotting against both beginning and ending, seems to suspend temporality and swing forever in the middle of both "return of" and "return to," thereby retrieving, rejoining, and unraveling the disheveled and obscure narrative networks dispersed discursively along numerous trajectories both forward and backward. In short, "somewhere" really means "elsewhere."

Years ago, I taught an undergraduate class on grotesque literature, of course, including those typical southern writers such as Flannery O'Connor, Nathaniel West, William Faulkner, Carson McCullers, Sherwood Anderson, and Eudora Welty. I anticipated some dis-ease (actually anxiety) due to some perplexing and disconcerting elements in this kind of narratives. Surprisingly, students not only loved the reading materials but also enthusiastically and intelligently assembled a comprehensive list of words to describe the grotesque in their group projects. Broken down into categories, here is what they came up with: "unusual, unexplainable, vague, weird, indeterminate, unbelievable, no synthesis, fragmented, displaced"; "supernatural, inhuman, subhuman, superhuman, demonic"; "isolation, alienation, violence, chaos, monster, other, horror, doom, misery, beyond ordinary"; "evil, gross, repulsive, ugly, bizarre, fearful, scary, twisted, distasteful, macabre, sickly, strange, disgusting, gothic, chill, dark, sinister, gloomy, psychological disorder"; "abnormal, unreal, unexpected, obsession, paranoia, deviation, aberration, deformation."

At this awesome list, they all laughed hysterically in class while, on my part, I was genuinely impressed by their remarkable command of vocabulary. They believed they had captured all, at least almost all, of the most essential features of this elusive topic. However, to their dismay, there was no *one single positive term* in this otherwise quite exhaustive list. So, in front of the massive pile of derogative terms that pervasively and erratically dominate the meanings of the grotesque, I asked the students what was missing on this extensive list. They seemed puzzled by the question and sat back somewhat tongue-tied. I felt, at that moment, a complicated matter gravely in hand. Is our cultural baggage really that heavy? Since then, the riddle of the grotesque, like a specter, occasionally haunts me.

Another book on the grotesque? I already feel apologetic. In the past few decades, theories of the grotesque have thrived for various reasons. In part, the disparate, indefinite, and uncanny nature of the grotesque alone provides intriguing opportunities for another book as well as books beyond this one. Nevertheless, I believe I may disappoint some readers in that, historical and theoretical speculations focusing on the nature, identity, and perception of the grotesque in art and literature, especially those limited to the modern era, are copious and splendid; and precisely because of that, I opt to sidestep this usual track. Instead, this project centers its research on an area that has hitherto been mostly neglected or entirely forgotten; that is, the issue of *the singular subject* in the context of, or more appropriately, *in the name of the grotesque*. In other words, the grotesque is *refashioned* as a cultural figure and a heretic theoretical trope to trace, explore, and expose the Western metaphysics of being—particularly the subject in the singular category—in a different light. Instead of merely *another book* tackling the *grotesque per se* in either art history or literary representation, this project is set to inquire, along the dubious and troublesome borderline between aesthetics and metaphysics: How *grotesque* is the subject? That is the question, and in effect, the very start of *unpacking* the question, both in terms of and in the name of the grotesque.

Decades ago, Wolfgang Kayser, one of the most authoritative critics on the topic, pointed out, "I tend to regard him [Hegel] as the last thinker whose analysis of the grotesque encompasses the metaphysical depth of the phenomenon, which was to be so totally lost sight of by his successors."[2] This book, partly responding to Kayser's concern, reevaluates the legacy of the metaphysical perspective that is assumed "totally lost sight of" *after* Hegel, but pursues this overlooked issue in a direction very much against both Kayser's point and Hegel's position. In *The Grotesque in Art and Literature*, Kayser grumbles, with some nostalgia and some grievance, "The metaphysical content of the grotesque, which was still essential to Hegel, now ceased to be recognized and was simply ignored."[3] Kayser opines that Hegel is the *last* and probably the *only* one who has ever *consciously* attempted to tackle the aesthetic issue of the grotesque from a metaphysical perspective. On this point, I see entirely the opposite. Tracing various paradigmatic configurations and varied rhetorical patterns of the grotesque evolved in different historical periods, I found out that theories of the grotesque have *rarely* left the metaphysical field at all. In other words, the aesthetics of the grotesque, from the very start, has always been circumscribed within and has ever hinged upon a metaphysical framework in spite of ceaseless shifts of directions and continuous alterations of patterns. Contrary to Kayser's observation, I contend that Hegel's metaphysical perspective is not the *last* one, but the *lasting* one in the discourse of the grotesque.

True, to retrieve Hegel's perspective appears to, *somewhat anachronistically,* run counter to the current ubiquitous discontents with the shaky metaphysical tradition since, as is well known, ontology is outmoded and offstage, ready to exit the critical scene amid vociferous ideological cant and political rant. To conjure up *an ontology for the grotesque*—the so-called "impossible subject"—alas, might as well be a preposterous self-mockery if not an abortive "suicidal discourse."[4] Hence, this grotesque project bears a precarious metaphysical body, perilous with heretic *revision* or *conjuration* of ontology—almost an extinct field in a postmodern age prevailed by the rhetoric of absence and difference. However, this allegorical *return*, to borrow de Man's term, only marks the start-point of going *elsewhere*. In effect, relocating the discourse of the grotesque to the outdated field of metaphysics offers a rare opportunity and a fresh point of view to discern the obscure and knotty relationship between grotesque art and the metaphysical subject and, moreover, to undertake an insurgent enterprise to topple down the Hegelian ontology of the singular subject precisely by means of what he has superciliously discharged as the disparate other.

In entirely different contexts, both Bakhtin and Lacan suggest that each word call for the other word. In this case, I propose, the subject calls for the grotesque. Foucault discovers *unreason* in *reason*, Derrida locates *absence* in *being*, Freud excavates *aggressivity* in *civilization*, and Nietzsche unveils *nihilism* in *divinity*. We are compelled to ask: What more unspoken and unspeaking words can be evoked within the lengthy and hefty tradition of metaphysics of presence that spells treacherously otherwise? In the same vein, I find the *grotesque* in the presence of *the singular subject*. Contrary to those prevalent theoretical hypotheses perpetuated previously, I contest that the grotesque does not at all suggest a disgraced ontological condition *after* the *loss* or the *disintegration* of the subject; instead, the grotesque is inherently latent within the *structurality* of the subject and it exposes the subject entirely *other-wise* as a delusional phantom generated by a solipsistic desire. This proposed *return to* the subject is in effect evoked by *a return of* the grotesque. Therefore, by unearthing the unconscious grotesque that lurks in the subject, I intend to dislodge the singular subject from its *onto-logical* locale of identity to a *hetero-logical* locus of disparity thereby collapsing the presumably polarized relationship between the subject and the grotesque. In short, the grotesque *dis-embodies* the subject.

To return to Hegel, nevertheless, means to uncover what he hides as well as to acknowledge what he *has sighted*. In his overall evaluation of art in his *Aesthetics*, Hegel tends to view the grotesque as a generic category of underdeveloped art stringently within the context of the Western metaphysical tradition. Most notably, Hegel identifies and appraises a specific enigmatic figure, an *unusual suspect* that so far has been largely ignored or merely forgotten, i.e., the *Sphinx,* as the emblematic embodiment of grotesque art in oriental cultures. Surprisingly, conjuring Hegel's specter evokes another ghost figure—the Sphinx that is buried as "a dead body" in Greek mythology in general and fossilized as a piece of rock in Hegel's metaphysical aesthetics in particular. Hence, resurrecting the Sphinx—the grotesque figure that Hegel defames not only as the most *primitive form of art*, but also the *most defective mode of being* according to his utmost standards of "Spirit"—opens up an utterly fresh perspective and a fertile territory to further explore the grotesque, not only as an aesthetic issue in the discourse of art, but also as an ontological query of being in Western metaphysics. In other words, Hegel has sharply sighted an overlooked grotesque (dead) body but completely missed the point in his forensic analysis.

The Sphinx is a *riddle that riddles*. To some extent, the issue of the grotesque can be allegorized in terms of the Sphinx's riddle; Hegel, Nietzsche, Freud, and numerous other thinkers across disciplines persistently returned to this ancient riddle to decode and unravel the mystery of man in one way or another. The structure of the book is partly organized around the infamous encounter, or more accurately, the intriguing *riddling* relationship between the two mythical figures, Oedipus and the Sphinx. According *Greek legend*, in their fatal confrontation or domination, Oedipus encrypts the Sphinx's riddle in a single word and with a singular subject—*Man*. To review this riddle as an allegorical game of identity and to revisit their encounter as a *riddling* relationship between the subject and the other, we have to inquire, beyond the bounds of all traditional models of conquest: Who is who in this guessing game? The standard positions tend to associate the riddle with the Sphinx, the symbol of the grotesque according to Hegel at least, whereas Oedipus stands for the singular subject—"Man" as he proclaims—in front of the monstrous other. Their relationship has consistently been characterized as a *unilateral domination* instead of a *specular reflection*. Hardly anyone suspected that the mystic riddle might unveil, and the alien other—the Sphinx—may mirror, the disparate and incongruous conditions that Oedipus attempts to conceal. Hence, I propose a disconcerting analogy between Oedipus and the Sphinx: this *unlikely pair* represents two forms of the grotesque even though, as they appear to be, irreconcilably opposed to each other. In fact, Oedipus' "Man" in singular form is conjured up as a sublime phantom of the singular subject according to his narcissistic desire or, probably, more due to his "ontological" lack. In other words, the grotesque may be the latent condition that haunts the subject as its repressed unconscious and expose its inherent disparity, incoherence, and multiplicity. In this case, the "grotesque Sphinx" is revived and employed as a deconstructive trope of *exorcising* in order to dispel the spectral presence of singular ontology and conjure away the phantom of the singular subject. Instead of repeating Oedipus' answer to encrypt the riddle of the Sphinx, I opt to reset the Sphinx's riddle to probe the problematic identity of Oedipus; that is, the Sphinx's *riddling* is deployed as a heretical "writing back" in a dissenting voice against the huge amount of narratives piled upon Oedipus alone.

To a certain degree, the mystic riddle *between* Oedipus and the Sphinx still haunts us. The current response to or the recent echo of the mystic riddle takes a different form in a new round of identity game: "*Who* comes *after* the subject?"[5] This question involves issues pertinent to both identity and temporality. Apparently, here *after*—a cunning pun—connotes both "post to" and "searching for." Moreover, as several critics already noted, numerous *others*, previously dismissed as either lesser than or deviation from what have been traditionally legitimized as the "standard" subjects, are desperately pursuing the singular subject positions through various kinds of negotiations, translations, or transgressions. In other words, every other, nameless or labeled, is trying to bring forth its "empowered" identity from its particular situation and distinctive perspective *after* the "death of the subject" declared by critics on several historical occasions and on various ideological fronts. However, despite the sincere disavow of never reverting to the essentialist position defined by Western metaphysics, some of these emerged and evolved positions of alterity, *other-wise* as they attempt to claim, do seem suspect of a repetition of singular ontology and remain captivated by the spectral presence of Western metaphysics. Therefore, "Who comes after the subject?" could be recapitulated in terms of "Who haunts the subject?" and consequently, the discourse of the subject slips from the field of ontology to that of *hauntology*. That is to say, the subject or the other, in either ontological or spectral form, is haunted by some ghosts that require invocation. After all, in Derrida's view, we are all haunted by ghosts of some sort. To parody Descartes, Derrida declares: "Therefore 'I am' would mean 'I am haunted.'"[6]

In response to Francis Fukuyama's theory of eschatology postulated in his book *The End of History and the Last Man*—the end of a certain concept of history and man in it without any other alternatives—, Derrida in *Specters of Marx* projects a different man, "man *as other*," along the line of *heterology*.[7] Derrida writes, "in the same place, on the same limit, where history is finished, there were a certain determined concept of history comes to an end, precisely there the historicity of history begins, there finally it has the chance of heralding itself—of promising itself. There where man, a certain determined concept of man, is finished, there the pure humanity of man, of the *other man* and of man *as other* begins or has finally the chance of heralding itself—of promising itself."[8] Here Derrida seems to envision "man *as other*" in terms of "radical alterity and heterogeneity, of *différance*,"[9] but promises, however, that this man comes *only at the end* of a certain concept of history and *after the death* of the subject in it. Apparently, Derrida intends to conjure away Hegel's ghost or Spirit of the *Same*, in fact all kinds of specters, toward the other in terms of alterity, disparity, and difference according to the heterodox of heterologies. In other words, Derrida assures us that the *other man*—"the pure humanity of man"—will come *after* the subject exits from history. But, it stands to debate to what extent Derrida has succeeded in dispelling the Hegelian specter and running out of Hegel's history; and to what degree he is still running *in* or *after* Hegel's time and haunted by Hegel's ghost. Does not the Derridean "pure humanity of man" sound similar to the Hegelian "pure spirit"—a phantom re-framed within an identical singular ontology? A return *of* the *same* or a return *to différance*? That certainly begs questioning.

Derrida's prediction of the *coming* of the *other man* overlooks, among other issues, the problematic *genealogy* of history itself and his *historicity* of history appears to repeat "the same limit" of temporality marked by the life or death of the subject and centralized by *his coming* or *going*. Consequently, "Who comes after the subject?" also prompts, anti-chronologically, another question preceding it: "Who comes *before* the subject?" Or, to further complicate the issue of *timing* or the lineal "historicity of history" centralized by the presumed priority of the subject, we might ask: Who comes *with* the subject? Hence, this project aims to investigate not only "*who* came *before*" or "*who* comes *after*" but also *who* is *with* the subject all the time as the unpresentable and invisible other. That is to say, the subject, as such, emerges as a subject laden with and haunted by some ghost others that require invocation. Thus, a radical proposal of an *unthinkable* history initiated by and starting with the *invisible* other is yet to be made beyond the *genealogy by the subject, of the subject, and for the subject*. Inevitably, we have to, *in the name of the grotesque*, retrieve, envision, and return to an *altered* discourse of the other based upon the heterodox tradition of *heterologies* and dispel the phantasmagoric ontology as hauntology. A word of caution: if the entire metaphysical tradition has consistently asserted that the history of the subject is a history of the *Same*, I opine carefully, then, genealogies of the grotesque, even if possible, are not exactly the whole histories of *the singular other*. There are others *and* others outside *singular heterology*. To transcend the hegemony of any singular paradigm, possibly heterologies may suffice to host a variety of diverse discourses for this impossible subject *as well as* the heterogeneous other. Therefore, this project invites us to rethink the entire discourse of being from a heretic perspective of the grotesque beyond the conventions of the fundamental tenets central to Western metaphysics—the singular being either in terms of *the total subject* or *the wholly other*.

Initially I started this project to explore the aesthetic issue of the grotesque as "an impossible subject" in metaphysics but unexpectedly turned it into a *wayward* speculation of the disparate and heterogeneous other in heterologies, a precarious theoretical journey from ontology and hauntology to heterologies. Despite kind advices and frightening warnings from close friends and past critics alike, I apologize to have put this project messily into modern and postmodern perspectives. Due to the chaotic and disparate nature of the grotesque, the book itself somewhat becomes a sort of carnival intertexts; it covers diverse cultural landscapes and various disciplinary fields, encompassing literature, art, aesthetics, psychoanalysis, ethnic studies, critical theories, philosophy, etc., in a sense, "monstrous" until it finds itself in the current form that probably only the nature of the topic might justify. By tracing the intricate relationship between aesthetics and metaphysics, this project interweaves an array of texts from different locales and different times: ancient myth of Oedipus and the Sphinx, modern discourses on the subject, and postmodern thoughts of the other, thereby bringing together several strands of inquiry that hitherto have not been connected in grotesque studies. The *riddling* relationship between Oedipus and the Sphinx underlines the overall structure of the project and figures as the central theoretical frame-narrative to probe the polemic relationship between the singular subject and the grotesque (other) in the perspectives of ontology, hauntology, and heterologies.

Structurally, the book is divided into six chapters in three parts and each part, in different theoretical frameworks and cultural contexts, examines the topic of the grotesque via the frame-story of Oedipus and the Sphinx. Part I traces the evolution of the grotesque from theoretical, cultural, and historical perspectives along the dubious borderline between aesthetics and metaphysics and interrogates the complex identity problem of the Sphinx, the symbol of the grotesque, in Greek legend and Egyptian mythology. Chapter One is comprised of inspections of the grotesque in three different discourse fields. Almost every single critic in one way or another acknowledges the unnerving difficulty of approaching the rambling topic of the grotesque that covers a vast theoretical field across a broad spectrum of disciplines. The first section surveys the chaotic and confounding situation of current speculations of the grotesque (in the works of Kayser, Bakhtin, Harpham, McElroy, Thomson, Russo, Connolly, and others) and then organizes the huge and desultory theoretical corpus of the grotesque into five distinct rhetoric patterns that have emerged repetitively and converged consistently on several key areas, such as intermixing and intermingling in composition; confusion and ambivalence in reception; negative or demonic attributes in nature; subversive or transgressive power in function; and a critical impasse on an "impossible subject." Departing from the typical methods employed by past critics, the second section revisits the archeological "primal scene" of the (re)discovery of grotesque art at the original site of Nero's *Domus Aurea*, or Golden House, an imperial palace mistaken as *grottoes* in the late fifteenth century and investigates in great depth the far-reaching consequences of its initial disfiguration or misnaming in terms of the "grotto-esque"—art from the underground—and the subsequent semantic ramifications and metonymic associations sparked by this cryptic *space metaphor* along various imaginary trajectories. The last section offers a short genealogical review of different alterations of the grotesque's elusive meanings construed according to the main aesthetic paradigms in several major historical periods from the Renaissance to the Postmodern in terms of "aesthetics of ambiguity," "aesthetics of the negative" or "aesthetics of paradox." Based upon the archaeological excavating and genealogical tracking, I attest that the aesthetic figuration of the grotesque has mostly been, in effect, a *metaphysical reconfiguration* of the grotesque *other-wise* because aesthetics and metaphysics have always been inextricably interlocked in expositions of the grotesque from the ancient to the present, and ultimately, I opine, ontology of the singular subject and metaphysics of presence constitute a kind of the "aesthetic unconscious" that regulates and normalizes the discourse of the grotesque.

Chapter Two provides a cultural analysis of the Sphinx as an emblematic figure of the grotesque that has been largely ignored so far and offers a heretical speculation of the alternative outcomes from the mystical encounter between Oedipus and the Sphinx as a case study of ontological difference. Several critics in the past, such as Bakhtin, Harpham, and Gombrich, noticed that the chimeric or sphinxlike figures stand prominently among the grotesque imageries re-discovered in the "grottoes" or Nero's imperial palace but none has contributed any extensive research on this phenomenon. Instead of interpreting the Sphinx and her role only from the perspective of Greek mythology and the Oedipus legend like past critics (Lowell Edmunds and Hegel in particular), the first section investigates the mystery of the Sphinx's origin by tracing multiple genealogies and varied metamorphoses of sphinx figures at three distinct historical and cultural locations respectively. That is, the Sphinx is regarded as a figure of grotesque art revived in Rome during the Renaissance, condemned as an alien monster that plagues Thebes in Greek mythology, and worshipped as the sacred guardian of mystic knowledge in ancient Egyptian culture. The second section interrogates the traditional views and standard assumptions both historians and critics hold in regard to the fatal encounter between Oedipus and the Sphinx in terms of conquest (human over beast, East over West, male over female, and logos over mythos—in each case, she occupies the position of the other), and then proceeds to problematize each paradigmatic shift that is allegedly inaugurated by the rise of Oedipus and the fall of the Sphinx by juxtaposing entirely different and, in effect, dramatically reversed outcomes that are generated respectively in the framework of the *Oedipus* legend or *going beyond* it, i.e., from the perspective of the *Sphinx* myth. Differing from all past theoretical hypotheses that are exclusively based upon the oppositional model, the last section provides a fresh angle to explore the ontological mystery between Oedipus and the Sphinx by analyzing the complex *riddling* relationship between them and proposes a heretic hypothesis of two discrete forms of the grotesque, latent or manifest, conscious or unconscious, physical and metaphysical, as embodied respectively by Oedipus and the Sphinx. The chapter ends with a radical conjecture: though seemingly opposed to each other in a dichotomous position, the grotesque actually constitutes the unconscious of the singular subject and, moreover, the desire for the phantom of a singular subject is in effect symptomatic of grotesque disparity.

Part II focuses on investigating the Sphinx and Oedipus as two discrete but analogical prototypes of the grotesque in the works of three German scholars, Hegel, Nietzsche, and Freud. Chapter Three explores the three modern critics' "aesthetic" speculation of the grotesque in general and its prototypical embodiment, the Sphinx, in specific in spite of their different theoretic foci. In "Introduction to the Philosophy of Art," Hegel proposes a premise of a "universal evolution" of art from the grotesque to the classical, and to the romantic. Hegel arbitrarily locates grotesque art in the East and specifically singles out the Sphinx as the *symbol* of grotesque Egyptian culture—excessive, disparate, and incoherent—not merely because it is a *defective art* figure lacking classical (Greek) harmony or order, but predominantly because it is an *inadequate subject* underdeveloped in spirit (the Christian Spirit), reflexive of a typical orientalist discourse. In the conclusion of *The Birth of Tragedy*, Nietzsche resurrects the Sphinx as the embodiment of an earth mother of heterogeneous nature; in the essay, Nietzsche mainly focuses on other chimeric figures in Greek mythology entirely ignored by Hegel, such as satyrs and Dionysus, as representations of the grotesque. Nietzsche returns to the Sphinx and other hybrids to challenge and overcome, via a Dionysian rupture, the bondage of the individual principle personified by Apollo and the confinement of the self-reflexive consciousness embodied by Oedipus. Nietzsche evokes the Dionysian principle to articulate a radical ontology, in fact, a *heterology* of the grotesque other to unsettle the modern subject of singularity. Ironically, Freud, the self-entitled master of Greek mythology, barely recalls the Sphinx as the latent mother figure in his aesthetic thesis "The 'Uncanny'" framed in his reading of Hoffman's story "The Sand-Man." After playing a labyrinthine linguistic game with "uncanny"—"*unheimlich*" and "*heimlich*" and toying with various concepts according to his Master-plot—the castration complex, Freud reluctantly unveils, at the very end, the dubious but horrific entrance of all human beings as the ultimate site of the uncanny, i.e., the maternal body, without acknowledging or recognizing the hidden Sphinx, the sacred guardian of life and death. In the name of his universal paradigm of the Oedipus complex, Freud *disembodies* the Sphinx without taking into account the full consequences of the *riddling* narratives by the mother figures in Hoffman's tale, i.e., the (m)other as the trickster like the Sphinx. I opt that it is not simply the father's dead body, but also the (m)other's *riddling* tongue, that haunts the Hoffman's protagonist Nathaniel and Freud's hero Oedipus alike.

Chapter Four shifts the focus of the grotesque studies by a change of character from the Sphinx to Oedipus. In this case, the grotesque is primarily characterized by Oedipus' narcissistic desire for the phantom of a singular subject in terms of "Oedipus Obsessed" in the context of hauntology. In *Specters of Marx*, Derrida coins the term "hauntology" not only to expose the subject's ontological absence but also to unravel the haunting relationship between the subject and some holy specter. This immanent haunting effect, I contest, is demonstrated respectively in the dispossession of Hegel's subject in *Phenomenology of Spirit*, annihilation of Nietzsche's priest in *The Genealogy of Morals*, and suppression of Freud's neurotic in *Civilization and Its Discontents*. The Hegelian subject's obsession with and deprivation by the Holy Spirit via negative signification, the Nietzschean priest's desire for and nullification by the Christian God via ascetic ideals, and the Freudian neurotic's identification with and negation by an omnipotent Father via an oedipal structure all attest to a "hauntological" coming into being or *nothing* under the spell of some Spectral Other. Hegel's *Phenomenology of Spirit*, in Derrida's words, can be translated as "*Phantom-ology of Specter*" due to the fact that Hegel arbitrarily ends his subject's ontological journey in an ethereal realm of theology and the Hegelian subject's transcendence unfolds an intra-spectral dialectics between a phantom subject and a Spectral Other. Nietzsche employs the self-denouncing and self-negating priest figure to parody Hegel's subject as a haunted character and comes up with an unauthorized version of the Hegelian subject in terms of *hauntology of the priest.* By tracing the genealogy of ascetic ideals, Nietzsche discloses a nihilistic will for self-annulation in the very obsessive pursuit of an identity invoked by a spectral other, Christ. Freud in *Civilization and Its Discontents* further investigates the escalation of a cultural pandemic of neurosis along Nietzsche's line of thought by uncovering an omnipresent and omnipotent superego, i.e., a holy father in transcendental terms. In varying degrees, each critic exposes the subject's narcissistic desire for the phantom of a singular being conjured up by some specter—actually a death wish in disguise. Oedipus' longing for an illusory "man" evoked by the Apollonian order exactly illustrates this kind of grotesque obsession. In this context, the modern grotesque, no longer distinguished exclusively by the hybrid agglomeration specific to chimeric or sphinxlike figures, is primarily associated with an obsessive narcissistic desire toward the singular subject. Consequently, the meaning of the grotesque undergoes a radical revision and a complete reversal from the Sphinx to Oedipus.

Part III shifts the analytical focus from the discourse of the subject to that of the other by relocating the locus of grotesque studies from ontology to heterologies. Chapter Five examines the dubious nature and polemic role of the other in Lacan's discourse of the subject by exposing a "hauntological" spell imbedded in the specular images and the oracular narratives invoked by the spectral other— reminiscent of the sublime phantoms and sacred oracles that initiate Oedipus' desire and determine his fate. Unlike other postmodern thinkers, Lacan refuses to give up the subject, but the *Lacanian subject* itself has been consistently labeled as "the subject of lack" by almost all critics including Felman, Ragland-Sullivan, Derrida, Butler, and others. Departing from this established position, I re-evaluate Lacan's subject in terms of *the subject qua other* because in both imaginary and symbolic orders his subject is inescapably meshed, infested, and dispossessed by some exorcising other. The mirror stage not only fabricates an optic illusion of a total self, but also situates the subject as *possessed* and *overtaken* by a spectral other. If the imaginary subject is fixed or transfixed by *a spectral other* in terms of a *specular* self-image, then the symbolic subject is under the spell of a linguistic other in a double signifying game of metonymic substitution and metaphorical transfiguration that renders the subject infinitely divided and decentered, i.e., grotesque. Further, I carefully set apart the poststructuralist Lacan and the psychoanalyst, or particularly, the *oedipalist* Lacan. The symbolic order, as is known, is centralized by the veiled phallus, the master signifier, the transcendental signified, or the Singular Other *without* any traces of alterity or difference. As a result, Lacan's other becomes highly problematic due to its *lack* of qualifications of otherness. In effect, Lacan's locus of the other, more than inhabited by generic "pure signifiers" or abstract "empty words," is loaded with "full words" from the (dead) father as the holy texts. Beyond the theory of language as a generic other as so noted by past critics, I contest that the unconscious subject is infested with a series of others: the oracular other (the father's speeches), the spectral other (the ghosts of the dead father), and the Holy Other (the sacred Phallus). Despite Lacan's claim of "no Other of the Other", the capital Other, I argue, figures as the Singular

Subject and henceforth the Lacanian subject is subjected to the *Same* instead of the *Other*. Instead of repeating the phallocentric mythology, I propose to relocate the discourse of the other from singular ontology to heterologies, that is, from Oedipus' perspective to the Sphinx's prospects.

Chapter Six examines otherness in terms of the carnival, the abject, and the mestiza as cases of different renegotiation with the grotesque in a postmodern context. The first part reviews the recent revival of "the other studies" after the demise of the central subject and traces the current discourse of the other by critics such as Levinas, Lyotard, Bataille, de Certeau, and Mark Taylor. Some of these others evolved in philosophical discourses, however, tend to be abstract or claim to be universal; they are suspect of returning to or repeating after metaphysical trends. Instead of tangling in the metaphysical sphere, I explore the alternative discourse of the other that is grounded in a concrete physical body in a specific social space. I select three distinct modes of discourse of the other as postmodern translations of the grotesque: Bakhtin's notion of the carnival in *Rabelais and His World* from social and ideological perspectives, Kristeva's concept of the abject in *Powers of Horror: An Essay on Abjection* from psychoanalytic and feminist perspectives, and Gloria Anzaldúa's idea of the *mestiza* in *Borderlands/La Frontera: The New Mestiza* from gender and ethnological perspectives. To Bakhtin, carnivalizing the grotesque signifies a jolly opening of the social body and an ecstatic celebration of its "unfinished metamorphosis." Against all official aesthetics of the past, Bakhtin develops a counter-aesthetic discourse by reviving the medieval and Renaissance folk culture, a marginal aesthetic mode to engage a politics of resistance and subversion. Instead of being confined to the Lacanian phallic order and undergoing castration, perversion, and melancholia, Kristeva initiates a radical semiotics of abjection, moving the discourse of the grotesque to a maternal space in terms of the *chora* and celebrating the *jouissance* of the heterogeneous female body via schizophrenic "self-dividing" desires. Transgressing all singular or binary paradigms of gender, border, and identity, Anzaldúa develops a new rhetoric of the grotesque based upon her *mestiza* body in the ethnographic borderlands. By resurrecting the sphinxlike figures of ancient mythologies in hybrid cultures, she argues strongly for a radical mestiza consciousness and a borderland subject position across the bounds between self and other, male and female, heterogeneous origins and singular identity. Hence, this postmodern refashioning of the grotesque moves "the other studies" outside the homogeneous domain of singular ontology and consequently the others arisen in heterologies are irreconcilably multiple, disparate, and heterogeneous. In other words, the Sphinx returns to "embody" a heretical locus of the other studies in a radical *jouissance* of disparity, diversity, and alterity in a postmodern age.

NOTES

1. Peter Brooks, "Freud's Masterplot," in *The Critical Tradition: Classical Texts and Contemporary Trends*, ed. David Richter (New York: St. Martin's Press, 1998), 1038.

2. Wolfgang J. Kayser, *The Grotesque in Art and Literature*, trans. Ulrich Weisstein (Bloomington: Indiana UP, 1963), 100.

3. Ibid., 103.

4. Barthes, Roland Barthes, *The Pleasure of the Text,* trans. Richard Miller (New York: Hill and Wang, 1975), 19.

5. In *Who Comes After the Subject?* edited by Eduardo Cadava, Peter Connor, and Jean-Luc Nancy, several essays, including articles by Derrida and Levinas, speculate on the issue of the other in generic terms; and most essays focus on interrogation of the singular subject in the context of the death of the central subject in Western metaphysics.

6. Jacques Derrida, *Specters of Marx: The State of the Debt, the Work of Mourning, and the New International*, trans. Peggy Kamuf (New York: Routledge, 1994), 133

7. Francis Fukuyama's book *The End of History and the Last Man* has provoked all kinds of responses for several decades and Derrida's *Specters of Marx* is just one of the recent works that still linger on the theory of eschatology in terms of hauntology. However, a decade after his declaration of "the end of history," Fukuyama revised his previous argument in *Our Posthuman Future: Consequences of the Biotechnology Revolution* (2002) and argued that there has emerged an alternative to the final form of humanistic history. That is, the human being itself is altered with the advancement of biotechnology and henceforth mankind and human ideals are remade differently from the perspective of post-humanism.

8. Derrida, *Specters of Marx*, 74.

9. Ibid., 75.

I

The Primal Scenes Revisited: Archeology and Genealogy of the Grotesque

Chapter One

The Uncanny Subject between Aesthetics and Metaphysics

I might as well repeat, after many other critics in the past, there is no single adequate definition of the grotesque and nor is there any single privileged perspective or point of view to approach the topic in hand.[1] Actually, singularity of all kinds, for me, presents precisely the problem of tackling the complex and knotty issue of the grotesque. The simple fact that so many contemporary critics from various disciplines have persistently returned to this topic indicates that this enigma cannot be easily dismissed in any single term or fully encrypted according to any single interpretative system. The current work intends neither to settle the final account to this topic nor to offer any tentative conclusion to its meaning. On the contrary, this project attempts to *unsettle* the discourse boundaries through both provocative departures and evocative returns across multiple textual, cultural, and historical spaces. Peter Brooks reminds us that Freud's "masterplot" of repetition not only drives toward the end or mastery but also desires to "generate new beginnings in relation to any possible end" and uphold "an indeterminate shuffling or oscillation."[2] Indeed, many critics during the past few decades have frequently come back to this topic and presented a copious amount of remarkable ideas from diverse disciplinary fields to throw light upon the cryptic nature of the grotesque. However, as several critics have noted, some of the theoretical endeavors, strenuous as they are, have contributed to further mystifying instead of illuminating this elusive figure.[3]

Alan Spiegel in "A Theory of the Grotesque in Southern Fiction" aptly summarizes the disconcerting situation: "The chief problem seems to be that the term 'grotesque' has been applied so frequently and so recklessly by so many contemporary critics to so many different literary occurrences that it now becomes increasingly difficult to use the term with any high degree of clarity and precision."[4] Hence, the daunting task confronting each critic at the onset is that one has to wade through a broad discursive field of profuse theoretical speculations in this *return to* the grotesque. To mitigate the confounding situation, this section ventures to organize those excessive signifiers that cluster around the term "grotesque" across a vast disciplinary spectrum into some discernible rhetorical patterns. Further, by tracing various "configured" identifications of the grotesque that have emerged and evolved at intersections of culture, paradigm, and history, I would like to probe the intricate enterprises of figuration, disfiguration, and transfiguration of the grotesque in terms of both an artistic figure and a dubious being.

I. THE CURRENT CRITICAL SCENES: FIGURATION OF THE GROTESQUE

In almost all cases, definitions of the term "grotesque" from dictionaries or literary handbooks, though varied in lexicological endeavors and theoretical purposes, tend to be limited, vague or ambiguous. Generally, it is either defined narrowly as a noun that stands for a particular style of decorative art characteristic of the interwoven and intermingled figures, partly human and partly animal, with foliage and flowers; or it is defined broadly as a generic adjective that can denote fantastic, playful, sportive, and fanciful as well as unreal, incongruous, horrific, and ugly. Though some meanings compiled in these reference materials are inclined to be widely apart and far-fetched in derivatives and associates, more or less the lexicologists seem to, surprisingly, share the same discourse strategy to approach this knotty term, i.e., a chain of binary structures, such as fantastic and bizarre, fanciful and eccentric, playful and ridiculous, comic and frightening—a dazzling interplay between synonyms and antonyms, or similarities and opposites. Typically, in some extended collocations beyond oxymoronic conjugation, a lot of more negative adjectives follow: ludicrous, absurd, monstrous, distorted, caricature, extravagant, ugly, unnatural, incongruous, ridiculous, eccentric, strange, abnormal, aberrant, horrific, terrifying, nightmarish, uncanny, unnatural, nocturnal, ominous, oneiric, surreal, supernatural.... And this awfully long list of gloomy terms, one may notice, is by no means an exhaustive inventory. (I merely picked them up at random from a few literary reference materials I respect.)[5]

If one cares to have a cursory look at the scholarship on the grotesque for the past several decades, the critical scene seems even more chaotic and confusing, so much so that one can easily get lost in these theoretical labyrinths across all fields. Suddenly everything becomes grotesque plus everything else we can think of. Theoretical speculations of the "grotesque" cover a broad scope and a wide spectrum, from reality to fantasy, from art to philosophy, from physicality to psychology, from spirituality to metaphysics, from disability to normalcy, from gender studies to post-humanism. . . . No wonder some critics assert, at the very start, the grotesque is prevalent in our culture and permeates our daily existence. In the "Preface" to his book *On the Grotesque*, Geoffrey Harpham alerts us that "the grotesque, in endlessly diluting forms, is always and everywhere around us—and increasingly invisible."[6] In another "Preface" to *The Grotesque in Art and Literature*, James Luther Adams and Wilson Yates provide a full catalogue: "The 'grotesque' in the arts calls attention to the monstrous, the absurd and the beastly—in the nature and consequences of mob violence, racial conflict, excessive sexuality, bureaucratism [*sic*], pollution of air and earth, the technology of destruction, the megadeaths and carrion of Hiroshima, Nagasaki and Songmy."[7] What more can we possibly add to this list? That is probably why Robert Doty in *Human Concern/Personal Torment* declares, mimicking the typical tone and rhetoric of the Enlightenment universalist, "the world is estranged, life is absurd, the grotesque is the *measure of all things* (italics added), spiritual or material."[8]

I believe several types of theoretical conjectures can be discerned amid these desultory and erratic signifiers dispersed along various planes of discourse. Careful readings of past scholarship uncover some particular rhetorical patterns that emerge repetitively and converge consistently on a number of central points in grotesque studies. Solely for the purpose of managing this vast and rambling topic, I break down past theoretical speculations of the grotesque into five distinctive groups of rhetorical prototypes or strategies. The first group anchors the grotesque's composition in a rhetoric of confusion and intermingling in structure; the second focuses on confusion and ambivalence in its reception; the third centers on negative and even demonic attributes pertinent to its nature; the fourth highlights the subversive and transgressive power in regard to its function; and the last group, in an overloaded postmodern jargon, declares a critical impasse on the grotesque as an "impossible subject."

The typical lexicons for the first group revolve around the con/fusing structure of the grotesque in composition: intermingling, merging, and coexisting of the opposites, the incompatibles, and irreconcilables. For instance, in his seminal book *The Grotesque in Art and Literature,* Kayser obsessively repeats this fusion model, and with con/fusions of all kinds: the grotesque is comprised of "the mixture of heterogeneous elements," "the monstrous fusion of human and nonhuman elements," and "the fusion of different realms, the coexistence of beautiful, bizarre, ghastly and repulsive elements."[9] Harpham in his extensive book *On the Grotesque* reiterates a similar rhetoric, citing a "co-presence of the normative, fully formed, 'high' or ideal, and the abnormal, unformed, degenerate, 'low' or material," a "structural confusion" or "a species of confusion."[10] Numerous other critics adhere to the same con/

fusion formula, for example, "the interweaving of totally disparate elements";[11] "[i]t commingles the animate and the inanimate and conflates such classifications as plant, animal, human";[12] "a process of hybridization or immixing of binary opposites";[13] and "a fusion of incompatible parts in parts."[14] For this group, the dichotomous positions co-exist but never cohere; the opposite parts intermix but never resolve. Difference is not negotiable into singularity; disparity is maintained *ad infinitum*.

The second rhetorical group focuses on the aesthetics of confusion *in response* to the grotesque, i.e., invoking incompatible and oppositional perceptions, such as, comic and tragic, ludicrous and monstrous, repulsive and attractive, gruesome and gleeful, horrifying and funny, fearful and delightful—demonstrating a typical oxymoronic wordplay. For instance, Phillip Thomson's *The Grotesque* centers its research of the grotesque on "*the unresolved clash of incompatibles in . . . response,*" "both comic and monstrous" or with "unholy glee and barbaric delight."[15] Several other critics also hold the same principle of aesthetic perception, for instance, "a heterogeneous mixture of fear and laughter, or horror and mirth; more generally, fascination and revulsion";[16] "playfully gay and carelessly fantastic" and "ominous and sinister,"[17] and "from the wondrous to the monstrous to the ridiculous."[18] For this group, incompatible feelings arising from polarized responses violently stand at the opposite ends without sympathetic resolution, therapeutic catharsis or emotional transcendence. Kayser succinctly sums up this ambivalent feeling: "The grotesque world is—and is not—our own world."[19] Probably the uncanny would most approximately characterize the aesthetic effect for this group.[20]

The third group centers on a negative discourse over the enigmatic as well as stigmatic nature of the grotesque. Critics employ the full linguistic capacity of negative conjugation along various trajectories. The grotesque figures are characterized as "incomprehensible," "inexplicable," and "impersonal" because they "point to an inhuman, nocturnal, and abysmal realm"[21] and are charged "with accusations of illegitimacy, bastardy, or hybridization";[22] and further, the grotesque represents "all the absolute antithesis of the harmony, order, dignity, and serenity,"[23] "associated with gross unnatural distortion and . . . the fearful, the unearthly, the nightmarish, and the demonic" and signifying "violation of harmony, symmetry, and proportion,"[24] in short, "the moral chaos of our world."[25] These definitions of the grotesque are overwhelmingly and pervasively dominated by negative tropes, or in effect, an overbearing critical condemnation of its uncanny and cryptic character. As a result, an enormous rhetoric corpus of derogative terms dances around the evasive word in a metonymic signification. Consequently, the nature of the grotesque is construed as irrational, inexplicable, inhuman, incompatible, and incongruous in a discourse prefixed by negative attributes across the board. In this case, the negative capacity appears to be not at all an accidental or derivative quality, but something absolutely essential and innate to the nature of the grotesque.

The fourth group, to a certain extent, also focuses on the "negative" edge of the grotesque—not in its essence, but in its power of negation or deconstruction, to use a fashionable phrase. That is, the rhetoric attention shifts from intellectual incomprehension and aesthetic illegitimacy regarding its nature to its negative function in terms of social subversion and cultural transgression in relationship to order, identity, border or center. For instance, in Kayser's view, the grotesque signals "the subversion of order and proportion," "the abolition of the law of statics," and "the destruction of personality."[26] Other critics concur that the grotesque figures significantly as a "subversive device to question the discourse of authority"[27] or to "overturn the bourgeoisie's own world of sanitary and sanctimonious normalcy and diurnal mediocrity."[28] In short, grotesque figures as a "deconstructive" trope to bust borders of all kinds—be they natural, physical, psychological or metaphysical. True to Connelly's observation, "The grotesque is defined by what it does to boundaries, transgressing, merging, overflowing, destabilizing them."[29] That is possibly why Harpham in "The Grotesque: The First Principle" poses: "Each age redefines the grotesque in terms of what threatens its sense of essential humanity."[30] In this historical sense and in terms of the way the group defines it, the grotesque is recapitulated as a dynamic power rather than a static essence.

The last group, if it claims a legitimate position, somewhat resigns itself to a postmodern posture of paradox. That is, their theoretical speculations seldom fail to end on any other note than a critical impasse or a discourse of the impossible. For instance, Harpham remarks: "The grotesque is concept without form" or "a word for this paralysis of language."[31] Thus, the grotesque is identified as either possessing "no subject"[32] or being "an impossible subject."[33] Many contemporary critics are acutely aware of the difficulty of approaching the grotesque because, as Harpham notes, it "either occupies multiple categories or that it falls between categories."[34] However, in spite of the exasperating theoretical aporia over its identity, rhetorical supplements keep coming, excessively so, as if attracted by some intriguing obscurity in the grotesque. It appears that something cryptic and uncanny in the grotesque not only invokes ambiguous feelings and confuses sense, but also suspends meaning and utterly aborts signification. In this context, the grotesque not only figures as a particular *insignificant other* in art but also embodies some mysterious *unsignifiable phantom* in ontology. As a result, what is aesthetically transcribed or theoretically formulated for the grotesque appears to be utterly dependent upon, arguably, the very untranslatability and unreadability of its identity, characteristic of a discourse fraught with slippery displacements and ironic erasures.

As the erratic contemporary discourses illustrate, there is neither systematic way nor comprehensive method to encompass the huge corpus of the grotesque. Instead, we see prolific meanings—either closely related or remotely derived—emerge and blend in a volatile field of rhetoric reconfigurations and theoretical contestations. The topics of the grotesque range from physical deformation to spiritual perversion, from natural distortion to social chaos, from religious fervor to moral decadence, from psychoanalysis of the id to metaphysics of void, from mythical consciousness to irrational desire, from supernatural whim to artistic sublimity, from demonic possession to neurotic obsession, from aesthetics of horror to politics of resistance, and so on so forth. Consequently, it is entirely unthinkable for one single word, i.e., grotesque, to host such an extravagant agglomeration of contradictory terms in synonyms and antonyms as well as evoke a monstrous assemblage of opposed emotions. That is why probably no survey of this notoriously vertiginous concept can ever hope to be exhaustive or conclusive. Descriptions or conceptualizations from any single point of view can by no means capture its varied and variable nature, and most critics have acknowledged, in one way or another, the impossibility of fitting the grotesque seamlessly into one rhetoric structure, one theoretical frame, one historical period, one domain of discourse, or one critical paradigm. Indeed, so far nobody has succeeded in locating any single adequate meaning that is commensurable to its slippery, cryptic, and heterogeneous conglomeration. To cohere it into a single subject or one discrete identity in any single category or paradigm would violate, so to speak, its *grotesque* nature. Henceforth, we feel compelled to inquire: What is so missing yet so overwhelming in the grotesque? Is there some essential lack that makes it *constitutionally* uncanny, enigmatic, and elusive?

To unravel this knotty issue, I intend to investigate the grotesque in two fields: archeology and genealogy, in the following section. The initial figurative and subsequent trans-figurative meanings of the grotesque can offer us two different trails of tracing; that is, how the grotesque is initially perceived and codified on the occasion of its re-discovery at the primal scene; and how it is subsequently ascribed and refigured in various historical contexts according to different aesthetic paradigms. Through this investigation, I attest that the grotesque has always been configured precariously between aesthetics and metaphysics in general, and between the singular subject and the disparate other in specific.[35] The following part will trace the grotesque in three discrete strands of its figuration: the initial (dis)figuration at the site of its re-discovery, the subsequent major historical and paradigmatic transfigurations since the Renaissance, and the theoretical con-fusion between aesthetics and metaphysics.

II. ARCHAEOLOGY OF THE GROTESQUE: DIS-FIGURATION AT THE PRIMAL SCENE

The short survey of the current critical scenes tells us that the grotesque, as an elusive, slippery, and cryptic figure, resists our intellectual efforts of categorization and confounds our sense of perception. It seems the baffling definitions of the grotesque are generated somewhere in the interstice between those enigmatic mute figures in the "grottoes" and the subsequent "lexicographic artifacts" ascribed according to various paradigmatic, linguistic, and cultural systems over centuries. Evidently, the grotesque's coming into light implicates archeology and cryptology, or hauntology in a (post)-Derridean sense. A return to the "primal scene" of its excavation in Rome during the Renaissance period could help ground our research of this slippery concept concretely in a specific historical context and reappraise what those mute figures in the "grottoes" could possibly suggest to Renaissance scholars and artists alike.

It is common knowledge that the term "grotesque" is initially coined to describe those decorative arts on the walls and ceilings of *Domus Aurea*, or Golden House, built by Roman Emperor Nero between Caelian and Esquiline Hills in Rome (AD 64–68) and buried by earth after his death. The ruins of Nero's imperial palaces were rediscovered by chance in the fifteenth century beneath Esquiline Hill close to the Coliseums. Alessandra Zamperini in *Ornament and the Grotesque: Fantastic Decoration from Antiquity to Art Nouveau* shares her research on the grotesque's coming into being in the Renaissance era.[36]

> The word appears for the first time in the work of an anonymous Milanese painter, written between 1496 to 1498, and was originally intended to evoke an atmosphere rather than signify a particular iconography or form. At the time, the newly rediscovered imperial residence had appeared as a dark and gloomy sequence of underground caverns which by their very nature had suggested the idea of grottoes, and as a result the fantastic and extravagant ornamentation found in the ruins were called 'grotesque.'[37]

In short, the origin of the word "grotesque," etymologically speaking, derives from a historical event, the excavation of Nero's *Domus Aurea* or Golden House in 1490's. When this *grotto-esque* was rediscovered in Nero's *Domus Aurea,* Renaissance artists were amazed by "a bizarre world of metamorphic and teratomorphic creatures, or other hybrids or deviations from nature, combined with isolated figurative or mythological scenes."[38] Merely by accident, re-discovery of the grotesque coincides with the historical movement known as the Renaissance or resurrection, a cultural event noted for its radical imagination to transcend the theologically based representation by seeking innovative ways to revive arts. In due time, the newly discovered art form, i.e., the grotesque, provided new avenues for Renaissance artists to refresh their creative vision. Zamperini points out, the grotesque could represent "an intriguing form of visual subversion," "a counter-cultural imaginative spirit," and a chance to refashion a new mode of representation beyond the aesthetic principles of classical culture.[39] As a result, "contemporary artists flocked there to explore its cavernous interior and to copy its striking mural decorations."[40]

Some critics, notably Mary Russo, have already pointed out that the discovery of the "grotto" painting is marked as a cultural and historical event. For me, it also signifies a *return*, a Derridean *'revenant,'* a return of the other, a spectral one—"the very coming of the *revenant* or the return of the specter."[41] Discovery of grotesque art in this case seems to signal, instead of the origin, both a *return to* and a *return of* an uncanny "other." When grotesque art was re-discovered from the buried grottoes, it represented to Renaissance artists a spectral return, from a cryptic locale, of a repressed art dated from the classical period. Contemporary artists, like Vitruvius, were critical of "the subtle subversion of imagery" in this sort of mural decoration due to its deviation from and violation of the dominant ornamental systems of the time. Zamperini notes, "What contemporaries found disconcerting in the grotesque was precisely its unreality, the monstrosity and the fantasy that animated its inventions: they were shocked by the nonchalance, or even the complacency . . . given to unreal images, bizarre forms that had never been seen in nature."[42] In other words, not only did Renaissance artists discover a previous art form, they also resurrected a style of decoration that had been marginalized as an unorthodox counter-art by contemporary artists.

Terminologically speaking, "grotesque" involves all kinds of ironic twists as a proper or "improper" noun. First, the word "grotesque" coined on the occasion of its re-discovery does not reflect any aspects of the intriguing subject matter painted on the walls and ceilings of Nero's *Domus Aurea*. Second, "grotesque," literally meaning art from *grottoes*, i.e., cave painting, is named after a mistaken space since the locale of its discovery is not at all a grotto, but a huge palace complex of imperial grandeur. Third, the sketchy etymology, as several scholars have noted, suggests that the word's coming into being is more associated with the gloomy "atmosphere" of the cavernous grottoes at the moment of its excavation rather than with either the artists or the period of its creation. As Kayser concedes, "the creator of grotesques, however, must not and cannot suggest a meaning."[43] Silence is what we encounter at the phantasmagorical but unspeaking walls. As we know, any creation or discovery is a complex incident that, though situated in a specific historical context, is interlinked with all kinds of cultural legacies and ideological networks. Hence, we have to discern cautiously what specific artistic figures are painted in Nero's Golden House and what those figures represent, suggest, evoke or recall beyond the "primal scene" at the site of discovery.

First of all, what was actually discovered in the so-called "grottoes"? The murals on the walls and ceilings are filled with images of hybrid creatures, mythical figures, sphinxes, Bacchus, satyrs, Dionysian and Apollonian symbols—magic, mythical, and supernatural. These figures in general remind us of those imaginary hybrids of primitive culture, fabulous creatures of pagan origins or chimerical deities of the ancient past, henceforth fantastic, playful, and fanciful in terms of *fantasia*. Specifically, these artistic images reflect some of the orgiastic themes and metamorphic creatures in Olympic mythologies, reminiscent of the Greek cultural legacy of a remote past. Hybrid creatures used to be mysteriously conferred with extraordinary gift and the "the subject in incompatible elements" is sometimes endowed with Titanic ability and supernatural power. However, in the Christian light of the Medieval Era, these images would associate with the fallen world of the lost souls, distorted figures, and fragmented bodies, half-human and half-beast in moral terms. This reversion of meanings occurs with a shift of perspective from aesthetics to ethics, from art to theology. These contrasts of meanings and responses in fact trace back to two different cultural heritages in two different eras: the pantheistic age of the classical period and the monotheistic time of the Middle Ages.

Secondly, *Domus Aurea,* the imperial palace complex where grotesque art is discovered, is owned by a specific infamous historical figure, the insane and despotic Rome emperor Nero Claudius Drusus Germanicus during the first century AD. Instantly, this persona reminds us of the legendary scandals of immorality, licentiousness, and debauchery in those orgiastic rites when lusty human beings have lost control and indulged in demoralizing self-abandonment, thus becoming half-human and half-beast from an ethical point of view. John Clark notes, among others, "Mere association of this ludicrous and effete art with the name of the mad tyrant Nero lent it more macabre qualities of the ominous and the berserk."[44] Consequently, the notorious legend of Nero's lusciousness more or less has contributed to the subsequent perpetuation of the "disreputable" meanings of the grotesque and authentication of its "underground" nature as if the darkened grottoes indeed overflow with horrific tales, orgiastic lust, macabre death, and bloody mysteries.

Lastly, perhaps the most important and ironic of all, the word "grotesque," etymologically rooted in space, derives from a mistaken location, a grand palace of imperial residence misconstrued as a frightening dungeon. As noted, such art was created prior to its naming in terms of "*grotto-esque*," and the designs were never intended to be placed in the underground. However, "*grotto-esque*" as a "space metaphor" contributes crucially to defining the "ex-centric" and dis-figurative meanings for this kind of decorative art since the dark interior explicitly expressed by the term poetically sparks all kinds of illusions associated with mysterious terrains.[45]

The word "grotto" metaphorically suggests a haunted cave despite the fact that the subject matters painted on the walls and ceilings of the palace complex speak entirely otherwise. This displaced *space metaphor* evokes an array of other terms in connection with dark interiors by connotation: gothic, mysterious, nocturnal, spectral, cryptic, and haunted. Projected along the imaginary trajectory of a mysterious interior, the meanings of the grotesque wildly exceed the figures of grotesque art. All the adjectives do not speak back to the artistic figures designated by the proper noun as a style of decoration, but to the thrilling dark hole of an unknown sphere. As a space metaphor, "*grotto-esque*" suggests not only a physical location, but also the cryptic part of culture—dark tales, dark passions, dark deeds, dark souls, the dark corners of humans and societies, (and by extension) religious visions of hell, the Romantic notion of an uncanny self, the psychoanalytic concept of the unconscious, and the modernist idea of the underground man. John Clark observes, "Man always associated the underworld with the shadowy, the chaotic, and the unnatural, and the popular imagination regularly peopled Hades . . . with monstrous creatures, . . . devils, and demons."[46] The linguistic evocations and semantic associations with *grottoes* exude a sense of unknown horror, a *terra incognita*, which draws and absorbs all floating signifiers like a black hole. Connelly in *The Grotesque in Western Art and Culture: Image at Play* suggests: "It is . . . an open mouth that invites our descent into other worlds."[47] In this context, the grotesque truly becomes a parable of the cave, shadowy, mysterious, and apprehensive, and archaeology of the grotesque turns into some sorts of aesthetic cryptology.

The brief archaeological account tells us that nomenclature of the grotesque is a dubious, slippery, and ex-centric one from the very beginning because, to some extent, the term "grotesque" is not so much a name as *lack* of one. The word we use to describe the style of decoration found in Nero's Golden House bears neither thematic or etymological connection to the subject matter, nor biological or genealogical linkage to the artists; instead, the word refers to a displaced location on the occasion of its rediscovery—disfiguration at the very origin. Thus, calling it "grotesque" on re-discovery implies lack of a better term, probably a case of failure of making sense after all.

The Foucauldian archaeology of knowledge reminds us that at the primal scene we do not expect to discover one truth or any singular origin; instead, the so-called primal scenes often lead us elsewhere, to disparate sources and manifold traces of textual and cultural networks. Ontology often lapses into *mystology* and *hauntology*. As Mary Russo argues, "This singular event cannot, however, be taken as the discovery, much less the origin, of the grotesque; art historians have identified many examples of drawings and objects in the grotto-esque style which predate both classical and renaissance Rome."[48] What we have been calling "grotesque art" had existed long time ago before it was named in the fifteenth century when rediscovered in Nero's Golden House. This form of art, as Zamperini suggests, "may be traced back to Hellenistic culture and to oriental decorative ideas" even though the grotesque mode of decoration is found to be displayed most fully in the murals of Nero's *Domus Aurea.*[49] Hence, the word "grotesque" as a "conjunctive sign" probably would not qualify to signify the origin. Instead, the term only points to a refashioning of a buried artifact, and furthermore, those figures excavated in the grottoes lead us to early centuries, other times, other locations, and other cultures.[50] This archaeology of its rediscovery merely uncovers multiple traces interlaced with each other, likely a palimpsest sans origin. In this case, it seems we have confronted a kind of "ontological absence" beyond retrieval or recall in spite of its intricate semantic complexity and etymological overload.

As a result of the fundamental lack of clues to the original context, these grotesque figures are inevitably destined to an uncertainty of constant reconfigurations and perpetual displacements in an ex-centric evolution. Arguably, the grotesque is considered one of the slipperiest aesthetic terms, a kind of wildly "floating signifier." Following the spirit of Nietzsche, Terry Eagleton in *Ideology of the Aesthetics* has the following remark: "Genealogy unmasks the disreputable origins of noble notions, the chanciness of their functions, illuminating the dark workshop where all thoughts are fashioned."[51] The genealogy of the grotesque is a case in point.

III. GENEALOGY OF THE GROTESQUE: TRANSFIGURATION IN DIFFERENT AESTHETIC MODES.

The brief archaeological review of the primal scene reveals that the term "*grotto-esque*" speaks neither to the style of decoration nor to the creators of the masterpiece. Instead, the noun simply points to a mistaken locale. But, as an adjective, its configurative meanings associated with grottoes are comprised of a whole metonymic chain of loosely related or entirely unrelated terms. As a noun, "*grotto-esque*" does refer to a style—cave art in effect; but as an adjective, it is highly unstable, elusive, and contradictory, possibly signifying everything else but the designated style of art itself—a kind of metaphorical exile in a sense. However, as time went on, the negative attributes of the term prevailed largely and expanded disproportionally in the aesthetic evolution through different historical periods. Ironically, the initial meaning of the grotesque has gradually lapsed into obscurity and its extended and associative meanings, in the meanwhile, have proliferated so erratically and diffusely that the current common usage of its ex-centric meanings to a great extent come to dictate the *essence* of the grotesque. Geoffrey Harpham notes that "the original 'grotesque' murals no longer form the center of our definition of the term . . . and one is left with a bewildering image of the grotesque as an aesthetic orphan, wandering from form to form, era to era."[52]

A brief genealogical exploration, in this circumstance, can help trace how meanings of the grotesque have been adopted, derived, and altered, and how they have evolved with various shifts of framework, *episteme*, and perspective, or in Eagleton's words, how the grotesque has undergone its perpetual refashioning via a series of "dark workshops" of aesthetical remodeling according to the dominant paradigms and the central subjects in different historical periods. In short, there is no fixed *proper meaning* of the grotesque except a history of convoluted conceptualizations and varied significations with different uses. To be pertinent to the point of my critique, I will focus on reviewing and analyzing a number of major aesthetic paradigms in grotesque studies rather than covering the entire aesthetic history or the complete genealogy of the grotesque even if it were possible. In this section, by surveying how configurative meanings of the grotesque have evolved in dominant aesthetic discourses in several major historical periods and cultural contexts, I intend to attest that aesthetics and metaphysics have always been inextricably interlocked in figuration and transfiguration of the grotesque.

Here is a brief summary. During the Renaissance era, the grotesque was considered a fantastic style of decoration in opposition to the classical aesthetic tenets of harmony, order, and perfection and beyond the reality principle of mimesis or any "natural" order of beings. Further, it was mostly placed on the margin to decorate a central artistic subject—usually human figures celebrated in an image of god. Eventually, an ambivalent response to its uncanny nature developed into what I call the "aesthetics of ambiguity." In the Enlightenment period, the grotesque got its identity somewhat "fixed" as the ignoble and ridiculous other to the social order and rational paradigm—no longer marginal, but oppositional. A "negative aesthetics" was generated for the grotesque in terms of the irrational, the unreal, and the animalistic according to the light of reason. It was conceived not so much upon an aesthetic principle as on a metaphysical order, i.e., the central subject of rationality. During the Romantic age, the grotesque became a fascination with the exceptional rather than the normal and, eventually, an "aesthetics of the negative" emerged to unearth the secretive interior of the subject—dark passions and obsessed souls in some uncanny cases. For modernism, the grotesque was adopted as both an aesthetic trope and an *ontological posture* to turn the negative (loss of the subject) into an absurd subject (a subject of loss), thus achieving its full ontological status of an uncanny being instead of simply an aesthetic figure. The "aesthetics of paradox" instituted a grotesque subject of loss, disintegration, and disfiguration, not as an *exception* as it was in Romantic culture, but as a shared living condition or even a *norm* of existence. For the postmodern, the grotesque morphs into a radical discourse of heterogeneity, disparity, and alterity outside the bounds of the singular subject, and it is translated into other terms like the carnival, the abject, and the hybrid in the prospect of a postmodern heterology.[53]

The Renaissance: Aesthetics of Ambiguity: Fantastic and Bizarre

Quite literally, the so-called grotesque art was resurrected with the Renaissance when rediscovered in the fifteenth centuries in Nero's Golden House. Renaissance artists were amazed at what they saw in the dark grottoes. But at first, artists like Raphael were not ready to embrace it. Zamperini explains, "Raphael's initial hesitation ought not to come as a surprise. For it was symptomatic of the ambiguity that, as we have seen, was inherent in the genre (classical in origin, anti-classical in substance)—an ambiguity that would remain a constant of its development in a culture strongly imbued with classicized restrains."[54] Raphael's hesitation represents the typical ambivalent attitude of Renaissance artists toward grotesque art due to its deviation from the classical principles. It was years later before Raphael gradually accepted the grotesque as a mode of decorative style and spread it from Rome to other parts of Italy.[55]

As a decorative style, the grotesque's revival poses an ironic return in that Renaissance artists were resurrecting, in this case, not the standard classical style, but what classicism had invalidated as an anti-aesthetic style. This mode of representation runs counter to the fundamental tenets of classical aesthetics such as unity, harmony, order, and coherence. On the one hand, Renaissance artists were intrigued by its fantastic, mythical, and supernatural charm and, on the other hand, they were also concerned over its blatant violation of the principal aesthetic doctrines of classicism. This explains, to some degree, when Renaissance artists revived the grotesque as a style of decoration, it humbly occupied a marginal position. By and large, the grotesque was usually placed as a fanciful and playful decoration on margins to highlight the more serious classical subject matter at the center—a minor art serving the major subject. All these indicate Renaissance artists had carefully positioned themselves to this uncanny art style. After all they were still struggling to liberate their artistic vision from past legacies or attempting to overcome the anxiety of influence. Connelly observes: "To some, these bizarre improvisations seemed a complete contradiction of the core values of the classical tradition; to others, they opened up exciting new possibilities for reinventing that tradition in startling ways."[56] This uncertainty evidently reflected Renaissance artists' ambivalent attitude toward this form of decorative art that, in due time, developed into an ambiguous aesthetics in response to grotesque art.

The two terms initially emerged to describe the grotesque are "fantastic" and "bizarre," *synonymous* by semantic association but *antonymic* in etymological connotation. Both words signify "strange," but their implied meanings project along different linguistic trajectories in subtle but crucial ways. "Fantastic" slightly bends toward creative imagination, fantasy, and fancy beyond the real whereas "bizarre" vaguely suggests some sense of delinquent deviation, perversion, and aberration from the normal. One closely associates with "fabulous" and "phantasmagoric" while the other resonates with "eccentric" and "irregular." The Renaissance aesthetics toward the grotesque, to a degree, appears somewhat to be oscillating between the divergent trajectories of these two terms. Nevertheless, both words refer to the affect and connote surprisingly strange, startlingly unexpected, blankly inexplicable, namely, amazed or astonished over something uncanny. In short, an aesthetic response arises from one's confused state of mind or overwhelmed emotion as if spellbound. Moreover, in spite of their different connotations, both terms—fantastic and bizarre—are semantically elusive and slippery. Hence, neither "fantastic" nor "bizarre" suggests so much a concrete conceptualization as a slippage, somewhat at loss for words. It is evident that the initial meanings of the grotesque in terms of "fantastic" or "bizarre" imply incomprehension in an undecided interplay between two elusive words rather than a precise clarification. I believe, this ambivalent response suggests Renaissance artists' astonishment, confusion, and incomprehension in front of grotesque art as well as their subsequent confused coming to term with it. In addition, the "hesitancy" and amazement of Renaissance humanists in front of the cryptic other in the cave painting probably suggests a situation of the Freudian uncanny, namely, a return of the repressed. The aesthetics of ambiguity reflects insecurity, uncertainty, and ambivalence of Renaissance artists' relation to the dubious and uncanny figure of the grotesque.

Harpham suggests, there are two systems of art, "the art of the center that had a subject... according to traditional and conventional schemata, and an art of the fringe that, at least in terms of the center, had no subject, yielded no meaning, and represented things that were not, nor could be, nor had ever been."[57] I think Harpham is not simply echoing Vitruvius here. This statement not only exposes the marginal position that the grotesque occupies in the arena of art, but also points out the ontological position it fails to occupy in the realm of metaphysics due to possessing "no subject." It is a mode of art short of a singular, central, and coherent being of presence. The Renaissance retained the ambiguous aesthetics of the grotesque instead of resolving the ambivalence. However, when the Age of Reason came along, the grotesque changed dramatically from the ambiguous to the ridiculous. The unstable binary sustained in the aesthetics of ambiguity collapsed into a solitary monologue of reason's allegation against the grotesque and, subsequently, a negative aesthetics against the grotesque came into being in due time.

The Enlightenment: Negative Aesthetics: The Irrational and the Ridiculous Other

Though grotesque art is rediscovered in the Renaissance period, it is during the Age of Reason that the ambiguous nature of the grotesque gradually resolves toward a negative signification. When reason ascends to the position of the hegemonic order and the rational being is extolled as the singular subject, all previous charms that characterize the grotesque as "fantastic" are lost in the unequivocal light of reason. The fantastic downgrades to the ridiculous or the bizarre, the mythical deflates into the supernatural or the unnatural, and the playfully intermixed hybrid creatures transform into monstrous beasts, distorted bodies, and lost minds. As a result, a *negative aesthetics* countering the grotesque is gradually implemented with the rise of neoclassical aesthetics that is based upon the classical tenets of the coherent subject, rational order, and balanced structure. Instead of occupying a marginal position in culture, the grotesque turns into the oppositional other embodying irrational, disruptive, and ridiculous elements that require elimination and repudiation.

Several critics, Kayser, Connelly, Thomson, and Clayborough among others, note that it was during the eighteenth century that the semantics of the grotesque developed into a generic concept that extended substantially beyond the realm of decorative arts into culture and literature. Foucault in *The Order of Things* marks the eighteenth century as the originating moment for cataloguing and classifying in an encyclopedic fashion the entire universe in line with a hegemonic rational order and a uniform social standard. Arthur Clayborough, for instance, in *The Grotesque in English Literature* observes: "The word grotesque thus comes to be applied in a more general fashion in English during the Age of Reason—and of Neo-Classicism—when the characteristics of the grotesque style of art . . . are the object of ridicule and disapproval. The more general sense . . . which it has developed by the early eighteenth century is therefore that of 'ridicule, distorted, unnatural' (adj.); 'an absurdity, a distortion of nature' (noun)."[58] Connelly in her "Introduction" to *Modern Art and Grotesque* also states: "The neoclassical foundations of art history and aesthetics, with their emphasis on ideated beauty and rational inquiry, set up an intrinsic hostility toward the grotesque."[59] Therefore, as the age turned steadily toward reason, the grotesque drastically deformed from the fantastic into the ridiculous, from the enigmatic into the stigmatic.[60]

Interestingly, several current critics point out that the professional essayists emerged with the Enlightenment became the frontrunners to articulate, in a prescriptive fashion, the new aesthetic standards and vehemently combatted anything that deviated from the neoclassical creeds of coherence and unity in structure or identity. The grotesque, a disparate figure in composition, became a protuberant oddity of ridicule. Michel de Montaigne adamantly argues against all "grotesque and monstrous bodies, pieced together of the most diverse members" without any definite shape, order, coherence, or proportion.[61] Joseph Addison specifically singles out the hybrid genre of "the tragi-comedy" in English Theatre as "one of the most monstrous Inventions that ever entered into a Poet's Thoughts."[62] According to John Dryden, the grotesque consists of "parts of different species jumbled together, according to the mad imagination."[63] Samuel Johnson, in his famous *Preface to Shakespeare*, compiled an extensive list of allegations against Shakespeare for his violation of the neoclassical aesthetic standards—grotesque mixture, incongruity, disunity, and discrepancy in character, plot, time, place, structure, genre, and so forth.[64] For them, anything less than morally uplifting and artistically unifying was construed as grotesqueries or mockeries. Indeed, the grotesque style was adapted into a genre of mockery for both writers and essayists. Henry Fielding, Alexander Pope, Jonathan Swift, and Lawrence Sterne, among others, had all employed the grotesque as a form of satire in one way or the other. For instance, in his famous novel *Gulliver's Travels*, Jonathan Swift used the grotesque not only to ridicule the political farce of England but also, more importantly, to address an ontological issue: the disproportional bodies of Lilliputians and Brodingnagians likely signified ontological disfiguration either in terms of shrinkage or inflation of the standardized subject. This trend of satirical and comic grotesque focusing on interconnections between physical, moral, and metaphysical deformations was later adopted and further refashioned by writers like Dickens, Thackeray, and others in the Victorian age.

In this context, if the Renaissance mostly perceived the grotesque as a mode of representation, the Enlightenment generally conceived it as a flawed being that strayed from the rational order and violated the basic criteria of the coherent and logocentric subject. Obviously, the grotesque failed the test to pose itself as a legitimate and valid subject of identical and uniform being due to its heterogeneous and incongruous agglomeration. Consequently, the grotesque changed from an ambiguous artistic figure into an irrational and ridiculous other—a delinquent being outlawed by the hegemonic order of reason. Ironically, the grotesque's "identity" was fixed precisely at the moment when it failed to qualify itself as a subject category in the rational system. As such, the grotesque's identity was clarified as the other to reason, designated as the pure negative of the culture, and reduced to a ludicrous figure to embody irrationality, animality, and insanity.

The Romantic: Aesthetics of the Negative: The Uncanny between the Sublime and the Monstrous

In a sense, the aesthetics of the negative continued to evolve in the Romantic era, but toward a different direction. If Enlightenment critics had come up with a *negative aesthetics* for the purpose of ridiculing, repressing or eliminating the grotesque, i.e. the irrational, the Romantics instead embraced it as a kind of creative avenue to explore and expand the subject's internal space for both transgression and transcendence. To a certain degree, the negative aesthetics of the grotesque in Enlightenment and Romantic cultures are two sides of the same coin: one suppressed it as the disruptive other while the other indulged it as the uncanny other-self; one was appalled by its chaotic disfiguration whereas the other was fascinated with its mysterious transcendence. Eventually, the eighteenth century's *negative aesthetics* that refuted and derided the grotesque evolved into an *aesthetics of the negative* that "romanticized" the grotesque in a new era marked by uninhibited imagination, unreserved passion, and untamed nature. Though both Kant and Hegel, as prominent aestheticians of the Romantic era, ardently promote a romantic sublime, each still echoes, more or less, some of the basic ideas central to the nature of the grotesque. In his *Critique of Judgment,* Kant argues for a sublime of the "boundlessness," but only in terms of "a formless object" with "the want of accordance" that generates "negative pleasure."[65] In "Introduction to the Philosophy of Art," Hegel believes that the romantic sublime, a kind subjective transcendence, predominantly lies in the *reappearance* of "the indifference, incongruity, and antagonism of spiritual ideas and sensuous form, the characteristics of symbolic art," i.e., the "grotesque art" in his vocabulary.[66] Both approach the romantic sublime by reverting to those essential ideas that previously define the grotesque in one way or another.

It is a kind of cliché to repeat that the Romantic period is known for its reckless desire to discover, expand, and unveil the inside of the subjective territory—a mystical and frightening interior full of chaotic drives, often in the *name* of a *return* to the genuine existence and authentic nature. Different from the Enlightenment that tried to jettison and restrain the grotesque, the Romantic instead appealed to the grotesque to represent the hidden self in psychic depth and uncover the dangerous passion in the unconscious. On the one hand, the grotesque was resurrected from its previous repression and evolved as an emotive power to transgress rational boundaries, destabilize egocentric identities, and disrupt normalized existence; and on the other, it simultaneously aroused horror and nightmare, anxiety and death, associated with the demonic, the monstrous, the nocturnal, and the freakish. Bakhtin observes, "The world of Romantic grotesque is to a certain extent a terrifying world, alien to man."[67] After all, the Romantic age is renowned for its fascination with the deadly, the morbid, the macabre, the ghostly, and the phantasmagoric. Russo also notes that "the grotesque goes underground in the course of the nineteenth century, becoming increasingly hidden and dispersed—a private and 'nocturnal' category."[68] Thus, the Romantic aesthetics of the grotesque resides in an uncanny space between the sublime and the monstrous.

Even today, we are still indebted to those Romantic authors for producing some, if not all, of the most notorious and monstrous figures, real or imaginary, in the course of the Romantic period: the anonymous and atrocious monster (nowadays known by his master's name and probably more as his master's *double* than as his *other*) in Mary Shelly's novel *Frankenstein*; the madly erotic, perverse, blasphemous, violent, and cryptic persona—Marquis de Sade who, through both writings and misconducts and in either public place or private confinement, discloses a petrifying secretive terrain of otherness; and the mysterious and scary character of the disfigured Quasimodo in Victor Hugo's fiction *The Hunchback of Notre Dame*, to name a few. Poe's collection of short stories entitled *Tales of the Grotesque and Arabesque* is packed with characters obsessed with morbid, sickly, and horrific provinces of the eerie interior. Further, even the physical shapes of gothic churches or ghastly castles assume a metaphorical dimension to embody the cryptic inside of the subject itself, such as Horace Walpole's *The Castle of Otranto.* Sir Walter Scott's in his essay on "The Novels of E. T. A. Hoffman" more or less points out the most distinctive usages and unique aspects of the grotesque in Romantic culture: "the grotesque . . . introduces the most strange and complicated monsters . . . by the unbounded fertility of the author's imagination."[69]

The Romantics bent the grotesque toward the haunted areas of the uncanny, the perverse, the mysterious, and the horrific in terms of cryptology. The most important of all, the grotesque, teaming up with the gothic, conjured up a negative sublime to represent a deranged subject that was lost, insane or perverse.[70] In this context, the grotesque subject in Romantic culture reflected the ontological condition of a few particular individuals who had lost their minds and were preoccupied with repressed passion, revealing an abysmal interior full of chaos, mystery, and terror. The Romantic aesthetics of the grotesque opened up an unknown space—the cryptic unconscious inside the striving romantic subject.[71] In "Introduction" to *Modern Art and the Grotesque,* Connelly observes: "The romantic period marked the entrance of the grotesque into the mainstream of modern expression, as a means to explore alternative modes of existence."[72] Of course, it is modernism that extensively remodeled the grotesque on a large scale and inaugurated a new subject in agony due to its alienation, division, disintegration or loss.

The Modern: Aesthetics of Paradox: The Absurd Subject of Loss

It is very much in the twentieth century that the grotesque dominated the literary scene and expanded to all domains of life, so much so that modern writers vied with one another to re-fashion the modern subject through a grotesque makeover by producing one pervert after another, more absurd and psychotic than the last one. Kafka's *Metamorphosis*, Dostoevsky's *Underground Man*, Hesse's *Steppenwolf*, Joyce's *Ulysses*, and Ellison's *Invisible Man*, all testify to this trend. Numerous critics have extended their comments on the revival of grotesque literature in the twentieth century. For instance, Bakhtin notes that "the grotesque became the prevailing form of various modernist movements"[73] while Thomas Man believes that for modern literature "the grotesque is its most genuine style."[74] Robert Dunne in *A New Book of the Grotesque* states that modern writers started to "experiment with the concept of the grotesque as the condition of modern life rather than as a fantastic or supernatural phenomenon"[75] while Bernard McElroy in *Fiction of the Modern Grotesque* observes: "Not supernatural demons or devouring chimeras, but external powerlessness and psychic dissolution are the fears with which the modern grotesque plays, and that is the most modern thing about it."[76] In a sense, the romantic unconscious has turned into a modern obsession. In the course of modernism, a shift of reference occurred for the grotesque from a purely aesthetic phenomenon of wild imagination to a concrete form of social existence, from a private psychological interior to a broad cultural milieu, from a supernatural whim to a metaphysical condition. Surprisingly, the grotesque has changed its status from an erratic exception in Romantic culture to a banal norm in modern society and henceforth assumed a new status in social, metaphysical, and existential categories.

The modern age has often been characterized in terms of repressive social conformity and mass production of uniform identity, i.e., loss of individuality, especially according to Marxist critics like Theodor Adorno and Max Horkheimer in their critique of mass society in *Dialectic of Enlightenment*. Under capitalist monopoly, all subjects became "identical" with "ruthless unity" like "ready-made cliché."[77] Further, Georg Lukács in "The Ideology of Modernism" argues, "Life under capitalism is, often rightly, presented as a distortion (a petrification or paralysis) of the human substance. . . . Distortion becomes the normal condition of human existence" and "eccentricity becomes the necessary complement of the average" and, consequently, "non-existence is the ground of all existence."[78] Clearly, Lukács holds the capitalist society responsible for producing a subject of "distortion," "eccentricity," and "non-existence," or in other words, a grotesque subject. Thus, according to the Marxist view, the grotesque is by no means a rare condition peculiar only to a few outcast perverts in modern society; on the contrary, the grotesqueness is prevalent and central to the normative constitution of modern man as well as the fundamental reality of his social environments.

In a broad scope, many modern thinkers across disciplines have contributed to disclosing the *grotesque* ontological status of man in a series of *essential* decenterments and losses. Prominently, it is Nietzsche that initially declared the death of God, or the loss of the absolute ontological center, thereby inaugurating a nihilist age of void fraught with anxiety. Both Darwin and Freud helped undermine the sublime illusion of the unitary ontological condition of the singular subject by either unveiling the unholy genealogical linkage to the animal origin sans divinity or uncovering the irrational unconscious inside the egocentric locus beyond logos. They all exposed a kind of primordial loss that unsettled the grand illusion of man as singular, rational or divine and led to a grotesque makeover of the ex-centric modern subject. Victor Strandberg in "The Crisis of Belief in Modern Literature" puts it sarcastically: "Under the double impact of Darwin's contention that man is only an animal and Freud's contention that he is hardly a noble animal at that, modern writers have indeed tended to scale man sharply downward in the great chain of being."[79] However, what was particularly upsetting in the ideas brought forth by Nietzsche, Darwin, and Freud was not so much the discovery of an unconscious linkage to *animality* per se as the devastating awakening to an *essential loss* of man's wholly or holy identity with the death of God. In other words, it was the disappearance of a divine center and the subsequent loss of a specular image reflected by God that traumatically erased human's narcissistic identity and reduced the human subject to the grotesque. If Hamlet could still indulge in a grand illusion of man as a remarkable "piece of work" during the Renaissance era, modern man, instead, found himself stripped of all the cultural ideals he had amassed in the course of civilization and mercilessly deprived of all the so-called "inalienable" fortunes of sublime rationality or holy divinity he had conjured up in his dreams. No wonder, existentialism became, so to speak, a *new metaphysics* in terms of loss, absurdity, void, alienation, and absence. "You are all a lost generation," to quote Gertrude Stein here. Ontology, in this case, became *hauntology*, with all sorts of ghost haunting the modern subject.

Consequently, the grotesque becomes *the* mode to represent and explore all fields of life and all aspects of society as William Van O'Connor in *The Grotesque* alerts that "our writers are terribly preoccupied with . . . the grotesque" on various fronts.[80] On the one hand, the grotesque is connected to disruptive power of unconscious desires as Robert Helbling in *The Power of Negative Thinking* points out that "though an aesthetic phenomenon, the grotesque may have psychological roots in the oneiric forces erupting in our mental life,"[81] and on the other hand, Michael Meyer, in his "Introduction" to *Literature and the Grotesque*, believes the grotesque "speaks to something profoundly basic about human nature and about the nature of existence itself."[82] According to Bernard McElroy, "The modern grotesque is internal, not infernal, and its originator is recognized as neither god nor devil but man himself," and he hastens to add that "perversity is the weapon with which the individual fights for his autonomy against the stupid conformity of the average man."[83] Hence, the grotesque is employed to depict all facets of our daily existence and, moreover, as Dieter Meindl reminds, the grotesque in modern literature "is used to initiate a humanizing and individualizing process" and to create "highly individualized literary characters."[84] In this case, the grotesque is adopted as a radical stance to mark oneself as a distinctive *subject* to challenge the social repression and resist normalized anonymity.

The grotesque subject in modernism emerges as a *posture* of an absurd being at the moment when the dominant subject of Western metaphysics has lost its ontological footing in the wake of the death of God. Correspondingly, a new type of absurd figure in literature arises ineptly in response to the void by the name of "*anti*-hero" after the demise of traditional heroes and loss of ontological centrality.[85] As a paradoxical figure, the antihero is not only haunted by a pervasive sense of loss, but also demonstrating a narcissistic obsession with the phantoms of all idealized heroic qualifications even though nowhere close to matching them. Holden Caulfield in *The Catcher in the Rye*, Quentin Compson in *The Sound and the Fury*, and Hazel Motes in *Wise Blood* are all infatuated, narcissistically, with phantoms of an impossible subject in the context of a significant loss. Kristeva's *Strangers to Ourselves* profoundly investigates the metaphysical homelessness and ontological ex-centricity of the modern subject in terms of an ontological "foreigner" as symbolized by the nameless protagonist in Camus' masterpiece *The Stranger*. Kristeva argues that "the foreigner has no self" and is constituted by "a fantastic of absence."[86] Despite the internal void, "the foreigner is a dreamer making love with absence" and "proudly holds on to what he lacks, to absence, to some symbol of other."[87] In short, as a foreigner, he has lost his idealized home both physically and metaphysically, i.e., ontologically dislodged and displaced elsewhere.[88]

In the due course of modernism, the grotesque that had been largely slighted in the past as the marginal other paradoxically took the central stage to represent the modern subject in alienation, crisis or demise. Decenterment, disfiguration, disintegration, and disparity, all the negative attributes that had previously been employed to disqualify the grotesque as a subject category were recalled to embody or *dis-embody* the modern subject. Ironically, the grotesque was invoked to represent the dominant ontological state of the modern subject for exactly the same reason it was dismissed before. The *grotesque subject*, I argue, was championed possibly as *the last mythology* to mark these protagonists as the "distinctive individuals" in history. All modern protagonists, in one form or another, attempted to ground their paradoxical posturing of an identity in alienation, disfiguration, and decenterment. In this case, the grotesque not only reflected the existential conditions of modern society (with organized repression and internalized alienation), but also figured as a paradoxical *desire* for subject formation. Instead of escaping the grotesque, the modern protagonists embraced the grotesque as a paradoxical mode of identification in disintegration. That is, a *paradoxical subject* of void, disintegration, disparity, and loss comes into being in the name of the grotesque. Ironically, loss of the subject is refashioned into a subject of loss and eventually the aesthetics of paradox and ontology of absence emerge as one.[89]

This brief review reveals that the grotesque, instead of being a unified and stable identity, has been continuously shaped and reshaped in a site of ongoing contestation in an amorphous field. It morphs from a marginal art in the Renaissance period to an irrational other during the Enlightenment era, from an uncanny figure in Romantic culture to a central but ex-centric subject in modern society. In this gradual alteration from an artistic figure in terms of *fantasia* to a human subject of social reality, the aesthetics of the grotesque changes variably in terms of a poetics of darkness, a psychology of perversion, a pathology of the mind, and an ontology of *essential loss*. This interminable alteration of the grotesque, with all kinds of twists and turns of paradigmatic drifts, unfolds its complex aesthetic evolutionary process as well as its linkage of and passage into the metaphysical area.

The Postmodern Turn toward Heterologies

In a nutshell, if the grotesque in modernism is characterized by an obsession with void, nada, or loss of the transcendental subject of singularity, i.e., God, then in postmodern culture the grotesque as a rhetoric trope plays a pivotal role of initiating disparity, maximizing difference, and inaugurating alterity. In the wake of the death of the metanarrative proclaimed by Jean-François Lyotard in *The Postmodern Condition*, i.e., the demise of all privileged central perspectives or singular paradigms, the grotesque in postmodern discourses figures crucially to articulate difference in the context of the *other* studies and henceforth has been translated into a variety of other terms, such as "carnival," "abject," "hybrid," and "mestiza," in an alternative aesthetics of art and a heterological discourse of "being otherwise" beyond the hegemonic paradigm of the singular, total, and unitary being. This return to a carnival mode of the grotesque *in the name of the other* helps ground the postmodern revision of human beings in terms of hybridization of identities, carnivalization of difference, and celebration of heterogeneity and diversity in a radical discourse along the trajectory of heterologies. (I will return to this issue in Chapter 6.)

IV: CONCLUSION: AESTHETICS OF ART AND METAPHYSICS OF BEING

The short genealogical account of the grotesque from the Renaissance to the modern era shows that the subject of the grotesque has always been configured along the conspicuously divisive but inextricably indivisible borderline between aesthetics and metaphysics. In *Aesthetic Theory*, Adorno asserts, "Art perceived strictly aesthetically is art aesthetically misperceived."[90] This is particularly true in this case since the aesthetics of the grotesque is, in effect, a metaphysical reconfiguration of the grotesque *otherwise*. Historically, the identity of art was initially defined within the academic discipline of philosophy, and aesthetics has always had an entangled relationship with metaphysics. Throughout history, Western aesthetics always has a tendency to evaluate art in the context of a metaphysical presence and according to a prior transcendental order. Ontology as the first principle of philosophy or metaphysics of presence is primarily dependent upon a unitary principle of singular identity to approach the question of being, or being qua identical and singular identity.

This relationship between aesthetics and metaphysics can certainly trace back to one of the earliest writings on art by Plato. In Plato's *Republic*, art is deemed inferior due to, mostly, the single fact that it lacks ontological presence, therefore a copy, a duplicate, a forgery, a shadow, several times removed from the real—the ultimate metaphysical order. In the court of metaphysicians, art is judged to be dubious, useless, problematic, misleading, and even dangerous predominantly due to its unreal nature and polemic ontology. Inevitably, as a philosopher, Plato launches his aesthetic thesis with a metaphysical locus so that art's nature precariously hinges upon the ontological framework. In this view, art is problematic because it lacks metaphysical qualification: being, truth, and reality. Consequently, the discourse of art becomes a metaphysical conspiracy against art. So, art is haunted and bounded by metaphysics.

However, the grotesque as an art category poses a special problem to the mimetic model because it cannot even be compared to a *bad copy* or *any kind of copy* of reality or nature. Put simply, it is not a copy at all. Plato's copy analogy aborts here. Different from mimetic art that aims to represent a prior superior metaphysical order such as reality, nature or truth, grotesque art deviates from reflection or imitation of any kind of ontological presence. It cannot refer back to the so-called real or natural. At best, pure illusion, and at worst, a nightmare of the most horrible kind: neither human, nor animal, nor plant, it signals a kind of confusion or distortion of all singular categories and, in effect, an ontological disfiguration. As an art in the mode of *fantasia,* it could be fantastic or playful, but from a metaphysical view, it is merely lack, confusion, violation, and impossibility. As classical architect Vitruvius believes, "it has never been, never is, and never will be."[91] Ultimately, most semantic "workshops" on the grotesque are not exactly definitions at all, but metaphysical reductions and disfigurations. Henceforth, what is discovered in discourse of the grotesque unveils the complicated and insidious underground work of metaphysical parlance. Ironically, the grotesque becomes the *unsignifiable* or *insignificant* precisely due to the fact that all the lexicographic efforts and semantic endeavors are so dependent upon the metaphysical frame to come to term with it.[92]

Kayser remarks, "I tend to regard him [Hegel] as the last thinker whose analysis of the grotesque encompasses the metaphysical depth of the phenomenon, which was to be so totally lost sight of by his successors."[93] Kayser laments that Hegel's metaphysical engagement with the grotesque in his *Aesthetics: Lecture on Fine Art* has been dropped from history ever since. On this point, I hold a different opinion. I believe the discourse of the grotesque in effect has never left the metaphysical arena at all because the aesthetics of the grotesque has been inescapably and inextricably interlocked with issues of subjectivity defined by the metaphysical tradition. The aesthetics of the grotesques, I contest, has always hung onto the framework of metaphysics. Reviewing the past scholarship of the grotesques, one cannot fail to notice that the discourse of the grotesque, to a great extent, remains captive of Plato's vision and still anchors the aesthetics of the grotesque to a metaphysical ground. In the official aesthetics throughout history, the grotesque has been mostly viewed as lack of realty and violation of coherence, counter to the fundamental principles of metaphysic of presence (real or natural), and in opposition to the basic criteria of ontological being (singularity and coherence). Due to this significant lack, the grotesque has been consistently placed in the position of the other in the entire history of dominant aesthetics. In other words, the long list of the derogative words accumulated in the history of Western culture is very much the collective labor to repress or eliminate it. In short, ontology of the singular subject and metaphysics of presence constitute a kind of "aesthetic unconscious" that governs and regulates the discourse of the grotesque.

Bakhtin in *The Dialogic Imagination* reminds us that the complicated cultural and linguistic network of each word unfolds a long history of "the inexhaustible wealth" and "the socially heteroglot multiplicity of its names, definitions and value judgments."[94] The word grotesque is a case in point: its history of meaning consists of a heteroglossia of inter-verbal and inter-cultural trans-acts. To trace the grotesque is like to trace the impossible, semantically as well as genealogically. Oftentimes, the critical efforts, instead of restoring its original meanings, uncover a complex cultural network of significations that lead us elsewhere. What we believe to be the primal scene of discovering the grotesque might simply be one clue leading to other scenes beyond the prior scene of revelation in the grottoes in Renaissance Italy. The "*grotto-esque*," true to its name, suggests a haunted space of the mystic other that evokes and recalls all kinds of historical, cultural, and artistic legacies.

Several critics, such as Harpham, Kayser, and Bakhtin, attended to clues linking to the mythological associations and oriental connections; however, only limited efforts have been devoted to further research along this line of thought. Past scholars in general only mentioned, in passing, vague implications or remote associations of chimera figures with the grotesque, but none has offered extensive analysis or substantial research on this issue. For instance, Harpham, in *On the Grotesque*, a huge work on the topic, only fleetingly reflects the lost track: "From the moment of its appearance in Western culture, *grottesche* represented an invocation of 'some other phase of being,' of mythological culture that was permanently lost."[95] The next chapter will attempt to retrieve this track.

NOTES

1. To date, most critics still reiterate the same rhetoric of impossibility of restricting the grotesque studies to one specific area. Justin D. Edwards and Rune Graulund state in *Grotesque*, one of the most recent books on the topic, "As a term, grotesque can thus never be locked into any one meaning or form, historical period or specific political function" (2013, 15).

2. Peter Brooks, "Freud's Masterplot," in *The Critical Tradition: Classical Texts and Contemporary Trends*, ed. David Richter (New York: St. Martin's Press, 1998), 1042, 1038.

3. In fact, there are many excellent books that trace the origin as well as the semantic development of the concept of the grotesque. Among them, several stand out brilliantly, offering either a succinct historical critique or a focused thematic analysis: Harpham's *On the Grotesque*; Russo's *The Female Grotesque: Risk, Excess and Modernity*; Clayborough's *The Grotesque in English Literature*; Kayser's *The Grotesque in Art and Literature*; Bakhtin's *Rabelais and His World*; Zamperini's *Ornament and the Grotesque: Fantastic Decoration from Antiquity to Art Nouveau;* Haar's *The Phenomenon of the Grotesque in Modern Southern Fiction: Some Aspects of Its Form and Function*; and Connelly's *The Grotesque in Western Art and Culture: Image at Play*. Historically, many writers and critics have also contributed to grotesque studies, systematically or sporadically, such as Dryden, Rustin, Hugo, Scott, and Vitruvius, to name a few.

4. Alan Spiegel, "A Theory of the Grotesque in Southern Fiction," *Georgia Review* 26, (1977): 426.

5. Here is a partial list of the reference sources: *Oxford English Dictionary*; *A Dictionary of Literary Terms and Literary Theory* edited by J. A. Cuddon; *A Dictionary of Modern Critical Terms* edited by Roger Fowler; *A Handbook to Literature* edited by William Harmon and Hugh Holman; *Encyclopedia of Contemporary Literary Theory: Approaches, Scholars, Terms* edited by Irena R. Markaryk; *The Bedford Glossary of Critical and Literary Terms* by Ross Murfin and Supryia Ray; and *Dictionary of Literary Terms and Motifs* by Jean-Charles Seigneuret.

6. Geoffrey Galt Harpham, *On the Grotesque: Strategies of Contradiction in Art and Literature* (Princeton: Princeton UP, 1982), xxi.

7. James Luther Adams and Wilson Yates, preface to *The Grotesque in Art and Literature: Theological Reflections*, ed. James Luther Adams and Wilson Yates (Michigan: William B. Eerdmans P, 1997), xiii.

8. Robert Doty, *Human Concern/Personal Torment: The Grotesque in American Art* (New York: Praeger Publishers, 1969), 4.

9. Wolfgang J. Kayser, *The Grotesque in Art and Literature*, trans. Ulrich Weisstein (Bloomington: Indiana UP, 1963), 36, 24, 79.

10. Harpham, *On the Grotesque*, 9, 5, xxi.
11. Philip John Thomson, *The Grotesque* (London: Methuen, 1972), 14.
12. Dieter Meindl, *American Fiction and the Metaphysics of the Grotesque* (Columbia: U of Missouri P, 1996), 15–16.
13. Peter Stallybrass and Allon White, *The Politics and Poetics of Transgression* (Ithaca: Cornell UP, 1986), 44.
14. Wilson Yates, "An Introduction to the Grotesque: Theoretical and Theological consideration," in *The Grotesque in Art and Literature*, ed. James Luther Adams and Wilson Yates (Michigan: William B. Eerdmans P, 1997), 2.
15. Thomson, *The Grotesque*, 27, 5, 9.
16. Robert E. Helbling, *The Power of Negative Thinking: The Grotesque in Modern World* (Salt Lake City: Reynolds Association, 1982), 5.
17. Kayser, *The Grotesque in Art and Literature*, 21.
18. Frances S. Connelly, introduction to *Modern Art and the Grotesque*, ed. Frances S. Connelly (Cambridge: Cambridge UP, 2003), 2.
19. Kayser, *The Grotesque in Art and Literature*, 37.
20. John Ruskin in the third volume of his monumental work *The Stones of Venice* (1851–1853) offered an elaborate description of the grotesque in a similar rhetoric of polarized response. To quote Ruskin in full here: "It seems to me that the grotesque is, in almost all cases, composed of two elements, one ludicrous, the other fearful; that, as one or other of these elements prevails, the grotesque falls into two branches, sportive grotesque and terrible grotesque; but that we cannot legitimately consider it under these two aspects, because there are hardly any examples which do not in some degree combine both elements; there are few grotesques so utterly playful as to be overcast with no shade of fearfulness, and few so fearful as absolutely to exclude all ideas of jest (Ruskin *Venice* 3:115)." Quoted in James Goodwin, *Modern American Grotesque: Literature and Photography* (Columbus: Ohio State UP, 2009), 10.
21. Kayser, *The Grotesque in Art and Literature*, 58.
22. Harpham, *On the Grotesque*, 5.
23. Bernard McElroy, *Fiction of the Modern Grotesque* (Basingstoke: Macmillan, 1989), 16.
24. John Clark, *The Modern Satirical Grotesque and Its Tradition* (Lexington: Lexington UP, 1991), 19.
25. Helbling, *The Power of Negative Thinking*, 25.
26. Kayser, *The Grotesque in Art and Literature*, 29, 185.
27. Dianne Marie Zandstra, *Embodying Resistance: Griselda Gambaro and the Grotesque* (Lewisburg: Bucknell UP, 2007), 16.
28. Clark, *The Modern Satirical Grotesque and Its Tradition*, 25.
29. Connelly, introduction to *Modern Art and the Grotesque*, 4.
30. Geoffrey Galt Harpham, "The Grotesque: The First Principle," *Journal of Aesthetics and Art Criticism* 34, no 4 (1976): 463.
31. Harpham, *On the Grotesque*, 3, 6.
32. Harpham, *On the Grotesque*, 32.
33. McElroy, *Fiction of the Modern Grotesque*, ix.
34. Harpham, *On the Grotesque*, 3.
35. Aesthetics can be defined narrowly as a distinct branch of learning, i.e., a philosophy of the beautiful or broadly as a critical discourse reflecting, perceiving, and evaluating the most general principles and nature of art. In this project, I use the term in the latter sense of the word and it involves and encompasses both emotional response toward art and intellectual judgment or critical reflection of the nature of art.
36. Alessandra Zamperini's *Ornament and the Grotesque: Fantastic Decoration from Antiquity to Art Nouveau* is considered one of the best books published recently. It traces the evolution of the grotesque as an art of decoration from Nero's Golden House to recent developments in *nouveau* art. She provides a succinct definition of the grotesque: "In the classic definition, the term 'grotesque' denotes a form of fanciful mural decoration based on a system of images comprising real and imaginary creatures, derived from both the plant and animal

worlds. These images are combined without any narrative or spatial connection between them, and their subjects are generally metamorphic in nature. Flowers, plants, animal, or mythological beings such as sirens, griffins or centaurs, to name a few, are painted against uniform grounds and undergo various kinds of transmutation" (2008, 6).

37. Alessandra Zamperini, *Ornament and the Grotesque: Fantastic Decoration from Antiquity to Art Nouveau*, trans. Peter Spring (London: Thames & Hudson, 2008), 9.

38. Ibid.

39. Ibid.

40. Ibid., 6.

41. Jacques Derrida, *Specters of Marx: The State of the Debt, the Work of Mourning, and the New International*, trans. Peggy Kamuf (New York: Routledge, 1994), 6.

42. Zamperini, *Ornament and the Grotesque*, 6.

43. Kayser, *The Grotesque in Art and Literature*, 186.

44. Clark, *The Modern Satirical Grotesque and Its Tradition,* 19.

45. In this case, the metaphorical implications of the world *grotto-esque* associated with a dark space would certainly have pleased Freud for multiple different reasons, maybe particularly due to its naming after a mistaken location. First, grotesque art in Nero's Golden House has been literally repressed for centuries till the end of the Middle Ages. Secondly, those so-called monstrous figures painted in the grottoes could be supporting evidence symptomatic of the unconscious desires or a carnival drive beyond the logocentric order or the egocentric subject. And lastly, the cryptic space of grottoes, a perfect metaphor for the unconscious, suggests underground, subjugation, repression, burial, death, haunting, womb-and-tomb, or Thanatos and Eros.

46. Clark, *The Modern Satirical Grotesque and Its Tradition,* 19.

47. Frances S. Connelly, *The Grotesque in Western Art and Culture: Image at Play* (New York: Cambridge UP, 2012), 1. In an epigraph to the book, Connelly cites Da Vinci's response to make a point: "After having remained at the entry [of a grotto] some time, two contrary emotions arose in me, fear and desire—fear of the threatening dark grotto, desire to see whether there were any marvelous thing within it" (2012, 1). Apparently, Da Vinci's reaction focuses on his entry of the grotto, the dark interior, or the mistaken location instead of the artistic representation *inside* the grottoes. In addition, the contradictory emotions of fear and desire invoked by the grotto reflect the typical uncanny response to the dark space metaphor of womb-and-tomb.

48. Mary Russo, *The Female Grotesque: Risk, Excess and Modernity* (New York: Routledge, 1994), 3.

49. Zamperini, *Ornament and the Grotesque*, 6.

50. I would like to acknowledge that, historically, some scholars also noted the connection between the grotesque and the arabesque. For instance, Swain states, "Although *grottesque* was the original name for the style, *arabesque* and *grotesque* were interchangeable terms well before the eighteenth century. The semantic confusion stems from the discovery of the arabesques in the cavelike ruins, or 'grotto,' of Rome and Pompeii. *Grotesque* therefore names the style with reference to its point of origin" (2004, 199). For Further reference, please see Virginia Swain's *Grotesque Figures: Baudelaire, Rousseau, and the Aesthetics of Modernity.*

51. Terry Eagleton, *The Ideology of the Aesthetic* (Malden: Blackwell P, 1990), 236.

52. Harpham, "The Grotesque: The First Principle," 461.

53. Bakhtin in *Rabelais and His World* traced, to some extent, and also discussed the altered meanings of the grotesque in several historical periods and literary movements. Here I reframe the survey, with a different focus and for a different purpose, along the hazy borderline between aesthetics and metaphysics. Also, in this historical survey, I do not intend to include Bakhtin's concept of the carnivalesque for several reasons. Critics familiar with the subject matter will notice that I have deliberately skipped Bakhtin's concept of the carnival that most critics tend to believe is identical to and synonymous with the grotesque. I hold a different opinion. In short, between the grotesque and the carnival, there is a difference and this difference deserves a thorough investigation in a separate chapter. I will return to this in Chapter 6.

54. Zamperini, *Ornament and the Grotesque*, 122.

55. One of the masterpieces of grotesque art was completed by Raphael, around 1515, on the pillars of the Papal Loggias in Vatican where the grotesque images and ornaments mostly occupy the position of the margins, seldom at the center. Many critics, including Kayser and Harpham, refer to this instance as evidence of Renaissance artists' use of the grotesque as a style of decoration.

56. Connelly, *The Grotesque in Western Art and Culture*, 32.

57. Harpham, *On the Grotesque*, 32.

58. Arthur Clayborough, *The Grotesque in English Literature* (Oxford: Clarendon P, 1965), 6.

59. Connelly, introduction to *Modern Art and the Grotesque*, 2.

60. Several other sources also point out this trend. For instance, in *A Dictionary of Literary Terms and Literary Theory* edited by J. A. Cuddon, the entry says: "But it does not seem to have been used regularly in a literary context until the 18th c., the period of the age of reason and Neoclassicism . . . when it was commonly employed to denote the ridiculous, bizarre, extravagant, freakish and unnatural; in short, aberrations from the desirable norms of harmony, balance and proportion" (1991, 393).

61. Quoted in Kayser, *The Grotesque in Art and Literature*, 24.

62. Quoted in Frances Barasch, *The Grotesque: A Study in Meaning* (The Hague: Mouton, 1971), 133.

63. Quoted in Maria Haar, *The Phenomenon of the Grotesque in Modern Southern Fiction: Some Aspects of its Form and Function* (Stockholm: Alquist and Wiksel International, 1983), 2.

64. Though a prominent authority to found and advocate proper decorum, coherent structure, and integral forms, Samuel Johnson himself ironically does not escape from a satirical critique in terms of the grotesque. Please refer to Rocco Coronato's *Johnson versus Bakhtin: Carnival and the Grotesque.*

65. Immanuel Kant, "From *Critique of Judgment*," in *The Critical Tradition: Classical Texts and Contemporary Trends*, ed. David Richter (New York: St. Martin's Press, 1998), 269–70, 273, 270.

66. Hegel, Georg Wilhelm Friedrich. *The Introduction to Hegel's Philosophy of Fine Art*. Trans. Bernard Bosanquet. London: Kegan Paul, Trench & Co., 1886.

67. Mikhail Bakhtin, *Rabelais and His World*, trans. Helene Iswolsky (Bloomington: Indiana UP, 1984), 38.

68. Russo, *The Female Grotesque*, 53.

69. Quoted in Kayser, *The Grotesque in Art and Literature*, 77.

70. The subtle difference between the grotesque and the sublime, though sometimes a vague one, can be discerned. In his *Critique of Judgment*, "Second Book: Analytic of the Sublime," Kant writes: "The feeling of the sublime is therefore a feeling of pain arising from the want of accordance between the aesthetical estimation of magnitude formed by the imagination and the estimation of the same formed by reason. There is at the same time a pleasure thus excited, arising from the correspondence with rational ideas of this very judgment of the inadequacy of our greatest faculty of sense, in so far as it is a law of us to strife after these ideas" (Richter 1998, 273). Thus the sublime, according to Kant, signifies a state of mind where the rational faculty fails to account for it or, in other words, the sublime defies the rational faculty. Whereas, I pose, the grotesque is more associated with the ontological chaos or it fails to fit into any ontological or metaphysical category of singular being. Though both as aesthetical phenomena, the sublime is inclined toward overwhelming and overtaking the logocentric subject whereas the grotesque is predisposed toward ambivalence, incomprehension, and confusion of the egocentric subject. One resides beyond the boundaries of rational and conceptual frameworks while the other signifies transgression of ontological and metaphysical order though both express failure of cognition and overriding of the subject. One indicates pain and pleasure, a kind of catharsis and therapeutics, while the other involves fascination and repulsion, a kind of confusion of horror and mirth. One links the aesthetic to the rational while the other resides between the aesthetic and the ontological.

71. Many critics have pointed out the polarized positions between Bakhtin and Kayser. In *The Grotesque in Art and literature*, Kayser sees the grotesque as sinister, nocturnal, and

ominous whereas Bakhtin, in *Rabelais and His World*, envisions the grotesque as joyous, festive, and carnival. However, it is interesting to note that, although differing on many other issues, Bakhtin and Kayser concur on the role of the grotesque in Romantic culture: subjective, monstrous, and alien. Both heavily rely upon the ideas initially introduced by Victor Hugo and Walter Scott to support their claims.

72. Connelly, introduction to *Modern Art and the Grotesque*, 1.

73. Bakhtin, *Rabelais and His World*, 51. However, Bakhtin's concept of "grotesque realism" in the context of "a new and powerful revival of the grotesque" in the twentieth century can be misleading because the writers he listed as evidence of support almost exclusively belong to what we now characterize as modernists instead of realists. In *Rabelais*, Bakhtin observes: "The latest development of this genre is considerably complex and contradictory. Generally speaking, two main lines of development can be traced. The first line is the modernist form (Alfred Jarry), connected in various degrees with the Romantic tradition and evolved under the influence of existentialism. The second line is the realist grotesque (Thomas Mann, Bertold Brecht, Pablos Neruda, and others)" (1984, 46). All writers on the list can be arguably labeled modernists.

74. Thomas Man, "Conrad's Secret Agent," in *The Art of Joseph Conrad: A Critical Symposium*, ed. R. W. Stallman (East Lansing: Michigan UP, 1960), 231.

75. Robert Dunne, *A New Book of the Grotesques: Contemporary Approaches to Sherwood Anderson's Early Fiction* (Ohio: Kent UP, 2005), 2.

76. McElroy, *Fiction of the Modern Grotesque*, 22.

77. Max Horkheimer and Theodor W. Adorno, *Dialectic of Enlightenment*, trans. John Cumming (New York: Continuum, 1998), 123, 125. According the Frankfurt school critics, especially Adorno and Horkheimer in their *Dialectic of Enlightenment* and Herbert Marcuse in his *One-Dimensional Man*, mass society is established upon repression, alienation, and disintegration, thus reducing each individual to an anonymous nonbeing in the very process of standardization. Some critics have developed this line of thought further in the postmodern discourse of technology. For further reference, please see *Pathology of the Modern Self: Postmodern Studies on Narcissism, Schizophrenia, and Depression* edited by David Michael Levin.

78. George Lukács, "The Ideology of Modernism," in *The Critical Tradition: Classical Texts and Contemporary Trends*, ed. David Richter (New York: St. Martin's Press, 1998), 1135, 1134, 1141.

79. Victor Strandberg, "The Crisis of Belief in Modern Literature," *The English Journal* 53, no. 7 (1964): 476.

80. William Van O'Connor, *The Grotesque: An American Genre and Other Essays* (Carbondale: Southern Illinois UP, 1962), 4.

81. Helbling, *The Power of Negative Thinking*, 3.

82. Michael Meyer, introduction to *Literature and the Grotesque*, ed. Michael Meyer (Amsterdam: Rodopi, 1995), i.

83. McElroy, *Fiction of the Modern Grotesque*, 21, 28.

84. Dieter Meindl, *American Fiction and the Metaphysics of the Grotesque* (Columbia: U of Missouri P, 1996), 11.

85. Many critics have noted that the modern protagonists, known as antiheroes, are more or less associated with the notion of paradox. For instance, Victor Brombert *in In Praise of Antiheroes* comments: "The term 'antihero,' as it has come to be used, is indeed linked to a paradoxical, at times provocative stance. . . . The last pages of Dostoevsky's narrative explicitly associate the word 'antihero' with the notion of paradox" (1999, 1). Brombert further clarifies, "The antiheroic mode, as we shall see, implies the negative presence of the subversive or absent model. But it is as much a question of mood as of mode" (1999, 1–2). In this context, I argue, more than a negative mode, the antihero signifies a subjective stance by translating the negative into a paradoxical *posture* with bravado of a bona fide hero. Recently, some critics have reframed the anti-hero in terms of the abject hero. See Michael Andre Bernstein in *Bitter Carnival: Ressentiment and the Abject Hero*.

86. Julia Kristeva, *Strangers to Ourselves*, trans. Leon S. Roudiez (New York: Columbia UP, 1991), 8, 5.

87. Ibid., 10, 15.

88. Louis Althusser in "Cremonini, Painter of the Abstract" collected in his *Lenin and Philosophy and Other Essays* also analyses modern art in terms of structural absence in the subject formation: "if Cremonini's faces are *deformed*, it is because they do not have the *form of individuality*, i.e. of *subjectivity*. . . . They are haunted by an absence: a purely negative absence, that of the humanist function which is refused them, and which they refuse; and a positive, determinate absence, that of the *structure* of the world which determines them, which makes them the anonymous beings they are, the structural effects of the real relations which govern them" (1971, 238–39).

89. For specific analysis of the paradoxical subject of loss, please refer to my article: "From Ideology of Loss to Aesthetics of Absence: The Endgame in Beckett's *The Lost Ones*" where I addressed how loss figures differently in modern and postmodern contexts.

90. Theodor Adorno, *Aesthetic Theory*, trans. Robert Hullot-Kentor (Minneapolis: U of Minnesota P, 1997), 6.

91. Around the first BC, Vitruvius's *De Architectura*, according to Kayser, already condemned this kind of ornamental style for subverting reality by the "unreasonable fashion" in "monstrous forms." "Such things, however, never existed, do not now exist, and shall never come into being" (Kayser 1963, 20). This frequently quoted remark from Marcus Vitruvius Pollio's *De Architectura* (27 BC) provides one of the earliest evidences of the classical critique of the grotesque as a deviant mode of decorative style.

92. Physical fragmentation and bodily distortion figure significantly to define the nature of the grotesque. In this context, I would like to shift our attention to the metaphysical realm, not just a linkage between them, but also a passage from one into the other. By moving the grotesque from the physical to the metaphysical arena, I intend to expose what is repressed and excluded in the grand illusion of the singular subject. By returning the discourse of the grotesque to ontology, I intend to uncover the grotesque within the self-contained, self-conscious, and self-enclosed totality of being and dismantle the myth of ontological singularity of the Absolute Subject (I will return to this in Chapter II).

93. Kayser, *The Grotesque in Art and Literature*, 100.

94. Mikhail Bakhtin, *The Dialogical Imagination: Four Essays*, ed. Michael Holquist, trans. Caryl Emerson and Michael Holquist (Austin: U of Texas P, 1981), 278.

95. Harpham, *On the Grotesque*, 51.

Chapter Two

The Mystical Encounter between the Sphinx and Oedipus

I. THE SPHINX: EMBLEM OF THE GROTESQUE AND THE PROBLEMATIC ORIGIN

Among the so-called grotesque images discovered in Nero's Golden House as well as other grotesque decorations created by Renaissance artists elsewhere, one figure stands, recurrently and prominently (sometimes in the center but mostly on the margin), as the typological embodiment and quintessential figuration of the grotesque. That is, the sphinx, partly human and partly animal (and partly divine in other contexts); sometimes birdlike with wings, and occasionally with a snake as its tail. Arguably the utmost mysterious enigma in history, the sphinx is the most characteristic representative of grotesque figures and hybrid creatures. This emblematic image inevitably directs us to the Oedipus legend in Greek mythology, and possibly to myths of other locales as well. As a chimera and an enigma, the sphinx has neither singular identity nor single origin: human and animal, male and female, demonic and divine, supernatural and mystical. Like a specter, the sphinx emerges from the grottoes to haunt the primal scene and the problematic origin of the grotesque.

In spite of different aesthetic views and varied linguistic spins by critics in all fields to decipher the "identities" of the grotesque, one single fact seems to stand indisputable and unequivocal. That is, the term "grotesque" is initially derived from the archaeological event of re-discovery of a form of decorative art with excavation of Nero's Golden House in the late fifteenth century. Most scholars have traced the "rediscovery" of the grotesque up to this historical occasion as its inaugural moment and few have inquired further beyond the grottoes or Nero's *Domus Aurea*. In this case, I am neither disputing nor debunking the grotesque's etymological coming into light as a "nominal" term. Instead, what I would like to investigate are the peripheral clues that might lead to, in Harpham's words, "some other phase of being" elsewhere that has "lost" its genealogical linkage to those fantastic and bizarre figures originally painted in the murals in Nero's imperial palaces and subsequently refashioned by Renaissance artists in Europe. As Foucault famously says in "Nietzsche, Genealogy, History," "What is found at the historical beginning of things is not the inviolable identity of their origin; it is the dissension of other things. It is disparity."[1] Thus, at the original site of the grotesque art, we might find *something else* that may lead us *elsewhere*, beyond the nominal event of its re-discovery in Rome.

To a certain degree, a number of critics have extended limited observations, either vaguely or tangentially, about the grotesque's association with mythological hybrids in general and images of oriental culture in specific. For instance, Bakhtin notices a "most characteristic" image among those grotesqueries in Nero's Golden House, i.e., "the chimera, this quintessence of the grotesque, which invades every sphere of painting."[2] Harpham suggests those grotesque decorative figures painted by Raphael in 1519 in the *Loggias* of the Vatican Palace are resonant with "a faintly mythological character, imparted by representations of fauns, nymphs, satyrs, and centaurs."[3] Walter Scott provides a full list of those Grecian mythical hybrids when he says that "the grotesque . . . introduced the most strange and complicated monsters, resembling centaurs, griffins, sphinxes, chimeras, rocs, and all other creatures of romantic imagination."[4] In *The Sense of Order: A Study in the Psychology of Decorative Art,* Gombrich hints that some of the monstrous images of the grotesque in Nero's Golden House are "linked with the enigmatic, the mysterious, through allusion to Egyptian or oriental divinities,"[5] i.e., the linkage between the monstrous images in the "grottoes" in Italy and the mythical figures in Egypt. However, these critics have merely noted, in sporadic and random manner, the lingering connection among grotesque images, mythical characters, and Egyptian culture; none has pursued further along these peripheral clues and fully developed this line of thought.

Without any doubt, as an iconic image found in Nero's Golden House, the sphinx casts much wider signification and implicates much broader issues than just grotesque images per se. How to unearth the cryptic meanings of the sphinx in terms of grotesque art, buried over centuries prior to its resurrection in the Renaissance period, certainly imposes intriguing and challenging issues. To situate my research in context, I would like to highlight a simple fact: the sphinx, though generally occupying a marginal or ex-centric position, stands as the central emblematic figure to represent the grotesque, and as such, I would venture to explore the sphinx, enigmatic as it is, as a typological embodiment of the grotesque[6] . Fully aware of all potential meanings of sphinx figures from different perspectives and in various discourses, I would like to stress that this project limits its parameter of research only to the issues of the sphinx's problematic identity in the context of ontological signification and metaphysical ramification.

Since Freud's "discovery" of the Oedipus complex, the founding principle of psychoanalysis, we are inclined to focus exclusively on Oedipus as *the legend* and, like Freud, we merely forget the Sphinx. We all know the famous riddle propounded by the Sphinx, but few bother to interrogate either the identity or the role of the Sphinx both *in* and *beyond* the *Oedipus* legend. We might as well suggest that the Sphinx probably *remain* to be the unsolved riddle for further inquiry. Solely from the perspective of narratology, some critics argue that the Sphinx is "structurally necessary" to the Oedipus legend as a rite of passage to justify Oedipus' intelligence whereas others contest that the Sphinx is only a variant, secondary, and unessential element in the legend. However, the dominant consensus is that the Sphinx as a mythical figure emerges somewhere in the evolution of *Oedipus'* legend and that is why most critics insist the Sphinx episode is nonessential—a bit redundant and maybe a late add-on that most likely distracts or misleads us from the legend. These contestations not only concern the Sphinx's polemic position in the Oedipus legend, but also discern its dubious status in Greek culture on a large scale.

Lowell Edmunds in "The Sphinx in the Oedipus Legend" seriously investigates "the question of the Sphinx's entry into the legend" and inquires "about her very raison d'être in the legend."[7] In his opinion, "the Sphinx motif as a whole is secondary in the legend" and "her riddle seems to bear no necessary relation to nag detail of the legend."[8] At best, Edmunds admits, "the Sphinx is a secondary element in the Oedipus legend, added at some point in the development of the legend in order to motivate the hero's marriage to his mother."[9] According to this view, as an unnecessary, redundant, and devious appendage, the Sphinx does not fit neatly within the circumscription of the Oedipus legend because she either exceeds the master plot, or misleads the master discourse, or sidetracks the master subject, King Oedipus. Thus, Edmunds concludes: "the Sphinx was the gravest problem in the logic of the narrative" because "the Sphinx is not integral to the plot of the Oedipus story."[10] As a result, the Sphinx poses not only as a threat to Oedipus personally, but also as a clandestine plot to disrupt *Oedipus'* legend in terms of narrative structure. Furthermore, the Sphinx becomes suspect in the Oedipus legend not only due to her illogical part in the narrative, but also possibly due to her illegitimate foreign origin as an *alien* monster that does not belong to Greek culture in the first place. In short, if some emphasize that the Sphinx is merely a sacrificial figure to the Greek hero and an alien beast *in* the Oedipus legend, then others insist that her entire part should be eliminated as a redundant narrative appendix *out of* the legend of Oedipus altogether.

Due to her polemic identity in Greek myth, the Sphinx becomes a suspect for all kinds of allegations. Some critics are doubtful of the Sphinx's validity and legitimacy as a logical element in the *Oedipus* legend while others are suspicious of her intelligent quota as a tricky *riddler*. Her mystery as a *riddle* that *riddles*, alas, seems to grow rather than diminish with all sorts of speculations. That is probably why Edmunds ends his essay with a tantalizing question: "The riddling of the Sphinx in the Oedipus legend remains a riddle."[11] So the *riddling* Sphinx stays with us. However, the efforts of cracking the riddle seems to have been often misplaced because most scholarship of the past tends to exclusively concentrate on the triad between Oedipus and his parents in the Oedipus legend. Here, I would like to shift our attention to two other areas that have hitherto been largely ignored, that is, the Sphinx's problematic identity or her polemic origin in *different* cultural contexts and the Sphinx's mystic riddle as the key to unravel their complicated relationship from two *contrasting* perspectives, namely, in the framework of *Oedipus'* legend or that of *Sphinx's* myth. Hence, I would like to pose a fresh analogy between Oedipus and the Sphinx, albeit *an unlike pair* for each other, that hardly existed before, and some might even be amused or amazed: how can one possibly compare *this* with *that*? One, arguably, represents a monumental prototype of philosopher in *Western* civilization whereas the other is merely an *alien* monster that no one cares where she comes from.

In fact, as mythical figures, sphinxes do not possess one single origin. Instead, there are multiple variations of their sources and contradictory versions from different locations in the evolution of the sphinx myth in European culture as well as in other cultures. The Sphinx that appears at Thebes in Greek mythology, far from the origin, is but one version of a story passed on from multifariously interlaced sources, and each version carries with it plural inscriptions and transfigurations across borders and cultures. Hence, the Sphinx emerges as a hybridized border figure of cultural crossings as Derrida says, and rightly so, "within a genealogy . . . is a cryptology or general *mystology*."[12] In *Positions*, Derrida reminds us that "there is already a *text*, a network of textual referrals to *other* texts, a textual transformation in which each allegedly 'simple term' is marked by the trace of another term."[13] Every text is necessarily and inextricably an inter-text, a palimpsest of various intricately interlinked cultural traces sans origin. The Sphinx is certainly a case in point. To situate the Sphinx in a cultural network will help us uncover a huge entangled web of intertextual transactions as well as multicultural interactions across histories and continents.

Several critics notice that the grotesque appears to be a chaotic *topos* of art devoid of a unified theme or a collage of diffuse narratives short of a coherent plot—a kind of "narrative paralysis." Zamperini notes the dilemma, "These images are combined without any narrative or spatial connection between them,"[14] but Harpham takes this "narrative" crisis as an exciting opportunity because "transcategorical hybrids also offer endless and compelling temptations to interpretation."[15] To align the shapeless corpus of the Sphinx into perspectives, I would like to conjure up a narrative of "spatial connection," a sort of "unauthorized" account of sphinx figures in three distinctive locations. Through a characteristic imaging, I attempt to "embody" the sphinx figure in the contexts of Egyptian mythology, Greek legend, and Italian "grotesque" art in the following section.

II. THE SPHINX AT DIFFERENT LOCATIONS: TRANSFIGURATION OF IDENTITIES

If the inauguration of a subject is always marked as a significant event, the "other" in most cases just pops up with obscure origination. Tracking the root of the sphinx figure, we encounter a knotty other with a tangled genealogic lineage interlocked discursively with various sources of cultures, histories, and mythologies instead of a singular origin.[16] Gilles Deleuze's opening remark in *Nietzsche and Philosophy* certainly speaks pertinently to the case here: "Genealogy thus means origin or birth, but also difference or distance in the origin."[17]

Unearthed among other grotesque images in the grottoes or the ruins of Nero's *Dumas Aurea* in Rome, those sphinx figures instantly remind us of the legend of the Sphinx's fatal encounter with Oedipus in Greek myth. However, the mythology of sphinxes goes beyond Greece and leads to other territories, such as Egypt. In this case, I have no intention, even if it were possible, to trace multiple origins and tortuous genealogies of sphinxes across cultures and centuries. Nor is it the purpose of the current project to debate about authenticity and primacy of sphinxes' origin or research all varieties of sphinx forms by tracking down, archaeologically, the entire evolution of sphinxes across the globe and throughout histories. To situate my research in context and stay relevant to my topic on the grotesque, I will limit the scope of my investigation to the typical embodiments of the sphinx inscribed in generic terms in three distinctive locales: ancient Egyptian culture, Greek mythology, and Renaissance art in Rome. Hence, I will focus on three different types of figuration of sphinxes: Egyptian sphinxes as royal guardians of sacred knowledge, divine and mystical; the Greek Sphinx as a demonic monster, enigmatic and alien; and Renaissance sphinxes as grotesque figures in decorative art, aesthetic and imaginary.

Generally speaking, the Egyptian sphinx, typically a recumbent lion with a human head but no wings, is an ancient totemic figure with mythical, spiritual, and divine status. Sphinxes in Egyptian culture play several significant roles: divine guardians of sacred temples or entrances to the next world, protectors of pyramids, mystic guardians of secrets of life and death, and guardians of the sacred knowledge of spirituality. To decode the sphinx means to gain access to the secret of life and death or the sacred knowledge of divine spirit. Sphinxes do not speak and their power resides in silence; and they are enigmatic and mystical. Several scholars point out that the sphinx, as an Egyptian mythical figure, is associated with the Sun God *Horemakhet.* Moreover, the sphinx in Egypt is predominantly male, with a man's head on a lion's body, symbolizing royal strength with both a regal posture and a divine position.[18]

If the Egyptian sphinx is prevalently male, the Greek sphinx is almost unanimously female. When the sphinx "migrates" from Egypt to Greece, it loses its royal status and mythic power as the guardian of sacred knowledge. *The Sphinx* that Oedipus confronts is an alien monster and a tricky temptress from a foreign land, demonic and destructive. It is in Greek mythology that she is reconceived as a monstrous creature that seduces and devours travelers. This Sphinx has lost her sacred power of silence and has become a beast speaking or singing riddles in an enigmatic tongue, an alien tongue perhaps. Also, the Greek Sphinx is notably a winged lion with a woman's head and she flies from other territories to Thebes—a foreign monster instead of a locale beast. If the sphinx in Egyptian myth is considered partly human, partly animal, and partly divine, then the human and divine parts are often elided in Greek culture; instead, the Sphinx turns into a frightening monster.[19]

Who sends the Sphinx over to Thebes in Greek myth? Some versions of the myth claim that the Sphinx is sent from Aethiopia by Hera to plague Thebes by asking passersby the famous riddle while other versions assert she is sent by Apollo from somewhere else, to avenge Laius, the king of Thebes.[20] Regardless who sends her, I just want to emphasize one aspect that has been consistently highlighted: she is sent from *elsewhere*, from a *foreign land* as an *alien monster*. While admitting her into the rank of Grecian deities or demonology, the Greeks never fail to remind us of the Sphinx's foreign origin—an outsider, a stranger, and an alien other—in Greek culture.

The sphinx that is revived and popularized by Renaissance artists during the fifteenth and the sixteenth centuries is based upon those cryptic figures unearthed from the dark caves or the ruins of Nero's imperial palaces among other grotesque images after a thousand of years of burial. Instead of possessing any royal and divine position as in ancient Egyptian culture or some alien status of the monstrous other as in classical Greek mythology, this refashioned sphinx of grotesque art entertains the imagination of Renaissance artists as a kind of fairytale figure of pure fantasy with mythical reference but absolutely no divine or spiritual ramification. Notably, in Raphael's paintings in the decoration of the *Loggias* of Vatican Palace completed around 1515, sphinxes as decorative figures stand out conspicuously in both background and foreground. This refashioned image is clearly taken after the Greek type of sphinxes, partly human, partly lion, partly bird, and sometimes with a reptile tail, but typically a female. Instead of demonizing her, Renaissance artists fantasize, feminize, and sexualize her with a complete trans-gendering: prominent breasts at front and an attractive woman's head on a lion's sleek body. No longer being a royal guardian at the entrance of sacred knowledge or a ferocious monster terrorizing travelers at Thebes, this sphinx becomes a fantastic figure of art. At this point, the image of the sphinx truly reflects a hybridized creature in composition and evolution, consisting of diverse features made and remade across cultures, histories, and centuries.[21]

In sum, from ancient Egypt to classical Greece and later to Renaissance Italy, the sphinx is perpetually refashioned with traces of various cultures, some with slight cosmetic touch-up and others with radical cosmological makeover. In Egyptian culture, the sphinx is a totemic figure of ancient spirituality and a divine guardian of sacred knowledge; in Greek myth, the Sphinx becomes a demonic female alien monster, speaking riddles to seduce and devour travelers in the context of the Oedipus legend; in the Renaissance era, it is adopted as a fantastic figure of decorative art. Since its revival in Italy in the late fifteenth century, artists across Western cultures have added all kinds of whims and fantasies to the sphinx's remodeling. It morphs into different genders with alteration of body, mutation of composition, and modification of meanings. Eventually, the sphinx becomes an ambiguous figure of *both* erotic beauty *and* vicious beastliness—an uncanny figure of exoticism: demonic and divine, feminine and masculine, seductive and terrifying, sacred and profane, mother and monster. If the typical hybrid components of the sphinx comprise animal body, human intelligence, and *divine spirit*, then the last part of her sacred nature gradually fades away. In short, the sphinx bears a complex cultural corpus of conglomerate composition and her genealogy is a confusing one at best. Despite confusion, one thing stands indisputable: in Greek culture, the Sphinx constitutes an archetypal image of the enigmatic other, *an alterity par excellence*: *female*, *alien*, and *monstrous*. It alters from divine to demonic, sacred to profane, holy to sacrilegious, that is, from a sacred guardian in mythology to an alien monster in demonology—in a word, an *evil spirit* to be dispelled.

III. THE ENCOUNTER: FALL OF THE SPHINX AND RISE OF OEDIPUS IN THE *OEDIPUS* LEGEND

It is common knowledge that in Greek mythology after Oedipus solves the Sphinx's riddle at their fatal encounter, the Sphinx is assumed to be dead for good and disappears forever regardless of its variable origins. Even though her dead body is unverifiable—a slight gap left in the legend, we do have a suspicious corpus of stories. In fact, there are several scenarios of supposition surrounding the mystery of the Sphinx's death. Popular versions in general assume that the monster Sphinx is killed singlehandedly by the hero Oedipus while others insist that the Sphinx jumps down the cliff and commits suicide out of despair, and still others, inferring from the structure of narrative logic, claim that the Sphinx merely exits from the scene after she plays her part: her riddle is solved, Thebes is saved, and the hero completes his rite of passage. No further inquiry is necessary as if that were the *whole* story. Somehow, something fundamental seems to be missing—as if Oedipus is suspect to play a "hide-and-seek" game with the Sphinx's spectral body, an ignored elision in the legend. Not surprisingly, as humanists, we are inclined to follow closely the trails of the famous Oedipus with his triumphant rise and tragic fall, but not so much the Sphinx, a dead body at this point. In short, dead or not, she is no longer relevant. So ends the story.

Let's review that pivotal and fatal encounter where names become games in Greek myth. Oedipus becomes the King because of a legendary deed, the conquest of the alien monster Sphinx who plagues the city with a riddle. Regardless of different assumptions of her origins or gender status, the Sphinx stays, in the *Oedipus* legend, a horrific *foreign female* monster coming from *elsewhere* to Thebes. Regardless who sends her or where she comes from, the Sphinx remains in *Greek myth* an enigmatic other that speaks an alien tongue of riddle, so to speak. As a kind of witch-bitch sorceress or temptress, the Sphinx for the most part plays a sacrificial role, henceforth to be dominated, decoded, eradicated, and forgotten. Put this way, in the *Oedipus* legend, the Sphinx occupies the position of an ignominious other to highlight a significant subject. She plays a central but subservient part to trigger the change of Oedipus' destiny from an anonymous character to a famous hero and a royal subject. So the absolute certitude of her "ending" is considered *utmost essential* as one of the most crucial evidences to support various theoretical claims of pivotal transition in the course of Western civilization. In this case, the unequivocal ending of the Sphinx in a definitive closure signals the demise of the other in various categories and with polysemous ramifications.

The meeting between Oedipus and the Sphinx, in this case, has the value of a founding myth as it registers an encounter between self and other with epistemological, historical, cosmographic, and cultural significations. To say the least, psychoanalysis has made a universal law in terms of the Oedipus complex. In addition, some historians in the past concur that this deadly encounter between the Sphinx and Oedipus signifies a critical transition and a defining moment of Western culture. In a scenario of the *conquest model*, past scholars have assembled a multitude of symbolic terminals associated with the death of the Sphinx. Some of the most common hypotheses of paradigm shifts are grounded in this conquest model, i.e., the *fall* of the Sphinx and the *rise* of Oedipus. However, all these theoretical projections regarding paradigmatic shifts, one might notice, are exclusively based on the presumptive outcomes brought forth from the perspective of the *Oedipus legend*, i.e., the Eurocentric and phallocentric point of view.

To solve the mystery of the Sphinx's disappearance or to envision different outcomes of her ending, we need to switch to other frameworks and reexamine the very "*raison d'être*" of the Sphinx from alternative perspectives by foregrounding the encounter differently—that is, beyond the *Oedipus* legend—in the *Sphinx* myth. To propose a dialogic model of exchange that involves both *shift* and *drift*, both opposition and reciprocation, we should consider *juxtaposing* the varied positions and designations of the sphinx in the light of both *Egyptian myth* and *Greek legend.* As I mentioned earlier, in Greek mythology, the Sphinx is usually perceived as merely demonic whereas in Egyptian culture, the sphinx is regarded as a sacred guardian and a divine deity. With a change of perspective, the encounter, instead of an occasion to make a legend for Oedipus' conquest, may be converted into an opportunity of a mystical exchange between the Sphinx and Oedipus. Moreover, the Sphinx's dead body, a kind of fort-da game, becomes an unsolved mystery that haunts *Oedipus'* legend like a specter or a ghost that has not only taken possession of Oedipus himself, but also cast a spell on the Greek legend.

IV. SHIFT AND DRIFT BETWEEN OEDIPUS AND THE SPHINX *IN* AND *BEYOND* THE LEGEND

Oedipus' encounter with the Sphinx might constitute what a psychoanalyst would call "the primal scene" where the subject's unconscious desires are played out in front of the terrifying other. Let's revisit this mysterious but decisive scene where the meeting concerns not only Oedipus' personal fate, but also probably the destiny of entire Western civilization. The primal scene, as we recall, might lead to "other scenes" and other territories, from the *Oedipus legend* to the *Sphinx myth.* This section interrogates what past critics have brought forth in the scenario of the so-called "paradigm shift" that is foregrounded in the premise of the conquest of the Sphinx as the other in various binary structures in several disciplines, such as the mother figure and the son-hero in psychoanalysis, the Oriental monster and the Western man in geopolitics, and the mystic cosmography and the rational order in epistemology. Most of these dichotomous positions, varied as they are, tend to perpetuate the same outcome: Oedipus, as a liminal hero, is to represent a chain of historical, cultural, and cosmographic transitions whereas the Sphinx, in a subordinate or sacrificial role, is to be conquered as *a rite of passage* to initiate Oedipus into an array of emergent symbolic positions. However, the contradictory outcomes generated by discrete readings from divergent perspectives, i.e., *framed in* or *going beyond* the Oedipus legend, collapse some of these hypothetical claims and prove many of the binary structures, specifically those in terms of "paradigm shift," to be delusive and fallacious.

Hero and Mother: The Dubious Rite of Passage

The orthodox Freudian encryption of the Sphinx's riddle is: "Where do babies come from?" So the Sphinx is assumed to be a mother figure, or perhaps more than that. Géza Róheim, one of the earliest scholars who have focused on the study of the Sphinx instead of Oedipus, points out that the Sphinx is a mother figure of creation and destruction, love and death, monstrosity and humanity. In *The Riddle of the Sphinx or Human Origins*, Róheim argues that the sphinx is "this ambiguous creature, enticing and dangerous, who loves but to devour, is, therefore, the mother of the hero."[22] In Greek mythology, the Sphinx plays the double role of mother-earth and mother-death, nurturing and destroying. As such, the Sphinx is sometimes presented in either recumbent or upright/erect posture, a kind of dubious image of the phallic mother that seduces as well as dominates: a bitch-witch figure. In *The Sphinx on the Table,* Janine Burke also states, as a dubious maternal figure, "she is the powerful and troublesome feminine, whom man needs to govern or who will destroy him."[23]

In Greek, the word "sphinx" is rooted in "strangle" and hence the Sphinx symbolizes the repressive and stifling mother who traps and suffocates the son as a devouring female monster—the monster-mother. The conquest of the Sphinx or any female monsters embodied by maternal figures signifies the triumph of the masculine principle over the feminine one, marks the son's liberation from the demonic mother's captivation or domination, and signals his independence and separation from the symbiotic relationship with the maternal body. Only when the hero becomes a "man," as Oedipus declares in front of the Sphinx, will the mother disappear and recede into the unconscious, as psychoanalysts postulate. Evidently, this interpretation of the Sphinx's ending as a demonic maternal figure and a symbol of the female principle merely reinforces the normative sacrificial rites for patriarchal culture. In other words, the demise of the Sphinx suggests that the initiatory (m)other has to be sacrificed to the emerging male hero so that he is able to develop into an independent subject of discrete being. In this case, Oedipus not only has to conquer the maternal bondage and overcome the strangulation by the female principle, but also, more importantly, to establish himself as an individual subject, a man, so to speak.

However, even from an orthodox psychoanalytic view, one may also suggest that this process involves not so much *conquering* the mother as *integrating* the female principle into one's unconscious. Instead of domination, this encounter may also initiate a return to the maternal space, a process of submerging or incorporating. All this implies that the Sphinx is not extinct, but falls into Oedipus' unconscious, symbolizing a return of the uncanny other that not only possesses, and sometimes, even may overcome him. Oedipus seems to be liberated as well as plagued by his suppression of the other. Consequently, the conquest model is not only challenged, but also, to some extent, reversed. In other words, the Sphinx ascribed as a maternal initiatory rite and in a sacrificial role makes sense *only when* she is entirely enclosed in the framework of the phallocentric order; that is, Oedipus is thus made into a man and the son achieves his independence from the mother. Oedipus, however, may fail even on that account because, after the rite of passage, he goes back to his mother, Jocasta and this return proves his undoing. This ambiguous return not only makes his separation from the mother doubtful, but also the whole schemata of initiatory rites problematic.[24] Therefore, how to dispose the spectral body of the Sphinx remains an issue in the Oedipus legend.

Human and Beast: Who is the Monstrous?

Some critics also propose that the legendary encounter between Oedipus and the Sphinx symbolizes the West's domination over the East in terms of different geopolitical body, or more specifically, it marks Greece's historical disjuncture from Egypt. It has been argued, predominantly by Hegel in *The Philosophy of History*, that the confrontation dramatizes the conquest of an alien monster from the Orient by an occidental man—a new genus of *Homo sapiens* in the true sense of the word. Oedipus has made himself a heroic figure of noble humanity, a representative of Western civilization, by eliminating the "brute body"[25] of the Egyptian savage beast—the monstrous other in a cultural initiatory rite. Thus, the meeting is brief but brutal, with the violent death of one and the glorious triumph of the other. Oedipus' legendary deed symbolizes the subjugation of oriental barbarianism and signals Greece's transition into a humanistic era with a pompous posture of what we might call "taming of the beast" from "a dark continent" perhaps.[26]

However, an alternative perspective may problematize the question: between Oedipus and the Sphinx, who is the monstrous? Monstrousness connotes "abnormal," "unnatural," and "horrific." If the Sphinx is condemned as a monstrous beast from Egypt that terrorizes the town, then Oedipus turns out to be no less than a monstrous man in Thebes. Though idolized as a man—a heroic and intelligent man who conquers the beast, solves the riddle, and saves the city, Oedipus later undoes all that by committing the most unnatural, abnormal, and horrific crime in violation of the social taboos—murdering his father and marrying his mother. If the Sphinx, an alien monster, terrorizes all young men in Thebes with a mysterious riddle, then Oedipus, the Greek human, plagues "Man" of Western society with a universal unconscious guilt (according to Freud at least). Alas, the very heroic and human self inconceivably turns out to be the monstrous other even after the cultural rite of passage toward civilization. The hero that saves the town turns into a monster that brings plague to it.

Janine Burke reminds us, "by defeating the Sphinx, Oedipus instigates a more terrible fate for himself. The Sphinx continues to act in the role of protector, as she did in Egyptian myth—she is trying to protect Thebes from Oedipus and Oedipus from himself."[27] On the one hand, according to the *Sphinx myth* in Egyptian culture, it is the Sphinx in the role of sacred guardian that tries to protect Oedipus and save the city from Oedipus the monstrous. On the other hand, the binary opposition between man and beast, the heroic self and the monstrous other in the *Oedipus* legend requires a radical revision. From a dialogic perspective, the Sphinx and Oedipus might not even oppose each other to some degree. Instead of being a confrontation, their "meeting" could be reframed as a reciprocal recognition, not only as *Man* and *Beast*, but also as monstrous doubles. René Girard in *Violence and the Sacred* suggests: "The monstrous double is also to be found wherever we encounter an 'I' and an 'Other' caught up in a constant interchange of differences."[28] In other words, the encounter between Oedipus and the Sphinx could be a chance of mutual reflection between them instead of an occasion of domination of beast by man. I opt for a heretical proposition regarding the relationship between Oedipus and the Sphinx in this re-vision and therefore put forward a counter-narrative against as well as beyond the orthodox interpretation of Greek mythology.

Logos and Mythos: Polemical Knowledge

Some past historians, especially Hegel, are inclined to believe that, in the name of *Oedipus*' legend, Oedipus' glorious deed of solving the riddle signals the triumph of a new intellectual tradition or the rise of a new epistemological paradigm and cosmographical order in terms of *Logos*. Different from traditional heroes who conquer with bloody murder in initiatory rites, Oedipus conquers by sheer intellect, or self-reflexive consciousness, henceforth marking a transition from the martial trial by arms to a philosophic trial by language. Jean-Joseph Goux in *Oedipus, Philosopher* suggests: "Oedipus alone triumphs through sheer intelligence, with his explanation of the famous riddle that is itself a trial by language."[29]

To translate Oedipus into a signifying legend, some argue that a new intellectual hero is born to represent the self-reflexive consciousness and the rational order. In *The Philosophy of History*, for instance, Hegel capitalizes on Oedipus' conquest of the Sphinx and solution of the Sphinx's riddle not only as the triumph of a Greek man, but also as the rise of a new Western cosmographical order, *Logos*. Rudnytsky in *Freud and Oedipus* observes: "Hegel equates the solving of the Sphinx's riddle with the advent of Greek culture, and thus sees Oedipus as the hero who raises humanity to self-consciousness."[30] As the embodiment of the logocentric tradition and the sovereign king of reason, Oedipus through his conquest of the Sphinx is to mark a transition from the era of superstition to the age of knowledge, from a mythical and supernatural cosmology to a conceptual and rational universe. Consequently, *Logos* prevails as the new epistemological and metaphysical order whereas mythos fades away as the archaic supernatural system. The death of the Sphinx in this case is not merely repeating the myth of sacrifice, but also simultaneously affirming the sacrifice of myth to initiate the transition from mythos to logos.

According to the *Oedipus* legend, the death of the Sphinx and the triumph of Oedipus signify a pivotal shift from the ancient mythical order of supernatural gnosis to a new symbolic order characterized by rational conceptualization and self-reflexive consciousness. The Oedipus legend, as Hegel argues, marks Greece's exit from the mythical world of the East and the ascent of the new logical order of the West. In Greek myth, Oedipus demonstrates the self-sufficient reason and self-conscious intellect by dismissing both the riddle and the Sphinx as mythical rites of passage via an inaugural term, "Man," in singular and capital form. It is interesting to note that this mythical encounter between Oedipus and the Sphinx, for some, almost constitutes a "real" historical event, or at least it is dramatized as a historical event in the frame of a mythical narrative.

However, others caution that the rational knowledge that wins Oedipus fame also dooms him as a villain, at most a tragic hero destroyed by the hubris of his solipsistic reason. Contradictory to the Delphi oracle—"Know Thyself," Oedipus certainly lacks self-knowledge, ironical to his pompous posture as the personification of self-consciousness. Instead of representing the epitome of knowledge, *Oedipus'* legend dramatizes precisely the failure of rational knowledge, impotence of self-consciousness, and limitation of the logocentric paradigm. Credited as the great intellect that solves the riddle, Oedipus is ironically a mysterious subject beyond his own knowledge. In *Powers of Horror: An Essay on Abjection*, Kristeva analyzes the abject Oedipus in terms of cognitive ambiguity and ontological uncertainty. Kristeva writes: "His abjection is due to the permanent ambiguity of the parts he plays without his knowledge, even when he believes he knows."[31] The Oedipus legend as a parable of the triumph of Logos and the new hegemonic order seems to turn into a satirical farce due to lack of self-knowledge, impotence of self-consciousness, and failure of narcissistic intellect.

Put in the alternative perspective of the *Sphinx myth*, the encounter between Oedipus and the Sphinx will inevitably have an entirely different trajectory than what Hegel could possibly perceive. As a divine guardian to the entrance of sacred knowledge, the Sphinx, instead of Oedipus, is the one that possesses the sacred knowledge of ontological mystique, concerning not only Oedipus' identity, but also the mystery of humanity. To conquer her is to bury that sacred knowledge, and in fact constitutes a sacrilegious violence. In this case, both Hegel and Oedipus fail to obtain this sacred knowledge protected by the Sphinx in terms of mythos, an alternative model to the cognitive system. They both remain outside the entrance to this mystical cosmography (for lack of a better term here) despite their presumptuous postures as emergent philosophers. Instead, Oedipus conquers and eliminates the Sphinx as the supernatural and monstrous other. That is to say, Oedipus fails to pass the initiatory rite by the Sphinx and fails to solve the mystery of his identity. In this instance, the *Sphinx* myth offers an alternative perspective to review the encounter heretically—a counter-narrative in opposition to the authoritative meanings defined by the orthodox *Oedipus legend.*

V. THE ONTOLOGICAL MYSTERY BETWEEN OEDIPUS AND THE SPHINX

If being can be postulated as a meta-physical event, probably no other event, factual or imaginary, in Western history could be more pivotal than the showdown between the Sphinx and Oedipus. Oedipus' challenge of the Sphinx represents both physical and symbolic confrontations with all sorts of ramifications. It involves not only "who won" or "who lost," but more significantly, "who is who" in this identity game in both corporeal and incorporeal terms. After all, what Oedipus encounters at the risk of his life is not only an enigmatic riddle in a battle of wits, but also a monstrous body of "an alien beast." As discussed previously, different "embodiments" of the Sphinx in different cultures generate different meanings for the Sphinx and, in addition, her physical body has always been a controversial site of metaphysical contention and ontological dispute. The Sphinx's physical body, not a being per se, is designated as a metaphysical locale to signify her ontological position, i.e., a *meta-physical* embodiment of the grotesque. In this context, I propose to examine the legendary meeting between Oedipus and the Sphinx as an ontological case study of meta-physical differences.

Ontological Difference: The Conquest model of Elimination

Being female, maternal, alien and disparate, the Sphinx embodies the grotesque other in spatial and physical form. Her corporeal body consists of multiple intermixed composites and her meta-physical corpus seems to represent diverse alterities in relation to human, to intellect, and to male. Most importantly, I argue, the Sphinx incarnates the ontological body of disparity in contrast to the singular subject cohered by the rational order and embodied by solipsistic Oedipus. As a hybrid, the Sphinx epitomizes a *typological image of difference* and *an emblematic figure of heterogeneity*. Her position as the disparate other poses a threat to the singular and identical constitution of subjectivity according to Parmenides' metaphysics of Oneness. In other words, a hybrid figure is designated as the monstrous other in the new order of singular ontology with the rise of logocentric and egocentric culture. To conquer her as a rite of passage is to initiate the singular ontology into presence.

The mythical encounter between the Sphinx and Oedipus in this circumstance transcends into an ontological confrontation between two distinctive paradigms of identity and two discrete modes of being. Their legendary meeting translates, in this case, from a physical confrontation into a metaphysical rite that initiates Oedipus as man or a particular kind of man in singular form. In front of the chimera, Oedipus seems to be entirely an independent individual, singular, autonomous, and alone. Hence, the rite of passage results in the conquest of the grotesque, i.e., the heterogeneous and disparate other and the triumph of the subject of singularity, and consequently the singular being comes to dominate the subject area as the exclusive ontological condition. The Sphinx as the alternative cosmographical mode of being (hybrid, disparate, and heterogeneous) is replaced by the new ontological mode of the singular subject, or in Goux's term, "a specific historical institution of subjectivity."[32]

According to the scenario of "paradigm shift," the mythical encounter between Oedipus and the Sphinx can be read as a metaphysical conquest: subjugation, elimination, or deletion of the disparate and hybrid other. The Sphinx as an ontological category disappears or elapses out of history. As a result, the Sphinx's meta-physical dead body seems to be disposed once for all. Ontologically, as some scholars have argued, the paradigm has thus *shifted* from *identity of difference* to *identity of the same*, toward the Parmenides' model of the singular subject with the demise of the Sphinx. Oedipus' declaration in front of the Sphinx spectacularly dramatizes the egocentric posture to herald in the era of a new mode of being: the self-reflexive singular individual, or at least, the phantom of it. However, we all know, philosophers profess not only ontology, but also hauntology in terms of phantoms, ghosts, and specters, as Derrida reminds us. Who knows if the monster after her death might not turn into a specter that haunts Oedipus from somewhere else?

Ontological Integration: The Internalization Model of Containment

Psychoanalysis, so it seems, has brought forth an alternative model or a modified version to the conquest model in terms of internalization. That is, the fall of the Sphinx means that the Sphinx *falls* into the unconscious of

Oedipus and ushers in the age of the "inner Sphinx." According to this model, Oedipus integrates the Sphinx that eventually constitutes his unconscious in terms of the famous Freudian Oedipus complex. In other words, Oedipus does not eliminate the Sphinx from earth; instead, he internalizes and contains her into his own unconscious, i.e., repressing an external alterity and suppressing a disparate alien to the unconscious level. In Goux's words, "to suppress the Sphinx . . . is to internalize her" so that "Oedipus's posture creates the site of the unconscious."[33]

However, the focus on internalization seems to be misplaced since the process of internalization still remains locked in the conquest model sustained by a presumptive binary structure. It implies the subjugation of *an external alterity* into one's coherent self and this integral assumption is based upon the premise of emergence of two discrete modes of being. That is to say, one is assumed originally singular, and the other, derivatively heterogeneous. The integration model presupposes a priori fact of Oedipus' primal singularity as if internalization of the disparate other contaminates and violates the sanctity of his pure being. Hence, the internalization model implicitly continues perpetuating *Oedipus'* legend as if the grotesque signals the *fall* from the grace of the singular being and contaminates the autonomous subject in terms of a divisive unconscious other. As Goux notes, the consciousness itself "is what establishes, simultaneously with itself, the dimension of the unconscious."[34] The singular subject is established upon subjugation and exclusion of the disparate other.

If the Sphinx falls into Oedipus' unconscious, then the heterogeneous other not only disappears, but also reappears in a spectral form to haunt Oedipus as an irreducible alterity, i.e., departure as return. The end of the Sphinx implies burial or installation of a spectral body within the subject's unconscious. Oedipus' ontological body, in this context, is plagued and dispossessed by a spectral other, a return of the departed body of the Sphinx. Instead of being internalized, contained, and repressed as a disparate "alter-ego," the spectral Sphinx seems to split *Oedipus singular* into *Oedipus complex*. In other words, the Sphinx does not at all vanish; instead, it goes underground, into the caves, the grottoes, and the unconscious like a cryptic other that haunts us like a ghost. Transmuted from a monster into a ghost, the Sphinx possesses and dispossesses Oedipus on the unconscious level. In short, the Sphinx haunts Oedipus as the irreducible and inexorable alterity, just like the grotesque haunts the singular subject in terms of the unconscious disparity.

Ontological Disparity: The Reflexive Double in a Mirror relationship

What if the purpose for which the Sphinx, as the guardian of sacred knowledge or cosmographical mystery, comes to Oedipus is to attempt to inform Oedipus' unconscious disparity by means of an allegorical and mystical discourse of riddle? What if the effort Oedipus has taken, by suppressing or eliminating the Sphinx, is to cover up his own internal discord and inherent disparity reflected by the Sphinx? What if this grotesque other embodies exactly what Oedipus tries to hide in order to entertain his narcissistic illusion of the singular subject? All these hypotheses center on the issue of how to speculate the spectacular confrontation differently and heretically.

As an uncanny subject, so exposes the riddle, Oedipus is structured between the conscious *one* and the unconscious *many*. Despite his claim to the singular sovereign subject, he occupies contradictory and incoherent positions in relation to himself, his family, and his society. Entering his hometown without being aware of it, Oedipus complicates his singular identity of a solitary being by complex and intricate social relationship. Assuming to be a single man without any complications in family, identity, society or history, Oedipus, in due time, finds himself to be both stranger and native to Thebes, both brother and father to his children, both son and husband to his mother, and both hero and villain to the community. In spite of Oedipus' posture of an inviolable singular identity, all these intermixed disparate positions qualify him for the grotesque. Contrary to his posture, as it turns out, Oedipus has violated nothing else but the delusional singularity of his identity.

In effect, Oedipus cannot eliminate the intrinsic disparity in his identity as symbolized by his own name. As legend has it, Oedipus solves the riddle by referring to his name and looking at his own feet (body). However, Oedipus' name consists of polysemic intermingling. Semantically speaking, Oedipus' name cannot be reduced to a single meaning. "Oedipus" as a noun can mean either "swollenfoot" or "knowfoot," and it contains multiple linguistic permutations: "Oide" means "swollen"; "oida" means "I know"; "pous" means "foot"; "dipous" means "biped" (man); and "pou" means "from where." This complicated interweaving of polysemous significations in Oedipus' name unveils a linguistic labyrinth that defies any single resolution of meaning or single solution to identity. Henceforth, Oedipus' name is a riddle, unconscious to himself, that plays a hide-and-seek game with his multiple and disparate identities.

From the perspective of Egyptian myth, if the Sphinx figures as the sacred guardian of mystic knowledge, i.e., Oedipus' ontological mystery, then what Oedipus has achieved is not merely that he has successfully internalized the Sphinx into his psyche or eliminated her out of his sight through the rites of conquest, but also that he has failed to realize his own ontological disparity as reflected by the Sphinx. In other words, instead of being the antithetical other, the Sphinx constitutes a double that Oedipus fails to recognize. On the physical level, the intermixed and disparate agglomeration of the Sphinx seems to be in sharp contrast to the inviolable purity of Oedipus' singular identity, but on a metaphysical level, the singular man and the disparate monster in effect mirror each other instead of being dichotomously opposed. As Goux points out, "To suppress the Sphinx is to free oneself from an agonizing link with a mysterious alterity."[35] In front of the mysterious hybrid monster, Oedipus encounters the hidden disparity in his own unconscious. In this case, the *Oedipus* legend appears to dramatize the encounter between man and beast as two distinctive modes of beings unequivocally opposed, i.e., the singular subject and the disparate other. However, reframed as a mirror relationship, the dangerous line that is supposed to demarcate their difference radically dissolves: self and other emerge as a reflexive dyad in a *specular relation* to embody two different forms and states of the grotesque. In this analogy between this unlikely pair, the Sphinx represents the manifest grotesque: physically disparate and cosmographically hybrid while Oedipus embodies the latent grotesque: psychologically incoherent and ontologically heterogeneous. The encounter as an occasion of a *specular relationship of doubling* has always been mistranslated into a *spectacular scene of conquest* through the *Oedipus* legend.

In this context, to subjugate the Sphinx implies a violent meta-physical desire for elimination of disparity already concealed inside Oedipus. To "dis-embody" the Sphinx or to make her disappear is to erase the external image that reflects and recalls Oedipus' internal disparity, and to dispel the physical mirroring other is to conjure away the metaphysical irreducible alterity, the so-called "inner Sphinx" in the unconscious. Put differently, the conquest of the Sphinx does not signal exactly repression of an exterior disparate other, but rather it means to masquerade what is already hidden inside the unconscious self for fear of be exposed by a mirroring (m)other. For Oedipus, Goux remarks, "Consciousness of self is the continuous suppression of the Sphinx."[36] As such, the encounter involves not so much a conquest of the other as a conjuration of a solipsistic self in front of the other. In other words, the obsessive desire for the phantom of the singular subject so much blinds Oedipus' vision to his ontological disparity or his grotesque condition.

Compelled by his narcissistic desire and solipsistic consciousness, Oedipus attempts to magically conjure up an illusory image of a singular subject, thereby unifying all that remain disparate and incongruous. However, this narcissistic image of a unified and integral subject is but a misrecognition or delusion because it exposes exactly what Oedipus ontologically lacks. Due to this lack, Oedipus strives to hail himself into presence by evoking a phantom-subject in singular form. Ironically, his obsessive desire for the singular subject demonstrates precisely the symptoms of his grotesque condition. In this case, the grotesque is characterized by an obsessive desire toward the phantom of the singular subject. From this perspective, what the Oedipus legend has dramatized is no more than a pompous posture of a delusory singular subject and an obsessive desire for the phantom of the autonomous individual. Consequently, the tragedy in the Oedipus legend is not simply due to the *Oedipus complex*, but also due to the phantom ontology or *hauntology* of the *Oedipus singular*.

VI: THE RIDDLE BETWEEN OEDIPUS AND THE SPHINX

To some degree, at least to Hegel, the destiny of Western civilization precariously hangs upon the solution of the mystic riddle in the legendary confrontation between Oedipus and the Sphinx. In Greek myth, the most common version of the Sphinx's riddle runs like this, "Which creature in the morning goes on four feet, at mid-day on two, and in the evening upon three?" And the riddle, so it goes, is solved once for all by Oedipus in a single word, "man," as told in the Oedipus legend. However, others believe that the mystery of the riddle remains.[37]

The Riddle: Allegorical Game of Intellect and Mystical Narrative of Ontology

In the Oedipus legend, there emerge three intricately interrelated figures: Oedipus, the Sphinx, and the riddle. In fact, there is a chain of riddles: the Sphinx as an alien monster is herself an enigma to Greeks in general, and Oedipus, the man who solves the riddle, is also a mystery to himself. Their fatal confrontation is centered upon Oedipus' reading of the Sphinx's riddle. Thus, the riddle is tripled and respectively embodied in three different forms.

Generally speaking, a riddle is a linguistic game of "hide-and-seek," a play of words with metaphorical condensation and metonymic substitution. The most common rhetorical pattern of riddles is based upon the lingos of "What is . . . ?" By extension, a riddle as an intellectual game informs an allegorical and enigmatic discourse with veiled meanings. The *Sphinx's* riddle centers on the mystery of a creature's ontological status in disparate and multiple positions in a temporal structure. If we take into consideration the Sphinx's status as the sacred guardian of mystical knowledge, i.e., ontological mystery, then the *Sphinx's* riddle, instead of an ordinary allegory of intellectual game in simple linguistic terms, implicates a mystical discourse with cosmographical or metaphysical ramifications.

The Sphinx's riddle unfolds a dialectics between *one* and *many*, one creature and many feet, or ontologically, one subject in multiple shifting positions in an allegorical and mystical mode. By introducing temporality and mystery into the hide-and-seek game, all subjects are configured as different rather than self-identical, mobile rather than fixed, and furthermore, the unconscious figures significantly in self-recognition and self-formation. Temporality, mobility, disparity, and the unconscious are essential and central to the riddle propounded by the Sphinx. Hence, encryption of the riddle depends upon the appropriate cultural contextualization or proper hermeneutic placement of the riddle. In other words, what the riddle means is ultimately determined by the textual space and the cultural location where meaning is made, or to be precise, whether the riddle signifies from the perspective of the *Sphinx's* myth or from that of the *Oedipus* legend. Different readings of the riddle as either a linguistic game in a logocentric order or a sacred discourse in a mystical cosmography generate entirely different solutions to the riddle.[38]

The Sphinx: The Sacred Guardian and Mystic Trickster

Sphinxes in Egyptian culture stand for the sacred guardians of mystical knowledge. In other words, instead of being simply a mother serving to initiate the son in psychoanalytic theory or a monster to be conquered by a hero in *Oedipus'* legend, the Sphinx represents the mystical *trickster* in *Sphinx's* myth. After all, who else talks only in riddles other than the tricksters? As I mentioned previously, the Sphinx's role as a *riddler* has been severely contested by past critics. Some do suspect whether this alien monster possesses any sensibility to wage a battle of wits with the Grecian intellectual. But this doubt is quickly dismissed as unfounded because the riddle the Sphinx propounds, as is noted, is not exactly hers to own after all. Instead, she is simply deployed to repeat what has been passed on to her by someone else in Greek culture, Muses, Apollo, or Hera herself. Every effort has been made to demean her as an alien, demonic, and monstrous other and downgrade her to a menial role of what has traditionally been labeled an "errant boy." However, if the riddle originates from the *trickster* Sphinx instead of a Greek god such as Hera, Muses or Apollo, then the mystic signification of the *Sphinx's* riddle goes immensely beyond the ordinary linguistic game. If the Sphinx assumes the role of the *tricky* guardian of sacred knowledge, i.e., ontological mystery, then, the *Sphinx's* riddle, in addition to an allegorical and enigmatic game of words, transcends into mystical and cosmographical dimensions concerning Oedipus' ontological mystery instead of simply testing his intelligence.

In *Alterity and Narrative*, Kathleen G. Roberts identifies the trickster as a crucial figure of alterity, "an animal or supernatural being" that exists "between multiple social worlds."[39] Jeanne Rosier Smith in *Writing Tricksters* also argues, "Interpreter, storyteller, and transformer, the trickster is a master of borders and exchange, injecting multiple perspectives to challenge all that is stultifying, stratified, bland, or prescriptive."[40] Without exception, tricksters are always inclined to, in one way or another, transgress boundaries and challenge all hegemonic models of singular orders and authoritative systems of interpretation. In general, as Smith observes, "tricksters dwell at crossroads and thresholds and are endlessly multifaceted and ambiguous."[41] Moreover, the tricksters are well versed in semiotic parlance and speak in an ambiguous double voice that calls for multiple meanings beyond the official designation. In this case, the Sphinx represents a typical trickster, "a master of borders and exchange," that speaks in an enigmatic and mystic mode of articulation.[42]

In Greek culture, Oedipus is regarded as the intellectual hero who has the answer to the Sphinx' riddle whereas in Egyptian myth, the Sphinx would be deemed the sacred guardian who holds the key to the ontological mystery of Oedipus' identity. To assume that the Sphinx uses the riddle simply to test the intelligence of Oedipus or as a rite of passage to Logos would seriously underestimate the issue or entirely miss the point, especially considering that sacred knowledge connotes a kind of "gnosis" of ultimate cosmographical mystery. In other words, the Sphinx' riddle is not simply an allegory of words that merely tests the intellect of Oedipus, but also, more importantly, the sacred knowledge that encrypts Oedipus' ontological secret. If we believe that the Sphinx is a guardian of sacred knowledge as well as a mystic trickster, then Oedipus must have failed to decode the latent meaning of the riddle in relation to his unstable ontological footing despite his pompous posture of intellect. The mystic knowledge to which the Sphinx safeguards the entrance is exactly the *mystery* of Oedipus' unconscious—multiplicity, disparity, and difference. In addition, the Sphinx who propounds the riddle also embodies the answer to the riddle—a typological body of diversity, disparity, and heterogeneity, thus a mirror to reflect the metaphysical condition of Oedipus.

Oedipus: The Solipsistic Reader

In Egyptian myth, the Sphinx is deemed a mystic trickster that guards the mystery of Oedipus' identity; in Greek legend, Oedipus is regarded (by Hegel at least) as an inaugural philosopher that solves the Sphinx's riddle. As a philosopher king, Oedipus assumes to be the embodiment of the solipsistic Logos. According to *Oedipus*' legend, the mysterious riddle is solved once for all as Hegel declares: "Oedipus found the simple answer: a man, and he tumbled the Sphinx from the rock."[43] However, as a trickster, the Sphinx speaks in a language of mystic knowledge beyond the realm of Logos. When Oedipus says "man," it merely reflects a voice of the self-sufficient and self-reflexive reason. Typical of a narcissistic reader, Oedipus reduces the disparate other hidden in a mystical riddle to a subject of singularity enclosed in a solipsistic discourse of the self-centered reason. Thus, Oedipus translates a complex mystical idiom of cosmographical mystery into a singular word of logocentric or phallogocentric language.[44] In this instance, Oedipus fails to gain access to the ontological mystery guarded by the Sphinx because her mystical riddle signifies beyond the terrain enclosed by the logocentric order. Those who rise with logos (or phallogos) also fall by it.

Moreover, Oedipus' singular "Man" not only expresses an arrogant posture, but also projects an obsessive desire toward a phantom. As a solipsistic philosopher, Oedipus reads the riddle *self-reflexively*, not just by referring to his body, his name, or his intelligence, but also more importantly, by resorting to his want. Instead of replying to a call from a disparate other, Oedipus simply attempts to hail himself into a singular presence according to his own narcissistic longing. By evoking "Man" in singular form, Oedipus tries to conjure up a sublime subject that he desires, thereby cohering into a singular and identical identity what remains incoherent and disparate. Actually, handicapped by his solipsistic reason, Oedipus' answer, "Man" in a unitary and singular fashion, constitutes ironically the *lack* of self-consciousness. His self-centered way of reading and thinking, instead of enabling, blinds him to his dubious ontological foothold. Cynthia Chase in "Oedipal Textuality: Reading Freud's Reading of Oedipus" observes: "Oedipus himself is the prime example of the bizarre being described by the Sphinx."[45] And Seth Benardete in "Sophocles' *Oedipus Tyrannus*" also notes: "Oedipus saw the heterogeneity that underlines an artificial homogeneity, but he does not see his own disparity."[46] Oedipus does not recognize he is the hidden subject of the mystic riddle, failing to note his latent disparity reflected physically by the Sphinx and signified allegorically in the mystic riddle.[47] To say Oedipus successfully solves the riddle in terms of "man" in singular form would mean to put the riddle only in the context of the *Oedipus* legend in order to realize *his* obsessive desire. In other words, Oedipus fails to encrypt the ontological mystery of his identity in this metaphysical theatre. Hence, the Freudian Oedipus complex turns into a kind of a solipsistic "Oedipus Singular." In this instance, Oedipus's case is much more complex than Freud's Oedipus complex.

In the Oedipus legend, "man" enters logocentric discourse as a universal, transcendental, and regal signifier, not just articulating an illusion of one's singular being as the sovereign subject of reason, but also positioning *Man* as the solipsistic center of a new order. As Charles Segal in *Oedipus Tyrannus: Tragic Heroism and the Limits of Knowledge* states: "The play is a tragedy not only of destiny but also of personal identity: the search for the origins and meaning of our life, our balance between one and many selves, our recognition of the large areas of darkness about who we really are, and the effort to explore the essential mystery of our selfhood."[48] Oedipus invokes just one single signifier, "man," not only to singularize his subject, but also to centralize himself as the royal subject, King Oedipus, a sovereign and hegemonic subject that exclusively dominates the ontological field. However, it is truly ironic that Oedipus, credited as the great intellect that solves the riddle, turns out to be a *riddle*-subject beyond his knowledge. The Oedipus legend dramatizes ultimately a tragedy of limitation of rational paradigm of the Western intellectual tradition as well as the illusion and impotence of rational thoughts to solve the riddle of the complex identity of humanity. Oedipus's answer "man" signifies the grandiose dream of a self-reflexive subject brought forth by a solipsistic philosopher, but due to his pierced feet, a limping philosopher at best.

The Riddle and Current Debates

To put the Sphinx's riddle into the context of our current debate, the question of "Who comes *after* the subject?" probably should be rephrased as "Who comes *before* or *with* the subject?"[49] I mean, before Oedipus comes onto the scene, there is the Sphinx. Oedipus' appearance seems to coincide with the Sphinx's departure in terms of either elimination or repression. The rise of Oedipus is always used to signal the fall of the Sphinx, i.e., the birth of the singular subject and the death of the grotesque other. It seldom comes to our attention that Oedipus and the Sphinx might represent two different forms of ontological disparity, i.e., manifest or latent, conscious or unconscious, spatial or temporal.

If the Oedipus legend is purported to justify various kinds of dominations, i.e., logos over mythos, man over beast, and male over female, from *logocentric*, *Eurocentric* or *phallocentric* points of view, the Sphinx myth, then, speaks entirely to a separate set of issues, that is, the human subject evolves in a temporal structure with multiple and disparate positions, often enigmatic and mystic in an unconscious form. The crux of the Sphinx's riddle is that the unconscious disparity of intermixed positions resides at the very center of being. Therefore, the grotesque comes back via an allegorical return to the mystical knowledge embodied in the *Sphinx's* riddle. Currently, many critics in one form or another *return* to the *Sphinx's* riddle or the Sphinx herself as the *riddler* and trickster to explore the fundamental issue of ontological mystery: "What constitutes the subject?" Or, more pertinent to our current debate: "Who comes after the subject?" Different readings of the *Sphinx's* riddle generate different answers for different purposes. However, man, both in and beyond the Oedipus complex, remains a riddle to himself. Man is not the solution to the riddle; on the contrary, man is the riddle itself.

In the past, we tended to, like Greeks, celebrate the death of the demonic Sphinx and owed our gratitude to the heroic Oedipus for solving the riddle and exorcising the monster. Thereafter, the Sphinx was entirely forgotten and lapsed out of history. In the past, historians hastened to join others to congratulate Oedipus, worshiping him as the savior of Western civilization whereas current critics tend to ceaselessly condemn Oedipus as a prototypical figure for plaguing modern man; some even have gone so far as to colonize the entire unconscious of Western men in terms of a universal desire or guilt in the name of the *Oedipus* complex. In short, *Oedipus* has consistently occupied the center of discourse and continuously absorbed all critical attention without disruption. We are compelled to ask: How to end the legend beyond Oedipus instead of perpetuating it? Here I propose, if this particular legend of Oedipus should end somewhere, why not end it in this *re-turning of* the myth of the Sphinx? Of course, it stands to debate that, by rewriting this fabled encounter between the Sphinx and Oedipus, I have radically revised this mythical confrontation through a provocative departure from the orthodox Oedipus legend and an evocative return to the *Sphinx myth*. No doubt, I take the risk of heretically counter-narrating Greek mythology by contextualizing the Sphinx as a guardian of sacred knowledge and a mystical trickster of divine spirit from the perspective of Egyptian culture.

VII. CONCLUSION OF PART ONE: THE UNCANNY SUBJECT OF THE GROTESQUE

Resurrected from Nero's imperial residence, the sphinx figure is epitomized as a typological image of the grotesque. Since then, it has been taken for granted that the grotesque inherently consists of incompatible and irreconcilable elements and its "identity" lies in its hybridity, disparity, and incongruity, that is, non-identical identities. From a metaphysical perspective, the grotesque is disqualified as a legitimate "subject" category due to its lack of singular, identical, and unitary being. Here we may inquire: Is there such a thing as *the grotesque subject*? Or more heretically: *How grotesque is the subject*? Is it possible that the two terms, i.e., the grotesque and the subject, so opposed to and exclusive of one another, might be in fact inherently related to each other in some ways still unconscious yet? Apparently, according to the orthodox ontology, one is constitutionally unitary, identical, singular, and total while the other is notoriously diverse, disparate, incongruous, and incoherent. In a word, non-negotiable?

The subject, as we know, has often been regarded as a haunted house of being or an uncanny subject, as Freud suggests. To evoke Derrida's specter in this case, what is haunting the singular subject? I propose, the grotesque, as embodied by the *grotto-esque* figure sphinx, returns to uncover the underground nature of the subject and dis-embody the subject like a ghost. In this case, I contend that the grotesque resides at the very unconscious center of the singular subject as its repressed alterity. Further, I postulate that there is no subject without the grotesque, and there is no subject outside the grotesque: alterity and identity, in this case, perilously emerge as one, undermining all metaphysical illusions of a total being and dispelling all ontological phantoms of the singular subject. Disparity, alterity, and incoherence reside at the very core of the sublime vision of the singular subject, and all subjects are inherently and constitutionally grotesque, that is, infinitely transformative and non-identical. Hence, man is permanently haunted by an irreducible and cryptic alterity, just like Oedipus, forever haunted by the Sphinx.

Previously, conceptualizations of the grotesque have always been framed in a temporal structure and in terms of "identity crisis" or in Luis Puelles' words, "an anthropology of the Fall."[50] That is, the subject *becomes* grotesque only after it *loses* its coherence, unity, and singularity as if the subject comes *before* the grotesque and assumes a prior presence of pure singularity. Departing from all past assumptions, I postulate that the grotesque is not external to, opposed to, or post to the subject as an alien monster like the Sphinx to Oedipus; on the contrary, the grotesque figures as the repressed unconscious lurking inside the singular subject. I insert the grotesque into the subject as its unconscious because within any singular subject there is hostage of diverse and disparate elements. Hence, the grotesque introduces a radical ontological opening of metaphysical issues of subjectivity in terms of non-identical alterity. Mary Russo suggests, "Subjectivity as it has been understood in the West requires the image of the grotesque body."[51] I contest that all subjects are diverse, disparate, and incoherent, and the obsessive desire to totalize oneself into a singular being in any hegemonic system reveals exactly inherent grotesque condition instead. Oedipus's answer to the Sphinx's riddle—a narcissistic desire to singularize and capitalize "Man" into an ontological phantom—is a case in point. In other words, the obsessive desire for the singular subject unveils the typical symptoms of the grotesque precisely due to the essential lack of coherence and totality. Peter Stallybrass and Allon White in *The Politics and Poetics of Transgression* observe: "The very drive to achieve a singularity of collective identity is simultaneously productive of unconscious heterogeneity, with its variety of hybrid figures."[52] It suggests that any desperate pursuit of the subject of singularity is accomplished with repression, subjugation, and exclusion of the grotesque.

To conclude, I evoke the grotesque as a trope, or a heretic figure to clarify, not to simplify, the debate of centrality and singularity of the "subject" in the context of the complex but interlaced relationship between aesthetics and metaphysics in general, and the elusive but inherent relationship between the singular subject and the grotesque in specific. I opine, the grotesque refigures the singular subject as ontologically *otherwise* if the grotesque is figured ontologically as an impossible subject. If we believe that the grotesque in aesthetic discourse has an identity issue, then, we might as well say that identity of the subject in metaphysical category is a grotesque issue. Moreover, as an ironic concept, the "grotesque subject" is a self-subversive and self-abortive figure; it exposes the inherent disparities and irreducible difference of any singular subject and discloses all singular ontologies in terms of metaphysical illusions and solipsistic desires. That is to say, the grotesque disembodies all unitary and singular beings and uncovers their latent disparity and heterogeneity. Consisting of non-negotiable difference and irreducible heterogeneity, the grotesque radically splits, undermines, and destabilizes all subjects of singular category.

NOTES

1. Michel Foucault, *Language, Counter-Memory, Practice*, ed. Donald F. Bouchard, trans. Donald E. Bouchard and Sherry Simon (Ithaca: Cornell UP, 1977), 142.
2. Mikhail Bakhtin, *Rabelais and His World*, trans. Helene Iswolsky (Bloomington: Indiana UP, 1984), 96.
3. Geoffrey Harpham, *On the Grotesque: Strategies of Contradiction in Art and Literature* (Princeton: Princeton UP, 1982), 26.
4. Quoted in Wolfgang J. Kayser, *The Grotesque in Art and Literature*, trans. Ulrich Weisstein (Bloomington: Indiana UP, 1963), 77. Kayser cited Walter Scott's notion of the grotesque in the essay "The Novel of E. T. A. Hoffman." Walter Scott believes Hoffman to be the first outstanding artist to represent the fantastic or supernatural grotesque in composition. Here is the full quote from Scott: "In fact, the grotesque in his compositions partly resembles the arabesque in painting, in which are introduced the most strange and complicated monsters, resembling centaurs, griffins, sphinxes, chimeras, rocs, and all other creatures of romantic imagination, dazzling the beholder as it were by the unbounded fertility of the author's imagination" (Kayser 1963, 77).
5. E. H. Gombrich, *The Sense of Order: A Study in the Psychology of Decoration Art* (Ithaca: Cornel UP, 1979), 280.
6. In the age of deconstruction, I am definitely aware that typology is certainly a dangerous trope amidst the death of all totalized narratives. But in this instance, typology serves well the purpose to qualify the sphinx as the most representative of a type of being, i.e., hybrid figures. Here typology figures as a paradoxical trope, based upon a fictional body, to signify an ontological position. Hence, instead of being postulated as an ontological presence, it is employed to render defunct any ontological singularity, thus a kind of self-subversive figure.
7. Lowell Edmunds, "The Sphinx in the Oedipus Legend," in *Oedipus: A Folklore Casebook*, ed. Lowell Edmunds and Alan Dundes (New York: Garland P, 1983), 155.
8. Ibid., 154, 148.
9. Ibid., 147–48.
10. Ibid., 156, 157.
11. Ibid., 161.
12. Jacques Derrida, *The Gift of Death*, trans. David Wills (Chicago: U of Chicago P, 1995), 20.
13. Jacques Derrida, *Positions*, trans. Alan Bass (Chicago: U Chicago P, 1972), 33.
14. Alessandra Zamperini, *Ornament and the Grotesque: Fantastic Decoration from Antiquity to Art Nouveau*, trans. Peter Spring (London: Thames & Hudson, 2008), 6.
15. Geoffrey Harpham, *On the Grotesque: Strategies of Contradiction in Art and Literature* (Princeton: Princeton UP, 1982), 21
16. In fact, there are plentiful sources on the enigmatic origin of the sphinx, some reliable while others highly speculative. However, even according to some of the most authoritative sources, the genealogy of the sphinx's origin is very tentative and contradictory. The huge tome edited by William Smith, *A Dictionary of Greek and Roman Biography and Mythology* (Boston: Little Brown & Co, 1867), lists the sphinx in a manner of uncertainty and multiplicity despite their extensive research of ancient literature. In the entry, the Sphinx, listed as "a monstrous being in Greek mythology, is said to have been a daughter of Orthus and Chimaera . . . , or Typhon and Echidna . . . , or lastly of Typhon and Chimaera" (1867, 895). So her origin is a mystery in Greek mythology. Interestingly, the *Dictionary* is forced to concede that,

in spite of various assumptions of her conception in Greek myth, "The figure which she was conceived to have had is originally Egyptian or Ethiopian" (1867, 895). Regardless of all lexicological efforts, we are left with confusion, contradiction, and uncertainty of the sphinx's multiple origins. In addition, despite contradictory sources about its genealogy, Greek mythology persistently confirms the alien status of the Sphinx: she is introduced into Greek mythology from other places, predominantly from Egyptian culture.

17. Gilles Deleuze, *Nietzsche and Philosophy*, trans. Hugh Tomlinson (New York: Columbia UP, 1983), 2.

18. Willis Goth Regier in *Book of the Sphinx* observes: "In Egypt is the Great Sphinx of Giza, flat on its belly amid ghosts of the gods. He has a very old name, *Horemakhet*, Sun on the Horizon" (2004, 3). Janine Burke in *The Sphinx on the Table* poses that the sphinx used to play the role of protector in Egyptian culture, as "an Egyptian symbol of justice and protection, and an emblem of pharaoh" (2006, 26–27). Burke elaborates: "In Egypt the Sphinx is a guardian, a benevolent protector of entrances and passages in palaces and temples, not the enigmatic temptress of Greek myth. The lion's body symbolizes strength and valour [sic]; the face was the pharaoh's. The Egyptians regarded monarchs as gods, so the sphinx represented both worldly and divine protection" (2006, 66).

19. In William Smith's *A Dictionary of Greek and Roman Biography and Mythology*, the entry says, "after her incorporation with Grecian story, her figure was variously modified. The Egyptian Sphinx is the figure of an unwinged lion in a lying attitude, but the upper part of the body is human. . . . The common idea of Greek Sphinx . . . is that of a winged body of a lion, having the breast and upper part of a woman" (1867, 895). Clearly, Greeks reconfigure her differently as a woman after she is adopted into Greek culture as a kind of "residential alien." Willis Goth Regier in *Book of the Sphinx* also notes: "In Egypt Sphinxes could be male or female; in the Roman Empire Sphinxes were carved with Caesar's faces on them; in Egypt and Rome Sphinxes were totemic, solar and powerful. But in Greece, with rare exceptions, Sphinxes were female and mortuary. A thoroughly feminized Sphinx entered the Oedipus myth and stayed there through the centuries" (2004, 141). Regier specifically points out that the Sphinx is a fusion of Phix, the Greek riddler, singer, and strangler and the Egyptian *Horemakhet*, "Sun on the Horizon" (2004, 3). The Greek Sphinx (Phix) only sings riddles with a gentle or idle tongue, but the alien Sphinx from elsewhere not only propounds riddles but also devours with a ferocious tongue. In some versions, she sings the riddle, seduces young men, and devours or strangles them. She is a sorcerer that tricks and destroys.

20. According to Willis Goth Regier's *Book of the Sphinx*, one version is that Phix is sent by Hera to punish Laius for kidnapping a beautiful boy, Chrysippus, for his pleasure. She sends Phix to Thebes to chastise the city, torment its king, and kill its young men. She sings the riddle (2004, 41). But in *A Dictionary of Greek and Roman Biography and Mythology* compiled by William Smith, the entry says, "According to some she had been sent into Boeotia by Hera.... She is said to have come from the most distant part of Ethiopia . . . ; according to others she was sent by Ares . . . , or by Dionysus . . . , or by Hades" (1867, 895). It is another case of uncertainty and plurality in regard to the Sphinx's confused and intricate origins.

21. Numerous scholars have pointed out the *composite* nature of the sphinx from various cultural locales. For further references, see Theodor Reik's *Dogma and Compulsion: Psychoanalytic Studies of Religion and Myths*; Géza Róheim's *The Riddle of the Sphinx or Human Origins*; Willis Goth Regier's *Book of the Sphinx*; and Lowell Edmunds' "The Sphinx in the Oedipus Legend."

22. Géza Róheim, *The Riddle of the Sphinx or Human Origins*, trans. R. Money-Kyrle (London: Hogarth P, 1934), 17.

23. Janine Burke, *The Sphinx on the Table: Sigmund Freud's Art Collection and the Development of Psychoanalysis* (New York: Walker & Co, 2006), 27.

24. From a psychoanalytic view, homogeneous crimes include incest, self-reproduction and self-duplication. Incestuous children are duplications and reproductions of the same subject. Oedipus' relation to womb-fantasy—to reproduce oneself from son to husband on the one hand and to return to the symbiotic state on the other—demonstrates his narcissistic obsession with the singular self. This return journey from womb to womb re-circulates and reproduces the self-identical subject. Irigaray in *Speculum of the Other Woman* specifically critiques Oedipus'

narcissistic desire in terms of self-production of the same: "Here is the womb in which he may reproduce (himself) the re-producer. What a triumphant revenge for the anxieties of an Oedipus who *sees himself coming out (again)* from a womb he has himself fertilized. In this way he would close the phallic circuit and circularity, and verify his power to endow the woman-mother with a child-phallus—identical to himself" (1985, 78).

25. Georg Wilhelm Friedrich Hegel, *The Philosophy of History* , trans. J. Sibree (New York: Dover, 1956) 199.

26. In *The Philosophy of History*, Hegel emphatically notes that the Sphinx as an Egyptian symbol "*appeared* in Thebes" in order to juxtapose the Egyptian Sphinx with the Greek Oedipus. Hegel intends to affirm a "fact" that the Sphinx that "shows up" in Greek culture does not belong to Greece, and she only stays there as a foreigner and a stranger. Apparently, readers familiar with postcolonial theory recognize the full implication of Oedipus' conquest of the Sphinx as a paradigmatic illustration of the West's domination of the East, especially in the context of Hegel's *The Philosophy of History*. This topic certainly deserves a book by itself.

27. Burke, *The Sphinx on the Table*, 212.

28. Girard, René Girard, *Violence and the Sacred*, trans. Patrick Gregory (Baltimore: Johns Hopkins UP, 1979), 164.

29. Jean-Joseph Goux, *Oedipus, Philosopher*, trans. Catherine Porter (Stanford: Stanford UP, 1993), 16. Critics like Goux raise important issues about this conquest and regard this linguistic contest as a deviation from the orthodox rite of passage for the mythical heroes. In *Oedipus, Philosopher*, possibly the most radical reading of Oedipus against Freud, Goux holds that "Oedipus does not kill the Sphinx in an act of warrior's daring. The Sphinx kills herself: she commits suicide by flinging herself into the abyss as soon as the riddle solved" (1993, 16). Judging from the fact that the riddle involves a battle of wits, one may presume that probably no bloody confrontation is necessary. Here tricks of tongue displace fling of staff, moving the contest from physical to mental arena, from arts of war to arts of wisdom, from martial to philosophical field. This actually constitutes one of the main evidences for Goux to argue for a deviation from the normal rites of passage for the mythical heroes.

30. Peter Rudnytsky, *Freud and Oedipus* (New York: Columbia UP, 1987), 172–73.

31. Julia Kristeva, *Powers of Horror: An Essay on Abjection*, trans. Leon S. Roudiez (New York: Columbia UP, 1989), 84.

32. Goux, *Oedipus, Philosopher*, 2.

33. Ibid., 194.

34. Ibid., 199.

35. Ibid., 179

36. Ibid., 178.

37. There are various versions of the riddle. For instance, in *Oedipus Tyrannus: Tragic Heroism and the Limits of Knowledge*, Charles Segal lists several versions. One version of the riddle runs like this: "What has one voice and four feet, two feet, and three feet?" Another version differs slightly: "What goes on four legs in the morning, two legs in the afternoon, and three legs in the evening?" The earliest known version goes like this: "There is on earth a being two-footed, four-footed, and three-footed that has one name and, of all creatures that move upon earth and in the heavens and in the sea, it alone changes its form. But when it goes propped on most feet, then is the swiftness in its limbs the weakest" (1993, 56). Regardless of some discrepancies between "creature," "name," and "voice" on the one hand, and "legs," "feet," and "limbs" on the other, all versions of the riddle play with the same dialectic game between *one* and *many*.

38. According to some versions of Greek myth, there are three separate riddles instead of one, but only the one about identity game stays with the Oedipus legend. For more information about different versions of the sphinx as well as multiple versions of riddles, please see Lowell Edmunds' *Oedipus: The Ancient Legend and Its Later Analogues*. However, Edmunds only explores the Sphinx *within* the legend of Oedipus, and regards it as an unnecessary and unjustifiable element instead of viewing the Sphinx as a discrete subject by itself.

39. Kathleen Glenister Roberts, *Alterity and Narrative: Stories and the Negotiation of Western Identities (*Albany: SUNY P, 2007), 173, 180.

40. Jeanne Rosier Smith, *Writing Tricksters: Mythical Gambols in American Ethnic Literature* (Berkley: U of California P, 1997), xiii.

41. Ibid., 7

42. Recently there has been a revived interest in trickster figures, especially in the context of ethnic literature and in the discourse of the other. For instance, Jeanne Rosier Smith in *Writing Tricksters: Mythical Gambols in American Ethnic Literature* argues, "At this new crisis (or carnival) of American literature, tricksters proliferate, disrupting tradition and mediating change" (1997, xii). And further, Smith adds, "Trickster is a profoundly cross-cultural and therefore truly American phenomenon" (1997, xiii). On the other hand, Kathleen G. Roberts in *Alterity and Narrative: Stories and Negotiations of Western Identities* states, "I am especially interested in the ethical positioning surrounding Trickster's 'rhetoric of possibility.' The implications of this positioning for alterity might, in a postmodern era, actually transcend Western perspectives" (2007, 173).

43. Georg Wilhelm Friedrich Hegel, *Aesthetics: Lectures on Fine Art*, trans. T. M. Knox (Oxford: Clarendon P, 1975), 361.

44. Please see Petro Pucci's *Oedipus and the Fabrication of the Father*. Pucci points out the connection between *pous* contained in Oedipus' name and its metaphorical meaning of male sex, and "the double etymology of the same 'Oidipous,' which emphasizes both knowledge and the swollen foot (erect penis)" (1992, 76).

45. Cynthia Chase, "Oedipal Textuality: Reading Freud's Reading of Oedipus," *Diacritics* 9, no. 1(1979): 63.

46. Seth Benardete, "Sophocles' *Oedipus Tyrannus*," in *Sophocles: A Collection of Critical Essays*, ed. Thomas Woodard (New Jersey: Prentice-Hall, 1966), 111.

47. Some critics, like Charles Segal, Peter Rudnytsky, and Jean-Pierre Vernant, already noted the direct connection between the riddle and Oedipus in terms of acting out, incarnation, or embodiment. For instance, Segal points out: "Oedipus both answers and acts out the riddle's answer, for he is himself the quintessence of the being to whom the riddle points. The answer to the riddle is both 'Man' and 'Oedipus'" (1993, 57). Rudnytsky comments, "Oedipus proves ultimately to be indistinguishable from the riddle he thinks he has answered" (1987, 265) and "by solving the Sphinx's riddle only to discover that he incarnates that riddle in himself" (1987, 200). In "Ambiguity and Reversal: On the Enigmatic structure of *Oedipus Rex*" collected in *Tragedy and Myth in Ancient Greece*, Jean-Pierre Vernant states: "Oedipus is double. He is, in himself, a riddle whose meaning he can only guess when he discovers himself to be in every respect the opposite of what he thought he was and appeared to be" (Vernant 1981, 90). However, no one pursues further to explicate and unravel the *specific* meanings of this embodiment in terms of ontological mystery in the context of a mystical narrative of sacred knowledge from the perspective of the *Sphinx myth* or to point out that the Sphinx herself meta-physically embodies the riddle in terms of the grotesque.

48. Charles Segal, *Oedipus Tyrannus: Tragic Heroism and the Limits of Knowledge* (New York: Twayne P, 1993), 13.

49. See *Who Comes After the Subject?* edited by Eduardo Cadava, Peter Connor, and Jean-Luc Nancy. This collection of essays focuses on the issue of the Western subject in the context of crisis of identity, i.e., the death of the central subject in Western metaphysics. However, the issue of the *other* in relation to or beyond the hauntology of the subject deserves more attention and investigation.

50. Luis Puelles, "Nothing under One's Feet: Approaches to an Aesthetic of the Grotesque," in *The Grotesque Factor* by Valeriano Bozal et al (Museo Picasso Málaga, 2013), 32.

51. Mary Russo, *The Female Grotesque: Risk, Excess and Modernity* (New York: Routledge, 1994), 9

52. Peter Stallybrass and Allon White, *The Politics and Poetics of Transgression* (Ithaca: Cornell UP, 1986), 194.

II

Reconfiguring the Grotesque between the Sphinx and Oedipus

Chapter Three

The Enigmatic Sphinx

The Grotesque Other in Aesthetic Speculation

In *The Grotesque in Art and Literature*, Wolfgang Kayser claims that in German culture "the monstrous fusion of human and nonhuman elements [figures] as the most typical feature" of the grotesque,[1] and he supports his argument by citing examples from Hoffman's short story "The Sand-man," Freud's essay "The 'Uncanny,'" and Hegel's idea of grotesque art in his aesthetical lectures.[2] In a broad sense, this basic theoretic premise postulated by Kayser defines most German scholars' aesthetic position to the grotesque. However, what constitutes human is subject to debate, and what accounts for the nonhuman is entirely controversial: is it divine or demonic? In spite of its agglomerate monstrosity, the Sphinx or sphinxlike creatures, more or less, seem to have inscrutably possessed German thinkers, especially Hegel, Nietzsche, and Freud, and each in his respective field has contributed to theoretical exploration of the grotesque in general and the Sphinx or sphinx-like figures in particular.[3]

Of note, all three Germany critics' approaches, though different in disciplines, theoretical contexts, and analytic foci, appear to share the same tradition, i.e., interrogating aesthetic issues within a metaphysical framework and engaging aesthetic theses in terms of metaphysical speculations. More or less, they all resort to metaphysical idioms to make sense of grotesque art. Therefore, Hegel's "Introduction to the Philosophy of Art," Nietzsche's *The Birth of Tragedy*, and Freud's "The 'Uncanny'" are all inextricably interlacing metaphysics with aesthetics and linking art to issues of identity in approaching the topic of the grotesque. Regardless of the difference in disciplines or contexts, i.e., Freud's framework in psychoanalysis, Nietzsche's anchorage in Greek tragedy, and Hegel's obsession with onto-theology, their aesthetic speculations of sphinx figures and grotesque images inevitably converge on the ontological issue of subjectivity in Western metaphysics.

Accordingly, the difference of their respective approaches to the grotesque, to a great extent, is marked distinctively by the specific strategy each adopts to negotiate with the Sphinx. For Hegel, it is by exclusion; for Nietzsche, with celebration; and for Freud, through repression. Hegel in *Aesthetics: Lectures on Fine Art* and "Introduction to the Philosophy of Art" excludes the Sphinx from Greece not merely because it is a defective art figure, but predominantly because it is an inadequate subject underdeveloped in spirit and cumbered by wild nature, or in Hegel's word, a symbol of *grotesque* Egyptian culture. To exclude the Sphinx from Greek culture means to deny any traces of its possession of spirit (i.e., Western spirit), and to disclaim its connection to Grecian territory is to protect the Western ideal representation of perfect harmony between a *human* body and a *divine* spirit (Christianity in fact). Nietzsche in *The Birth of Tragedy* resurrects, at the conclusion, the Sphinx as the embodiment of an earth mother figure, full of rejuvenating power of mystic nature; but in the entire essay, he focuses on sphinxlike creatures or chimeras in Greek mythology totally ignored by Hegel, such as satyrs and Dionysus, as representatives of disparate, hybrid, and grotesque beings. Nietzsche celebrates the return of the Sphinx and other hybrids alike from ancient Greek mythology to challenge and overcome, via a Dionysian rupture, the bondage of the individual principle embodied by Apollo and the confinement of the self-reflexive consciousness exemplified by Oedipus. Ironically, Freud, the self-entitled master of Greek mythology, either unconsciously represses or deliberately ignores the cryptic Sphinx at the precise moment when he elaborates on the legend of Oedipus in his *Interpretation of Dreams*. Instead, Freud later returns to the issues of the grotesque in one of his short essays "The 'Uncanny,'" where he tactfully plays with the uncanny like a fort-da game in terms of ambivalent feelings of both "familiar" and "strange" but demurely ends it at the dubious entrance of all human beings, i.e. the maternal body, without acknowledging or recognizing the hidden Sphinx, the sacred guardian of life and death.

I. HEGEL'S SYMBOLIC ART: A METAPHYSICAL SPECULATION OF THE GROTESQUE

Hegel's Dialectics of Art: Form and Content

Typically, Hegel's aesthetic discourse is based upon a dialectic relationship between form and content, and, still, both are subject to the final determination by and conclusive deliberation of spirit, the uttermost *telos* of all Hegelian ideals. The essential value of art exclusively relies upon its relationship with spirit; or in other words, art has meaning only *when* or *if* it transcends into spiritual arena. To be art at all, in Hegel's view, is to be spiritual, i.e., metaphysical and theological. Hence, the highest art embodies the most self-determined form of spirit and, ultimately, Spirit, or the Christian God in specific, inexorably functions as the infinite and absolute essence of all art. That is to say, the metaphysical or theological principles thoroughly dominate and permeate Hegel's entire aesthetic theory of art and, henceforth, his aesthetic speculation, so to speak, becomes a suspicious undertaking in the name of, if not for the sake of, metaphysics.

At the very onset of "Introduction to the Philosophy of Art," Hegel makes it clear that, to be "worthy" of a philosophical discourse, art has no other avenue but to join "the same sphere with religion and philosophy."[4] Therefore, the *telos* of art is to embody and express "the most universal truths of spirit" because "spirit only is the true essence and content of the world."[5] It is absolutely unequivocal for Hegel that aesthetics of art is a matter concerning metaphysical being, i.e., spirit because, as he insists unswervingly that "the beauty of art is beauty born—and born again—of spirit."[6] The Hegelian *Spirit* seems to be defined tautologically or spectrally as something like "in and by itself," absolutely solipsistic and transcendental. Moreover, Hegel professes that spirit in metaphysics is in fact embodied by the *Christian God* and "Christianity" figures "as absolute and universal spirit."[7] Evidently, religion and philosophy, metaphysics and theology emerge as one to frame art stringently in a spiritual realm or an onto-theological sphere. In this case, Hegel's speculation of art appears to be haunted prevalently by an omniscient spectral other in terms of an absolute and eternal spirit. Perhaps more a metaphysician or a theologian than an aesthetician in this context, Hegel sees art exclusively in the sacred light of a holy ghost of the West.

Hegel postulates a "universal evolution" of art based upon his dialectic principle and claims that art has to develop through a series of stages of dialectic resolutions between content and form. For the ideal art to emerge, Hegel contends, the spiritual content and sensuous form have to "reconcile into a united whole."[8] Different negotiations between content and form, that is, how the two sides—"the spiritual content and its sensuous embodiment"[9] —come to terms with each other, yield different forms of art, i.e., symbolic, classical, or romantic art. Ultimately, each form of art is judged exclusively by how close it stands by or how far it goes toward the transcendental presence: *Spirit*. Along the trajectory of the Hegelian theory of a "universal evolution," art is supposed to develop from symbolic to classical and finally to romantic model.

Art in Different Forms: Symbolic, Classical, and Romantic

According to the Hegelian "evolution" theory of art, symbolic art, or grotesque art, is irrefutably the lowest in rank: underdeveloped in spirit and deficient in form. Form in symbolic art is "defective and whimsical" and its spiritual idea is "still indefinite and obscure and ill-comprehended,"[10] hence, abstract, one-sided, and lacking distinctive individuality. Since the spiritual idea has not yet found "its adequate form,"[11] symbolic art demonstrates unrest, struggle, and inadequacy. In Hegel's words, incongruity, incoherence, and incompatibility between the two sides "makes the relation of the spiritual idea to objective reality a negative one."[12] Therefore, grotesque art as an insufficient art form fails to satisfy spiritual demand and is thus incapable of embodying Spirit or the Christian God. In short, Hegel equates "symbolic art" to "grotesque art" for particular reasons: its form is imperfect and inadequate; its spirituality is vague and deficient; and, consequently, their dialectic relationship is characterized as incongruous, incompatible, and antagonistic. As a result, due to its "excesses of imagination," symbolic art "distort[s] the objects of the outer world into a bizarre and grotesque medley."[13]

Hegel's prejudice against symbolic art is evidenced by a long list of derogative terms he has compiled to inscribe its grotesqueness, such as distortion, monstrous, bizarre, incongruity, foreignness, boundless, disfiguration, and incompatibility. In line with the past critical assessments, Hegel's discourse of the grotesque continues to perpetuate the "aesthetics of the negative." Therefore, Hegel's critique of symbolic art in terms of its grotesque nature seems not so much an *aesthetic* evaluation of its artistic merits as a *theological* accusation of its illegitimacy and disqualifications, especially due to "the foreignness of the spiritual idea."[14] If the Greek beauty, according to Hegel's standards in his *Aesthetics*, "displays the inner life of spiritual individuality as entirely embodied in its corporeal shape,"[15] then symbolic art demonstrates precisely the opposite: "confusion and grotesqueness in the mixture of elements striving against one other."[16] Thus, symbolic art is marked by it lack of individual containment, failure of coherence into a singular subject, and an essential absence of humanity and spirituality. In a word, *grotesque*!

By comparison, in classical art, Hegel is delighted to announce, there is the "free and adequate embodiment of the spiritual idea in the form most suitable to it," henceforth, a perfect "conformity of content and form" and a harmonious wholeness of beauty.[17] Instead of the incomprehensive "foreignness" imbedded in the symbolic art, "Spirit" in classical art is characterized "as human mind" and furthermore, the form to embody the "spiritual and individual . . . is the *human form.*"[18] In sharp contrast to the natural chaos and monstrosity of grotesque art (or oriental art in specific), Greek art, or Western art in this case, is featured by a perfect human body with a fully developed individuality and a thoroughly cultivated mind, i.e., the ideal embodiment of the singular subject. Consequently, Hegel affirms that the shape of the Greek god is "the bodily shape of man . . . and his essence is individual and confined."[19] Hegel's ideas here, evidently fraught with typical Eurocentric sentimentality, defend rather than define Greek art which, according to him, possesses both a *specific* (i.e., Western) singular subject and a *particular* (i.e., Western) transcendental spirit in a human form. In addition, the dialectic relationship between the incorporeal form and the spiritual ideas is characterized as a complete correspondence, coherence, and harmony, with a concrete human body as the ideal site to host a sublime spirit.

Romantic art, according to Hegel's dialectic negation, once again destroys the unity of the spiritual idea and its sensuous form and returns to "the difference and opposition of the two, which the symbolic art left unreconciled."[20] Hegel insists that romantic art is no longer content with expressing itself in the confinement of the bodily form because "the true essence of Spirit is its infinite subjectivity."[21] Hence, the subject matter in romantic art would transmute into a sublime domain of pure spirit instead of being bounded within any corporal reality because no physical, natural, or corporal form suffices to embody Spirit. No wonder Hegel believes that romantic art "transcends itself" and carries on "this process of self-transcendence within its own artistic sphere and artistic form."[22] For Hegel, pure spirit, though ephemeral and invisible, poses no problem whatsoever to his onto-theology because the infinite subject exists only in and by spirit, immaterial and incorporeal. In this case, romantic art becomes, so to speak, an art *disembodied* by pure spirit, a ghost without any body or substance. Hegel confirms: "This content . . . coincides with what Christianity declares to be true of God as Spirit."[23] Here Hegel sounds more like a fanatic priest than a logical philosopher, obsessed perhaps?

If Greek art in general is characterized by gods in individual forms, i.e., a perfect unity of a human body and a divine nature, Hegel suspects that art as such is still bounded, on the one end of the dialectic binaries, by corporeality in an earthly world. Aside from classical art where spirit is lodged in a concrete human body, romantic art transcends corporeality or the boundaries of any discrete individual body. Subsequently, the infinite, absolute, and universal spirit negates or "disembodies" everything. As Hegel argues in his *Aesthetics*, the true spirit (or the infinite and universal content) "is the absolute negation of everything particular," and the complete unity with itself "has dissipated all external relations."[24] In short, Hegel's romantic art comprises a solipsistic, self-enclosed, self-identical pure subject of infinite spirit *in* and *by* itself. In Hegel's view, only when *pure spirit* dominates and permeates infinitely and entirely, or in other words, when art approximates religion, does art reach its highest form. To put it ironically, it is only when art *ceases* to be art, and when art's materiality, substance, and corporeality completely dissolve and miraculously transcend into pure spirit, that art paradoxically evolves into a kind of true art *sans* art altogether. Hegel's theory of fine art is in fact a theory of *disappearance* or *desertion* of art, or more precisely, a philosophical and theological conjuration or conversion of art into solipsistic spirituality. In a word, spectral!

Evidently, Hegel's thesis of romantic art entails an unsolved dilemma to his dialectic negotiation between content and form; and actually it signals the unavoidable demise of his hypothesis of the "universal evolution" from symbolic (grotesque), classical (beautiful) to romantic art (sublime). His dialectics of art does not end with perfect harmony or coherence featured by classical art; instead, the continual incompatible strife and struggle between form and content ends with the triumph of spirit, a pure transcendent of a self-enclosed spectral subject. In fact, Hegel betrays and forsakes the dynamics of his dialectic principle when he tries to arbitrarily form a closure of art within an ethereal sphere of pure spirit—a dead-end of his art theory. Instead, his aesthetic speculation of art submerged in a metaphysical or theological discourse is subject to and centralized by a spectral figure, an ephemeral ghost of divine spirit.

Further, although symbolic art and romantic art share the same strife between form and content, i.e., incongruity, incoherence, and antagonism between "spiritual ideas and sensuous form," Hegel insists, nevertheless, there is "but this essential difference."[25] He opines that symbolic art is grotesque because its spirit is underdeveloped and insufficient to accommodate the excessive form whereas romantic art is sublime because its abundant spirit transcends its insufficient form. On this point, I believe their difference lies elsewhere. If Hegel centralizes the Christian God as the embodiment of the romantic spirit, then the "essential difference" does not reside in the incompatibility between form and content, or in the incoherence between body and spirit. Instead, their difference is located in the geopolitical distance between the *East* and the *West*.[26] In Hegel's opinion, compared with classical art, the oriental symbolic art lacks "substantial individuality," "the *human* form," and coherent identity embodied by *Greek* culture. In contrast with romantic art, the oriental symbolic art lacks "superior spirit," consciousness, and infinite subjectivity embodied by *German* culture. In other words, the oriental art is constituted by a significant lack of both *humanity* and *spirituality* according to the European standards, thus grotesque is its true name.

To recapitulate the universal evolution of art according to Hegel's dialectical theory: it starts with symbolic or grotesque art that is marked by its incoherence between form and content due to its "under-developed spirit" in improper form and lack of distinctive subjectivity; for classical art, form and content, body and spirit cohere and harmonize, featured by the perfect embodiment of the individual subject with the best suitable form; and in the final stage, romantic art transcends into pure spirit without form, i.e., disembodied, ethereal, ineffable, spectral, or meta-physical. Hegel arbitrarily ends art in spirit in a theological discourse toward the final *telos* of "pure subjectivity" defined by the Holy Spirit of Christianity. All this reveals that an omnipresent metaphysical specter inhabits and haunts Hegel's aesthetic speculation of art, to evoke Derrida's hauntology here. That is to say, Hegel's discourse of grotesque art is largely grounded in the Eurocentric position of the individual subject (Greek classicism) and the Christian spirituality (German romanticism). However, in one way or another, both the Greek individual subject and the German solipsistic spirit, particularly the Hegelian spirit, are dependent upon the same fundamental principle of ontological singularity.

The Grotesque and the Sphinx: Oriental Art

In "Introduction to the Philosophy of Art," Hegel arbitrarily locates grotesque art exclusively in the territory of the Orient, i.e. "Chinese, Indians, and Egyptians," regardless of the immense cultural differences among these nations. Hegel asserts that oriental artistic objects, i.e., "their representations of the gods," "adhered to formlessness . . . and were not able to arrive at genuine beauty."[27] Further, Hegel believes that their spiritual idea inflicts violence upon them, and "distorts and disfigures them into grotesque shapes."[28] All these deficiencies and disfigurations constitute, in general, "the character of the primitive artistic pantheism of the Orient."[29] As the first form of art, as Hegel points out, symbolic art is characterized by "its endless quest, its inner struggle, its sphinxlike mystery, and its sublimity."[30] In this case, oriental art is not simply infested with strife and incongruity, but also permeated with mystery as well as sublimity, exotic indeed.

Particularly in his *Aesthetics: Lectures on Fine Art*, Hegel opines that the primitive nature of grotesque art in the Orient is characterized by its lack of individuality, or more specifically, lack of singularity of the subject and thus "the individual figures are wildly tugged apart from one another into the colossal and grotesque."[31] In general, oriental art, Hegel contends, "does not get beyond the grotesque intermixture of the natural and the human."[32] Specifically, Hegel targets Egyptian art, accusing it of "worshipping an actual existence of the Divine in living animals like the bull, cats, and many others."[33] "Moreover," Hegel alarms, "the animal form is used intermingled with the human; we find human figures with lions' heads."[34] To Hegel, this is absolutely blasphemous from the orthodox Christian view: how could animals possibly embody "true spirit"? To intermingle animals and humans not only violates, in a most outrageously barbaric manner, the purity of sacred spirit but also commits the sacrilegious crime against the Hegelian infinite Spirit, the Christian God.

Hegel specifically singles out the Sphinx itself as the embodiment of symbolic or grotesque art. He situates the Sphinx in a specific territory of the Orient, Egypt, and bars her entrance into Greece, the West. He denies her legitimate "citizenship" in Greece since Greek art, for him, represents the perfection of art embodied by the harmonious unity of human body and divine spirit while the Sphinx is better left out of the West due to its grotesque status: half-man and half-beast. The following paragraph from Hegel's *Aesthetics: Lectures on Fine Art* is worth quoting at some length for it provides a comprehensive view of his aesthetic appraisal of sphinx figures as the symbol of grotesque art and an "objective riddle," full of mystery and puzzlement.

> The works of Egyptian art in their mysterious symbolism are therefore riddles; the objective riddles *par excellence.* As a symbol for this proper meaning of the Egyptian spirit we may mention the Sphinx. It is, as it were, the symbol of the symbolic itself. In innumerable quantities, set up in rows in hundreds, there are sphinx shapes in Egypt. . . . [One] near Cairo is of such colossal size that the lion's claws alone amount to a man's height. Some of them are recumbent animal bodies out of which as an upper part, the human body struggles; here and there again there is a ram's head, but elsewhere and most commonly a female head. Out of the dull strength and power of the animal the human spirit tries to push itself forward, without coming to a perfect portrayal of its freedom and animated shape, because it must still remain confused and associated with what other than itself.[35]

The Egyptian Sphinx is not only enigmatic, but also stigmatic. Hegel reduces the Sphinx to a symbolic object, a piece of rock of "colossal size," bounded on earth without any possibility of spiritual transcendence. In addition, the Sphinx represents domination of humanity by animality, signifying the futile struggle of a monstrous figure shackled by an *animal* body and controlled by an *alien* spirit. In Hegel's view, the Sphinx is an emblem of lack: lacking (right) spirit, humanity, and singularity of the subject. In other words, her material body is used as an ontological site to symbolize her monstrous otherness. Therefore, either in terms of aesthetics or metaphysics, the Sphinx lands herself squarely in the same category: the grotesque.

In another context, in *The Philosophy of History,* Hegel also reiterates similar ideas regarding the Sphinx as a "riddle" in "an ambiguous form, half brute, half human." Even consenting to her role as "a symbol of the Egyptian Spirit," Hegel insists, "[t]he human head looking out from the brute body, exhibits Spirit as it begins to emerge from the merely Natural . . . without, however, entirely freeing itself from the fetters Nature had imposed."[36] That is to say, the Sphinx as the symbol of the Egyptian spirit exhibits the *deficiency* of an *alien and primitive* spirit that is restrained by the brute body of materiality and confined by the barbaric power of wild nature. Moreover, Hegel observes: "The multiform sphinxes, with lions' bodies and virgins' heads—or as male sphinxes . . . with beards—are evidence supporting the view, that the meaning of the Spiritual is the *problem* (italics added) which the Egyptians proposed to themselves."[37] And Hegel hastens to offer a solution: "The Greek Apollo is its solution; his utterance is: '*Man, know thyself.*'"[38] To Hegel, Oedipus, the Greek man embodying the Apollonian principle, is the hero who solves the *problem* of the Egyptian *alien* and *inadequate* spirit of disparity and incoherence. In this case, as an enigmatic "symbol of Egyptian spirit," the Sphinx epitomizes exactly the *problem* of spirituality that requires subjugation, encryption, or liberation by the Occident. That is why in his *Philosophy of History* Hegel declares triumphantly: "Oedipus, giving the solution, *Man*, precipitated the Sphinx from the rock" and presented the "solution and liberation of that Oriental Spirit."[39] In Hegel's opinion, Oedipus is not only a man, but also a paragon of human intellect, an icon of Greek civilization, and an emblem of Western Logos.

Hegel uses the legend of Oedipus as an exemplary tale to illustrate that in their primitive stage of civilization Egyptians have only "advanced so far as to propose the problem" of a confused and cryptic spirituality in the form of "objective riddles" and it is the fully developed Greek human that solves the riddle in terms of individual consciousness and singular ontology thereby eliminating, once for all, the disparate other embodied by the Sphinx. Willis Goth Regier in *The Book of the Sphinx* points out: "Hegel's Sphinx is the symbol of the defeat of the Sphinx. His Sphinx commemorates the overthrow of Egypt by Greece, the overthrow of enigma by thought, of nature by man, of mystery by clarity."[40] Hence, the Egyptian Sphinx not only displays internal incongruity and disfigured composition in Hegel's aesthetic discourse but also represents the monstrous other due to its ontological disparity and pagan spirit according to Hegel's Christian onto-theology.

II. NIETZSCHE'S DIONYSUS: MYTHICAL DESIRES TOWARD THE GROTESQUE

Dionysus, Satyrs, and the Grotesque

As if attempting to directly challenge Hegel, at the start of *Ecce Homo*, Nietzsche declares: "I am a disciple of the philosopher Dionysus; I should prefer to be even a satyr to being a saint."[41] At the end of *Twilight of the Idols, Or, How to Philosophize with the Hammer*, Nietzsche also proclaims: "I, the final follower of the philosopher Dionysus—I, the teacher of the eternal recurrence."[42] At different ends of two separate books, Nietzsche repeats the same position: he intends to revive Dionysus as a new philosopher to represent the disparate other. Nietzsche's posture through Dionysus is not only different from but also thoroughly antithetical to the other emergent philosopher proposed by Hegel, i.e., Oedipus. It seems that the spectral body of the grotesque Sphinx, conjured away by Oedipus in his legendary conquest, mysteriously returns with a carnival deity of Greek mythology, Dionysus, in Nietzsche's aesthetic discourse of the grotesque. After all, Dionysus is too intoxicated to gain any self-reflexive consciousness or to hold on to any singular and integral subjectivity symbolized by Hegel's Oedipus. Apparently, Dionysus goes the opposite way against the prediction of the Hegelian history of philosophy.

In "A Critical Backward Glance" prefaced to his *The Birth of Tragedy*, Nietzsche inquires: "What meaning did the tragic myth have for the Greeks during the period of their greatest power and courage?"[43] In other words, at the height of Greek civilization marked by the triumph of the rational order and the individual subject, why did tragedy take the central stage? To rephrase the question differently, Nietzsche is asking: "What does the union of god and goat, expressed in the figure of satyr, really mean? What was it that prompted the Greeks to embody the Dionysiac reveler—primary man—in a shape like that?"[44] Nietzsche is profoundly interested in probing and interrogating what specific parts these grotesque and hybrid figures, such as satyrs and sphinxes, play in the context of Grecian remarkable cultural achievements, particularly, in terms of individuality and rationality. Hence, Nietzsche returns to these odd figures entirely neglected by Hegel and reappraises Greek art previously defined in terms of the complete harmony and perfect wholeness of a human mind in a human body for which, unfortunately, neither Dionysus nor satyrs qualify. Instead of being "a united whole," satyrs embody the Hegelian concept of grotesque art, i.e., "a bizarre and grotesque medley"[45] and "grotesqueness in the mixture of elements."[46] Moreover, the satyr represents what Hegel believes to be the most sacrilegious crime against the Christian Spirit. Neither entirely a "human form" nor totally a "human mind," the satyr is comprised of "the grotesque intermixture of the natural and the human" and "the animal form . . . intermingled with the human."[47]

Generally, in ancient festivals, satyrs always play a crucial part in the Dionysian rites. Similar to the Sphinx, the satyr also consists of, in Hegel's words, "an ambiguous form, half brute, half human."[48] In other words, as a chimera, the satyr resembles the sphinxes or is a kind of sphinx figure in a broad sense. Throughout ancient civilization, Nietzsche affirms, "we find evidence of Dionysiac celebrations which stand to the Greek type in much the same relation as the bearded satyr, whose name and attributes are derived from the he-goat, stands to the god Dionysos."[49] These mythical chimeras, in Nietzsche's view, represent "those brutal and grotesque Dionysiac forces,"[50] and, as a grotesque character, the satyr is considered a prototypical embodiment of the Dionysian spirit closely associated with and similar to sphinxes. Hence, Nietzsche in *The Birth of Tragedy* resorts to the Sphinx and sphinx-like figures of Greek culture in general to explore the function of the grotesque in terms of disparity, disintegration, and transgression.

In Hegel's view, as we recall, the Greek classical ideal is represented by a coherent wholeness of a perfect body with a divine spirit and Greek culture signals a pivotal transition from mythos to logos, a radical departure from the disparate grotesque toward the singular subject anchored to the rational order, as evidenced by the rise of Oedipus and the fall of the Sphinx. Nietzsche, on the contrary, identifies the grotesque epitomized by the Sphinx as the redemptive and transgressive power and henceforth argues for a return to the primordial nature in order to overcome the self-enclosed individual consciousness exemplified by Oedipus. By retracing the relationship between Dionysus and satyrs, and the Dionysian rites and the final resurrection of the Sphinx as the emblem of nature or the earth mother, Nietzsche attempts to revive and reinstate an alternative cosmographical mode of being discarded by Hegel. In this context, Nietzsche intends to conjure up, through the Dionysian rites, the grotesque beings of heterogeneity, multiplicity, and disparity subjugated in the past as well as to exorcize the Hegelian model of individual consciousness and the singular subject defined by the Apollonian principle. The Greek tragedy, Nietzsche seems to contest, demonstrates this powerful desire for self-disintegration as well as self-transformation according to a radical alternative cosmographical order beyond the confinements of logocentric and egocentric culture.

In sharp contrast to Hegel's metaphysical aesthetics, Nietzsche declares, at the very start of *The Birth of Tragedy,* "art . . . constituted the essential metaphysical activity of man."[51] Hence, aesthetics for Nietzsche constitutes the essence of existence rather than metaphysics, and further, any kind of metaphysics is but an "esthetic metaphysics."[52] In other words, Nietzsche appears to start his project with metaphysics of art but ends it with art of metaphysics. Instead of perpetuating metaphysics of art advocated by Hegel, Nietzsche contends that the very metaphysical issue of being can only be resolved in an aesthetic negotiation between Dionysian and Apollonian principles, and therefore, the entire subject of ontology becomes an aesthetic *topos.* In this case, we might as well say Nietzsche not only challenges German metaphysicians' postulations of art in general but also responds directly to Hegel's metaphysical or onto-theological aesthetics in particular.

The Art of Being: The Apollonian and the Dionysian

The Apollonian principle epitomized by self-control, self-knowledge, and self-consciousness informs the basic foundation of the Hegelian self-conscious subject of the *same* as Hegel asserts in *The Philosophy of History* that "[t]he Greek Apollo is its solution."[53] Whereas, the Dionysian principle proposes a drastically different model as it involves a transformative process of self-abandonment, self-division, and self-transcendence toward a heterogeneous alterity. Via a Dionysian rite of rupture, Nietzsche intends to disrupt the boundaries circumvented by the Apollonian mode of singular identity and refashion an alternative being of disparity. Evidently, Nietzsche is engaged in an ontological enterprise rather than merely tackling the issue of tragedy in a paradoxical aesthetic speculation on the metaphysical subject.

"As a moral deity," Nietzsche remarks, "Apollo demands self-control from his people and, in order to observe such self-control, a knowledge of self."[54] In opposition to Hegel's idea, the self-reflexive knowledge for Nietzsche means not simply control of the self, but also bondage and confinement, or worse, delusion. Nietzsche argues, Apollo "reigns also over the fair illusion of our inner world of fantasy."[55] As "the apotheosis of the *principium individuationis,*"[56] the Apollonian subject of individuality means "nothing much" but a fantasy. Furthermore, Nietzsche exposes that Apollo himself figures as "the marvelous divine image of the *principium individuationis,*"[57] that is, a *narcissistic image* of self-reflection. Ironically, instead of embodying "the moral deity," the Apollonian individuality represents "the source of all suffering" as well as "the root of all evil."[58] Apparently, from Nietzsche's perspective, Apollo invokes a *phantom* as an ontological locus that anchors the singular subject in the solipsistic self-reflexive consciousness or self-enclosed hallucination—Oedipus's evocation of man is an exemplary case.

Nietzsche challenges the myth of sublime subjectivity associated with the self-indulged artist. The hyperconscious individual in this instance is the obstacle rather than the motor of art and, as Nietzsche contends, "the subjective artist is simply the bad artist."[59] Contrary to the Hegelian ideal of a solipsistic subject, Nietzsche recommends, instead, "a triumph over subjectivity" in all undertakings of arts. In other words, Nietzsche believes art possesses the power to disrupt the boundaries of the subject whereas the self-conscious subject will restrict art to a solipsistic closure. A true artist, in Nietzsche's opinion, has "abrogated his subjectivity" in the "Dionysiac phase" and "what recent writers on esthetics speak of as 'subjectivity' is a mere figment."[60] Hence, the idealized subject that Hegel brings forward is dismissed as an illusory image that deludes and misguides artists by the Apollonian light. All true artists have to undergo, as Nietzsche proposes, a "mystical process of un-selving" since "the subject . . . can be thought of only as an enemy to art, never as its source."[61] In this context, the sublime subjectivity is not construed as the originating source, but instead is regarded as a pure phantom that inhibits and misleads art.

If Apollo embodies a "god of individuation and just boundaries," then by contrast Dionysus "appears in a multiplicity of characters."[62] In Nietzsche's view, the Dionysian rites dispel the illusion of the individual self and precipitates dissolution of all boundaries of discrete beings. Nietzsche suggests that, through the Dionysian rites of rupture, one is able to overcome the delusional ontological order or the "artificially restrained and discrete world of illusion";[63] and only by shattering "the *principium individuationis*" and dissolving the "just boundaries," can one undergo the "strangest metamorphosis" of "mystic self-abrogation" and embraces a mythical self-transcendence toward multiplicity and disparity. Nietzsche states: "The mystical jubilation of Dionysos . . . breaks the spell of individuation and opens a path to the maternal womb of being,"[64] i.e., an open space for self-disintegration and self-transformation. Instead of repeating the Apollonian oracle, "Know Thyself," Nietzsche suggests to go beyond the self. Rene Girard in *Violence and Sacred* observes that the Dionysian state "is not a synthesis of elements, but a formless and grotesque mixture of things that are normally separate" and Dionysus "reenacts the hysterical trance and the crazy mixture of differences."[65] Hence, the Dionysian principle involves self-abandonment, intoxication, self-forgetting in ecstasy, and it purports to transgress the bounds of the delusional individual principle through a radical dismemberment or rupture of totality of being. Interestingly, the birth of tragedy for Nietzsche implies the death of Apollo and rebirth of Dionysus because the death of Dionysus signifies "a rebirth of Dionysos, which we can now interpret as meaning the end of individuation."[66]

As a figure similar to the sphinx, the satyr stands for the grotesque. Nietzsche believes that "the satyr expressed nature in a rude, uncultivated state" and "the satyr was man's true prototype."[67] Instead of being demonic or monstrous, the satyr in Nietzsche's view represents the "sublime and divine" spirit of nature. In contrast, the modern individual "is but a replica of the sum of cultural illusions which he mistakes for nature."[68] Through the Dionysian rites, man is "cleansed of the illusion of culture," "tending toward the shattering of the individual," and "entering a strange being"; and eventually he "sees himself metamorphosed into the satyr."[69] If Hegel uses the Sphinx as a sacrificial rite of passage for Oedipus to conquer the disparate grotesque and initiate the illusion of the singular subject, Nietzsche suggests, via a carnival rite of Dionysus, the modern individual can get rid of the alluring delusion of the singular subject and return to the grotesque state of disparity in an ecstatic transformation like satyrs. Nietzsche asks, rhetorically, "If we could imagine an incarnation of dissonance—and what is man if not that?"[70] Hence, the proposed new cosmographical order of being rests upon transformative grotesque mixture or "an incarnation of dissonance" as represented by disparate figures like satyrs, sphinxes, and Dionysus.

Nietzsche argues elsewhere, in *The Will to Power*: "The assumption of one single subject is perhaps unnecessary. . . . My hypotheses: The subject is multiplicity."[71] The Dionysian principle promoted by Nietzsche inaugurates multiple and discontinuous affects that disintegrate the totality of the subject. It discards the Hegelian dialectic tendency to assimilate difference into identity and multiplicity into singularity. Instead, this *Nietzschean will* cannot be cohered into an identical subject or unified into a total being because the

Dionysian rites, by introducing an ecstatic alterity of disparity and multiplicity, utterly decenters and completely dissolves the Hegelian model of the self-sufficient and self-enclosed subject. Andrew Bowie notes in *Aesthetics and Subjectivity* that, for Nietzsche, "[t]he will is 'divided in itself.' This fact is most obviously manifested in us through desire, which entails an inherent incompleteness and a need on the part of that which desires to move beyond itself."[72] This "*Nietzschean will*" precipitates transcendence toward the grotesque other and shatters the illusory bondage of the singular and identical being. This Dionysian desire of self-undermining and self-dismembering is not at all deemed a preparatory process oriented towards a high synthesis of the *same* as predicted and prescribed by Hegel; on the contrary, it opts for an alternative mode of being altogether. The Dionysian principle henceforth unsettles the subject of singularity via an ecstatic and orgiastic revelry—with hybrid figures of man-goat, satyrs—and transforms the modern man into the grotesque other. Jűrgen Habermas in *The Philosophical Discourse of Modernity: Twelve Lectures* specifically highlights that the Dionysian ecstasy will bring forth "ceaseless transformations" "at the cost of a painful de-differentiation, a de-delimitation of the individual" toward "a merging with amorphous nature within and without."[73]

The Mystic Oneness and Disparate Multiplicity

Different from the orthodox romantic notion of nature in terms of a unified wholeness, Nietzsche's concept of a "primal unity" of nature can be confusing or even misleading. In Nietzsche's view, "the primal Oneness" represents the *dissonant* and *heterogeneous* nature itself in its contradictory and chaotic form—an alternative cosmography that unbinds human beings. Therefore, Nietzsche anticipates that "nature itself, long alienated or subjugated, rises again to celebrate the reconciliation with her prodigal son, man."[74] It is important to note, man aligns himself with and returns to nature—the earth mother instead of Logos or the Hegelian Spirit. In *Nietzsche's Philosophy of Art*, Julian Young reminds us that "it is important to resist the temptation to read Nietzsche's Dionysian solution as a matter of identifying with other *human* beings."[75] Via the Dionysian rites, one is initiated "back into the original oneness of nature,"[76] instead of being subjugated by any other singular system or hegemonic order. And this nature, according to Nietzsche, consists of "the original Oneness, the ground of Being, ever-suffering and contradictory,"[77] in short, a dynamic and heterogeneous oneness of becoming and transforming.

In Nietzsche's opinion, the primordial and heterogeneous nature is epitomized by the Sphinx, an incarnation of the primal power abhorred by Hegel in his meta-aesthetic discourse of the grotesque. Nietzsche writes: "That same nature addresses us . . . in a voice that rings authentic: 'Be like me, the

Original Mother, who, constantly creating, finds satisfaction in the turbulent flux of appearances!'"[78] In this case, the Sphinx returns as an earth mother figure to embody all disparate and multiple elements of nature in a ceaseless flux. To be "wholly identified with the original Oneness, its pain and contradiction,"[79] for Nietzsche, means to be a subject of heterogeneity and disparity. Therefore, Nietzsche's Dionysian principle in effect radically reconceives the "Primordial Oneness" in terms of disparate, multiple, and diverse elements, and henceforth, to submerge in the mythical nature of the original Oneness means to reform oneself in a process of contradiction, alteration, and multiplicity instead of unification or singularity.

Similar to Hegel, Nietzsche also returns to Oedipus and the Sphinx in Greek mythology, but reviews their legendary encounter from a completely different angle. Nietzsche contests that *Oedipus'* legend dramatizes man's futile attempts to dominate the dissonant nature by a rational order. Instead of signaling the glorious rise of logos or the individual subjectivity as Hegel suggests, Nietzsche sees in Oedipus' triumphant deed a tragic fall due to the self-sufficient reason and the egocentric consciousness. Further, Nietzsche associates the riddle with the mystic nature and regards the Sphinx as the incarnation of grotesque nature. And here is Nietzsche's conclusive remark regarding "the terrible triad of Oedipean fates":

> [T]he same man who solved the riddle of nature (the ambiguous Sphinx) must also, as murderer of his father and husband of his mother, break the consecrated tables of the natural order. It is as though the myth whispered to us . . . that whoever, in pride of knowledge, hurls nature into the abyss of destruction, must himself experience nature's disintegration.[80]

Here the Sphinx as the emblem of nature is violated by the hubris of human intellect and as a result of the crime of wisdom (the Apollonian principle) Oedipus has to suffer the consequence of self-dismemberment and self-disintegration. Contrary to Hegel's position, Nietzsche argues that the true meaning of Oedipus drama resides precisely in the tragedy or futility of delusional intellectual wisdom and the phantom of the singular subject.

To a great extent, Nietzsche's Sphinx appears to be a Greek one, but her mythical meaning lies substantively and substantially beyond the legend of Oedipus and outside Sophocles' plays, but closely related to the Egyptian Sphinx as the embodiment of an alternative cosmography. Instead of being a monstrous other that plagues Thebes, Nietzsche ecstatically resurrects and completely restores the Sphinx as a sacred power of mystic nature in sharp contrast to the Greek Oedipus. To Nietzsche, Oedipus figures no more than a tragic hero with restrictive knowledge who, tempering with the power of nature, has to repay with his life—thus a sacrificial and sacrilegious character. In this instance, entirely in opposition to Hegel's supposition, *Oedipus* is sacrificed instead in order to resurrect the sacred Sphinx as the new cosmographical order. Hence, Nietzsche's heretic reading reverses the outcome of the legendary encounter postulated by Hegel: the Oedipus legend unfolds the sacrifice of the individual self and initiation of the disparate other, that is, the *fall* of Oedipus and the *rise* of the Sphinx. Apparently, Hegel seems to have shifted the polarized paradigmatic structure represented by Oedipus and the Sphinx toward the wrong direction.

Gilles Deleuze in *Nietzsche and Philosophy* qualifies Nietzsche's notion of Dionysus in terms of radical disparity and fundamental transgression. Deleuze identifies Nietzsche's Dionysus as "the god of transformations, the unity of multiplicity, the unity that affirms multiplicity and is affirmed of it."[81] In the "Foreword" to Deleuze's *Nietzsche and Philosophy*, Michael Hardt aptly summarizes: "In Nietzsche's concept of *multiplicity* Deleuze finds a notion of difference that does not refer back to (and thus depend on) a primary identity, a difference that can never be corralled into an ultimate unity."[82] Therefore, in Deleuze's view, Nietzsche's idea of becoming posits an eternal recurrence that proliferates and expands difference and multiplicity, a vital strategy that circumvents the Hegelian dialectics toward the ultimate unity or singularity of being. In other words, the eternal recurrence initiates an infinite self-transfiguration and self-transgression, not toward *one*, but toward the mythical multiplicity and disparity. Nietzsche contests elsewhere in *Ecce Homo*, "*becoming*" is actually "a radical repudiation of the very concept of *being*,"[83] in fact, a radical positioning of a new mode of being *otherwise*. The self-dismemberment involves both joy and pain as Nietzsche declares, at the end of *Twilight of the Idols*, "beyond terror and pity, in order to *be oneself* the eternal joy of becoming—that joy that also includes in itself the *joy of destruction*."[84]

What Nietzsche has proposed is in effect a provocative philosophical heterodox in which the diverse and excessive Dionysian desires obliterate the boundaries of individual confinement and precipitate the grotesque transformation. Hence, Nietzsche's aesthetics of the grotesque projects an alternative cosmographic or ontological position of difference, multiplicity, and becoming in terms of eternal recurrence. It is a radical ontology, or more precisely, a heretic *heterology*, that carnivalizes difference in a way that destruction is deemed an affirmative and reproductive power in an infinite process of modifications and reconstructions. Nietzsche has fundamentally ruptured the metaphysical concept of being—the singularity of the subject—into irreducibly multiple, diverse, and recurrent fragments. That is to say: coming into *being* means coming into *differences*. Later, Deleuze and Guattari in their *Anti-Oedipus* ground their theory of the schizophrenic subject in Nietzsche's Dionysian principle and further develop the Nietzschean will into a radical desire for disruption, difference, and transgression.

III. FREUD'S "THE 'UNCANNY'" AND THE GROTESQUE: MOTHER AND THE OTHER

"Uncanny," a slippery term itself, has been as an essential trope to characterize the nature of the grotesque over the past few centuries. Perhaps nobody else has contributed more to the topic than Freud; in particular, his seminal piece "The 'Uncanny'" provides a fertile place to explore the complex issues of the grotesque. Like Nietzsche and Hegel, Freud has been persistently preoccupied over the riddle of man, or more specifically, the grotesque nature of the human subject. As a critical theory, psychoanalysis has been, indisputably, instrumental and central in refashioning the literature of the grotesque.

Freud's "The 'Uncanny,'" published in 1919, positions itself uniquely in Freud's engagement with psychoanalysis in general and art in specific. Typical of him, Freud provides more questions than answers in his research. From the very start of "The 'Uncanny,'" Freud apologetically confesses that he is "impelled to investigate the subject of aesthetics," a topic that has been "neglected in the specialist literature of aesthetics."[85] If Hegel is relentlessly critiquing grotesque art on a metaphysical ground, and Nietzsche is adamantly arguing for a replacement of metaphysics by a Dionysian aesthetic principle, Freud, so it seems, postures to dodge the topic altogether. As a rule, Freud's apologetics are often employed as a discourse strategy to *conceal* and then *reveal* something profound that he is *not supposed* to know. His apologetics are in fact a routine narrative of hide-and-seek, signifying both secrecy and schematic plot. So we guess, in spite of his reluctant posture to enter the discourse of a "neglected" topic, is it possible that Freud is compelled to probe a repressed area that is remotely related to his own unconscious? What is he hiding in this "neglected" topic and why is he not quite at home about the aesthetic discourse on the uncanny? In general, resistance is often construed as a symptom of repression that would certainly arouse the interests of psychoanalysts. Freud frames his analysis of the uncanny in his reading of Hoffman's short story "The Sand-Man." As a gothic tale, what horror is it going to evoke for Freud, and what would figure as the horror itself for Freud?

Between Aesthetics of the Negative and Aesthetics of Ambiguity

Freud starts by saying that the uncanny in general "is undoubtedly related to what is frightening—to what arouses dread and horror."[86] Further, Freud makes the distinction between normal aesthetic processes that focus on the positive feelings of "what is beautiful, attractive and sublime" and the uncanny that mostly deals with "the opposite feelings of repulsion and distress."[87] Apparently, Freud starts the topic of the uncanny by situating his speculation in a typical aesthetics of the negative, that is, what evokes "dread and horror." In fact, throughout the essay, Freud compiles a comprehensive list of negative words from various languages in reference to the meanings of the uncanny: lost, unknown, frightening, unhomely, strange, foreign, uneasy, gloomy, dismal, ghastly, haunted, ghostly, repulsive, daemonic, gruesome, hidden, secret, mystic, ambivalence, and so forth.[88]

As a master of words, Freud traces the origin of the word "uncanny" to its full etymological ramifications and semantic conjugations. He elaborates, "The German word '*unheimlich*' is obviously the opposite of '*heimlich*' ['homely'], '*heimisch*' ['native']—the opposite of what is familiar; and we are tempted to conclude that what is 'uncanny' is frightening precisely because it is *not* known and familiar."[89] At this moment, one is led to believe that the uncanny simply means "strange," "foreign" or "alien." However, by tracing the word "uncanny" in a binary position between *heimlich* and *unheimlich,* Freud finds out, astonishingly, the meanings of these two antonymous terms eventually become identical and overlap somewhere along the long etymological extension and semantic evolution. As Freud observes, "among its different shades of meaning the word '*heimlich*' exhibits one which is identical with its opposite, '*unheimlich.*' What is *heimlich* thus comes to be *unheimlich.*"[90] Thus, Freud concludes: the uncanny is structured between "familiar" and "unfamiliar," "known" and "unknown," "at home" and "not at home." The initial aesthetics of the negative gradually evolves into an aesthetic of ambiguity in terms of "intellectual uncertainty; so that the uncanny would always, as it were, be something one does not know one's way about in."[91] Somewhat like Renaissance artists' initial response to the grotesque art in the grottoes, Freud seems to posture the same attitude of incomprehension, uncertainty, and loss in front of the uncanny other.

The Castration Complex and Oedipus

Regardless of his aesthetic position of ambiguity toward the uncanny, Freud typically reads Hoffman's tale "The Sand-Man" through his master plot and the metaphysics of psychoanalysis: the Oedipus complex. Freud founds the Oedipal complex to solve all riddles he encounters in his exploration of human psychology—a kind of metanarrative to decode all mysteries. The castration theory is positioned as the cornerstone for the Oedipus complex and Freud's reading of Nathaniel's fear of the blinding of his eyes by the Sand-Man inescapably points to the castration complex. As Freud says, "A study of dreams, phantasies and myths has taught us that anxiety about one's eyes, the fear of going blind, is often enough a substitute for the dread of being castrated."[92]

Furthermore, Freud directly refers to the legendary hero Oedipus himself to make his case: "The self-blinding of the mythical criminal, Oedipus, was simply carrying out a mitigated form of the punishment of castration."[93] Framing his investigation of the uncanny within the grounding theory of the Oedipus complex, Freud can only see Oedipus, only that far, as the inevitable outcome since, he believes, his universal formula is the master code that defines all plots and encrypts meanings of all stories. In this case, Freud is simply using Hoffman's "The Sand-Man" to rehearse his Oedipus drama in terms of castration or its mitigated form, blindness. In fact, in *Speaking the Unspeakable: Religion, Misogyny, and the Uncanny Mother in Freud's Cultural Texts,* Diane Jonte-Pace points out that castration theory ascribes "not only a paradigm for the structure of the psyche, but also a system for the evaluation of culture."[94] In other words, the Oedipus complex provides a universal theoretical structure and overall critical framework to explore all social, cultural, and human existences. His speculation on the uncanny is no exception.

However, the Oedipus complex as a universal paradigm not only provides insight for Freud, but also limits his vision and blinds him to all other positions. When the father figures as the singular and central presence, the mother simply disappears, absent and invisible—repressed. That is to say, if Freud's reading is grounded in the castration complex, the key to decode all meanings, his probing of the uncanny in terms of castration theory will inevitably go back to the same enclosed system of the Oedipal structure centered by the father figure, and a dead one too. By reducing "The Sandman" to an exemplary story of Oedipus, Freud can only "investigate" the uncanny in a framework of absolute certainty and centrality, i.e., his universal formula of castration. In this context, the uncanny is not at all ambiguous or enigmatic, but prefixed by a pre-determined meaning despite his sophisticated linguistic jugglery and elaborate word play. However, something else, more *unheimlich* than *heimlich,* seems to haunt Freud's Oedipal theory of the uncanny, just like the Sphinx's spectral body in the Oedipus' legend.

Return of the Repressed: The Maternal Body

As Freud prescribes initially, the uncanny is concerned with what is "concealed and kept from sight";[95] further, Freud warns us that the uncanny is associated with "what is frightening—to what arouses dread and horror,"[96] and it certainly takes him a long time to reach the locale of terror after all the games of hide-and-seek. Indeed, after his labyrinthine linguistic game and complex maneuvers of fort-da, Freud stages his final revelation of the uncanny as a surprising denouement by introducing, hesitatingly, another avenue to approach the uncanny, a kind of "dark continent," so to speak.

Near the end of the essay, Freud is ready for his conclusive remark and presents all the sources relevant to the uncanny: "animism, magic and sorcery, the omnipotence of thoughts, man's attitude to death, involuntary repetition and the castration-complex comprise practically all the factors which turn something frightening into something uncanny."[97] Surprisingly, Freud perfunctorily adds something as a kind of appendix as if only to offer a minor revision to his project, as he says, "we have now only a few remarks to add."[98] However, what he adds entirely changes the focus and points to a locale beyond the Oedipus paradigm as well as exposes the very unconscious of psychoanalytic theory: the womb-fantasy associated with the maternal genitals. In fact, Freud himself identifies the return of the repressed as the key factor of the uncanny because, as he states, "this uncanny is in reality nothing new or alien, but something which is familiar and old-established in the mind and which has become alienated from it only through the process of repression" and "the uncanny [*unheimlich*] is something which is secretly familiar [*heimlich-heimisch*], which has undergone repression and then returned from it."[99]

However, what has returned for Freud evokes not so much desire as fear of the enigmatic maternal body, the horrific cryptic site of the uncanny. Freud presents the feeling of the uncanny as if one confronts the mysterious maternal body at the primal scene, probably the same as when Oedipus stands in front of the Sphinx as the earth mother figure as well as the sacred guardian of mysteries of life and death. To furnish the "beautiful confirmation of our theory of the uncanny,"[100] Freud exposes the monstrous female body. Let's quote Freud at some length at this point:

> It often happens that neurotic men declare that they feel there is something uncanny about the female genital organs. This *unheimlich* place, however, is the entrance to the former *Heim* [home] of all human beings, to the place where each one of us lived once upon a time and in the beginning. . . . [W]henever a man dreams of a place or a country and says to himself, while he is still dreaming: 'this place is familiar to me, I've been there before,' we may interpret the place as being his mother's genitals or her body. In this case too, then, the *unheimlich* is what was once *heimisch*, familiar; the prefix 'un' ['un-'] is the token of repression.[101]

After various detours and delays, Freud, at the end of the essay, demurely unfolds the secret space that he plays with by covering and uncovering: the castrated female genitals—the locus of the uncanny, the horror of lack. Freud associates the uncanny with a dreadful feeling one has at the entrance of a haunted dark continent—the castrated maternal body. The sight of castrated female genitals unveils, instead of a locale of desire, pure horror of absence: death and dismemberment. In short, the uncanny, instead of correlating to "the mysterious and terrifying death of his beloved father,"[102] becomes a horrific primal scene at the sight of the genitals of a castrated mother, and here the womb figures as the tomb.

On the surface, Freud seems to uncover two effects associated with the origin of the uncanny, the Oedipus complex and the womb-fantasy. On the one pole stands the Oedipus complex, linked to castration, fear, dread, dead father, blindness, and *unheimlich*; and on the other pole stands the womb fantasy, signifying death and rebirth, desire and fear, the grotto and home, *heimlich* as *unheimlich*. Freud carefully draws the linkage between them: "this terrifying phantasy [dismemberment associated with castration-complex] is only a transformation of another phantasy which had originally nothing terrifying about it at all, but was qualified by a certain lasciviousness—the phantasy, I mean, of intra-uterine existence."[103] Hence, the womb figures as *the* uttermost repressed source of all "terrifying phantasy." In spite of Freud's insistence on its pleasure or "lasciviousness," this substitute of fantasy from dismemberment to absence involves more terror than pleasure, the horror of a primal erasure. Freud uses the typical castration paradigm to evoke uncanny feelings associated with a kind of primal scene when little boys visualize the female genitals for the first time and are shocked at the dark hole with its significant lack, the lack of phallus. Thus, Freud starts his discourse of the uncanny in a typical frame of the Oedipus complex with the master code of the castration complex, but ends the discourse elsewhere, with a return of the repressed, in the womb-fantasy, exposing the repressed (m)other, the maternal body, the mother-death, or the spectral Sphinx, the hidden enigma in the Oedipus legend.

Helen Cixous in "Fiction and Its Phantoms: A Reading of Freud's *Das Unheimliche* (The 'Uncanny')" observes: "What lies on the other side of castration? 'No meaning' other than the fear (resistance) of castration. . . . It is this dodging from fear to fear, the unthinkable secret since it does not open on any *other* meaning."[104] While this *other* meaning, as the hidden figure in the hide-and-seek game, constitutes the unconscious of the Freudian discourse, i.e., the repressed Sphinx, the sacred guardian of mysteries of life and death. Therefore, the entire purpose of Freud's sophisticated play of fort-da is to veil and unveil the maternal body as the ultimate site of the uncanny. Unlike Freud's other theoretical trajectories, this time, at the primal scene, the specter is not the father's penis or father's dead body (too familiar), but the mother's body as the dark hole, the uncanny site that haunts Freud.

The mother's body in this case becomes a riddle for Freud, and apparently that leads us back to the specter of the Egyptian Sphinx, the sacred guardian at the entrance to all mysteries of life and death. Both Freud and Oedipus seem to stand at the same entrance of life and death guarded by the sacred mother—the Sphinx. In an uncanny blindness, Freud forgets that the Sphinx might be the guardian to the entrance of secrets hidden in the Oedipus legend. In *The Spectral Mother: Freud, Feminism and Psychoanalysis,* Madelon Sprengnether correctly points out, "For the most part, however, Freud had trouble thinking about the figure of the mother."[105] Not simply trouble, but simply that he cannot think beyond the father.

As a famous collector of ancient figures and sphinxes, and, especially, with one antique sphinx figure facing him on his table, how could Freud possibly forget the Sphinx—the riddle of riddles?[106] How could Freud, an authority on myths and ancient literature, at the very moment of defining Oedipus, neglect both the Sphinx and her riddle? Possibly, for Freud, the Sphinx is assumed dead, or death itself. Goux exposes, "Freud attributes the threat of castration to a father with a human face, whereas the most radical, unnamable threat comes from a 'monster' who is female."[107] In a sense, it is the Sphinx that haunts Freud as the uncanny spectral other. As to the sphinx as a goddess, Freud has offered full resistance, as Sprengnether notes, "Freud struggles to subdue her in his various attempts to account for the phenomenon of mother-goddess worship, and finally he imagines her as an avatar of death."[108] The dead body of the spectral Sphinx, assuming to be buried long ago in the Oedipus legend, seems to return as the uncanny other to possess Freud.

Freud develops his extensive negative aesthetics of the uncanny in terms of the grotesque female body—the castrated female sexual organ as an unhomely home, a haunted house, a dark continent, the horror of lack and dismemberment, in short, *Thanatos* as *Eros*. As an uncanny maternal body, the hidden Sphinx is exposed as the mother-death, and as a hysterical other, her speech remains a riddle in an alien tongue—the language of the unconscious. Similar to Oedipus in this case, Freud fails to solve the riddle of the Sphinx, so that the Sphinx, as a mother figure, remains a riddle, and her words, as the words from the (m)other, still haunt both Oedipus and Freud.

The (M)other Tongue: A Horror Story

Hoffman's tale "The Sand-Man" itself possesses multiple meanings beyond the restrictive framework of the Freudian analysis. It can be interpreted differently as how the young Nathaniel is haunted and dispossessed by stories from mother figures, and how Nathaniel, as an obsessional neurotics, arbitrarily relates the fictive story to his anxiety of loss of vision, and how he fails to comprehend his mother's story of "The Sand-Man" as an allegorical tale of linguistic play, i.e., a riddle-narrative.

Freud's theory of the uncanny is contextualized within Hoffman's story "The Sand-Man." And Hoffman's tale begins with a story, a kind of "gothic" tale of a Sand-Man, told first by the mother, and later by the nurse, to Nathaniel, in fact a night time fairy tale to scare children who refuse to sleep. This tale about losing one's eye is deeply buried in little Nathaniel's mind and haunts him for the rest of his life. Freud writes:

> This fantastic tale opens with the childhood recollections of the student Nathaniel. In spite of his present happiness, he cannot banish the memories associated with the mysterious and terrifying death of his beloved father. On certain evenings his mother used to send the children to bed early, warning them that 'the Sand-Man was coming'; and sure enough, Nathaniel would not fail to hear the heavy tread of a visitor, with whom his father would then be occupied for the evening. When questioned about the Sand-Man, his mother, it is true, denied that such a person existed except as a figure of speech; but his nurse could give him more definite information: 'He is a wicked man who comes when children won't go to bed, and throws handfuls of sand in their eyes so they jump out of their heads all bleeding.'[109]

Clearly, a fairy tale turns gothic, so the narrative itself becomes the source of horror. Freud observes: "Although little Nathaniel was sensible and old enough not to credit the figure of the Sand-Man with such gruesome attributes, yet the dread of him became fixed in his heart."[110] Eventually, a fairy tale, transferred to his anxiety over the death of his father, haunts him like a ghost story. And Freud reminds us that readers "will not fail to recognize in the child's phantasy the persisting influence of his nurse's story."[111] Consequently, Nathaniel is obsessed with a phantom of horror in the context of a text, a dark fairytale from the other or mother; and more interestingly, each time he has to decode his life in the context of this fairy tale by translating himself into a disoriented character in a horror story. As Freud postulates, an uncanny effect is produced "when the distinction between imagination and reality is effaced . . . [and] when a symbol takes over the full functions of the thing it symbolizes."[112] As a result, the distinction between the mother's night time story as a linguistic game and Nathaniel's reconfiguration of the tale as his social reality blur into one. So the uncanny stems from not so much the death of his father as the enigmatic words from his mother. In this case, it is the playful words from the mother that inhabit the neurotic subject and produce the uncanny effect. If Oedipus fails to comprehend the mystic and enigmatic riddle from the Sphinx, then Nathaniel is also confounded by the fairytale stories from the (m)others.

The Spectral Sphinx: The Riddle of the Unconscious

Without doubt, Freud likely identifies with Oedipus, the intellectual hero, as his double, who is going to solve the riddle of man.[113] Furthermore, Oedipus' answer, "man," itself in turn becomes a riddle that obsesses Freud. This enigmatic creature, in a typical Freudian term, is full of internal divisiveness and chaotic drives that destabilize and decenter the singular subject. Ironical enough, in the name of the Greek hero and in terms of the *Oedipus complex*, Freud seems to insert the grotesque Sphinx as well as her riddle—incoherence, disparity, and multiplicity—into the unconscious of Oedipus. In this context, Freud's Oedipus complex as the universal law to decode the riddle of the unconscious hides the mystic narrative of Sphinx's riddle and the spectral body of Sphinx. Therefore, as the embodiment of the grotesque and the unconscious of the Freudian discourse, the Sphinx emerges as the answer to the riddle of man's identity that Freud either fails to acknowledge or intentionally ignores.

In his rebuttal against the orthodox Freudian interpretation, Goux points out: "The riddle of the Sphinx? An expression to be taken in two senses: the riddle that the Sphinx proposes, and the one that the Sphinx herself constitutes. Oedipus thought he had resolved the first, and Freud the second. But what if neither had found the answer?"[114] Goux seems to mock both Freud and Oedipus for their futile or misplaced encryption of the riddle in triple forms, namely, the Sphinx, Oedipus, and the mystic riddle. In this instance, the Oedipus complex is not only more complex than, but also entirely other than, what Freud has brought forward. What is hidden, elided, or missing in the famous Freudian Oedipus complex turns out to be the uncanny grotesque—the spectral Sphinx. Freud has persistently repressed her in his theory of psychoanalysis just as Oedipus has suppressed her in Greek myth. Freud assumes that he is using Oedipus to answer the Sphinx's riddle in terms of the Oedipus complex; but contrary to his hypothesis, Freud is secretly positioning the grotesque Sphinx at the center of his Oedipus complex and decoding Oedipus' unconscious, a riddle itself, in terms of an uncanny grotesque. Unlike Hegel who uses Oedipus' answer to solve the mystery of the Sphinx's riddle, Freud unconsciously uses the Sphinx's riddle to decode the mystery of Oedipus' answer, man, or Oedipus as the man. Hence, Freud fails to see that the Sphinx figures as the unconscious of his Oedipal principle. Instead, Freud closely—possibly too closely—identifies with Oedipus the Greek *tragic* hero, as his intellectual double, with all his blinding hubris of knowledge. Rather than confronting the Sphinx and reading her riddle, Freud must have been too profoundly preoccupied with and too deeply absorbed in reading himself and his own desire all the time, just as Oedipus keeps looking at his own feet (symbolic penis) and evoking his own solipsistic phantom instead of looking at the Sphinx. In this case, Freud seems to have unconsciously repeated exactly after Oedipus: he "disembodies" the Sphinx one more time.

To conclude, Hegel, Nietzsche, and Freud in their respective disciplinary fields explore the issue of the grotesque via different terms, such as symbolic art, the Dionysian principle, or the uncanny. For Hegel, the grotesque predominantly associates with the sacrilegious intermixture of humanity and animality, lacking both the Christian Spirit and the classical singular identity; contrary to Hegel, Nietzsche negotiates with the grotesque by proposing a Dionysian principle, a carnival desire in effect, to transcend the bondage of the individual principle and overcome the confinement of the self-conscious subject; for his part, Freud positions the grotesque in an uncanny territory of "in between" that evokes feelings both familiar and strange, pleasurable and horrifying until he unveils at the very end the uncanny site in terms of womb-and-tomb. In one way or another, the Sphinx, as "the symbol of the grotesque," to borrow Hegel's words here, emerges inevitably and figures crucially as the convergent point in their respective aesthetic speculations of the grotesque. To a degree, each of them configures the Sphinx as a maternal figure, either in terms of a primitive mother of the wild nature that requires domination for Hegel, or an earth mother of some heterogeneous primal power that precipitates transgression and transcendence for Nietzsche, or a spectral mother of both life and death, signifying both Eros and Thanatos for Freud. Nevertheless, all of them, in one way or another, framed their analysis of the Sphinx in the context of the *Oedipus* legend, and Oedipus has persistently played a central ghost figure that looms largely over the discourse of the grotesque. Apparently, to *riddle out* Oedipus, particularly his subjectivity in the context of grotesque studies, requires further inquiry despite Hegel's supposition—Oedipus as a paragon of the singular subject as if immune to the grotesque. In this case, we may inquire: What other allegorical meanings might be conjured up in the Oedipus legend and, furthermore, could the paradigm of the grotesque be shifted from the theoretical center of the Sphinx, the usual suspect, to the locus of Oedipus, the hero that subjugates the grotesque monster?

Hegel regards Oedipus as a type of intellectual hero who solves the Sphinx's riddle—a Greek man of wisdom, and moreover, a kind of Apollonian figure standing for the singular subject of Western civilization, in fact, a kind of prototype of modern man. If Hegel evokes Oedipus' "man," illusory or not, to inaugurate the singular subject or the self-conscious modern man, Nietzsche sees in Oedipus the inevitable fall of the modern subject due to the bondage of individual consciousness. That is why Nietzsche marks Oedipus as a *tragic hero*, a victim of individual subjectivity in Greek culture. Anchoring his universal theory of humanity (as well as of culture to some extent) in terms of the Oedipus complex, Freud views Oedipus as a "mythical criminal" that embodies the neurotic modern subject due to some unnamable, unsettling, and irreconcilable unconscious desires in the context of civilization or its discontents. Despite their different deployments of Oedipus to advance their discrete theories either in aesthetics, metaphysics, or psychoanalysis, they all identify Oedipus as a potential riddle-subject for further investigation. More or less, most modern critics point out that Oedipus brings more plague rather than solution to the identity of the modern subject in Western civilization. In other words, his answer, "man," to the Sphinx becomes a riddle for further inquiry. In fact, in the modern era, Oedipus gradually takes the central stage as the new focus of grotesque studies and emerges as a new prototype of the grotesque subject precisely due to his obsession with the solipsistic desire and dispossession by the phantom of singular ontology.

NOTES

1. Wolfgang J. Kayser, *The Grotesque in Art and Literature*, trans. Ulrich Weisstein (Bloomington: Indiana UP, 1963), 24.
2. This chapter mostly focuses on close readings of three texts by three German thinkers: Hegel's "Introduction to the Philosophy of Art"; Nietzsche's *The Birth of Tragedy*; and Freud's "The 'Uncanny'." To some extent, this chapter returns to and expands on the three general speculations outlined in Chapter 2 by a thorough investigation of the three German thinkers' ideas of the grotesque. Hegel's metaphysical speculation of the grotesque is based upon the Eurocentric model of the conquest—the West over the East in the context of his "universal evolution" of art. Nietzsche's aesthetic discourse of the grotesque challenges the supposition of the paradigm shift from Logos to Mythos via a return to the Dionysian principle. Freud's aesthetic discourse of the grotesque (m)other rewrites the son and mother model in terms of the uncanny.
3. I am not making a stretch here. For instance, there are two definitions of the Sphinx from *OED*: a hybrid monster, usually having the head of a woman and the (winged) body of a lion, that infested Thebes until the riddle it propounded was solved by Oedipus; or any monster of a similar form and character. Thus, the satyr is a case in point. In generic terms, any monstrous figures of similar forms and characters belong to the sphinx category. *OED* defines chimeras and all hybrid figures, in a broad sense, as sphinxes.
4. Georg Wilhelm Friedrich Hegel, "Introduction to the Philosophy of Art," in *The Critical Tradition: Classical Texts and Contemporary Trends*, ed. David Richter (New York: St. Martin's Press, 1998), 362.
5. Ibid., 362, 361.
6. Ibid., 361.
7. Ibid., 367.
8. Ibid., 363.
9. Ibid., 364.
10. Ibid., 365, 364.
11. Ibid., 365.
12. Ibid.
13. Ibid., 367.
14. Ibid., 365.
15. Georg Wilhelm Friedrich Hegel, *Aesthetics: Lectures on Fine Art*, trans. T. M. Knox (Oxford: Clarendon P, 1975), 531.
16. Ibid., 428.
17. Hegel, "Introduction to the Philosophy of Art," 365.
18. Ibid., 366.
19. Ibid., 367.
20. Ibid., 366.
21. Ibid.
22. Ibid., 367.
23. Ibid., 366.
24. Hegel, *Aesthetics: Lectures on Fine Art*, 519.
25. Hegel, "Introduction to the Philosophy of Art," 367.
26. Obviously, it is neither the intended focus nor the defined scope of this research to pursue Hegel for his Eurocentric position and the orientalist attitude toward grotesque Egyptian culture. Such a project would deserve at least another book if not more. In short, the oriental art in this context constitutes an exotic object, or "objective riddles" like the Sphinx, both fantastic and grotesque, in Hegel's philosophical speculation of art.
27. Hegel, "Introduction to the Philosophy of Art," 364.

28. Ibid., 365.
29. Ibid.
30. Ibid.
31. Hegel, *Aesthetics: Lectures on Fine Art*, 338.
32. Ibid., 341.
33. Ibid., 357.
34. Ibid.
35. Ibid., 360. As a meticulous writer, very carefully Hegel chooses his words to hide the specific location of the *other* type of sphinxes with "a female head" and leaves us with a vague hint of its position in an obscure area of "*elsewhere,*" thus concealing Greek sphinxes from the list. In general, the sphinx transfigures its gender from male to female when it is adopted by Greek culture. Here we get a sense that Hegel takes extreme caution to protect the purity of Greek culture from contamination by the Oriental grotesque.
36. Georg Wilhelm Friedrich Hegel, *The Philosophy of History* , trans. J. Sibree (New York: Dover, 1956), 199.
37. Ibid., 213.
38. Ibid., 220.
39. Ibid.
40. Willis Goth Regier, *Book of the Sphinx* (Lincoln: U of Nebraska P, 2004), 5.
41. Friedrich Nietzsche, *On the Genealogy of Morals and Ecce Homo*, trans. Walter Kaufman (New York: Vintage, 1967), 217.
42. Friedrich Nietzsche, *Twilight of the Idols, Or, How to Philosophize with the Hammer*, trans. Richard Polt (Indianapolis: Hackett Publishing, 1997), 91. In Greek mythology there are various versions regarding the origin of Dionysus. One version claims Dionysus is the son of Zeus and Semele, and another version contends that he is a son of Zeus and Persephone. But both versions involve his birth and rebirth in origination. The rebirth, regardless of variations in different versions, is the primary reason why Dionysus is worshipped in mystic religions since his death and rebirth are events of mystical reference. As god of wine, Dionysus is a major figure of orgiastic rites of madness, ecstasy, and revelry in Greek mythology. He is also known as Bacchus, with horns, either those of a ram or a bull. As potent power of nature, Dionysus is strongly associated with satyrs, centaurs, etc. In Greek mythology, satyrs are usually described as having the upper half of a man and the lower half of a goat.
43. Friedrich Nietzsche, *The Birth of Tragedy and the Genealogy of Morals*, trans. Francis Golffing (New York: Doubleday, 1956), 4.
44. Ibid., 8.
45. Hegel, "Introduction to the Philosophy of Art," 367.
46. Hegel, *Aesthetics: Lectures on Fine Art*, 428.
47. Ibid., 341, 357.
48. Hegel, *The Philosophy of History* , 199.
49. Nietzsche, *The Birth of Tragedy and the Genealogy of Morals*, 25. Several critics also point out the connections between the Sphinx, satyrs, and the Dionysian rites. In *Oedipus, Philosopher,* Jean-Joseph Goux observes: "There is thus a close connection between the Sphinx and the Dionysian Satyrs in their function as markers of the final phase of initiation" (1993, 55) and further, specifically for the Sphinx, "[h]er emergence is greeted by the ecstatic dance of goat-footed Pans and horse-tailed Satyrs" (1993, 53). Also, as evidenced by unearthed Greek vases, the Sphinx is always depicted together with satyrs in the Dionysian rites. In fact, their connection, beyond the initiatory rites as participants, is also indicated by a shared position as hybrid figures in composition, i.e., ontological disparity. According to the *Dictionary of Literary Terms and Motifs* edited by Jean-Charles Seigneuret, "The grotesque has its origins in the pre-literary festivals of Dionysus, which were celebrated with sacrifice and solemnity as well as feasts and revels. The celebrants dressed as satyrs and sang abusive songs in the belief that degradation and destruction would assure birth and renewal" (1988, 560).
50. Ibid., 26.
51. Ibid., 9.
52. Ibid., 13.
53. Hegel, *The Philosophy of History* , 220.

54. Nietzsche, *The Birth of Tragedy and the Genealogy of Morals*, 34.
55. Ibid., 21.
56. Ibid., 33.
57. Ibid., 22.
58. Ibid., 66, 67.
59. Ibid., 37.
60. Ibid., 38.
61. Ibid., 39, 41.
62. Ibid., 65, 66.
63. Ibid., 34–35.
64. Ibid., 97.
65. René Girard, *Violence and the Sacred,* trans. Patrick Gregory (Baltimore: Johns Hopkins UP, 1979), 160, 165.
66. Nietzsche, *The Birth of Tragedy and the Genealogy of Morals*, 67.
67. Ibid., 52.
68. Ibid., 53.
69. Ibid., 56, 55–56, 53.
70. Ibid., 145.
71. Friedrich Nietzsche, *The Will to Power*, trans. Walter Kaufmann and R. J. Hollingdale (New York: Vintage, 1968), 270.
72. Andrew Bowie, *Aesthetics and Subjectivity: From Kant to Nietzsche* (Manchester: Manchester UP, 1990), 265.
73. Jürgen Habermas, *The Philosophical Discourse of Modernity: Twelve Lectures,* trans. Fredrick Lawrence (Cambridge: MIT Press, 1996), 94.
74. Nietzsche, *The Birth of Tragedy and the Genealogy of Morals*, 23.
75. Julian Young, *Nietzsche's Philosophy of Art* (Cambridge: Cambridge UP, 1992), 53.
76. Nietzsche, *The Birth of Tragedy and the Genealogy of Morals*, 27.
77. Ibid., 32.
78. Ibid., 102.
79. Ibid., 38.
80. Ibid., 61.
81. Gilles Deleuze, *Nietzsche and Philosophy*, trans. Hugh Tomlinson (New York: Columbia UP, 1983), 77.
82. Hardt, Michael Hardt, foreword to *Nietzsche and Philosophy*, by Gilles Deleuze, trans. Hugh Tomlinson (New York: Columbia UP, 1983), ix.
83. Nietzsche, *On the Genealogy of Morals and Ecce Homo*, 273.
84. Nietzsche, *Twilight of the Idols, Or, How to Philosophize with the Hammer,* 91.
85. Sigmund Freud, "The 'Uncanny,'" in *The Standard Edition of the Complete Psychological Works of Sigmund Freud,* trans. James Strachey, vol. 17 (London: Hogarth P, 1955), 219.
86. Ibid.
87. Ibid.
88. Apparently, this recalls the long list of the negative terms related to the grotesque in Chapter 1. Also, specifically, Freud in this essay explicates the uncanny in three different languages: in Greek: "strange, foreign"; in English: "ghastly," "haunted," and "repulsive"; in Arabic: "daemonic, gruesome" (1955, 221). The rhetoric patterns here remind us of the genealogical traces of different terms that are used to denote the typical nature of the Sphinx in various cultural locales and historical sites.
89. Freud, "The 'Uncanny,'" 220.
90. Ibid., 224.
91. Ibid., 221.
92. Ibid., 231
93. Ibid.
94. Diane Jonte-Pace, *Speaking the Unspeakable: Religion, Misogyny, and the Uncanny Mother in Freud's Cultural Texts* (Berkeley: U of California P, 2001), 16.
95. Freud, "The 'Uncanny,'" 223.
96. Ibid., 219.

97. Ibid., 243.
98. Ibid.
99. Ibid., 241, 245.
100. Ibid., 245.
101. Ibid.
102. Ibid., 227.
103. Ibid., 244.
104. Hélène Cixous, "Fiction and Its Phantoms: A Reading of Freud's Das Unheimliche (The 'Uncanny')," *New Literary History* 7, no. 3 (1976): 536.
105. Madelon Sprengnether, *The Spectral Mother: Freud, Feminism, and Psychoanalysis* (Ithaca: Cornell UP, 1990), 2. Several critics share similar theoretical positions, such as Jane Tod in "The Veiled Woman in Freud's '*Das Unheimliche,*'" Robin Lydenberg in "Freud's Uncanny Narrative," and Ruth Ginsburg in "A Primal Scene of Reading: Freud and Hoffman." They all exposed the veiled primal scene of the mother in Freud's "The 'Uncanny'," but none has named the Sphinx yet.
106. In *The Sphinx on the Table: Sigmund Freud's Art Collection and the Development of Psychoanalysis*, Janine Burke claims that Freud had a Greek Terracotta Sphinx on his table and "Freud collected different images of the Sphinx, as if exploring the various meanings she offered. His free-standing, terracotta Sphinx (1st–2nd century A.D.) has the face and breasts of a woman, together with the lower quarters of a lion and beautifully curled wings" (2006, 203). Though being surrounded by a large collection of ancient figures of goddesses and female sphinxes, Freud seems to be single-mindedly concentrating on Oedipus alone.
107. Jean-Joseph Goux, *Oedipus, Philosopher*, trans. Catherine Porter (Stanford: Stanford UP, 1993), 181.
108. Sprengnether, *The Spectral Mother*, 182.
109. Freud, "The 'Uncanny,'" 227–28.
110. Ibid., 228.
111. Ibid.
112. Ibid., 244.
113. In the essay, Freud decodes the uncanny in terms of "double" as one of its connotations. In addition to persons who look alike, Freud also suggests that this double relationship "is accentuated by mental processes leaping from the one of these characters to another—by what we should call telepathy—, so that the one processes knowledge, feelings and experience in common with the other. Or… the subject identifies himself with someone else" (1955, 234). Peter Rudnytsky in *Freud and Oedipus* writes that Freud's biography Ernest Jones noted that, in 1906, on the occasion of Freud's fiftieth birthday, "Freud was presented by a group of his adherents with a medallion, engraved on one side with his portrait in profile and on the other with a design of Oedipus answering the Sphinx, inscribed with a line in Greek from *Oedipus the King*: 'Who knew the famous riddles and was a man most mighty'" (Rudnytsky 1987, 4). According to Jones, Freud "became pale and agitated" because when he was "a young student at the University of Vienna he used to stroll around the great arcaded court inspecting the busts of former famous professors of the institution. He then had the phantasy, not merely of seeing his own bust there in the future, which would not have been anything remarkable in an ambitious student, but of if being inscribed with the *identical* words he now saw on the medallion.'" Ernest Jones, *The Life and Work of Sigmund Freud,* 3 vol., New York: Basic books, 1953-1957, quoted in Rudnytsky, 1984, 4.
114. Goux, *Oedipus, Philosopher*, 24.

Chapter Four

Oedipus Obsessed

Grotesque Desires and the Phantom Subject

The previous chapter examines how Hegel denigrates Egyptian sphinxes as the embodiment of the grotesque in terms of an alien other lacking spirituality and individuality while Nietzsche extols the Sphinx as an incarnation of the mystical and primordial power of nature, celebrating other chimeric figures like satyrs in the Dionysian rites. For his part, Freud secretes, in a labyrinthine game, a cryptic sphinx figure represented by an uncanny maternal body—the dark entrance full of dread and terror. All three thinkers, more or less, engage sphinx figures either as the grotesque, the Dionysian, or the uncanny in their respective aesthetic discourses. In this chapter, I will return to them by reframing the topic of the grotesque differently, with a shift of focus and a change of character.

To some degree, their distinctive strategies of approaching the Sphinx, either in terms of condemnation, glorification, or repression, correspond to the different ways they engage the *central subject*, Oedipus. Instead of pursuing a case study or an exemplary tale of psychological exploration of incestuous desire in a domestic space, I would like to probe *Oedipus'* "Man" or his obsession with the singular man in the metaphysical arena. In this case, I propose "Oedipus Obsessed" as an ontological prototype through which to investigate the obsessive desires for the phantom of the singular subject in the context of grotesque studies. Hegel's sees in Oedipus' evocation or conjuration of a singular "man" the western subject's coming into being via the Apollonian order whereas I find in this evocation, instead, a subject's subordination to and dispossession by a spectral other in terms of hauntology. This immanent haunting effect, I contest, is demonstrated respectively in the disembodiment of Hegel's infinite subject by the Holy Spirit in *Phenomenology of Spirit*, negation of Nietzsche's morbid priest by the Christian God in *The Genealogy of Morals*, and suppression of Freud's neurotic individual by an omnipotent Father in *Civilization and Its Discontents*. Though for entirely different purposes, each of them discloses, intentionally or not, the subject's narcissistic obsession with the phantom of a singular being—actually a death wish in disguise. In fact, the subject's ontological coming into being, as presented in their respective works, somewhat parallels Oedipus' philosophical adventures in Greek mythology. Oedipus' uncanny homeward journey can be translated into a sort of metaphysical allegory illustrative of his quest for the singular Oedipus, a phantom-subject in this instance. In this case, Oedipus constitutes the central figure of, and the central problem for, the modern subject.

The Oedipus legend, from an ontological perspective, unfolds a story of Oedipus' pursuit of the singular subject—autonomous, self-reflexive, and self-enclosed—, a narcissistic illusion of a phantasmagoric identity conjured up by the Apollonian order and anchored to an egocentric or logocentric ground. In this context, the grotesque is no longer distinguished exclusively by the peculiar hybrid agglomeration specific to chimeric figures like sphinxes or satyrs. Instead, the grotesque is characterized by an obsessive desire for the singular subject under the spell of some spectral conjuration.[1] Consequently, the meaning of the grotesque undergoes a radical revision and a complete reversal from the exterior to the interior, form the corporeal to the ontological, from the physical to the metaphysical, from the disparate to the singular, and from the manifest heterogeneous body to the latent homogeneous desire—in short, from the Sphinx to Oedipus. In effect, Hegel's "unhappy consciousness," Nietzsche's "bad conscience," and Freud's "unconscious" are all symptomatic of a haunted subject spellbound by some spectral and specular other. In other words, the longing for the singular subject does not necessarily mean possession of totality; on the contrary, Oedipus' appeal reveals precisely the *lack* of singular presence that provokes his obsessive desires for an illusory being in the first place. Instead of being an impossible subject due to incoherence and disparity, the grotesque, in this case, is inherently associated with an ontological wanting toward the phantasmagoric sublime singularity and totality. To some degree, all desires for the total subject involve some sorts of *obsession and dispossession* under the spell of some specter. Oedipus' narcissistic fixation with the phantom of the transcendental singular "Man" spelled out by the Apollonian specter is a case in point. Henceforth, we enter a new realm, hauntology as ontology.

I. DERRIDA'S HAUNTOLOGY: THE SPECTRAL AND SPECULAR OTHER

In general, theories of ghosts are usually construed as nonsensical or supernatural and few take the risk to claim authority of any sorts on this ephemeral and ethereal topic. Nevertheless, it is certainly intriguing that nobody else has contributed more to this spectral topic than one of the most *destructive* thinkers, Derrida, especially in his *Specters of Marx,* where he intends, in the name of *hauntology*, to expose "all the forms of a certain haunting obsession that seems . . . to organize the *dominant* influence on discourse today,"[2] or in other words, to unveil the spectral conjuration in all ideological, hegemonic, and ontological systems. Hamlet's Ghost warns, "I am thy Fathers Spirit. . . . But that I am forbid/ To tell the secrets of my prison house."[3] True, a ghost story is always a forbidden narrative, laden with both dark secrets and dispossessed bodies.

To expose the unconscious of all symbolic systems, Derrida conjures up a new word in *Specters of Marx*, "hauntology." Derrida remarks, "We will take this category to be the irreducible, and first of all to everything it makes possible: ontology, theology, positive or negative onto-theology."[4] Hauntology as a critical trope is instrumental and central to unraveling mysterious operations and insidious functions of all kinds of ontological, theological, and ideological orders or hegemonic systems. Ghosts share one uncanny quality: they all haunt by a powerful presence of absence.[5]

All ideological systems, Derrida contends, involve "production of ghosts, illusions, simulacra, appearances, or apparitions" and especially, Derrida alerts, "Haunting belongs to the structure of every hegemony."[6] In other words, at the center of each hegemonic order resides a ghost as a spectral other, haunting, inhabiting and possessing. To differentiate ontology from its near homonym hauntology, Derrida clarifies: "Ontology opposes it [hauntology] only in a movement of exorcism. Ontology is a conjuration" and a magic "exorcism of the spectral simulacrum."[7] Further, Derrida explicates: "For the singular ghost . . . , the arch-specter, is a father."[8] Hence, this singular ghost, in either sacred or secular form, occupies a transcendental position of the absolute authority. Paradoxically, the arch-ghost, though ontologically absent, lurks at the center of ontological presence. True, the other haunts; but, in both theological and metaphysical senses of the word, what could haunt more than the absolute transcendental subject in terms of the omniscient and omnipresent Holy Ghost?

Perhaps more importantly, Derrida untangles the mysterious relationship between "spectral" and "specular" by uncovering a speculating conjuration of the ghost. Through the figure of the armored Ghost of Hamlet, Derrida discovers that the specter always produces what he calls a "visor effect": "This spectral *someone other looks at us*, we feel ourselves being looked at by it."[9] In other words, the "visor effect" is produced by *someone other*, or some omniscient as well as omnipotent *spectral other,* in an absolute distance and a priori space, that speculates, gazes, invades, or possesses us. That is to say, to speculate is to conjure up or frame up a ghost reflection. In this context, Derrida employs the full semantic capacity of the word "spectral" in terms of both possessing and gazing.[10]

Derrida explicates, "Speculation always speculates on some specter, it speculates in the mirror of what it produces, on the spectacle that it gives itself and that it gives itself to see", i.e., "in representations."[11] That is to say, the spectral figure, itself an incorporeal phantom, does not give back a reflection. Instead, like a magic mirror, it produces or conjures up a phantom of a specular image *as if* it were a reflected mirror-image. As Derrida teases, "How do you recognize a ghost? By the fact that it does not recognize itself in the mirror."[12] In fact, this image, Derrida asserts, is but "the body of some*one* as some*one other*. And of some*one other* that we will not hasten to determine as self, subject, person consciousness, spirit, and so forth."[13] In this case, the *specular* image "reflected" by the *spectral* other is nothing else but a self-reflexive phantom projected by a ghost figure onto the other because it does not "return the right reflection . . . , it phantomalizes."[14] Derrida concludes, "The specular becomes the spectral at the threshold of this objectifying naturalization."[15] Consequently, the *spectral* plays the mysterious function of the *specular* despite its phantasmagoric simulation or naturalization. The "visor effect" as an uncanny specter both looks and reflects, gazes and mirrors, haunts and seduces by conjuring someone into someone *other*. In this case, an arch-ghost, in the name of the *Spectral Other*, does not so much reflect as fantasize an image for the subject *as if* it were a specular mirror-image while the subject takes a "naturalized" image, a simulation in fact, *as if* it were his true identity.

Derrida's hauntology intends to "disembody" the subject and strip the subject of its illusory ontological presence. Derrida defines hauntology as a rite of conjuration or sorcery through which a spirit comes back as a specter with a paradoxical incorporation, i.e., taking possession of somebody to repeat itself as a phantom. Put differently, Derrida evokes the specter to haunt the subject and to disembody it into a ghost figure. As a result, the ghost-subject becomes a paradoxical incorporation, an uncanny apparition, something unnamable and incorporeal, i.e., a subject of absence. To parody Descartes, Derrida declares: "Therefore 'I am' would mean 'I am haunted.'"[16] In this case, Oedipus' declaration of "Man," a haunted phantom, certainly casts out a broad and far-reaching spell on all modern subjects.

II. SOLIPSISTIC DESIRE, NEGATIVE SIGNIFICATION, AND THE GHOST SUBJECT IN HEGEL'S *PHENOMENOLOGY OF SPIRIT*

Hegel's *Phenomenology of Spirit* collapses three discrete perspectives in his speculation of the subject: the theological *telos* of Spirit, a philosophical dialectics of desire, and an ontological position of negative signification. However, his philosophical principle of dialectics that drives the ontological quest for the subject is eventually sacrificed to a theological conjuration. Hegel's subject, haunted by and obsessed with the Holy Ghost of Christianity, ends with the death of dialectics in a theological ontology or onto-theology. Both infinite desire for and negative signification toward the singular subject are captivated within the same grand illusion of a solipsistic phantom-subject under the spell of the Holy Ghost in terms of the Spectral Other.

Let's begin with Hegel's "Preface" to his *Phenomenology of Spirit*:

> Further, the living Substance is being which is in truth *Subject*, or, what is the same, is in truth actual only in so far as it is the movement of positing itself, or is the mediation of its self-othering with itself. This Substance is, as Subject, pure, *simple negativity*, and . . . it is the doubling which sets up opposition, and then again the negation of this indifferent diversity and of its antithesis [the immediate simplicity]. Only this self-*restoring* sameness, or this reflection in otherness within itself . . . is the True. It is the process of its own becoming, the circle that presupposes its end as its goal, having its end also as its beginning.[17]

The above paragraph from Hegel's "Preface" succinctly summarizes both the subject's fundamental nature and the dialectic processes the subject undergoes in its journey toward the telos of Being. First, the Subject is posited as "what is the same," that is, the Subject, capitalized as the finale, is self-identical; to reach this Subject, mediation or negation of "self-othering with itself" is transformed into the "self-*restoring* sameness," and the dialectics between self and other turns into a self-reflexive "doubling" or "reflection in otherness within itself" in a narcissistic self-closure; then, the dialectics of "opposition" becomes a negation of "this indifferent diversity and of its antithesis," i.e., all otherness, diversity, and multiplicity; and finally we are back to the same place where we start, and thus the Subject's becoming turns out to be a tautological, circular, and solipsistic return journey to itself. In other words, the Hegelian dialectics between self and other, presumably a dialogic exchange between diversity and similarity, self and the other, negation and position, are circumscribed within a self-enclosed circular space. All the differing and othering transforms into self-doubling and self-restoring, all negations convert into positions, and the quest for others is reversed to a return to the same.

Hegel's dialectics for the subject can be viewed as two discrete but equally contradictory movements. The dialectics of desire and the dialectics of negative signification are both entrapped within the same metaphysical framework of singular ontology. Instead of infinitely moving the subject toward the other, both dialectics are ensnared by a solipsistic desire for the closure of the self and oriented toward the phantom of a singular being ascribed by a theological ontology. Oedipus' hallucinatory "man" in a singular term, invoked as an ontological longing, exactly illustrates this kind of solipsistic desire or grotesque obsession under the spell of the Apollonian Spirit. That is to say, the Hegelian singular subject, similar to Oedipus' illusory "man," is haunted by the Spectral Other in terms of the Holy Spirit in his *Phenomenology*.

Dialectics of Desire and the Unhappy Consciousness

For Hegel, "self-consciousness is *Desire* in general."[18] Hegel intends this desire or self-consciousness to be a dialectic process that involves a complex negotiation between self and other. This desire gestures toward a "double move." On the one hand, desire is postulated as a dynamic process that mobilizes the subject toward the other and difference beyond itself; on the other hand, it also appropriates all otherness and integrates all difference into the same. Eventually, this nominal "double move" turns out to be disguised maneuvers toward the same goal—the solipsistic subject of the self-same *sans* alterity. Hence, the Hegelian dialectics of desire not only seems to be a dubious "dialectics limited" or a finite dialectic, but also is a "self-reflexive" dialectics in the true sense of the word in that: everything is tautologically reflected back to and enclosed within this "self-mirroring" space of the singular subject.

According to Hegel's dialectic hypothesis, desire in terms of infinite self-consciousness is predisposed to generate a dialogic process of both self-becoming and self-overcoming that keeps destabilizing, dividing, and decentering the subject eternally instead of anchoring the subject in any fixed position or achieving any possibility of its final unification. Desire as such postures to move the subject toward the other, difference, and alterity. Hence, this dialectic of infinite desire, on a philosophical level, precludes any probability of a final resolution and undermines any anticipation of a total subject. In the very process of desiring, the Hegelian subject is supposed to disrupt totality, rupture closure, and disintegrate unity.

If that *were* the case with the Hegelian dialectic practice, Hegel's ideas of "the unhappy consciousness" might as well characterize the alienated situation of his own subject. Hegel believes that "the *Unhappy Consciousness* is the consciousness of self as a dual-natured, merely contradictory being."[19] This unhappy consciousness stems from the irreconcilable contradictions that internally split and divide the subject. Alas, what is the immanent condition of Hegel's subject engrossed in its infinite desire for difference if not inherently contradictory, internally divided, and eternally unstable, i.e., grotesque? In spite of its relentless drives toward the illusion of a singular subject, his dialectics of desire in terms of philosophical practice seems to contradict and sabotage the final ontological *telos* of an enclosed self-identical subject *as far as* this self-reflexive consciousness keeps generating self-division, self-dislocation, and disparity.

Walter Davis in *Inwardness and Existence* characterizes the "unhappy consciousness" as "the grand theme of the *Phenomenology*" and "Hegel's essential contribution to a theory of subjectivity";[20] and we might add, the ontological condition of Hegel's subject itself is an example *par excellence*. In Davis' opinion, the unhappy consciousness is entailed as the consequence of the subject's inability to coincide within itself all its "reflections" because "Subject is defined by the impossibility of achieving the very thing it desires."[21] Further, Davis points out, generally, "All consciousness is unhappy consciousness, the condition of a 'divided and merely contradictory being.'"[22] Constituted by infinite desire, the subject becomes a subject of continuous transgression and transfiguration, ontologically unstable and interminably incoherent, in short, grotesque. The Hegelian dialectics of infinite desire in this case produces exactly this "unhappy unconsciousness," and, consequently, a term that Hegel uses to critique skepticism ironically backfires at his own position.

As a result, the ultimate ontological goal of desire in terms of infinite self-consciousness substantially overrides Hegel's hypothetical dialectic exchange between self and other. In fact, latent in the Hegelian self-consciousness underlies an inherent hostility toward every other it encounters and, as such, desires incessantly move to appropriate all otherness for self-expansion in a kind of imperialist enterprise. The Hegelian subject is totalizing insofar as it reduces all otherness to the inevitable same, assimilates all disparity into identity, and incorporates all heterogeneity into a homogenous body of the singular subject. Consequently, the infinite dialectics of desire between self and other, similarity and difference, identity and diversity becomes a "dialectics limited" toward the final destination of an absolute subject of singularity. Similar to Oedipus' quest, the Hegelian subject's metaphysical journey toward the other becomes an ironic return trip back to the same home; as Hegel admits, "it is just this unrest that is the self . . . that which has returned into itself."[23] The dialectics of desire turns into a self-departing and self-returning circular movement enclosed within a homogeneous subjective space.

Hegel made it clearly that "this movement of becoming an *other to itself*" is in effect a process of "suspending this otherness."[24] The other in this dialogic process is suspended, overcome, and converted into a self-identical same. William Desmond in *Desire, Dialectic, and Otherness* outlines the fundamental principle central to all metaphysicians: "The metaphysical coup de grace was rather to subsume otherness within a dialectical *aufhebung*. . . . Otherness thus seems to be both saluted and domesticated within a larger, overarching totality."[25] In this context, desires in Hegel's "dialectics limited" are characterized by appropriation and occupation of the entirety of exteriority or otherness so that the solipsistic subject imposes its authority and asserts its sovereign autonomy in a totalized subjective domain. In other words, the dialectic negotiation is operationalized as a strategy for domination or conquest. Mark Taylor in *Altarity* points out: "Within Hegel's dialectic economy, identity *works* through difference; identity *is* the working through difference."[26] Eventually, as Taylor notes, "Each subject becomes itself through relation to the other, and thus includes the other *within* it as constitutive of *its own* being."[27] The previous model of conquest or integration, allegorized by Oedipus' domination of the Sphinx, exactly illustrates this process.

From the perspective of a totalizing and self-reflecting subject, probably there may be no real other or alterity at all in Hegel's *Phenomenology*. The other emerges, according to Hegel, only as an internal "reflection" of the self in a narcissistic mirror. To quote Hegel here: "This self-identical essence is therefore related only to itself; 'to itself' implies relationship to an 'other', and the *relation-to-self* is rather a *self-sundering*; or, in other words, that very self-identicalness is an inner difference."[28] Indeed, the interior differences in this "*self-reflexive*" dialectics function only insofar as an intra-subjective self-modification, self-distancing as self-embracing, circumscribed within the closure of a self-identical being. Taylor in *Altarity* mocks: "In this dialectical interplay, difference, the other of identity, is identity's *own* other. Such ownership of difference is essential to identity."[29] Hegel himself admits without any hesitancy: "For mediation is nothing beyond self-moving selfsameness, or is reflection into self."[30] Mediation of consciousness is self-directed, self-absorbed, and self-oriented since the Hegelian other differs from the self only as a reflexive image of the self in terms of internal doubling or duplicating. In *The Tain of the Mirror: Derrida and the Philosophy of Reflection*, Rodolphe Gasché observes, "The mirroring subject's self-mirroring is the goal of the whole process."[31] Here Gasché identifies the narcissistic gaze of Hegel's subject into oneself, and infinitely, as a self-enclosed consciousness in a totalizing process of self-reflection.

Hegel's dialectics of desire as a theoretical hypothesis seems to project the most intriguing process that is lent to opening up possibilities for difference, otherness, and diversity, *ad infinitum*. In other words, infinite desire is presumed to preclude any possibility of the subject's completion and renders the singular subject unrealizable. However, this dialectics of infinite desire, entrapped within a self-reflexive space, becomes an abortive circular moment as the "finite dialectics." Butler in *Subjects of Desire* mocks: "Like Don Quixote, Hegel's subject is an impossible identity who pursues reality in systematically mistaken ways."[32] Instead of a subject that desires, Butler hints that it is desire itself that projects the phantom of a singular subject without any ontological presence in the first place. Thus, the Hegelian subject emerges as an impossible identity, or more precisely, as an impossible subject invoked by desire, similar to Oedipus' apparitional "man." In short, Hegel's dialectics of desire in a contradictory move toward both self and other falls into this dilemma: in the infinite desire toward the other, the subject ends in an inner contradiction and internal division that yields the unhappy consciousness; in the infinite self-consciousness toward the self, the subject ends in a pure desire of a phantom-subject.

Dialectics of Negative Signification and the Singular Subject of Absence

To fulfill the desire for a singular subject as well as to end the unhappy consciousness (and implicitly all consciousness and desires), Hegel resorts to a theological conjuration in terms of what he calls the "negative signification"—a paradox of negation as position, or what I call a "negative ontology." Hegel's solution to the unhappy consciousness and resolution of the impossible subject actually imply negating not only all desires and consciousness, but also, ironically, the subject per se. That is, when *the subject as desire* negates all its substance, otherness, and self-consciousness, when it transcends into a pure phantom of a being, the negative dialectics inaugurates a subject of absence in a negative ontology. It is truly ironic that negation of otherness inevitably ends with deletion of the self and, eventually, the subject's ontological coming into being turns out to be a subject's metaphysical going into nothingness. Teleology elapses into aschuaelogy. In this context, if dialectics of desire yields the unhappy consciousness, then dialectics of negative signification entails ethereal death wish.

As a philosophical principle, dialectics of negative signification operates on two different planes. On the metaphysical level, the dialectic negation is predisposed to terminate all otherness toward a self-identical subject and henceforth negation is carried out in terms of a return to the same rather than to difference. In Hegel's view, "*negativity* is the differentiating and positing of *existence*," therefore a "return into self."[33] That is why Hegel believes negation has "a positive significance" since "the absolute antithesis is posited as a self-identical essence."[34] The negative dialectics in this case becomes a self-serving operation in a solipsistic mode to eliminate all difference toward an all-encompassing totality of the same. Hegel asserts that "the absolute negation of all otherness" is "a purely *self*-relating negation."[35] Negation as a vital strategy of subjugation intends to overcome, purify, and domesticate all desires for the other toward the final unity and internal integrity of the subject.

On the theological level, the negative signification operates according to "the principle of the void"—a self-vacating and self-erasing exorcism in a negative or spectral ontology. In other words, the subject, via a negative signification, is supposed to inaugurate itself by self-voiding toward an ephemeral being sans substance—a subject of absence in effect. To anchor the subject in a negative ontology means to initiate it into the ethereal status of a spectral position marked as a ghost subject. In this case, Hegel's negation of negation can be comprehended as a death wish in disguise toward a negative ontology. Here the subject devoid of all desires, self-reflexive consciousness as well as the unhappy consciousness entailed by them is fully redeemed blissfully as if paradise regained. That is to say, all dynamics of negation results in a final resolution of a sacrificial transcendence toward the phantom of a spectral subject sans presence.

Indeed, the real challenge of this negative dialectics involves not simply elimination of otherness, but the most important of all, nullification of the subject itself, as the ultimate effect of negation of negation, so to speak. In *Subjects of Desire,* Butler alerts: "If one resolves the aims of desire into the aims of a singular identity to discover and reflect itself, one dispenses with the realm of alterity and thereby loses the self as well."[36] In other words, to negate all otherness implicates total deletion of the self, an irresolvable dilemma for Hegel's subject because, ironically, negation *for* the self becomes negation *of* the self. Despite the dilemma, Hegel advocates adamantly that "the moment of the 'I' which is for itself pure negativity," and furthermore, he insists, it is "*being-for-itself* or pure negativity."[37] Paradoxically, "to be" is "not to be," to parody Hamlet's here. The Hegelian "to be" means to be "pure negativity"; but what else could Hegel's "pure negativity" possibly conjure up if not a subject of absence? Consequently, the negative dialectics that gestures towards eradicating otherness for the subject ends with a paradoxical erasure of the subject itself. In this self-abortive dialectics of negation, the subject is initiated in such a way as never capable of being ontologically present. The final solution via a negative signification turns the subject into a ghost figure, a subject of nothingness.

Hegel's dialectics of desire and dialectics of negative signification become almost synonymous toward the same *telos*. On the one hand, both involve appropriation of all alterities into a self-enclosed subject of singularity, and on the other, both facilitate pursuit of the illusion of a phantom-subject of desire. If the dialectics of desire only misleads the subject in a *wanting* position with the unhappy consciousness in its infinite self-division and self-decenterment, then the dialectics of negative signification certainly ends the subject in a regained illusory paradise of pure absence—a total self-negation. In spite of all the intricate negation and position, departure and return exorcised in the double dialectics, none is able to make the singular subject ontologically present.

Despite the assumption of the dialectics of infinite desire to radically suspend the subject from ever achieving its ontological finality, Hegel arbitrarily postulates an absolute end to his subject in the realm of theological ontology in terms of Spirit. Consequently, his negative signification slips into a dubious project of theological hauntology. Hegel asserts: "Spirit is this power only by looking the negative in the face, and tarrying with it. This tarrying with the negative is the magical power that converts it into being."[38] Or nothing? By evoking Spirit, Hegel intends to redeem the subject in a negative signification, that is, negation of negation means the final submission to and ultimate dispossession by Spirit. In this case, his philosophical inquiry is inescapably absorbed into a theological hauntology, his dialectic method is surrendered to a spectral metaphysics, and his negative signification is converted into a phantom ontology. Eventually, the subject's coming into being unveils an intra-spectral dialectics between the phantom subject and the Spectral Other.

The Ghost Subject and the Spectral Other

Hegel's *Phenomenology of Spirit* can be read as a Christian fable of the subject's transcendence from substance to Spirit or from a subject to a specter in the context of the full etymological capacity of the German term "*Geist*." The subject as phenomenon, mediated in the double processes of an ironic dialectics of desire and a paradoxical negative signification, is transfigured into a phantom of singular absence under the spell of some spectral other, i.e., the Holy Ghost of Christianity.

Hegel's discourse on the subject, in an ironic mode, taunts the futile journey of the subject toward its own end as an impossible and absent being. In order to reach the absolute Subject in terms of Spirit, the subject has to negate itself substantively by eliminating its substance, desire, and consciousness altogether. To embody Spirit, the ultimate *telos* for Hegel, means to *disembody* the subject into an incorporeal and ethereal phenomenon, i.e., a ghost figure, or a grotesque subject of singular absence in effect. Eventually, the subject's return to itself becomes a self-departing journey toward a spectral other that takes possession of the subject; and this obsessive desire to transcend into Spirit inevitably loses the subject altogether to the spectral other. Hence, the desire for the final identification with Spirit signifies a kind of death wish, enthralled by the phantom of a holy ghost. In fact, if the subject ends in a theological home of Spirit, it indicates precisely the death of all living substance as well as the demise of all desires—a total negation.

In this context, the Hegelian desire in transcendental terms does not intend on any general exterior objects at all; instead, the real object of desire for the Hegelian subject is the Spectral Other. Butler in *Subjects of Desire* remarks that "the initial self-consciousness no longer seeks to consume the

Other, as it sought to consume objects, but *is instead consumed by the Other*" and, further, "self-consciousness is convinced that the Other has occupied its own essence—self-negation—stolen it even, and in this sense self-consciousness finds itself besieged by the Other."[39] As a result, the initial desire for the self and the subsequent negation of the other is reversed in Hegel's paradoxical dialectics. Instead of appropriating the other, the subject submits itself to the Spectral Other in an "ecstatic self-sacrifice." Instead of "a reflection of its own identity through the Other," as Butler points out, the subject finds itself lost to "the enslaving and engulfing" Other.[40] Instead of possession of a self, the subject ends with an ironical dispossession.

What constitutes Spirit? Hegel is not at all equivocal about this: the Holy Spirit of Christianity. In various contexts, Hegel has consistently asserted this onto-theological position regarding Spirit in terms of the Christian God. In this case, Hegel, very much a Christian philosopher, argues explicitly that Spirit, or the Holy Ghost of Christianity, is at work shaping the destiny of man. For instance, in "Introduction to the Philosophy of Art," Hegel posits, "The Christian God is . . . purely spiritual, and can be known only as spirit and in spirit" and "Christianity, in depicting God as Spirit . . . as absolute and universal spirit."[41] In *The Philosophy of History,* Hegel believes that "Infinite Spirit itself therefore is posited . . . in the Divine Being" and "God is thus recognized as *Spirit*."[42] Moreover, Hegel hastens to add, "The nature of God as pure Spirit, is manifested to man *in the Christian Religion*."[43] Here, the Christian God is centralized as the Absolute Subject and, henceforth, Hegel's phenomenology of the subject is inescapably haunted by "absolute and eternal spirit." In a word, Hegel's wholly subject is besieged and dispossessed by the Holy Other.

Derrida in *Specters of Marx* has specifically named "the father Hegel" as the one who inaugurates "the subject of becoming-specter of the spirit" as well as "the theory of the specters."[44] Derrida suggests, with the term *Geist*, we might as well take the full range of its etymological implication, as *spirit*, *specter* and *ghost*. Clearly, Derrida's hauntology undermines the Hegelian ontology by exposing the ghost lurking in the Absolute Subject. To Derrida, the Hegelian Spirit is but a "ghostly simulacrum" and the Hegelian subject's coming into the holy light illustrates exactly this process of "ghosting" the subject in terms of the "spectral apparition" of Spirit.

In *Specters of Marx*, Derrida inquires rhetorically: "What is a *phenomenology* if not a logic of the *phainesthai* and of the *phantasma*, therefore of the phantom?"[45] Hegel's *Phenomenology of Spirit* might as well be translated into *Phantomology of Specter,* as Derrida suggests, because the subject's coming into being demonstrates "a phenomenological reduction *to the* ghost. . . . The reduction as subjectivization of the corporeal form of the external phantom is but a super-idealization and a supplementary spectralization."[46] Moreover, as Derrida reminds us, "all phenomenology is a phenomenology of spirit (let us translate here: phenomenology of specter), and that, as such, it cannot hide its Christian vocation."[47] Derrida pinpoints the theological locus of Hegel's phenomenology where a holy ghost resides at its center; and he further reveals that "[t]he arch-specter . . . , the capital ghost (*das hauptgespenst*) is man himself with a capital M."[48] This "Man-God," as exposed by Derrida, "play[s] the same role in *The Phenomenology of Spirit*."[49] Thus, the Hegelian subject's pursuit of the singular subject via a theological anchor echoes similar obsessive desire of Oedipus for the phantom of the singular and transcendental "Man" under the spell of the Apollonian specter.

Apparently, Hegel's pure subject means pure absence and pure lack, and to be a Hegelian subject means to be haunted and dispossessed by the Spectral Other. As a result, Taylor in *Altarity* observes: "Divine substance and human subject are reconciled in the self-conscious identity-in-difference of God and man. Subject and substance, self and other, humanity and divinity are internally related in such a way that each becomes *itself* in and through the other."[50] It seems that the Holy Ghost and the human subject emerge *almost* as one and the same in the final resolution for the Hegelian subject, or more precisely, in an intra-spectral and specular "self-reflexive" dialectics, i.e., a conjuration of a ghost by the Holy Ghost.

All subjects, defined in Greek terms, are subject to something other. For Hegel, all subjects are subjected to Spirit or the Holy Spirit. The Hegelian subject's coming into being (or nonbeing) via an obsessive desire toward singularity turns out to be a process of subjection to the Divine Being of Christian theology. In order to identify with God, all subjects have to be negated, and infinitely negated so that, as Hegel suggests, "the absolute melting-away of everything stable, is . . . absolutely negativity, *pure being-for-itself*."[51] In other words, only by dissolving and absolving all substance and desire can one expect to transcend into a spiritual or ghost subject; and this negative signification actually reveals a Freudian death wish at the center of Hegel's subject of desire for singular presence or at the end of Hegel's philosophy of history for the ghost-subject. This certainly reminds us of what Nietzsche says in *The Will to Power* in his critique of nihilism in terms of hauntology:

> Nihilism as a psychological state is reached . . . when one has posited a totality . . . [and] has wallowed in the idea of some supreme form of domination and administration. . . . Some sort of unity, some form of 'monism': this faith suffices to give man a deep feeling of standing in the context of, and being dependent on, some whole that is infinitely superior to him, and he sees himself as a mode of the deity.[52]

III. THE ASCETIC IDEAL AND NIHILISTIC DESIRE: THE DISEMBODIED SUBJECT AND BAD CONSCIENCE IN NIETZSCHE'S *THE GENEALOGY OF MORALS*

Deleuze in *Nietzsche and Philosophy* states: "we will misunderstand the whole of Nietzsche's work if we do not see 'against whom' its principal concepts are directed. Hegelian themes are present in this work as the enemy against which it fights. Nietzsche never stops attacking *the theological and Christian character of German philosophy*."[53] Particularly in *The Genealogy of Morals* and *The Anti-Christ*, Nietzsche is engaged in an "unholy" war against the theological *telos* of the Hegelian subject and the Christian God. In *Genealogy*, Nietzsche pointedly alerts, without calling names: "Let us, from now on, be on our guard against the hallowed philosophers' myth of a pure, will-less, painless, timeless knower."[54] In *The Anti-Christ*, he also warns: "Among German one will understand immediately when I say that philosophy has been corrupted by theologian blood. . . . German philosophy is at bottom—a *cunning* theology."[55] Nietzsche relentlessly critiques the theological exorcism by metaphysicians, possibly more at Hegel himself than anyone else, when he says: "These have spun their web around him so long that . . . he himself became a spider, a metaphysician. Thence forward . . . he transformed himself into something ever pale and less substantial, became an 'ideal,' became 'pure spirit.'"[56] To Nietzsche, those metaphysicians who spin metaphysical webs appear to have lost their minds in their labyrinthine speculations and eventually their hallucinated subject itself gradually evaporates when transcending into an ontological locale of pure being or pure nothingness.

In *Genealogy*, Nietzsche tactfully translates Hegel's incorporeal subject into a physical body and moves it from an onto-theological site to a concrete social space. Hegel's hypothetical subject lodged in a metaphysical locale, in this case, takes the form of a material body, in fact, a disembodied body, of the morbid priest. Specifically, Nietzsche uses the self-denouncing priest figure spellbound by the ascetic ideal to parody the Hegelian subject entrapped in the so-called dialectics of infinite self-reflexive consciousness and eternal negative signification. More or less, so it seems, Nietzsche sort of rewrites, in a parodic mode, an unauthorized account of the Hegelian subject postulated in his *Phenomenology of Spirit* in terms of *hauntology of priests*. In other words, the priest in Nietzsche's *Genealogy* figures as a dis-embodied typological Hegelian character that is obsessed with the grotesque subject of singularity under the spell of a negative will to being or nothing.

In contrast to Hegel's delusional projection of the subject's blissful salvation or happy transcendence into Spirit by submerging itself in a Divine Being, Nietzsche sees the opposite: the soul is terribly sickened and horrifically plagued precisely due to the fact that it is excessively satiated with

Spirit or Divinity. For Nietzsche, Christianity provides neither promised transcendence nor foretold redemption of the self; on the contrary, it is exposed as the very "original" cause of prevalent psychological anxiety and ontological disease that transforms the modern subject into a grotesque one. By uncovering the hauntological exorcism in terms of a ravaging self-negation and an inquisitive self-interrogation, Nietzsche holds Hegel's Holy Ghost responsible for invoking and conjuring the priestly type of grotesque humanity—the dis-embodied subject with "bad conscience." When Hegel ends his singular subject in an illusion of an ephemeral holy specter, Nietzsche ends Hegel's subject in dispossession, death, and nihilism.

Nietzsche's Priest: The Ascetic Ideal and Bad conscience

Instead of probing scandals of prevalent corruption in terms of corporal sin due to sexual lust, Nietzsche in his *Genealogy* exposes a more seductive as well as more devastating desire that possesses the priest, i.e., the longing for self-abnegation incited by a negative ideal—the ascetic ideal. Reframing Hegel's philosophical dialectics of negative signification in a different context of the ascetic ideal of self-renunciation, Nietzsche demystifies how the secretive spell of negative desire haunts, dispossesses, and disembodies the priest. Moreover, Nietzsche uses "bad conscience" as a theoretical trope to inquire the effect of the Hegelian unhappy consciousness as a case of self-inquisition and self-dividing. We might as well say Nietzsche comes up with a satirical version (or perversion) of Hegel's negative signification in terms of the ascetic self-annihilation and Hegel's self-reflexive consciousness in terms of the nihilistic self-flagellation.

Nietzsche's diagnosis of the modern subject's disease in terms of "bad conscience" certainly recalls the Hegelian subject's ineradicable unhappy consciousness for failing to achieve the subject of singularity. To Nietzsche, this sickness is *metaphysical* or "*hauntological*." In *Genealogy,* Nietzsche remarks: "I take bad conscience to be a deep-seated malady to which man succumbed under the pressure of the most profound transformation he ever underwent."[57] In other words, this "deep-seated malady" precipitated by the unbearable pressure points to a prevalent metaphysical sickness exorcised by a spell, i.e., the spell of the ascetic ideal of self-abnegation. That is why Deleuze in *Nietzsche and Philosophy* states emphatically that "his (Nietzsche's) whole theory of bad conscience must be seen as a reinterpretation of the Hegelian unhappy consciousness."[58]

In *Genealogy,* Nietzsche inquires: "How could such a brave and resourceful animal but be the most precarious, the most profoundly sick of all the sick beasts of the earth?"[59] In other words, how could the ascetic principle, with all its perverse effect of self-denial and self-repression, be possibly exorcised into a singular ideal desire for the subject? The following paragraph from

The Genealogy of Morals seems to parody, through the priest figure, the Hegelian subject's transcending into Spirit via the dialectics of negation in a Christian light:

> He projected all his denials of self, nature, naturalness out of himself as affirmations, as true being, embodiment, reality, as God . . . , as transcendence, as eternality, as endless torture, as hell, as the infinitude of guilt and punishment. In such psychological cruelty we see an insanity of the *will* that is without parallel: man's will to find himself guilty, and unredeemably so; his will to believe that he might be punished . . . ; his will to erect an ideal (God's holiness) in order to assure himself of his own absolute unworthiness. What a mad, unhappy animal is man![60]

Here, Hegel's negation of self and obsessive desire to transcend into Spirit are reinterpreted, from Nietzsche's view, as an endless self-persecuting will to and an insane yearning toward self-elimination. It seems that the subject has to negate oneself eternally and absolutely in order to be identified with God. Furthermore, this ascetic ideal initiates nothing else but self-suffering and self-torture, i.e., "the desire for self-mortification" and "the will to extinction."[61] Paradoxically, the more one is pursuing the ideal of the singular subject defined by "God's holiness," the more one proves to be guilty and more one seeks further torture to redeem oneself, a vicious circle no true believer can ever expect to escape. Ironically, the negative desire for self-purification and self-punishment is conjured up as a pleasure and a blessing. As Nietzsche alarms, "People no longer complained of pain but were insatiable for it."[62] Hence, Nietzsche might as well have rewritten a haunted version of Hegel's philosophy of history or his phenomenology of Spirit in terms of hauntology of the priest—a grotesque subject indeed.

Nietzsche accuses particularly Christianity for creating "negative ideals and humanity's bad conscience."[63] According to Nietzsche's *Genealogy*, human beings become morbidly sick by "taking arms against" themselves since the ascetic ideal initiates a "secret violation of the self," and "a soul divided against itself."[64] In this context, the animal instinct is no longer regarded as the insurgent other subversive to humanity in Nietzsche's view; there lurks in the unconscious a more threatening other, a spectral figure embodying the antihuman and anti-life power that insidiously represses, subjugates, and endangers the human species. To Nietzsche, the way theologians conjure up the ghost-subject via a nihilistic will to nothing parallels that metaphysicians evoke the subject of absence in a dialectics of negative signification toward a negative ontology.

Nietzsche's *Genealogy* exposes the death wish initiated by the ascetic ideal and negative desires. If Hegel sees "void" as a fundamental productive principle to his negative signification that "magically" converts the subject into a divine being, Nietzsche sees void as entirely a counter-productive desire that bewitchingly turns the subject into a ghost. "The ascetic ideal expresses a *will,*" Nietzsche alerts, "to nothingness."[65] When the Christian order invokes the negative as the ideal for identification, the incurred desire to embody this ascetic ideal can only result in violation, dispossession and disembodiment of the subject itself. Consequently, the very identification with the spectral other coincides with loss of the self, nihilistic indeed. In short, the absolute subject erected by the Christian ascetic ideals serves a "holy purpose," i.e., negation and disintegration of all existence.

Nietzsche observes in his *Genealogy*, "Wherever we look we meet the hypnotic stare of the sinner, fixed on the same identical thing—his 'guilt,' the sole cause of his suffering. Everywhere guilty conscience."[66] Here guilt and bad conscience, as the perverse effect inflicted by the internalized spectral gaze in an omniscient and omnipotent fashion, turns man into a disembodied ghost. The Hegelian self-reflexive consciousness translates into a kind of self-inquisition and self-torture under the spell of the spectral other. Nietzsche mocks that in spite of all the sufferings or pleasures the priest can endure, there is slim hope for the priest to transcend into a Divine Being. Instead, the irresolvable conflict and irreconcilable fissures emerge within to split the subject into a grotesque one in terms of the Hegelian unhappy consciousness or the Nietzschean bad conscience.

In addition, Nietzsche in *Genealogy* alerts that, rather than devoid of purpose, self-torture and self-negation become the purpose of a haunted life under the omnipresent gaze of the "sadistic conscience." Thus, Nietzsche discloses, "the sinner became wide-awake, eternally wide-awake."[67] Hence, a spectral other is speculating infinitely into the soul of the priest as "this guilt-ridden man seized upon religion in order to exacerbate his self-torment to the utmost. The thought of being in God's debt became his new instrument of torture."[68] In this case, indebted to God means a forfeited existence and a disowned life. Here, the Hegelian self-reflexive desire toward Spirit and the Nietzschean self-conscious torture for the Christian God emerge as an identical drive toward a holy order that ends either in a bad conscience or a ghost position. More striving toward God in theological terms, more sickening in biological terms, the subject is made despairingly aware of the infinite distance between the corporeal reality and the spectral divinity.

Derrida in *Specters of Marx* points out that "the specter is a paradoxical incorporation, the becoming-body, a certain phenomenal and carnal form of the spirit."[69] Nietzsche's priest is a prime example of this paradoxical incorporation of the specter. Hegel's ideal subject of pure being, represented in a parodic mode by Nietzsche's priest, is obsessed with and disembodied by Christianity or the Hegelian Spirit. The Hegelian desire to identify with the Spectral Other via a negative signification is satirically paralleled by the priest's nihilistic will to nothing under the spell of the Christian God. Where Hegel sees blissful transcendence, Nietzsche sees only horrific despair. By lifting the veil of its metaphysical facade, Nietzsche's *Genealogy* exposes Hegel's theological foundation as a negative ontology and further demystifies the ascetic ideal of self-abnegation as a grotesque desire of death instinct. Nietzsche warns that the priest's ascetic ideal "as *absolute* values allowed him to deny life and even himself."[70] And Nietzsche adds, "It was here, precisely, that I sensed the greatest danger for humanity, its sublimest delusion and temptation—leading it whither? Into nothingness?"[71] In short, by tracing the genealogy of the Christian morality, Nietzsche discloses the entire theological sorcery of how human beings, under the spell of the ascetic ideal, would willingly choose nonbeing as being, suffering as pleasure, negation as position, disembodiment as identification.

Nietzsche in *Twilight of the Idols* declares: "I already defined *modernity* as a physiological self-contradiction."[72] Actually, the modern subject starts with the Hegelian subject of infinite negation, unhappy consciousness, and hauntology. In other words, the modern subject, in fact a grotesque one, at the very inauguration is obsessed with and dispossessed by the singular subject under the spell of some spectral other. To identify with the absolute subject of Christianity via the ascetic ideal generates a paradoxical conjuration to divide, negate, and disembody oneself; and by extension, to submit oneself to any hegemonic system is destined to be dispossessed, and to desire the phantom of any singular subject means to succumb oneself to the spectral other. For Nietzsche, the priest represents the prototype of the modern grotesque subject and the embodiment of the negative ideal towards a nihilistic end in nothingness.

Metaphysics of Absence: The Spectral Other and Nihilism

Entirely different from Hegel, Nietzsche declares that Christianity is "the greatest misfortune of humanity."[73] For Nietzsche, Christianity, instead of offering redemption as Hegel believes, yields suffering and leads to nihilistic desire. If Hegel defines God as divine, holy, and transcendental, Nietzsche sees it as fiction, illusion, and evil spell.

Throughout his career, Nietzsche has consistently attacked the Christian God as a phantom of empty words. In "A Critical Backward Glance" prefaced to his *The Birth of Tragedy,* Nietzsche sarcastically entitles "God as the supreme artist"[74] or a magician who conjures up the ascetic ideal as the utmost goal for identification. Further, the "Christian doctrine" or "God's absolute truth" is deemed to be "at best, an artistic fiction; at worst, an outrageous imposture."[75] In *Twilight of the Idols*, Nietzsche also introduces God as an empty signifier: "The last, the thinnest, the emptiest is posited as the first, as a cause in itself, as *ens realissimum* [the most real thing]."[76] In addition, Hegel's pure subject and Spirit as the "highest concepts" are, in Nietzsche's view, "the most universal, the emptiest concepts, the final wisp of evaporating reality."[77] In regard to the notion that "God is truth, and truth divine," Nietzsche inquires suspiciously in his *Genealogy*, "But what if this equation becomes less and less credible, if the only things that may still be viewed as divine are error, blindness, and lies; if God himself turns out to be our *longest* lie?"[78] This means that God or the Holy Spirit turns into a ghost that is posited as the absolute presence sans presence. That is probably why Nietzsche in *The Anti-Christ* sacrilegiously states, "'Pure spirit' is pure stupidity," and Nietzsche regards "Christianity . . . as the art of holy lying."[79]

Further, Nietzsche aligns the Christian ideals with nihilism that sanction death against life. In *The Anti-Christ*, Nietzsche observes: "The Christian conception of God . . . , God as spirit—is one of the most corrupt conceptions of God. . . . In God nothing deified, the will to nothingness sanctified."[80] In *Twilight of the Idols*, Nietzsche remarks: "The concept of 'God' was up to now the greatest *objection* against existence" instead of the final salvation for human beings.[81] Nietzsche contests that the subject's desire for the spectral Other is "nothing other than a belief in the ascetic ideal in its most radical form, though an unconscious one."[82] Hence, Nietzsche unveils in Hegel's subject's mysterious transcendence an unconscious desire for nothingness. Now, let's quote Nietzsche's conclusive remark at the end of his *The Genealogy of Morals*:

> Until the advent of the ascetic ideal, man, the animal *man*, had no meaning at all on this earth. . . . Finally the ascetic ideal arose to give it meaning—its only meaning, so far. . . . It signifies . . . a will to nothingness, a revulsion from life, a rebellion against the principal conditions of living. . . . Let me repeat . . . man would sooner have the void for his purpose than be void of purpose.[83]

When God is established as the Absolute Subject that ordains all to identify with it through self-negation, and when the ascetic ideal is inscribed as the normative morality that demands all to implement self-denial and self-interrogation, human beings truly become grotesque in this obsessive quest for the void as the single purpose of life because, in Nietzsche's view, coming into being by submitting oneself to Spirit signals disembodiment of humanity.

In *The Will to Power*, Nietzsche identifies two characteristics of nihilism. The first is marked as "when we have sought a 'meaning' in all events that is not there."[84] That is to say, something absent or spectral postures as a fundamental and transcendental presence. And the second refers to the domination of a hegemonic order, that is, "when one has posited a totality . . . , some supreme form of domination and administration. . . . Some sort of unity, some form of 'monism.'"[85] The first characteristic uncovers delusion or absence, and the second points to a totalized system, i.e. the metaphysics of presence; henceforth, nihilism becomes synonymous with metaphysics. Any subject, subjected to hauntology of Spirit, transforms itself into a grotesque one with a bad conscience as Nietzsche discerns in "'Nihilism' an ideal of the highest degree of powerfulness of the spirit."[86] If Hegel believes that only Spirit—the highest ideal and ultimate *telos*—can redeem humanity, Nietzsche sees the opposite. The desire toward the phantom of the singular subject leads to nihilism instead of identity, grotesquery instead of totality. In Nietzsche's view, human beings are lost not because they do not believe in God anymore; on the contrary, human beings are lost precisely due to the fact they are single-mindedly obsessed with and horrifically haunted by God.[87] Interestingly, only Nietzsche is "in-sane" enough to cry out aloud: God is haunting even though it is dead.

As we recall, Nietzsche's scandalous words "God is dead" come from a mad man that looks "lost."[88] In *Gay Science*, Nietzsche's mad man is haunted by "an infinite nothing" or an "empty space" left by the death of God. This mad man or the dispossessed man, I guess, has to be a priest. Or put differently, God is dead, so man is mad due to the loss of the absolute subject. Like Hamlet, father is dead, man is mad, or, at least, pretends to be so. In this context, Christianity neither "improves" nor saves human beings; instead, human beings turn increasingly neurotic due to the spectral exorcism. Nietzsche in *The Anti-Christ* observes: "The religious man as the Church *desires* him to be is a typical *décadent*; the moment when a religious crisis had gained the upper hand of a people is always characterized by epidemics of neurosis."[89] From Nietzsche's prophetic statement here, we can certainly hear future echoes from Freud's diagnosis of neurosis as avoidable rampant conditions of the modern man in his *Civilization and Its Discontents* and *The Future of an Illusion*.

IV. FREUD'S *CIVILIZATION AND ITS DISCONTENTS* AND *THE FUTURE OF AN ILLUSION*: BETWEEN OEDIPAL RITES AND NARCISSISTIC DESIRE

Perhaps no other discipline has contributed more to the literature of the grotesque than psychoanalysis, and some even suggest psychoanalysis itself is an exemplary grotesque narrative par excellence. From an orthodox Freudian point of view, human beings are grotesque by nature due to some irreconcilable internal conflicts. Thus, the typical subject formation in psychoanalytic discourse is identical to the normative figuration of the grotesque: heterogeneous, disparate, and incoherent elements co-habiting the psychic space.

Freud's model of the psyche, far from static or stable, is founded upon a dynamic and chaotic space with all kinds of drives, strives, and desires and the Freudian subject itself has always been a complex site of contention, full of discord, division, and uncertainty, in a word, grotesque. However, the traditional binary structure in regard to human beings since the Enlightenment or the onset of humanism is polarized between certain notions of animal instinct and various projections of human ideals. In his philosophical speculation of human conditions in *Civilization and Its Discontents* and *The Future of an Illusion,* Freud reframes this binary differently by situating human beings in a precarious position between the basic animal instinct and the lofty divine spirit. In other words, the human ego is constantly at the mercy of two kinds of mutinous power of alterity: on the one hand, the irresistible disruption of basic animal instinct, i.e., the *id* in a broad sense, and on the other, the omnipresent surveillance of an austere *superego* in terms of the Christian God. The alluring animal instinct as the other accounts for part of Freud's interests, and possibly the banal part, while a more threatening and powerful other for Freud, far beyond the animal kingdom, stems from the phantom of a terrifying spectral other in terms of the Holy Father.

In this case, the Oedipus complex, far beyond the domestic theatre, is enacted on a cultural stage, substantially exceeding the original meanings intended by Freud and arching into a narcissistic terrain along a patrilineal trajectory. If Nietzsche translates, in a parodic mode, the Hegelian subject's submission to Spirit by means of a negative signification into the priest's dispossession by the Christian God via a nihilistic desire of asceticism, Freud simply translates the Hegelian subject's preoccupation with God in onto-theology into a narcissist's neurotic obsession with an omnipotent spectral father figure in a discipline called psychoanalysis. If Nietzsche's priest is fanatically embracing his Christian God and dispossessed like a ghost with both torture and pleasure, Freud's neurotic is caught half-heartedly between this world and the next with both fear and desire. To bend the Freudian term of the uncanny to this occasion, the psychoanalytic subject's ontological or egological anchorage is structured ex-centrically between "home" and "not home," *heimlich* and *unheimlich*, or displaced somewhere between some animal drives and a divine will.

The Unconscious Other in Question

Arguably, the most subversive idea that radically challenges stability and certitude of the human subject is Freud's concept of the unconscious, an otherness full of heterogeneity, contradiction, and conflict. In Freud's view, the subject is inescapably a subject of the unconscious. But what exactly constitutes the enigmatic otherness in the unconscious probably still remains a riddle and is subject to debate. It is a kind of cliché to repeat that Freud discovered the unconscious, and it functions as an instrument that fundamentally undermines the traditional paradigm of the psychic structure defined by the rational cogito. To Freud, the stabilized and centralized rational ego is but a dream of yesterday, a philosophical illusion, reminiscent of the lingering residue of the Enlightenment legacy. In other words, the human being as a subject has always already been dispossessed by some unconscious otherness that renders it ex-centric and ex-singular, i.e., grotesque.

In general, past humanists are always inclined to single out the animal nature or basic instinct as the absolute otherness lurking in the unconscious that menaces and subverts the centrality of the rational ego established since the Enlightenment. From "Wolf-Man" to "Rat-Man," the title characters of Freud's case studies seem to profess nothing else but grotesque images of the wild nature.[90] However, I believe, these scary animal tales tell only the sensational part of the pop stories for generic psychoanalytic theories while the other part, possibly the most disturbing part that frightfully haunts the psychoanalytic subject, lies elsewhere in some spectral sphere beyond nature.

On the one hand, especially in pop psychology, it seems that Freud animates the subject by excavating in the unconscious a repressed other in terms of animal instinct or primitive drive that dispels the illusory myth of the singular subject and disrupts the stable totality of rational being. The ego, so it goes, is no longer the master in one's own house, or probably anybody else's for that matter, due to the uncontrollable animal nature. To claim and protect the legitimate status of humanity, the subject has to engage a life-long and often precarious struggle to subjugate eruptions of the animal other. In this case, the human subject somewhat looks like a typological grotesque figure, partially human and partially animal, an unstable and incoherent being infested and periled by an unconscious alterity. Therefore, nature and culture are put in a polarized position so that the very destination of civilization seems to depend upon keeping the animal other under tight control or eradicating it out of the mind.

On the other hand, especially in his philosophical essays on civilization and religion, Freud discerns a more imminent threat that endangers humanity from another source, in fact, a much more powerful other than animality, that is, the omnipotent authorial figure in terms of the superego. The Oedipus complex as the central rite of passage instills into the subject an inherent fear of castration from a dominating father, spectral or corporeal. This centric concept, if extended beyond the domestic theatre into a larger cultural context, grounds the subject under the spell of an omnipresent and omnipotent Holy Father in terms of the Spectral Other. Henceforth, the civilized man is no longer merely opposed to nature as his adverse other. Instead, humanity is forever at the mercy of an overwhelming divine power, a kind of uttermost opponent, as the result of civilization. More than erupting stability of the rational ego like the basic instinct, this internalized Spectral Other—the real culprit in Freud's view—haunts and threatens the very existence of the subject in a much more insidious manner. In a way, the subject that Freud brings forward is inhabited, invaded, haunted, and taken possession of like a hostage.

Hence, Freud seems to say that the repressed animal instinct and the desired divine power cohabit in the unconscious space in terms of either *id* or *superego*, but the horrible panic Freud prophetically points out directs us elsewhere. The images that Freud extricates from the unconscious of his patients usually lead to a wild animal kingdom in terms "wolf-man" or "rat-man," but Freud's universal paradigm of the unconscious in terms of the Oedipus complex points to other awesome and awful figures, such as the castrating father, the omnipotent God, and the omnipresent superego. Therefore, human beings are far less haunted by the natural animal instinct than by the culturally engineered divine demand—all kinds of commandments from religious doctrines, ethical codes, and social ideals. It is interesting to note that the "other" proposed by Freud the philosopher appears to be drastically different from that speculated by Freud the psychoanalyst.

Superego and Neurosis: Spectral Haunting and Self-Aggression

In *Civilization and Its Discontents* and *The Future of an Illusion*, Freud focuses on exploring origination of neurosis not merely as a random individual case study in isolation, but also as a prevalent social epidemic on a massive scale. Freud is convinced that, due to the restrictive power of civilization to tame animal desires, human beings feel increasingly eroded and violated by those internalized social values and religious doctrines. In other words, in pursuit of spiritual ideals, the human subject turns repressively neurotics not because he fails to resist the seductive pleasure of animal instinct, but because he lives in fear of punishment from the omnipotent God if he fails. It is not the id, the locus of primordial drives, that renders us neurotic or grotesque; instead, it is the terror of the inescapable omnipresent superego, the patrolling agency of a spectral father figure that produces the neurotics and perverts in modern society. The real threat stems from some divine authority in a spectral sphere rather than from a corporeal locale of animal instinct. In this case, the superego in the name of civilization conjures up the adverse effect similar to the Hegelian unhappy consciousness and the Nietzschean bad conscience combined.

In *Civilization and Its Discontents*, Freud testifies that "a person becomes neurotic because he cannot tolerate the amount of frustration which society imposed on him in the service of its cultural ideals."[91] As a result, it is the lofty ideals of civilization that turn human subjects into neurotics. In Freud's view, "Neurosis was regarded as the outcome of a struggle . . . in which the ego had been victorious but at the price of severe sufferings and renunciations."[92] Here, self-renunciation and severe torments certainly recall the ravaging effect of Nietzsche's ascetic ideal on the priest in terms of self-denial and life-negation. Neurotic symptoms emerge as the result of the uncanny spell of the superego.

In addition, under the spell of the internalized cultural ideals, the aggressive instinct toward others is redirected inward toward one's ego as a self-destructive desire. In *Civilization and Its Discontents*, Freud unfolds the perverse outcome of civilization's devastating power upon the individual, drastically different from what humanists would like to believe. The following is Freud's diagnosis of how threat turns into desire due to the sacred order of the executing and exacting superego:

> There . . . as super-ego, and which now, in the form of 'conscience,' is ready to put into action against the ego the same harsh aggressiveness that the ego would have liked to satisfy upon other, extraneous individuals. The tension between the harsh super-ego and the ego that is subjected to it is called by us the sense of guilt; it expresses itself as a need for punishment. Civilization, therefore, obtains mastery over the individual's dangerous desire for aggression by weakening and disarming it and by setting up an agency within him to watch over it, like a garrison in a conquered city.[93]

Hence, all subjects are inescapably subjected to an interior persecuting agency in terms of "conscience' or "bad conscience," to quote Nietzsche here. In other words, under the gaze of the omnipresent surveillance of the superego, the subject, like "a conquered city," is permanently occupied and inherently haunted by a terrifying spectral other in the name of civilization. In this case, we may say that Freud is simply repeating Nietzsche's notion of "bad conscience" in different terms.

Further, as Freud points out, the more one adheres to the decreed of the ideal subject, the more punishment one flints upon oneself. In *Civilization and Its Discontents*, Freud observes: "For the more virtuous a man is, the more severe and distrustful is its behavior, so that ultimately it is precisely those people who have carried saintliness furthest who reproach themselves with the worst sinfulness."[94] Consequently, similar to Nietzsche's priest, human beings' fear of punishment, according to Freud, is perverted into a desire for punishment as Freud notes, "when misfortune befalls him, he searches his soul, acknowledges his sinfulness, heightens the demands of his conscience, imposes abstinences on himself and punishes himself with penances."[95] Eventually, one is caught in an inextricable vicious circle: the more one renounces oneself, the more one calls for renunciation "under the influence of a sadistic super-ego."[96] As a psychological embodiment of some theological authority, the superego possesses the subject so much so that this spectral phantom becomes, so to speak, normalized as an inherent psychic structure and naturalized as an integral component of the subject's haunted existence. Victoria Hamilton in *Narcissus and Oedipus* states: "Freud's super-ego has its base in paranoia—in watching, ordering, judging, threatening and punishing."[97] Fear of authority furthers renunciation of instinct, but fear of the superego presses for punishment for the subject. As a result, every renunciation of the basic instinct strengthens the authority of the superego and intensifies the sense of guilt. Like Nietzsche's priest, the obsessive desire for the holy subject turns the subject toward neurosis, psychosis, and self-destruction—in a word, grotesque.

Particularly in *Civilization and Its Discontents*, Freud critiques religion for seducing mankind into mass neurosis when he says that "by forcibly fixing them in a state of psychical infantilism and by drawing them into a mass-delusion, religion succeeds in sparing many people from an individual neurosis."[98] That is to say, religion is responsible for generating a mass neurosis in the name of the Holy Spirit. Similarly, in *The Future of an Illusion*, Freud remarks: "Religion would thus be the universal obsessional neurosis of humanity; like the obsessional neurosis of children, it arose out of the Oedipus complex, out of the relation to the father,"[99] or the Holy Father. Ironically, religion, which is supposed to save human beings from suffering, becomes the intoxicating media that converts human beings into obsessional neurotics and leads to a mass-delusion "in a state of blissful hallucinatory confusion."[100] Consequently, religion produces the sublime loss of self, reality, and sanity. Freud warns that even those religious ideas "are prized as the most precious possession of civilization"[101] and the absolute value of the utmost importance, "they are illusions, fulfillments of the oldest, strongest and most urgent wishes of mankind,"[102] i.e., the phantoms of spectral presence. In this case, Freud's superego occupies exactly the same position as Hegel's Specter and it misleads and haunts the modern subject.[103]

Terry Eagleton in *The Ideology of Aesthetic* observes: "The superego is not only self-contradictory, but in a certain sense self-undoing."[104] Both Freud and Nietzsche would certainly agree to this point. The subject becomes neurotic or grotesque due to exorcism of the relentless commandments from the superego, the embodiment of those sacred laws of the father figure, secular or divine. Similar to the effect of Hegel's self-reflexive consciousness, Freud's superego generates endless guilt through self-repudiation and self-aggression. Therefore, Freud alerts, the subject is not merely disoriented toward elsewhere or ex-centric, but misled toward nowhere or extinction, a death wish toward non-being. As a result, Freud predicts that we could all end up like Nietzsche's priest, losing oneself to the spectral other with fallacious convictions of either salvation or condemnation. Moreover, by installing this omnipotent father figure as the ideal image of identification, a narcissistic relation is established behind the scandalous and sensational drama of the Oedipus complex.

Oedipus or Narcissus: The Problematic Object of Desire

It is well known that the primal scene of psychoanalysis is the discovery of the Oedipus complex, and the legendary Oedipus is supposed to decode the riddle of man's enigmatic identity. It seems that Freud mythologizes Oedipus as the universal structure of human psychology in general and the unconscious in particular. In other words, Freud makes the Oedipus legend not merely the basis of his psychoanalytic theory, but also the founding myth of all civilization as well as its discontents.

Deleuze and Guattari in *Anti-Oedipus* declare: "Psychoanalysis has its metaphysics—its name is Oedipus" and "Oedipus," they remind, "is the ultimate private and subjugated territoriality of European man."[105] In *A Thousand Plateaus,* they also point out that psychoanalysis is founded on "an Oedipal apparatus, which Freud considers the sole motor, the immobile motor that must be found everywhere."[106] Henceforth, the multiple, diverse, and heterogeneous desires that characterize the unconscious are compressed and territorialized into a single domestic space to enact the romance of the bourgeois family. The imperialism of the Oedipal myth, according to them, underlines the paranoiac nature of the patriarchal law and theological order. By forcing all subjects to go through the Oedipal rites of passage, Freud installs and institutes an omnipotent figure in terms of the spectral other into the unconscious.

In effect, Freud inserts into the unconscious a master text, a master code, a mono-myth of neurotic obsession with and phobic fright of the Holy Father. In other words, this quest for the origin of man and the solution to the riddle of psychoanalysis goes back to Freud's analogy of man's relationship to a spectral presence. To some degree, Freud's Oedipus complex appears to rewrite a psychological version of the Hegelian *hauntological* ghost story of God's relationship to humanity. In *Oedipus and the Fabrication of the Father*, Petro Pucci points out: "The Father figure is the figure of the anchorage of any discourse to a fixed origin, to a transcendental signified."[107] Evidently, Freud's subject is totally subordinated to an omnipotent transcendental father, an uncanny figure of both the primal father and the spectral other, fraught with both dread and desire.

Freud, in this case, discerns in the awesome rite of the Oedipus complex not only fear, but also unconscious desire. On the one hand, the Oedipal subject is overanxiously haunted by the horror of castration by an omnipotent father, and on the other, the subject is secretly longing to replace him or act on his behalf, narcissistically identifying with the father figure in order to repeat after him, like Oedipus. In other words, the Oedipal desire on an undercurrent side aims at the *object of identification* as the *object of desire.* This unconscious return to the father constitutes for Freud a return to the very beginning of civilization, the *imago* or the phantom of a primal father. In *The*

Future of an Illusion, Freud observes: "Fundamentally this was a return to the historical beginnings of the idea of God. Now that God was a single person, man's relations to him could recover the intimacy and intensity of the child's relation to his father."[108] In Freud's view, the image of God is founded upon the projection of a person's relation to a father figure as the result of desire. This means that man creates the image of an omnipotent God out of the need of protection from nature on the conscious level; but simultaneously this projection also reveals an unconscious desire for identification with God. Freud argues, "God was the exalted father, and the longing for the father was the root of the need for religion" and "the primal father was the original image of God."[109] Thus, the father in spectral terms, or the *imago*, constitutes a subject for identification out of a narcissistic desire.

In *The Future of an Illusion*, Freud notes, "The narcissistic satisfaction [is] provided by the cultural ideal."[110] Therefore, all symbolic systems justifying their ideal subject are founded upon a narcissistic model of self-imaging and self-duplicating, very much like the dialectic or "self-reflexive" relationship between Hegel's subject to Spirit. A narcissist is characteristic of obsession with a perfect self-image conjured up by some spectral other, typically reflexive of a grandiose mirror image of the cultural ideals prescribed by some sacred father. As we know, Hegel's subject is self-wrapped, self-absorbed, and self-centered, and the subject's relationship to Spirit is in fact enclosed in a narcissistic space of intra-subjectivity and intra-spectrality. True to what Freud says, a narcissistic cannot tell the difference between me and not me, between the self-image and the spectral other.

In "On Narcissism: An Introduction," Freud states: "The subject's narcissism makes its appearance displaced on to this new ideal ego, which, like the infantile ego, finds itself possessed of every perfection that is of value."[111] In addition, Freud observes: "What he projects before him as his ideal is the substitute for the lost narcissism of his childhood in which he was his own ideal."[112] And this ideal self-image, as it turns out, is actually nobody else but a regressive or nostalgic illusion or *imago* of the primal father, or theologically, of God. Victoria Hamilton in *Narcissus and Oedipus* remarks: "He fell in love with an insubstantial hope, mistaking a mere shadow for a real body."[113] In other words, the subject is nothing else but a phantom image conjured up by the spectral other, likely a dream of the past.

In *Civilization and Its Discontents*, Freud points out the difficulty or impossibility of bridging the distance between the human and the divine in terms of a narcissistic reflection: "God has made them in the image of His own perfection; nobody wants to be reminded how hard it is to reconcile the undeniable existence of evil . . .with His all-powerfulness or His all-goodness."[114] Evidently, it is absolutely impossible to coincide entirely with the ideal or the illusory subject of spectral nature. As Nietzsche illustrates that the priests, with both pain and pleasure, testify the failure rather than achievement of perfect identification. Paradoxically, in its narcissistic pursuit of the phantom of a singular being, the subject is deprived of its substance like a body being overtaken by a ghost. Therefore, the grotesque is not merely associated with the lack of identity, unity, and totality; on the contrary, the grotesque is predominantly related to an obsessive desire for the subject of singularity. Any subject, regardless of Hegel's subject, Nietzsche's priest, or Freud's neurotic, is subject to haunting by a spectral other, the absolute subject of some divine order. Oedipus' narcissistic desire for the singular man under the spell of the Apollonian specter is a case in point. Goux in *Oedipus, Philosopher* remarks, and rightly so, "The modern subject . . . is initially determined by the posture of Oedipus."[115]

Freud shares Nietzsche's diagnosis of the modern subject's disease and repeats Nietzsche's "bad conscience" in terms of the cultural unconscious in his critique of Hegel's subject of infinite consciousness and negative desire. Different from either Hegel's sublime prospect of an onto-theological myth to redeem the subject in a utopian future or Nietzsche's evocation of the mythic desire of the Dionysian principle as a redemptive power in a nostalgic past, Freud patiently analyzes the middle passage of the modern subject in terms of neurosis. When Nietzsche suggests going back to a mythical past of the Dionysian self-abandonment, and Hegel proposes going forward to an angelic future of pure subjectivity, Freud does not share their dreams of either the past or the future. Instead, Freud offers illusion and disillusionment for future humanity in the context of both civilization and its discontents. Insofar as we assume to be human, Freud seems to be saying, we have to live abjectly with our neurosis, or in other words, *our* grotesqueness.

V. CONCLUSION OF PART TWO: THE MODERN SUBJECT

As I proposed, the grotesque desire embodies the single-minded narcissistic obsession with the singular subject. Hegel's subject's dispossession by Spirit via a negative signification, Nietzsche's priest's deprivation by Christianity via the ascetic ideal, and Freud's neurotics' obsession with a primal father via an Oedipal structure all attest the grotesque coming into being under the spell of some spectral other. The Spirit in Hegel's *Phenomenology of Spirit*, Christ in Nietzsche's *The Genealogy of Morals,* and the "Father" in Freud's *Civilization and Its Discontents* are all presented, more or less, in spectral terms. Hegel's subject, Nietzsche's priest, and Freud's neurotic all hang onto the same Holy Ghost of Christianity in terms of the Spectral Other. In one way or the other, each of them returns to the Oedipus legend and, in varying degrees, each repeats the same Oedipal story of a subject's narcissistic obsession with a spectral father figure in an ontological, cultural, or familial context. To repeat Freud's "Masterplot," there is no mastery or end, only return or eternal return perhaps.

Roland Barthes in *The Pleasure of the Text* remarks, "Death of the Father would deprive literature of many of its pleasures. If there is no longer a Father, why tell stories? Doesn't every narrative lead back to Oedipus? Isn't storytelling always a way of searching for one's origin, speaking one's conflict with the Law, entering into the dialectic of tenderness and hatred?"[116] Apparently, the Oedipus legend in this case not only tells a story of "searching for one's origin," but also figures as the originating locus of all storytelling. In effect, *Oedipus'* legend discloses precisely the problem of centrality of the patriarchal culture and patrilineal mythologies: everything is defined by the father's name, the father's words, and the father's law, even after his death. This phallic narrative certainly sounds like Lacan's theory of the symbolic order. In the next chapter, we will see how the same Oedipus story is repeated one more time, in *other* terms, by Lacan after Freud.

NOTES

1. In *Winesburg, Ohio*, Sherwood Anderson tells us: "It was the truths that made the people grotesques. . . . It was his notion that the moment one of the people took one of the truths to himself, called it his truth, and tried to live his life by it, he became grotesque and the truth he embraced became a falsehood" (1997, 25–26). Here Anderson proposes a new paradigm by exposing the unconscious of the modern grotesque in terms of an obsessive desire, i.e., a single-minded obsession with and inevitable dispossession by a singular presence or the singular subject. The grotesque, in this context, signifies a single-minded desire to embody the phantom of a grandiose subject of singularity.

2. Jacques Derrida, *Specters of Marx: The State of the Debt, the Work of Mourning, and the New International*, trans. Peggy Kamuf (New York: Routledge, 1994), 37. Derrida's *Specters of Marx* is the most sustained study of ontology in terms of hauntology among his several other writings on the same topic. For instance, in *Of Spirit: Heidegger and the Question,* Derrida also points out that the issue of ontology lies precisely in the neglect of the ghost—the metaphysical ghost residing at the center of ontology. See also Derrida's *The Gift of Death* and *On the Name* for further discussions of hauntology.

3. Shakespeare, William, *The Tragedy of Hamlet, Prince of Denmark* (New York: Pocket Books, 1992), 57.

4. Derrida, *Specters of Marx,* 51.

5. For more materials on theories on haunting, please see *Ghosts: Deconstruction, Psychoanalysis, History* edited by Peter Buse and Andrew Stott. In the past few decades, critics have developed various scenarios based upon Derrida's notion of hauntology for different purposes. Colin Davis in *Haunted Subject: Deconstruction, Psychoanalysis and the Return of the Dead* focuses on the hauntological uncanny effect: "Hauntology supplants its near-homonym ontology, replacing the priority of being and presence with the figure of the ghost that which is neither present nor absent, neither dead nor alive" (2007, 9). Warren Montag in "Spirits Armed and Unarmed: Derrida's *Specters of Marx*" speculates on the same uncanny position: "To speak of specters, the lexicon of ontology is insufficient. Ontology speaks only of what is present or what is absent; it cannot conceive of what is neither. Thus, it is replaced by a 'hauntology' adequate to the task of interrogating the spirit, that which is neither living nor dead" (1999, 71). Jodey Castricano in *Cryptomimesis: The Gothic and Jacques Derrida's Ghost Writing* explores Derrida's hauntology specifically in the context of internalization for the subject: "Haunting, then, implies interiority: the necessary construction of an 'inside' whether of . . . a system of

representation, or a 'subject'" (2001, 22-23). Besides, Derrida also addresses the difference between hauntology and cryptology. Please refer to "Fors: The Anglish Words of Nicolas Abraham and Maria Torok" and *The Ear of the Other*. A provocative reading of Derrida's hauntology comes from Nancy J. Holland's "The Death of the Other/Father: A Feminist Reading of Derrida's Hauntology." From a feminist perspective, Holland raises interesting issues of seeing and blindness: "But what if the ghostly apparition that looks at us sees not we ourselves, we daughters as we are, but only its own ghost, the spectral image of what it wants to see, desires to see, must see when it looks at a female form?" (2001, 67). In this case, Derrida's hauntology is equally suspect of being haunted by the ghost of the phallic mythology because he focuses only on the father-son relationship in *his* hauntology. In addition, the term hauntology has become seminal and instrumental in ethnic studies. For instance, Kathleen Brogan in *Cultural Haunting: Ghosts and Ethnicity in Recent American Literature* argues, "The ghosts haunting contemporary American literature lead us to the heart of our nation's discourse about multiculturalism and ethnic identity" (1998, 4).

6. Derrida, *Specters of Marx*, 45, 37.
7. Ibid., 161, 170.
8. Ibid., 139.
9. Ibid., 7.
10. According *OED*, the word "spectral" is defined either as an apparition, a phantom, a ghost or an unreal object of thought; a phantom of the brain or an image or a phantom produced by a reflection (mirror). The word "specular" is defined as either vision by reflection, (shared with the third definition of "spectral") or relating to, and having the qualities of a mirror. Clearly Derrida employs the full etymological capacity of the word "spectral" in his theory of specters by playing with overlapped meanings between the two words "spectral" and the "specular."
11. Derrida, *Specters of Marx*, 146.
12. Ibid., 156.
13. Ibid., 7.
14. Ibid., 156.
15. Ibid.
16. Ibid., 133.
17. Georg Wilhelm Friedrich Hegel, *Phenomenology of Spirit*, trans. A. V. Miller (Oxford: Oxford UP, 1977), 10.
18. Ibid., 105.
19. Ibid., 126.
20. Walter A. Davis, *Inwardness and Existence: Subjectivity in/and Hegel, Heidegger, Marx and Freud* (Madison: U of Wisconsin P, 1989), 43.
21. Ibid., 46.
22. Ibid., 43–44.
23. Hegel, *Phenomenology of Spirit*, 12.
24. Ibid., 21.
25. William Desmond, *Desire, Dialectics, and Otherness: An Essay on Origins* (New Haven: Yale UP, 1987), 1.
26. Mark C Taylor, *Altarity* (Chicago: U of Chicago P, 1987), 18.
27. Ibid., 21.
28. Hegel, *Phenomenology of Spirit*, 100.
29. Taylor, *Altarity*, 16.
30. Hegel, *Phenomenology of Spirit*, 11.
31. Rodolphe Gasché, *The Tain of the Mirror: Derrida and the Philosophy of Reflection* (Cambridge: Harvard UP, 1986), 20.
32. . Judith Butler, *Subjects of Desire: Hegelian Reflections in Twentieth-Century France* (New York: Columbia UP, 1987), 23.
33. Hegel, *Phenomenology of Spirit*, 32.
34. Ibid., 80.
35. Ibid., 76.
36. Butler, *Subjects of Desire*, 89.

37. Hegel, *Phenomenology of Spirit*, 10, 12.
38. Ibid., 19.
39. Butler, *Subjects of Desire*, 48.
40. Ibid.
41. Georg Wilhelm Friedrich Hegel, "Introduction to the Philosophy of Art," in *The Critical Tradition: Classical Texts and Contemporary Trends*, ed. David Richter (New York: St. Martin's Press, 1998), 364, 367.
42. Georg Wilhelm Friedrich Hegel, *The Philosophy of History* , trans. J. Sibree (New York: Dover, 1956), 324, 319.
43. Ibid., 323.
44. Derrida, *Specters of Marx*, 122, 121.
45. Ibid., 122.
46. Ibid., 129–30.
47. Ibid., 133.
48. Ibid., 138.
49. Ibid., 144.
50. Taylor, *Altarity*, 29–30.
51. Hegel, *Phenomenology of Spirit*, 117.
52. Friedrich Nietzsche, *The Will to Power*, trans. Walter Kaufmann and R. J. Hollingdale (New York: Vintage, 1968), 12.
53. Gilles Deleuze, *Nietzsche and Philosophy*, trans. Hugh Tomlinson (New York: Columbia UP, 1983), 162.
54. Friedrich Nietzsche, *The Birth of Tragedy and the Genealogy of Morals*, trans. Francis Golffing (New York: Doubleday, 1956), 255.
55. Friedrich Nietzsche, *Twilight of the Idols and The Anti-Christ*, trans. R. J. Hollindale (London: Penguin, 2003), 133.
56. Ibid., 140.
57. Nietzsche, *The Birth of Tragedy and the Genealogy of Morals*, 217.
58. Deleuze, *Nietzsche and Philosophy*, 157.
59. Nietzsche, *The Birth of Tragedy and the Genealogy of Morals*, 257.
60. Ibid., 226.
61. Ibid., 221, 230.
62. Ibid., 278.
63. Ibid., 220.
64. Ibid., 221.
65. Ibid., 284.
66. Ibid., 278.
67. Ibid.
68. Ibid., 226.
69. Derrida, *Specters of Marx*, 6.
70. Nietzsche, *The Birth of Tragedy and the Genealogy of Morals*, 154.
71. Ibid.
72. Nietzsche, *Twilight of the Idols, Or, How to Philosophize with the Hammer*, trans. Richard Polt (Indianapolis: Hackett P, 1997). 77.
73. Ibid., 82.
74. Nietzsche, *The Birth of Tragedy and the Genealogy of Morals*, 9.
75. Ibid., 10.
76. Nietzsche, *Twilight of the Idols, Or, How to Philosophize with the Hammer*, 20.
77. Ibid., 19.
78. Nietzsche, *The Birth of Tragedy and the Genealogy of Morals*, 288.
79. Nietzsche, *Twilight of the Idols and The Anti-Christ*, 137, 169.
80. Ibid., 140.
81. Nietzsche, *Twilight of the Idols, Or, How to Philosophize with the Hammer*, 37.
82. Nietzsche, *The Birth of Tragedy and the Genealogy of Morals*, 288.
83. Ibid., 298–99.
84. Nietzsche, *The Will to Power*, 12.

85. Ibid.
86. Ibid., 14.
87. In a different context, Luce Irigaray in *Speculum of the Other Woman* identifies this obsession with God as a kind of *male hysteria*. Irigaray writes: "The conception of the hysteric is still *paternal*, set on fire only by its fantasies of copulating with Him who is recognized as the sole source of Sameness. . . .God-the-Father, the Self-Same-He" (1985, 357). Further, Irigaray mocks in her critique of the patriarchal tradition since Plato: "For only the philosopher's thought is truly winged, though this earns him with the crowd the reputation of being 'mad.' Whereas, although he is indeed beside himself, delirious and out of his own control, he is rather 'inspired,' possessed by a God" (1985, 322). This certainly sounds like Nietzsche's priest or Hegel's subject.
88. In *The Gay Science*, Nietzsche writes that the madman cried: "God is dead! God remains dead!" and that is the death of "the holiest and mightiest thing the world has ever possessed" (2001, 120). Then, the madman asks: "Aren't we straying as though through an infinite nothing? Isn't empty space breathing at us?" (2001, 120).
89. Nietzsche, *Twilight of the Idols and The Anti-Christ*, 179.
90. Many critics have written substantially on the topic of animality in psychoanalysis, especially in Freud's case histories popularized as *Wolf-Man* and *Rat-Man*. Please see *Freud and the Rat Man* and *Cries of the Wolf Man* by Patriack J. Mahony as well as *Rat Man* by Stuart Schneiderman.
91. Freud, *Civilization and Its Discontents*, trans. James Strachey (New York: Norton, 1961), 39.
92. Ibid., 76.
93. Ibid., 84.
94. Ibid., 87.
95. Ibid.
96. Ibid., 100.
97. Victoria Hamilton, *Narcissism and Oedipus: The Children of Psychoanalysis* (London: Routledge and Kegan Paul, 1982), 278.
98. Freud, *Civilization and Its Discontents*, 36.
99. Freud, *The Future of an Illusion*, trans. James Strachey (New York: Norton, 1961), 55.
100. Ibid., 56.
101. Ibid., 24–25.
102. Ibid., 38.
103. In general, Freud seldom argues with philosophers and possibly for good reasons. However, in *Civilization and Its Discontents*, he did occasionally express his doubt about the dubious subjects the philosophers invoked for possible redemption of the self or the subject of spirit. For instance, he mocks the vain efforts of those philosophers "who think they can rescue the God of religion by replacing him by an impersonal shadowy and abstract principle, and to address them with the warming word: 'You shalt not take the name of the Lord thy God in vain!'" (1961, 22–23). This statement might as well be interpreted as a slant against Hegel's idea of Spirit/Specter in terms of the abstract metaphysical Subject to replace the Christian God. In *The Future of an Illusion*, Freud also critiques conjurations of philosophers: "They give the name of 'God' to some vague abstraction which they have created for themselves; . . . notwithstanding that their God is now nothing more than an insubstantial shadow and no longer the mighty personality of religious doctrines" (1961, 41). It certainly reminds us of Hegel's Specter or Spirit that is identified as the Christian God; for Freud, pure spirit is pure illusion or mere phantom.
104. Terry Eagleton, *The Ideology of the Aesthetic* (Malden: Blackwell P, 1990), 270.
105. Gilles Deleuze and Felix Guattari, *Anti-Oedipus: Capitalism and Schizophrenia*, trans. Robert Hurley, Mark Semm, and Helen R. Lane (Minneapolis: U of Minnesota P, 1987), 75, 102.
106. Gilles Deleuze and Felix Guattari, *A Thousand Plateaus: Capitalism and Schizophrenia*, trans. Brian Massumi (Minneapolis: U of Minnesota P, 1983), 37.
107. Pietro Pucci, *Oedipus and the Fabrication of the Father* (Baltimore: Johns Hopkins UP, 1992), 9.

108. Freud, *The Future of an Illusion*, 24.

109. Ibid., 28. 54.

110. Ibid., 16.

111. Freud, "On Narcissism: "An Introduction," in *The Standard Edition of the Complete Psychological Works of Sigmund Freud,* trans. James Strachey, vol. 14 (London: Hogarth P, 1955), 94.

112. Ibid.

113. Hamilton, *Narcissism and Oedipus*, 23.

114. Freud, *Civilization and Its Discontents*, 79.

115. Jean-Joseph Goux, *Oedipus, Philosopher*, trans. Catherine Porter (Stanford: Stanford UP, 1993), 82.

116. Roland Barthes, *The Pleasure of the Text,* trans. Richard Miller (New York: Hill and Wang, 1975). 47.

III

The Subject of the Other(s) in Ontology and Heterologies

Chapter Five

Oracles and Ghosts

The Dubious Other in Lacan's Discourse of the Subject

I. REPEATING AFTER FREUD AND THE SACRED WORDS FROM THE SPECTRAL OTHER

In "The Freudian Thing, or the Meaning of the Return to Freud in Psychoanalysis," Lacan situates himself conspicuously as well as dubiously in the so-called poststructural "return to the meaning of Freud." Lacan suggests, "One began only to repeat after Freud the word of his discovery: *it speaks*."[1] In Lacan's view, the unconscious that "speaks" resides in the field of the other. He clarifies, "The Other is, therefore, the locus in which constitutes the I who speaks to him who hears."[2] In this dialogue between "I" and "him," the speaking subject postulated by Lacan seems to be inescapably circumscribed by a centric, encompassing, and spectral Other. Thus, the proposed return to Freud in this case initiates an infatuated repetition, i.e., "only to repeat" Freud's words after his death. After all, Freud is acknowledged as the father of psychoanalysis, a kind of "Holy Father" to some degree. Eventually, the return to Freud somewhat turns into a repetition of the sacred words from a holy father in a spectral sphere, symptomatic more of an *oedipalist's obsession* rather than a *poststructuralist's différance*.

In "The Subversion of the Subject and the Dialectics of Desire in the Freudian Unconscious," Lacan implicitly refers to Hamlet's expectation from his father's ghost to illustrate the subject's position to the Other in terms of anticipation of an oracle. Lacan writes: "That is why the question *of* the Other . . .comes back to the subject from the place from which he expects an oracular reply."[3] To evoke Hamlet's Ghost here, "remember me" are the ghost's departing words or a kind of "*afterword*" from the dead father that reappears in a *postmortem* form. Similarly, by returning to Freud and repeating after his words, Lacan likely intends to resurrect Freud's Ghost and haunt the psychoanalytical discourse with the sacred words from the spectral Freud. Ironically, the return *to* Father Freud becomes a return *of* the ghostly other, and Lacan's post-Freudian discourse turns into a neurotic repetition after the Ghost Freud. In contrast, if Freud attempts to identify with Oedipus the master-reader and decodes the riddle of man in terms of a "neurotic subject" according to his master text, the Oedipal paradigm, then Lacan, more or less acting out like the neurotic Oedipus, is obsessed with the oracles or the sacred words from the ghost-father Freud and endeavors to encrypt the mystery of the subject from where "*it speaks,*" i.e., the locus of the uncanny and spectral Other.

In "Desire, Life and Death," Lacan directly cites Oedipus as an exemplary case to attest to the subject's relation to the other in terms of an oracular fulfillment: "Oedipus achieved the full realization of the speech of the oracles which already named his destiny even before he was born."[4] Hence, Oedipus, as "the central knot of speech," is in effect neurotically enacting and implementing "an order of gods" or the mystical words from some divine father. These oracles prefigure his life, his destiny, and his history. Lacan reminds us: "Oedipus' history has for a long time, forever, been written. . . . Everything happens as a function of the oracle."[5] Thus, oracles are deemed the enigmatic sacred texts inscribed by a spectral or divine other, i.e., the *afterword* of a spectral father. By inserting words into the unconscious in terms of the other, Lacan reconfigures the subject, I believe, as *the subject qua other* or the subject conjured up by the "mystic" words of the uncanny other. To some extent, the oracles as the sacred words and the holy laws of the divine fathers are comparable to the linguistic and phallic structures of the Lacanian symbolic order.

In Lacan's view, the constitution of Oedipus' desire, or the subjectivities of Oedipus, is predestined by oracles or holy scripts prior to his birth. That is to say, the very stuff of his being and the very content of his unconscious are dictated, inscribed, and prescribed by a symbolic order or some sacred texts. Instead of possessing himself, Oedipus finds his subject dispossessed and disposed by the oracles issued from those holy-father figures. His relentless efforts to escape the power of the mystic oracles paradoxically demonstrate his neurotic obsession with them. In this context, this oracular other figures as the signifying locus that both inaugurates and possesses the subject like a riddle. Consequently, Lacan situates his speculation of the subject in various spheres and capacities of otherness in terms of what I call the *subject qua other*. The other in this context becomes the crux to figure out the Lacanian cryptic subject as well as his enigmatic desire.[6]

II. THE GROTESQUE: SURREALISTIC IMAGES, POSTSTRUCTURALIST IDEAS, AND MODERN ETHOS

Lacan has diagnosed all kinds of grotesque symptoms in his psychoanalytic discourse of the subject—neurotics and psychotics haunted by images and words. It remains to investigate how much Lacan has contributed to the grotesque studies or to what extent the grotesque as a trope has influenced Lacan's appraisal of his subject, and moreover, to what degree the Lacanian subject itself, either in the imaginary or the symbolic order, is inherently grotesque in the first place. It is worthwhile to track, briefly, the contextual frameworks of the Lacanian subject's coming into being, i.e., his entangled relationship with Surrealists and his close connection with poststructuralists. In fact, surrealistic images inhabit Lacan's imaginary subject and poststructuralist ideas pervade Lacan's symbolic order.

Most postmodern theorists (poststructuralists in particular) have suspended the concept of the subject because in principle they refute any possibility of language's capability to install the subject in its ontological locus or any other pre-established unitary systems; instead, the subject subsists along the chain of signifiers, disposed as one word among others, without final signification or sublime transcendence. Jean-François Lyotard argues, for instance, that the subject has disintegrated due to the slippery effect of excessive signifiers. His famous *The Postmodern Condition* reiterates this position: "The social subject itself seems to dissolve in this dissemination of language games."[7] In other words, language games become the fundamental postmodern condition to recuperate the subject in terms of dispersion. The subject, in a postmodern context, has no interior except mosaic textures of interlinked linguistic networks. Derrida's *Positions* fully represents the typical poststructuralist posture toward the current state of the subject. Derrida observes: "It confirms that the subject, and first of all the conscious and speaking subject, depends upon the system of differences and the movement of *différance*."[8] Thus, what is called "the subject" as an ontological category is actually constituted by various tissues of differences, and as such, the subject is meshed in an infinite network of word play, deferred and suspended in a chain of signifiers. In short, according to Derrida and his likes, "There is no subject who is agent, author, and master of *difference*. . . . Subjectivity—like objectivity—is an effect of *différance*, an effect inscribed in a system of *difference*."[9]

Unlike his contemporaries (Derrida, Foucault, Barthes, and others) who have suspended, dismissed, or dismantled the subject without any hesitation, equating *lettre* and *l'être* with or without *différance,* Lacan, for some obscure reasons, is reluctant to relinquish the tenacious subject altogether. In *Subjectivity and Intersubjectivity in Modern Philosophy and Psychoanalysis: A Study of Sartre, Binswanger, Lacan, and Habermas*, Roger Frie notes: "For

Lacan, the subject is dislocated and decentered, though it is never entirely subverted."[10] Instead, Lacan seems to retain the subject and positions himself precariously in this linguistic game by anchoring the subject in the context of the other and in terms of *the subject qua other*. For Lacan, even though decentered, the subject has to figure as a subject of some sort. Put this way, Lacan remains one of a handful of postmodern thinkers who desperately hang onto the subject and obstinately insist on keeping the "proper name" of the subject, probably *in the name of* someone or some other—a father in a *postmortem* condition perhaps? (Otherwise, why is there a return to or a repetition after Freud?)

We have to remember, it is not Freud alone who creates the psychoanalytical discourse. Instead, it is the grotesque narratives (articulated, repressed, silenced, or hidden) from neurotics, psychotics, perverts, and hysterias that provide both the elusive subject matter and the enigmatic speech for psychoanalysis. The subject of psychoanalysis can in no way be a normal one except fragmented, decentered, incoherent, and disintegrated. From this perspective, the psychoanalytic subject would be "inconceivable" without the *riddling* words from the grotesque other, or "the system of differences and the movement of *différance,*" to bend Derrida's idea to this occasion. Hence, Lacan proposes, "Psychoanalysis should be the science of language inhabited by the subject. From the Freudian point of view man is the subject captured and tortured by language."[11] Further, Lacan argues: "If the neurotic inhabits language, the psychotic is inhabited, possessed, by language."[12] That is to say, all subjects, neurotic or psychotic, are subject to a de-centric language, namely, obsessed with or dispossessed by the cryptic words in the field of the other.

Despite Lacan's departure from the Surrealist movement, in *Jacques Lacan: The French Context*, Marcelle Marini notes, "Paradoxically, it was among the surrealists that Lacan became famous."[13] Indeed, Lacan has maintained a close relationship with surrealists like Dali, Crevel, and others in his early academic years and even contributed to their periodical *Minotaure*.[14] However, Lacan did eventually distance himself from them because he did not share their enthusiasm, indulgence, and exaltation of madness, feigned or real. However, the Lacanian subject, the imaginary in specific, is structurally shaped by the contagious surrealistic imageries, especially those grotesque images of the fragmented bodies and distorted torsos. In fact, there are plentiful explicit references and implicit allusions to surrealistic images in Lacan's speculation on the imaginary subject.

Particularly in his essay "The Mirror Stage," more than once, Lacan refers to grotesque images to illustrate his theory of the fragmented body in the imaginary order. For instance, he writes, "It then appears in the form of disjointed limbs, or of those organs represented in exoscopy, growing wings and taking up arms for intestinal persecutions—the very same that the visionary Hieronymus Bosch has fixed, for all time, in painting, in their ascent from the fifteenth century to the imaginary zenith of modern man."[15] Also in "Aggressivity in Psychoanalysis," he alludes to surrealistic images to demonstrate the disintegrated corporeality of the imaginary subject: "These are the images of castration, mutilation, dismemberment, dislocation, evisceration, devouring, bursting open of the body, in short, the *imagos* that I have grouped together under the apparently structural term of *imagos of the fragmented body*."[16] Lacan frequently evokes Bosch, the precursor of Surrealism, to address the narcissistic desire of aggressivity in the imaginary order; for instance, Lacan writes: "We must turn to the works of Hieronymus Bosch for an atlas of all the aggressive images that torment mankind."[17] These surrealistic imageries impart a fervent sense of otherness; and moreover, the grotesque vision in effect constitutes the cognitive framework and theoretical base for Lacan to formulate his theory of *the subject qua other* in the imaginary order.

Hence, Lacan's figuration of the imaginary subject is associated with the grotesque images produced by Surrealists while his configuration of the symbolic subject is grounded in the de-centric linguistic operations postulated by poststructuralists. Furthermore, the subject of the other in terms of decenterment and disintegration more or less resonates with the lingering ethos of the modern culture. Lacan argues that one of the most important discoveries by Freud is that "the very centre of the human being was no longer to be found at the place assigned to it by the whole humanist tradition."[18] Clearly, the Lacanian subject qua other to a great extent epitomizes the grotesque modern subject, decentered, divided, disintegrated, or lost. Further, Lacan points out that "man only deludes himself when he believes his true place is at their axis, which is nowhere."[19] This certainly sounds like a tragic modernist, recalling the pessimistic doctrines of existentialism and, especially, echoing Nietzsche's prediction: we are all mad after the death of God, i.e., lost and decentered in the wake of the central void.

In "Introduction" to *The Subject of Lacan: A Lacanian Reader for Psychologists*, Malone and Friedlander observe: "The image of the *self* as integral (wholistic) and autonomous has virtually defined Western culture since beginning."[20] This statement succinctly sums up the central issue Lacan intends to contest—the singular and unitary subject. Lacan dismisses any idea of a total subject as he says, "The idea of the unifying unity of the human condition has always had on me the effect of a scandalous lie."[21] Specifically, Lacan demystifies the illusory image of the narcissistic totality in the imaginary as well as disrupts the egocentric mythology of the singular subject in the symbolic order. In both cases, the subject of the other is exposed as a subject of lack, that is, a ghost-subject lacking both singularity and presence.

In the tragic spirit of modernism, Lacan positions his subject in a *postmortem* form: the imaginary subject is construed as a lost subject that is nostalgically recuperated as a narcissistic illusion, and the symbolic subject is projected as a phantom-subject that is abolished at the moment of representation. Therefore, beyond the fragmented images of Surrealism and the decentering signifiers of poststructuralism, the Lacanian subject's *hysterical* coming into being or nothing repeats to a certain degree the last mythology of the neurotic modern individual that is centralized on a void in the wake of the death of God and subsequently haunted by the return of a ghost father in a *postmortem* fashion. Lacan writes, "In the 'emancipated' man of modern society, this splitting reveals, right down to the depths of his being, a neurosis of self-punishment, with the hysterico-hypochondriac symptoms of its functional inhibitions . . . ; it is our daily task to open up to this being of nothingness the way of his meaning in a discreet fraternity."[22] In a word, the human subject is lost to and haunted by some spectral Other.

In various contexts, Lacan reiterates that the subject in either the imaginary or the symbolic sphere is instituted in relation to the other or the Other. As Lacan repeats Freud's discovery that "man isn't entirely in man,"[23] he further points out "it is in the space of the Other that he sees himself and the point from which he looks at himself is also in that space. Now, this is also the point from which he speaks . . . , it is in the locus of the Other that he begins."[24] Henceforth, the subject appears like a hostage captivated by some omnipotent Other, and among the various others named by Lacan are the mirror image, the unconscious, language, and speeches. Surprisingly, the phallus, the central figure of the symbolic order, is seldom explicitly erected as the other, probably elided in the slippery chain of substitutions in the metonymic discourse of desire. Evidently, if the poststructuralist Lacan perceives language as the other, then the *oedipalist* Lacan leans upon the Phallus as the Other. However, what seldom gets attention so far points to another other in the context of the modernist void. That is, the Other in a *postmortem* condition emerges as the spectral Other.

In the past, most scholarship has primarily focused on speculating the Lacanian subject in terms of lack. To sustain the subject in name, Lacan positions *the subject of lack* in a locus of complicated structures and entangled relationships in three different orders, the imaginary, the symbolic, and the real. He absolutely refuses to speculate on the subject in the real because, he insists, the real is the impossible. In other words, the subject never emerges in the category of reality at all. Instead, the subject, to repeat (after) Lacan here, is essentially a subject of lack, want-of-being or desire. In "Desire, Life and Death," Lacan writes, "Desire is in a relation of being to lack. This lack is the lack of being properly speaking. It isn't the lack of this or that, but lack of being whereby the being exists."[25] In other words, the subject arises merely as some sort of fantasy projected by desire or is "immanent" in hallucination in either the imaginary or the symbolic order. Therefore, Lacan argues: "The subject situates himself as determined by the phantasy. . . . The subject sustains himself as desiring in relation to an ever more complex signifying ensemble."[26] In this case, I propose *the subject qua other* as an alternative term to further explore what is concealed in *the subject of lack*; that is, the subject comes into being or lacking due to mediation, institution, and dispossession by some enigmatic and captivating *other*. The other, initiating desire in the subject, anchors the subject in fantasy or impossibility, i.e., want-of-being. Thus, either via an optic illusion of a specular image or through an immanent hallucination of a linguistic system of *différance*, *the subject qua other* yields a subject of lack—lacking both totality and presence. In this context, the ontology of the Lacanian subject is not only grounded in lack or wanting of being, but also that the subject finds itself ontologically changing into a ghostly other haunted by some spectral other. As a result, both imaginary and symbolic subjects turn out to be *a subject qua other* under the spell of some exorcising other.

III. THE SPECULAR OTHER AND THE IMAGINARY SUBJECT

Lacan discusses the subject's imaginary relation to the other in several seminars, particularly in "The Mirror Stage" and "Aggressivity in Psychoanalysis" collected in *Ecrits*.[27] He analyzes the optic illusions reflected in the mirror to speculate on the subject's formation in terms of "the imaginary." He observes that, at the age of six months old, a child sees in the mirror a reflected image that initiates a paradoxical process of both unification and separation. The mirror stage is based on the hypothesis of a dialectic game of "both me and other than me," real and unreal, identification and alienation. In the mirror relation is constructed a paradox, a duality, a distance, and a fissure between self and other, namely, an *uncanny subject qua other*.

In "The Mirror Stage," Lacan postulates that the mirror initiates a deceptive relationship when "the *I* is precipitated in a primordial form," and eventually "the transformation that takes place in the subject when he assumes an image," and "man projects himself, with the phantoms that dominate him."[28] The hallucinatory phantom of the imaginary "ideal-I" resides in a space of fantasy, seducing the subject in terms of *projection* rather than *reflection*. The mirage, or the *imago* as Lacan calls it, in the imaginary order is but a specular illusion of a coherent, autonomous, and total subject. Similarly, in "Topics of the Imaginary," Lacan demystifies the illusionary mirror-image by saying that "man, for the first time, has the experience of seeing himself, or reflecting on himself and conceiving himself as other than he is . . . , which entirely structures his fantasy life."[29] In effect, it involves more *conceiving* than *reflecting*, and in addition, as Lacan observes, the imaginary subject is instituted and inscribed by *an other* or a phantom that prefigures the subject in the sphere of fantasy. As Lacan points out, "it is in the Other that the subject is constituted as ideal . . . , as ego, or ideal ego."[30] Hence, the imaginary subject as the "ideal ego" is constituted by an illusory other or phantom, more in terms of *projection* than *perception*, desire than reality, conjuration than reflection. In other words, the subject perceived in the imaginary as an ideal ego or an integral and total being is but a phantasmagoric *alter-ego* conjured up in a fantasy space.

The imaginary order in this case, consisting of illusive images and narcissistic fantasies, opens ways for the child to anticipate the delusion of a unified body and an integral subject that he objectively lacks. Contingent upon perceptual confusion between self and other, the subject is "caught up in the lure of spatial identification" with a succession of fantasies that transform it "from a fragmented body-image to a form of its totality."[31] The imaginary, Lacan argues, constitutes the locale of misrecognition where the phantasmagoric other, an idealized image of a unitary subject, is *introjected* as the totality of a singular self. In his return to Freud, Lacan has been consistently battling against the egocentric object-relation theory. For Lacan, the ego is a fetish, an obsession, and an uncanny apparition. As an illusionary and a deceptive mirage, the ego camouflages a subject of lack. Lacan strongly objects to egology: "It's a function of mirage, in which the subject refinds himself only as misrecognition and negation."[32] That is why he insists, "psychoanalysis isn't an egology."[33] Particularly in "The Mirror Stage," Lacan denounces the autonomous and total subject based upon "egology" because, as he explicates, it is "the *function of méconnaissance* that characterizes the ego in all its structures" and it is "the *méconnaissances* that constitute the ego, the illusion of autonomy" via "the visual *Gestalt* of his own body."[34] It is via *misrecognition* that the subject is misconceived as total and integral and further, based upon the optic illusion of a corporal totality, the subject is projected as an *imago* of singular presence. Consequently, the entire dialectic of the subject's coming into being in the imaginary is staged between reflection and projection, lack and desire, reality and fantasy, perception and misrecognition.

Lacan identifies the mirror stage as the site of primary narcissism that "determines the formal structure of man's ego."[35] That is to say, the subject falls in love with a projected ideal ego as the object of desire and forms a narcissistic closure with an optic illusion in the magic mirror. As a structural concept, the mirror serves to conceive the subject in its primordial narcissistic form in an enclosed self-reflexive specular space. Moreover, this imaginary self-reflexivity in the mirror stage precipitates a narcissistic quest for the subject of totality as the object of desire, but what eludes him is actually the integral ontological presence the mirror never gives back. Eventually, the subject is caught in this intra-subjective space of self-mirroring—a narcissistic movement of self-duplicating and self-doubling. In other words, primary narcissism is fundamental and instrumental to the structure of the total subject in terms of an illusory *alter-ego* conjured up by a magic mirror. The ego qua other in the imaginary projects a subject of fantasy and this phantomlike alter-ego figures as a spectral other that entraps, alienates, and possesses the subject.

From Freud, we learn that a narcissist is incapable of recognizing the difference between me and not me, or, in this context, the self and the specular image in the mirror—in effect a hallucinatory other.[36] Instead, the subject is fixed and transfixed by an image from the other as a form of an idolized ideal-I. The narcissistic mode of identification characterizes the general ontological principle for all subjects of totality and singularity as Lacan points outs that "[t]his narcissistic moment in the subject is to be found in all the genetic phases of the individual, in all the degrees of human accomplishment in the person."[37] In addition, Lacan notes, in "this erotic relation," "the human individual fixes upon himself an image that alienates him from himself"[38] and creates "his discordance" with reality. Due to the impossible coincidence between oneself and the optic image, the subject is forever hunting for and haunted by an elusive mirage of a total being. As a moment of both alienation of the self and paralyzing fixation to the mirrored double, the mirror stage initiates a complex process of both identification and estrangement. This yearning for the specular other, or the other as the idealized object of desire, displaces, divides, and decenters the subject. In short, this dialectics of desire marks the subject's permanent alienation from and impossible coincidence with the misleading "ideal-I" in a futile narcissistic quest.

Further, the mirror stage not only fabricates a falsified image of the self, but also situates the subject as *possessed* by a phantom other. This means, what is dramatized in the imaginary stage is not only that the projected phantom-other is mistaken as an idealized object of desire for the subject, but also the subject is overtaken and disposed by an alluring other in a spectral space. If the subject is fixed or transfixed by *a specular image of the self* in terms of *a spectral other* in the mirror, then the process of the subject's "ontological coming into being" becomes a sort of the Derridean hauntology. The imaginary subject in this case translates into a ghost figure, both *specular* and *spectral*. Here the ontology of the *subject qua other* turns into a hauntology of a *ghost qua specter*.

In Lacan's view, subjectivization of the subject in the imaginary begins with a series of narcissistic fantasies of the lost object. The image in the mirror, the myth of totality and wholeness, is nostalgically reconstructed as loss: loss of a symbiotic paradise and loss of an integral subject. As Jane Gallap in *Reading Lacan* notes, "The mirror stage is thus high tragedy: a brief moment of doomed glory, a paradise lost."[39] It is no wonder, according to Lacan's diagnosis, all neurotics and psychotics are obsessed with this specular and spectral other in a narcissistic quest. In other words, the Lacanian subject in the imaginary is based upon an irretrievable "primordial loss" of a fantasized totality and symbiosis, characteristic of the grotesque obsession of all modernist protagonists.

Anthony Wilden's remarks in his "Lacan and Discourse of the Other" certainly throw light on all modernists' quest for lost identity. Wilden observes: "Since the discovery of the lack of object is for Lacan the condition and the cause of desire, the adult quest for transcendence, lost time, lost paradises, lost plenitude, or any of the myriad forms the lack of object may take, including the most grotesque and the most absurd—can be reduced, if one wishes, to the question at the root of neurosis and psychosis, the question asked by Oedipus: 'who (or what) am I?'"[40] Lacan believes that the symptoms of neurotics, "hysterical or obsessional," are distinguished by an obsession "with the imaginary dialectic of himself and the other."[41] This means the neurotic is typically fixated on an imaginary other as the lost object that is retroactively recuperated as desire. Lacan notes: "In the desires of obsessional neurotics we have already encountered the impossible as object of desire. . . . What characterizes the obsessional neurotic in particular is that he emphasizes the confrontation with this impossibility. In other words, he sets everything up so that the object of his desire becomes the signifier of this impossibility."[42] Especially in the context of the modernist ethos, though the ideal ego is lost, the narcissistic pursuit of the illusion of a lost paradise or a singular subject is never lost. On the contrary, the neurotics take this loss as an impossible desire—the grotesque desire—and are engrossed with an illusory object of impossibility.[43]

In sum, the singular subject in the imaginary is symptomatic of a psychotic obsession with and a fixation on the illusion of a presumed total being retroactively instituted as loss, in effect a narcissistic pursuit of a misleading grandiose subject in terms of an illusory other. In this case, the imaginary subject in the mirror stage is not simply delusional or deceptive, but also hauntological in the sense that an ephemeral image of the other dominates and overtakes the subject as a phantom. *The subject qua other,* in this case, turns into *a subject qua specter.*

IV. THE LINGUISTIC OTHER AND THE SYMBOLIC SUBJECT

If the imaginary subject is noted as *a subject qua other* in terms of images and phantoms, then the subject in the symbolic is characterized as *a subject qua other* in terms of language games. Either way, the Lacanian subject seems unable to escape its inevitable destiny of being besieged, dislodged, and dispossessed by the other. The symbolic subject, though usually marked as a subject of *lack*, does not exactly connote "lack of signification" or "unsignifiable" as most postmodern scholars would like to argue. On the contrary, the subject is lacking precisely due to *over*-signification, that is, the subject is lost, displaced, and dissipated in an incessant flow and flux of words that keep the subject sliding along a slippery chain of signifiers. The subject in the field of the other becomes a puppet chained to the signifying games of words. In *Jacques Lacan: The French Context*, Marcelle Marini notes that "the Lacanian texts turn the human world into a puppet theater where the puppets are manipulated by the threads of the signifier."[44] As Lacan remarks: "The subject is subject only from being subjected to the field of the Other."[45] Hence, signification implicates subjection and, further, inauguration of the subject turns into subordination to the locus of the Other. The subject's coming into being in the symbolic order is initiated via the rites of passage of the other—a linguistic conjuration.[46]

In general, the symbolic subject meshed in language is subject to "the double play" of the signifying games: metaphorical transfiguration and metonymic displacement. The moment it is initiated into the symbolic order, the subject is represented and overtaken by the other in an indefinite linguistic process that both sustains and dislocates the subject toward elsewhere, ex-centric and de-centric. In the field of the other, the subject thus emerged is never self-identical or self-present, but always disparate and deferred in an infinite process of dispersion along the chain of signifiers that forecloses any possibility of its ontological presence or totality. In "The Subject and the Other: Alienation," Lacan clarifies, "The Other is the locus in which is situated the chain of the signifier that governs whatever may be made present of the subject."[47] It is the Other, the field of signifiers, that both evokes the subject into being and simultaneously exorcises it into absence in a linguistic rite of conjuration. Lacan observes: "The signifier, producing itself in the field of the Other, makes manifest the subject of its signification. But it functions as a signifier only to reduce the subject in question to being no more than a signifier, to petrify the subject in the same movement in which it calls the subject to function, to speak, as subject."[48] Put differently, the subject that is called into being in the field of the other is reduced to a figure of other's signification.

Further, the subject "in the field of the Other," as Lacan observes, "represents the subject for another signifier, which other signifier has as its effect the *aphanisis* of the subject."[49] Represented as a signifier, the subject is chained to other signifiers that render the subject divided and lost in a linguistic labyrinth. That is why Lacan insists, "There is no subject without, somewhere, *aphanisis* of the subject, and it is in this alienation, in this fundamental division, that the dialectic of the subject is established."[50] Hence, the subject qua other in the symbolic order is constitutionally, fundamentally, and irremediably schizophrenic, characterized by its ex-centric and de-centric position in terms of alienation, division, and disappearance. Put simply, born as an uncanny figure to fade, the subject disappears at the moment of its entrance into the symbolic order and is subsequently reduced to a ghost figure and disembodied as a subject of absence. So Lacan postulates, "It is necessary to find the subject as a lost object."[51] As a result, the subject, founded on a primal loss at its inauguration, comes into being only to lose itself in the field of the other.

In "The Function and Field of Speech and Language in Psychoanalysis," Lacan illustrates the subject's "ever-growing dispossession" and incessant displacements by a chain of others. Lacan mimics, "For in this labour which he undertakes to reconstruct *for another*, he rediscovers the fundamental alienation that made him construct it *like another*, and which has always destined it to be taken from him *by another*."[52] Hence, the subject finds himself caught in an infinite metonymic game of substitution by other signifiers like a purloined letter. Malcolm Bower in *Lacan* mocks the Lacanian subject's "adventures in being" since "the other-infested subject can have no other destiny than that of successive disappearance and return, entity and non-entity, sense and nonsense, concentration and dispersal, being there and being gone."[53] Indeed, in his adventures in the field of the other, the subject finds himself in an uncanny state and a slippery position between identification and loss, designation and displacement, presence and absence. Consequently, subjection of the subject to the effects of signifiers prefigures the subject to be *other-wise*.

Lacan writes: "So, it is between the signifier in the form of the proper name of a man and the signifier that metaphorically abolishes him" that the subject emerges paradoxically.[54] In receiving a name from the other, the subject is deprived of his being and displaced elsewhere. Symbolically designated in the *name* of a subject, the subject finds itself a subject of lack, i.e., *aphanisis*. Subjected to the effect of signifiers, the subject is no longer the master in possession of itself; instead, the subject is denounced, disowned, and deprived by the very discourse that is supposed to represent it. Symbolic identification becomes symbolic dispossession and nullifying erasure. The moment one assumes the position of a subject in terms of a proper name, he discovers himself to be disposed as another signifier under the sliding power of words, losing his property as a subject altogether.

The Lacanian subject centers on the notion of "splitting," "the *spaltung*," a primary discord as the fundamental ontological condition that renders the subject internally divided and permanently incoherent. Lacan writes: "the moment of a 'fading' or eclipse of the subject . . . is closely bound up with the *Spaltung* or splitting that it suffers from its subordination to the signifier."[55] The subject's subordination to the signifier introduces a gap or self-division in the ontological structure of the subject, i.e., decentered at the origin and born divided, so to speak. Hence, *the subject qua other* as the effect of the signifier is configured in a perpetual displacement, decenterment, and disembodiment. Therefore, the inherent 'hysterical' structure of the symbolic order deforms and disfigures the subject into a grotesque one.

Due to the sliding effects of the signifiers, the subject can hope neither to be whole nor to cohere into a singular or unitary being. Coming into being for Lacan means subordination to the other and hystericization of the self. The dream of retrieving a whole, autonomous, unitary, and total subject is but another metaphysical illusion of impossible desire. Lacan observes: "In any case, man cannot aim at being whole" because "the 'total personality' is another of the deviant premises of modern psychotherapy."[56] Moreover, Lacan argues strongly against "any conception of the unity of the psyche, of the supposed totalizing, synthesizing psyche,"[57] or any myth of singular ontology. Put this way, the subject, deferred to infinity on a sliding chain of the signifiers, can never expect to escape its radical ex-centricity.

In this context, the Lacanian subject is immanently doomed to be schizophrenic, so to speak. However, John P. Muller in "Language, Psychosis, and the Subject in Lacan" points out, "The alternative is either death or psychosis."[58] Indeed, Lacan has offered nothing else but death as the alternative for the psychotic subject. He believes that "the death instinct is only the mask of the symbolic order. . . . The symbolic order is simultaneously non-being and insisting to be."[59] Lacan opines that symbolization of being is a death wish in disguise, contending that the subject is "entering into the play of the signifiers only in the mode of death" and "the subject enters the game as the dymmy (mort)."[60] What would that be if not a ghost in a haunted spectral space? It is as if the subject enters the discourse in a dead mode, or in a post*mortem* condition.

All these language games point us to one convergent point: after all, the symbolic order belongs to the Other, be it oracular, spectral, or hauntological. In "Seminar on 'The Purloined Letter'," Lacan states: "If what Freud discovered and rediscovers with a perpetually increasing sense of shock has a meaning, it is that the displacement of the signifier determines the subjects in their acts, in their destiny, in their refusals, in their blindnesses, in their end and in their fate . . . , everything . . . will follow the path of the signifier."[61] However, if the subject "will follow the path of the signifier" as Lacan claims, then it is extremely important and absolutely crucial to figure out *which signifier* the subject will follow toward his destiny or *which letter* will displace or *misplace* his identity. In "The Agency of the Letter in the Unconscious or Reason since Freud," Lacan mocks: "I think where I am not, therefore I am where I do not think."[62] This is not merely a parody of the Cartesian cogito or Descartes' motto: "*Cognito ergo sum*" (I think therefore I am), it also points to a perplexing field of the uncanny other where "*it speaks*."

V. THE DUBIOUS OTHER(S) IN THE UNCONSCIOUS

Desire, Language, and Other(s)

When Lacan says the discourse of the unconscious is the discourse of the other, we have to take his word *differently*, not only because the unconscious is designated as a space of alterity, full of incoherent and heterogeneous drives, but also predominantly because language itself is regarded as a field of the other, rife with linguistic *différance*. In this "other" domain, language generates desire for the subject; but due to its inherent metonymic structure, signifiers both initiate desire and at the same time postpone desire on a sliding chain, thus leaving a gap or fissure in the subject and rendering the subject impossible and its desire unrealizable. Lacan notes that "the Other, the locus of speech, is also the locus of this want, or lack."[63] The other, the locus of speech, issues the subject's desire and inaugurates a lack of being for desire to function in place of the posed subject. Evoked by language, desire remains strictly in a linguistic sphere as a symbolic articulation. Past critics have primarily focused on speculating the complex relationship between language and desire in terms of evocation, lack, displacement, and impossible fulfillment.

However, we do need to exercise some caution to carefully set apart the poststructuralist Lacan from the psychoanalyst, or particularly, the *oedipalist* Lacan. Though hardly distinct, the poststructuralist Lacan speaks in a language *different* from the psychoanalyst or *oedipalist* Lacan, especially in configuring the unconscious in terms of otherness. In other words, there is no *one single other* in Lacan's discourse of the unconscious. We need to distinguish that, on the one hand, the field of the other seems to be technically mediated via a generic linguistic game in abstract terms, and on the other hand, this "other" realm is governed by specific speeches and distinctive metaphors that prescribe its value, meaning, and culture. Therefore, we have to discreetly discern, beyond the general state of abstract linguistic mediation, *whose speeches* function as the authoritative articulation to institute the unconscious desire, and ultimately, *which word* figures as the "mystical" or "cultic" signifier in the name of the transcendental other to dominate the entire unconscious territory in absolute terms.

The other assumes manifold postures and possesses varied meanings in Lacan's discourse of the subject. I believe that the term "other" in the symbolic order is posited in three inter-related and overlapped areas: the unconscious (desire of the other), language (discourse as the other) and the phallus (law of the other). Many critics, like Ellie Ragland-Sullivan, have extensively discussed the effect of signifiers upon desire in a poststructuralist framework, i.e., the linkage as well as gap between words and desire in generic and abstract terms.[64] However, I notice, Lacan's return to the unconscious exposes and highlights the father's words and a mystical figure of desire in particular, i.e., oracles and the phallus. Here, the words from the father are anticipated as the sacred speeches and the phallus is worshipped as a holy signifier. Thus, Lacan's sophisticated metonymic game unravels a chain of the others in a complicated configuration of unconscious desires. In this linguistic fort-da game of the others, we have to demarcate carefully what is veiled or exposed, slipped or elided. In this circumstance, the locus of the other is not just inhabited by generic "pure signifiers" or abstract "empty words" in general; instead, the field of the other is loaded with the privileged "full words" from the (dead) father or particular proper names and specific holy texts.[65] Therefore, beyond the general theory of language as the other, I would like to focus on analyzing how the unconscious desire of the subject is conjured up in terms of the oracular other (the father's speeches), the spectral other (the *afterword* of the dead father), and the mystical or Holy Other (the phallus). Lastly, despite Lacan's declaration of "no Other of the Other," I intend to inquire into the status of the "other others" *outside* the Lacanian symbolic order—the phallocentric mythology.

The Oracular Other: The Father's Speech and Unconscious Desire

To repeat after Lacan here, the discourse of the unconscious is the discourse of the other. In many of his seminars, Lacan frequently comes back to this theme in terms of the effects of speech on the unconscious of the subject. In one seminar, Lacan states, "The unconscious is constituted by the effects of speech on the subject" and in another, he repeats, "The unconscious is the sum of the effects of speech on a subject."[66] Hence, the site of the unconscious for Lacan is occupied by speeches, or more accurately, the desire of the subject is structured, woven, and possessed by speeches from the other. Thus, according to Lacan, "the unconscious is something that speaks within the subject, beyond the subject."[67] The other in the unconscious appears to speak in an elusive and prophetic idiom that predestines the subject to carry out the "speeches of oracles." That is why Lacan believes that the subject in the field of the other "expects an oracular reply."[68]

Lacan insists "the subject inhabits the world of symbol, that is to say a world of others who speak,"[69] and hence, he asks rhetorically: "Who is this other who speaks in the subject . . . ?"[70] Put differently, Lacan inquires: Who is this other in the unconscious that speaks *in* as well as *to* the subject? The other speaking in the unconscious is by no means an *unknowable other*. Lacan makes it extremely clear that the symbolic order, instead of being organized by any random word, is centered on a specific privileged signifier—*le-Nom-du-Pere* or the Name-of-the-Father—as the locus of the signifying Other. Kristeva, for instance, exposes the privileged position of the speaking other: "The subject exists only inasmuch as it identifies with an ideal other who is the speaking other, the other in so far as he speaks."[71] Since woman constitutes the unspeakable and unspeaking in the symbolic, the only one that is granted the privilege to speak in the unconscious is inalienably a paternal figure. In other words, the father's speech functions in the capacity of the sacred oracles that institute the unconscious desire for the subject. When Lacan claims to insert the words into the unconscious of the subject, he is in effect installing into the subject the father's words in terms of the oracular other. If the unconscious of the subject is dominated by the words from the father in terms of a central other, then the subject qua other is saturated with the authoritative speeches of phallocentric culture in the name of the father.

Lacan believes all speech is demand from the other.[72] Ultimately, the subject comes into being at the other's command or upon the call of the oracles from the father. In "Position of the Unconscious": "Lacan argues that in "his advent as subject . . . was first produced at the other's summoning."[73] It is the father's oracular words as a symbolic demand that initiate the subject's desire and install the subject's position. As a result, the desire *of* the self turns out to be the desire *by* and *for* the other. In "The Subversion of the Subject and the Dialectic of Desire in the Freudian Unconscious," Lacan reminds us, "it is *qua* Other that he desires";[74] in "Position of the Unconscious," he insists "he is but the Other's desire";[75] and in "The Symbolic Order," he reiterates: "the subject exhausts himself in pursuing the desire of the other . . . because his own desire is the desire of the other."[76] Consequently, instead of owning his own desire, the subject pursues what the other desires for him; that is, his desire is subject to the laws, codes, and orders from the other, or the sacred words from the father. By submitting to the father's command and subordinating to the father's law, the subject inescapably follows the symbolic order of the other: inheriting the father's name, repeating (after) the father's words, enacting the father's desire, and imitating the sacred father. Lacan believes that the desire of the subject is determined by "the code of the Other" "since it is from this code that the subject is constituted, which means that it is from the Other that the subject receives even the message that he emits."[77] In other words, the subject is no longer the master to host its own discourse or desire; instead, he is held as a hostage by the names, speeches, and laws from the other.

In "The Function and the Field of Speech and Language in Psychoanalysis," Lacan clarifies: "It is in the *name of the father* that we must recognize the support of the symbolic function which, from the dawn of history, has identified his person with the figure of the law."[78] The symbolic order is constituted and centralized by the father's name and father's law, in fact, the father's words as the sacred law. The dissemination of the father's words impregnates the subject as desire and the subject's entry into the symbolic order is marked by his appropriation of the father's name, words, and laws.

For instance, upon the call from the ghost, Hamlet is commanded to remember his father's name as the cultural legacy and repeat his father's words as the sacred oracles. That is to say, it is the father's name that guarantees him the legitimate ownership of the symbolic order. Thus, the Oedipal rite gains new meaning: the subject undertakes his initiation into the symbolic order by adopting the father's name and repeating the father's words. "The father, the Name-of-the-father," Lacan reminds us, "sustains the structure of desire with the structure of law."[79] In this context, this law does not refer to the generic laws governing the linguistic operation, i.e., metaphor and metonymy, but the phallocentric laws sustained and centralized by the father's name and words.

The Spectral Other: The Dead Father and the Sacred "Afterword"

"The symbolic Father, in so far as he signifies this Law, is the dead Father."[80] The father, for Lacan, is always a "dead" one, a ghost figure that is re-constituted after his disappearance and returns in a spectral apparition. Thus, the demise of the father does not mean the ending of the father at all; on the contrary, his power is generated precisely in this exorcism of departure and return. In other words, Lacan translates the dead body of the father into a spectral phantom of the father, an ontological absence into a spectral presence, consequently initiating a return of a spectral other or some kind of holy father figure. Therefore, the Lacanian subject, as the neurotic Hamlet demonstrates, is not haunted so much by the *disappearance* of the father's dead body as by the *return* of the father's ghost. Mark Taylor in *Altarity* observes: "Never identical with itself, the faulty subject is haunted by an unknowable Other."[81] Actually, the *unknowable Other* reflects very much the familiar image of the dead father in terms of the uncanny Other in a spectral guise.

In "Desire and the Interpretation of Desire in *Hamlet*," Lacan argues that, for Hamlet, "his fate is expressed in terms of a pure signifier."[82] Metaphorically, "a pure signifier" connotes a "ghost signifier," a sort of *afterword* from his dead father or the ghost other in a spectral sphere. That is to say, Hamlet's fate is sealed by a mystical message from his dead father or the ghost's words as the enigmatic oracles. Further, Lacan writes, "In the fantasy . . . , an essential relationship of the subject to this being is localized and fixed."[83] In other words, Hamlet's subject is fixed and transfixed by an elusive specter as Hamlet inquires perplexingly, "Who is speaking?" In this case, it is the cryptic words of a ghost-father that institute Hamlet's unconscious desire and predestine his fate. It is this apparition that provides the oracular narratives directing him towards his mortal rendezvous with his destiny. At the spell of a spectral father, Hamlet's subject is written as a ghost narrative and his life is disposed by the sacred *afterword* of the dead father. Derrida writes: "The one who says 'I am thy Fathers Spirit' can only be taken at his word. An essentially blind submission to his secret, to the secret of his origin."[84] Hence, as Hamlet repeats his father's final words of "remember me" and promises "thy commandment all alone shall live," he follows faithfully the path of the *afterword* from the spectral father and never questions the truth of the enigmatic words from the ghost. Instead, Hamlet regards it as revelation of a sacred oracle and is determined to carry it out for fulfillment.

Lacan regards the symbolic order as a death wish in disguise. In this case, the field of the other that the subject enters is not merely a linguistic domain of words, but a haunted landscape of ghosts. The territory of the other is not only resonant with father's words, but also fraught with the ghostly *afterword* of the spectral father as the sacred oracle in a kind of *postmortem* terrain. Lacan explicates, "The subject's world will essentially consist of the relationship with that being who is the other for him, namely God himself."[85] Lacan might as well say that the subject is subjected to the father as a divine spirit as he points out that "it was the appeal of the void . . . the subject has come compliantly to reply."[86] Hence, the subject comes into being at the call from the spectral other or a spell exorcised by a ghost figure.

In sum, the subject, so it seems, finds himself turning into a ghost figure haunted by a spectral other. In this case, the relationship between the subject and the other is marked by subordination of a ghost to a holy ghost, doubly "ghosting" the subject, i.e., a ghost-subject qua a spectral other in the perspective of hauntology. Consequently, the discourse of the unconscious translates into a discourse of the sacred words/oracles or *afterword* from the spectral others; or, in other words, the unconscious is rife with phallic mythology or the holy texts of the dead fathers. For Lacan, the dead father, as a phantasmagoric apparition, is transubstantiated into a sacred figure of some holy other. It is by submission to this spectral other—the ghost, the dead father, the structural absence or mystic scriptures—that the subject finds himself displaced, decentered, and erased. Hence, the grotesque characters, like Hamlet, are obsessed with and dispossessed by an impossible desire prescribed to him by an oracular narrative from a spectral other, and they are summoned to live up to the full capacity of a phantom subject under the command of a holy ghost.

The Phallic Other: The Holy Arch-Ghost and the Cultic Meta-Signifier

In "The Function and the Field of Speech and Language in Psychoanalysis," Lacan concludes his seminar in this way: "The psychoanalytic experience has rediscovered in man the imperative of the Word as the law that has formed him in its image."[87] Which "Word" in capital letters embodies the universal law that governs the symbolic order and figures as the originating signifier that founds the Lacanian subject? Lacan insists that "it was certainly the Word (*verbe*) that was in the beginning, and we live in its creation."[88] This statement apparently echoes certain speeches from the holy text, specifically St John's words: "God is the Word and the Word is God." In other words, in the beginning there exists this *God-Word*, an original and generative *Word* that hosts the symbolic order. That is why Lacan alerts his subject: "he should see, beyond this signification, to what signifier . . . he is, as a subject, subjected."[89] This means that the subject is not subjected to any random signifier, but to a particular holy word of scriptural significance, a primal metaphor with inseminating power, and a transcendental and originating signifier in the field of as well as in the name of the Other, i.e. Phallus—the cultic meta-signifier. Displacing Freud's corporeal penis with a mystic signifier, Lacan wags a hyper-sign, "Phallus," as the sacred law of social taboo (castration) and the fetishistic object of universal desire (narcissistic obsession). In other words, a phallic specter haunts Lacan's theoretical body in his return to Freud.

In "The Signification of the Phallus," Lacan states, "The fact that the phallus is a signifier means that it is in the place of the Other that the subject has access to it."[90] Though in the field of the other, Lacan reminds us, "The position of the phallus is always veiled."[91] We are compelled to inquire: Why is the phallus as a signifier always *veiled* in the field of the other? Is it possibly that in this hide-and-seek game, the phallus masquerades itself in the field of the other only in *name*, or more precisely, in the *pseudonym* of the other? No wonder, Lacan insists that the phallus is forever disguised as *the Other* in order to cover its transcendental and central position. In this case, the phallus appears to be misplaced into this *other* territory where it does not belong or it is misnamed the other without any appropriate property of otherness. Instead, the *capitalized Other* as a singular signifier metonymically stands for another signifier in disguise, i.e., the *Absolute Subject* in a metaphysical sense of the word. By interrogating the phallus in the dubious field of the other, we uncover the metaphysical center of Lacan's symbolic order and reveal a *transcendental Subject* in the unconscious, that is, the Phallus as the ontological locus of signification even if called by any *other* names.

Many critics point out the centrality of the phallus as a signifier in Lacan's symbolic order. In *Positions*, Derrida critiques the phallus as "a transcendental signifier," "the correlative of a primary signified," "the central truth," and "the generating (disseminating) void."[92] From a poststructuralist perspective, Derrida discloses the full complicity between signifiers and the ultimate signification of the phallus as well as the logocentric locus of Lacan's symbolic order. As a kind of original and mythical meta-signifier, the phallus occupies a primal position in relation to all signifiers in Lacan's symbolic order. From a feminist position, Luce Irigaray also exposes that the phallus, erected as the singular paternal metaphor, centrally organizes the symbolic order in the name of the father and in terms of a universal desire. In *This Sex Which Is Not One*, Irigaray observes that "we might suspect the *phallus* (Phallus) of being the *contemporary figure of a god* . . . , to be the ultimate meaning of all discourse . . . , the signifier and/of the ultimate signified of all desire . . . , as emblem and agent of the patriarchal system, to shore up the name of the father (Father)."[93]

Samuel Weber in *The Return to Freud: Jacques Lacan's Dislocation of Psychoanalysis* notes sarcastically: "The signification of the phallus is constituted through castration, even and especially if 'nothing' is castrated."[94] Here, the phallus unveils itself as the central agency of hegemonic power that regulates the subject through castration. The subject's entry into the symbolic order or the cultural law is completely subject to the Oedipal rite of passage, i.e., castration, so that the phallus is worshipped as the ultimate (lost) object of desire. The phantom of the phallus in terms of the cultic object of desire and the mythical authority of the patriarchal law commands and demands the subject to sacrifice himself in his father's name as Lacan clarifies that "it is this whim that introduces the phantom of the Omnipotence, not of the subject, but of the Other in which his demand is installed."[95]

John Brenkman in "The Other and One: Psychoanalysis, Reading, the *Symposium*" observes: "The phallus is *at once* the signifying mark of desire and the symbol for object loss, since it derives its signifying function from the very possibility of its disappearance or absence."[96] By invoking a lost object, Lacan exorcises Freud's physical penis into a metaphysical metaphor and conjures up the phallus as a mythical signifier to return from the field of the other in a spectral form. In this Oedipal rite, the lost penis is resurrected as a holy fetish that stands for the universal desire to all subjects. As a symbolic simulacrum, the phallus occupies a position of the arch-ghost that haunts the entire symbolic order as "the generating (disseminating) void." In "The Signification of the Phallus," Lacan states, "The phallus is the signifier of this *Aufhebung* itself, which it inaugurates (initiates) by its disappearance."[97] The departure of the physical object is conjured up as a return of a metaphysical phantom in a disembodied supernatural shape. To a certain degree, for Lacan, to be the phallus is to be a ghost or host of the symbolic order—the arch-ghost in the name of the Holy Other. In the phallic order, as Irigaray exposes in *Sexes and Genealogies*, there is "a transcendental and unique God-Father" and the phallus is erected as a God-term in Lacan's symbolic order. Irigaray warns us: "The god Phallus, indeed, because even though many people go around saying God is dead, few would question the fact that the Phallus is alive and well."[98]

In Lacan's Oedipal return to Freud, the Freudian castrated penis returns in a spectral field as a mythical signifier; namely, the phallus as a supernatural fetish is erected as a cultural relic to memorialize the dead fathers or *imagos* of all ghost fathers. Instead of being a concrete biological organ, the Lacanian Phallus reappears as a sacred cult or a holy symbol. Lacan reminds us, "one cannot strike the phallus, because the phallus, even the real phallus, is a *ghost.*"[99] This enigmatic arch-ghost, the very embodiment of the cultural unconscious and remains of the sacred law of the dead father, centrally anchors the symbolic order in terms of the Holy Other. Samuel Weber in *The Return to Freud* observes: "The phallus thus operates as the pure representation of absence,"[100] similar to a Baudrillardian simulation where absence assumes the central presence.[101] In short, the Oedipus complex, the hauntology of psychoanalysis, rests upon a phallic mythology that represents the father's name, words, laws, and desire in a spectral fashion.

However, though desire claims to be the other's desire, desire for the phallus in the name of the father constitutes exactly the same desire for the subject in the symbolic order. Via an Oedipal rite of passage, the subject pursues nothing else but the desire ascribed by father's sacred orders. By repeating after the dead father the same language, same name, and same law, the subject inescapably reincarnates the same desire of the ghost father and perpetuates the same mono-myth of patriarchal culture. Under the spell of the solipsistic phallic order, the subject is in effect reduplicating the identical subject, genealogically speaking, from the father to the son and circulating the same property of father's symbolic order so that the *afterword* from the spectral Other can be memorialized to eternity. In this case, the Oedipal exorcism becomes a narcissistic rite.

As we know, the unconscious as the locus of the other is irreducible to the Oedipus complex alone, but Lacan, in his return to Freud, stays on the same track as Oedipus, repeating the father's (Freud's) sacred words, the Oedipus complex. Eventually, the other in the unconscious is *oedipalized* by the father's singular speeches alone—"Remember me," to repeat Hamlet's Ghost here, revealing in the patrilineal order a narcissistic identification within an oedipal structure. Franco Rella in *The Myth of the Other: Lacan, Deleuze, Foucault, Bataille* observes: "The unconscious in Freud does not speak the language of the Other but speaks 'many dialects,' which cannot be composed or translated into a *single* language."[102] Henceforth, the Lacanian field of the other appears to be a territory over-populated by father's ghosts, rampant with the *afterword* of the spectral other.

The Oedipal rites of castration are pivotal as the central ideological apparatuses to perpetuate and monopolize the same desire within the patrilineal circle. The Phallus as the locus of signification reveals the hidden mythology or *mystory* of the Lacanian subject's coming into being via a dubious Other. Hence, the subject is conceived as a phallic product in insemination and dissemination, in effect, a narcissistic self-reproduction according to the same master code or master-text. The holy father in terms of a spectral other calls on the subject to perpetuate the same phallic mythology via the oedipal rite of "repeating (after) the father" and to reinforce the same symbolic order along the patrilineal genealogy. Deleuze and Guattari note in *Anti-Oedipus* that ironically one gets out of the Oedipal complex only by initiating someone else into it. The Lacanian other, true to Lacan's theory, operates in a metonymic substitution for the spectral father, that is, a symbolic other *only in name*. In short, what lurks behind the veiled Other in Lacan is not at all an *other*, but the holy ghost of the *Absolute Subject*, the Spectral Other of the Singular Same that embodies and mythologizes the same law, same culture, same language of the dead fathers. In this case, Lacan's other is a pseudo-other *without any traces of alterity or difference*, informing a narcissistic desire for self-identical being.

The irreconcilable contradiction in the Lacanian discourse of the symbolic other lie in this: on the one hand, in the field of the other, there is an infinite language game of difference via metaphorical configuration and metonymic displacements; and on the other hand, in the name of the father, there is the centric phallus as the holy other or transcendental presence that restricts the incessant play within the structure of an oedipal mythology and anchors the ghost subject in a hegemonic phallic order. Here, the poststructuralist Lacan inevitably conflicts with the *oedipalist* Lacan. The spectral Phallus as the mythical embodiment of the dead father's sacred *afterword* limits the free linguistic play or the poststructuralist *jouissance*.[103] In short, Lacan's others are highly problematic because they *lack* otherness. The imaginary other turns out to be a projected illusion of the self, a self-reflexive image of totality *without alterity,* whereas the symbolic other, anchoring in the phallus, goes back to the symbolic father or the sacred words of the father *without difference*. Hence, Lacan's scheme of the symbolic order is decided between the structure of language, the sliding power of metonymies and metaphors, and the unconscious of the culture, the universal law of the patriarchal culture in terms of oracles and ghosts.

VI. NO OTHER OF THE OTHER? THE WHOLLY OR HOLY OTHER WITHOUT ALTERITY OR DIFFERENCE

Lacan in *Television* declares: "[T]here is no Other of the Other."[104] What could Lacan possibly mean by this? Further, in "The Subversion of the Subject and the Dialectic of Desire in the Freudian Unconscious," Lacan explains that there is "no metalanguage that can be spoken, or, more aphoristically, that there is no Other of the Other."[105] In spite of Lacan's denial of a hegemonic "metalanguage," the Lacanian Other does seem suspect of the Singular Other or the Absolute Subject. Put differently, the Lacanian Other, when exposed behind the veil, seems to possess a kind of metaphysical status of ontological singularity and totality. Therefore, the Lacan's Other appears not at all a wholly other, but a Holy Other in the name of the father, a hegemonic Other lacking otherness.

Lacan's statement evokes various response and speculations. In *Subjectivity and Otherness: A Philosophical Reading of Lacan*, Lorenzo Chiesa observes: "The fact that there is a (symbolic) Other of the (symbolic) Other indicates that the Other as the order of signifiers is guaranteed by another transcendental Other, namely the paternal Law. The Other as Law, the Other of the Other, corresponds to the Name-of-the-Father."[106] In "The Other of the Other?: Cultural Studies, Theory, and the Location of the Modernist Signifier," Christopher Bush remarks: "In Lacanian terms there can't be an Other of the Other because the very formulation assures the unconditional singularity of the Other."[107] In her critique of Lacan's "No Other of the Other," Irigaray in *This Sex Which Is Not One* simply states, "there is no meta-language, except inasmuch as the Other *already stands for it*, suspending in its own eksistence the possibility of an other."[108] All critics note that Lacan tends to essentialize and totalize the other according to the metaphysical tradition of singular ontology, especially in the context of a phallic mythology.

Kristeva observes: "A ghost . . . , this Other . . . is indeed the size of a Master."[109] Lacan also states: "The Other . . . holds the master position . . . as absolute Master."[110] In other words, the phallus is erected as the absolute master that monopolizes the entire symbolic order in terms of the father's law. As the meta-Other and the locus of signification, the phallus excludes all alternative others from its solipsistic culture and prohibits their emergence. In this tautological discourse, the phallus is posed as the absolute and singular Other without alterity—a narcissistic and solipsistic subject in effect. In this case, it is not only, as Lacan says, there is no other of the other, but *there is no other at all.* In *This Sex Which Is Not One,* Irigaray exposes, "Phallicism" has been in fact "sustaining itself upon the Other, nourishing itself with the Other, desiring itself through the Other, even without ever relating it as such."[111] Further, Irigaray adds that "the body of the Other," "the place of the Other," and "the desire of the Other" are all spelled in Phallic terms.[112] Thus, as the privileged signifier in the position of the absolute Master, the Lacanian Other postures as the other without other's properties. Interestingly, *the subject qua other* becomes a metonymic displacement for a *subject qua same*. The subject is captivated within a narcissistic space without any possibility of going beyond the father's territory circumscribed by the sacred myth of the Oedipus complex.

To see Lacan's Other from a different perspective, Althusser's "Ideology and Ideological State Apparatuses" might as well be a case study of the Lacanian Other as the Absolute Subject. Althusser translates the Lacanian Other into the spectral and specular Absolute Subject in his analysis of ideological apparatuses. Similar to Lacan's symbolic summon, Althusser also identifies the ideological call to being in terms of interpellation. Althusser explains, "*all ideology hails or interpellates concrete individuals as concrete subjects.*"[113] Further, Althusser exposes that "the interpellation of individuals as subjects presupposes the `existence' of a Unique and central Other Subject, in whose Name the religious ideology interpellates all individuals as subjects."[114] That is to say, inauguration of the subjects is dependent upon one unique condition: "there is a Unique, Absolute, *Other Subject*, i.e., God."[115] As such, the subject realizes itself through subjection to the Absolute Subject, i.e., the Holy Ghost or Holy Father. Althusser demonstrates: "God thus defines himself as the Subject *par excellence* . . . and he who interpellates his subject, the individual subjected to him by his very interpellation."[116] Althusser's analysis of God's relationship to the subject runs parallel to Lacan's theory of the Other's relation to the subject. Moreover, Althusser observes that "he who was called by God, recognizes that he is a subject, a subject *of* God, subject subjected to God, *a subject through the Subject and subjected to the Subject.*"[117] Lacan's subject relation to the Other is a case in point. Paul Smith in *Discerning the Subject* also remarks: "Lacan's symbolic, Althusser's Law of Culture, Law of Order, or ideology take on the same connotations and functions and then mark inexorably toward a view of the subject/individual as entirely *sub-ject.*"[118] In this case, Lacan's Singular Other is synonymous to Althusser's Absolute Subject as the phallus plays the central and spectral role in Lacan's "symbolic state" apparatuses.

From a Marxist perspective, Althusser exposes the ideological unconscious of Lacan's symbolic order and demystifies the relationship between the subject and the Spectral and Specular Other in terms of interpellation by the Absolute Subject. Similarly, from a feminist perspective, Luce Irigaray in *This Sex Which Is Not One* exposes the gender unconscious in the symbolic order. Lacan's heteronomy predominantly centers on a male-to-male relationship from the father to the son, thus Oedipal through and through. In the Lacanian discourse of the other, Irigaray discerns that there is "[n]o desire for a difference" because it is "trapped within the economy of 'sameness,'" based upon the "*hypothesis of a single identical genital apparatus—the male organ*" and locked in "the entire autoerotic, auto-positional, auto-reflexive economy."[119] Further, Irigaray points out that the Lacanian symbolic order aims to perpetuate itself in a solipsistic circulation by "a means of . . . masculine self-production or reproduction, or self-generation or self-representation—himself as the self-same, as the only standard of sameness."[120] Hence, Irigaray mocks, "If we keep on speaking the same language together, we're going to reproduce the same history. Begin the same old stories all over again. . . . The same. . . . Same. . . . Always the same."[121] In short, the Lacanian symbolic order is founded upon a male genealogy, and through the Oedipal rite, it intends to perpetuate the same phallic mythology by repeating after the father infinitely and narcissistically.

When Lacan says there is no Other of the Other, he probably assumes there is nothing outside his symbolic order. However, there are always others outside the phallic order, and perhaps abundantly so. Luce Irigaray, for instance, asserts that there are *other others* beyond the Lacan's Other, especially if we take into consideration psychoanalysis as a discourse of the other in terms of silence, the unspeaking and unspoken other of the female subjects. Irigaray challenges the hegemonic model of the Lacanian Singular Other and articulates a different other, the other to the Other in terms of multiplicity, difference, and heterogeneity outside the boundaries of the symbolic order that is grounded in a solipsistic phallic mythology. By excavating the other scenes of the other, Irigaray develops the *other others* along the heterological or heterogeneous models. These "different others" cannot be contained, assimilated or qualified as the same subject inseminated in Lacan's symbolic order; they reside out of the bounds of the metaphysical framework or the ontological system of singular, total, and self-identical being. Athena Athanasiou and Elena Tzelepis in "Thinking Difference as Different Thinking in Luce Irigaray's Deconstructive Genealogies" observe: "Irigaray offers the means with which to encounter the question of alterity without allowing heterology to disintegrate into heteronomy, without allowing the politics of the other to lapse into mere identity politics."[122] Evidently, heterology does not repeat heteronomy; instead it puts the *other* studies on a different trajectory. In *The Speculum of the Other Woman*, Irigaray argues strongly for an emergency of "a store of in(de)finite alterity, a multiplicity of not-yet-beings."[123] As for the Lacanian other, Irigaray simply says, "*that other is lacking in principle.*"[124] In prospect, we need to come up with "different others" in the principle of alterity outside the enclosed territory of singular ontology and relocate the discourse of the other to a radical heterogeneous and disparate locale of *heterologies*. In other words, instead continuing to linger in the same sphere of hauntology and probe the singular subject embodied by Oedipus, I suggest we return to the riddle of the grotesque embodied by the Sphinx and conjure up different others in terms of disparity and heterogeneity.

NOTES

1. Jacques Lacan, *Ecrits: A Selection,* trans. Alan Sheridan (New York: Norton, 1978), 125. Hereafter, all quotations from Lacan's works will be referenced by book titles, whereof appropriate, instead of seminar titles in the endnotes.
2. Ibid., 141.
3. Ibid., 312.
4. Jacques Lacan, *The Seminar of Jacques Lacan: Book II,* trans. Sylbvana Tomaselli, ed. Jacques-Alan Miller (Cambridge: Cambridge UP, 1988), 229.
5. Ibid., 209.
6. Michel de Certeau in *Heterologies: Discourse of the Other* notes: "Lacan belongs to no one. . . . He is Other, as he signs in this final declaration of 1980: 'If it should happen that I

leave, you may say that it is only in order to be at last Other. One can be happy being Other like everybody else after a life spent, in spite of the Law, trying to be Other'" (1986, 48). This declaration, dated January 15, 1980, figures as an epigraph in a special issue of *Liberation* (September 11, 1980), the best among a number of periodical issues devoted to Lacan since his death.

7. Jean-François Lyotard, *The Postmodern Condition: A Report on Knowledge*, trans. Geoff Bennington and Brian Massumi (Minneapolis: U of Minnesota P, 1988), 40.

8. Jacques Derrida, *Positions*, trans. Alan Bass (Chicago: U Chicago P, 1972), 29.

9. Ibid., 28. Specifically, Derrida lists qualifications or, to be precise, disqualifications of the subject in "'Eating Well,' or the Calculation of the Subject: An Interview with Jacques Derrida." Derrida clarifies that the so-called subject is neither "the absolute origin, pure will, identity to self, or presence to self of consciousness" nor "the figure or mastery of self, of adequation to self, center and origin of the world"; instead, the subject, or "this non-coincidence with self," is defined "as the finite experience of nonidentity to self, as the underivable interpellation inasmuch as it comes from the other, from the trace of the other" (Cadava 1991,103). In other words, the original, central, coherent, and singular subject is invalid as an obsolete idea of the past. The subject is inherently structured by heterogeneous elements that exceed what is called the individual being that used to assume an autonomous and singular posture. Significantly, Derrida points out "the *other*" without naming the specifics. Other poststructuralists, like Paul de Man, emphasize deletion instead of incoherence of the subject. Paul de Man in *Blindness and Insight: Essays in the Rhetoric of Contemporary Criticism* states, "Here the human self has experienced the void within itself and the invented fiction, far from filling the void, asserts itself as pure nothingness, *our* nothingness stated and restated by a subject that is the agent of its own instability" (1971, 19). Also in *Allegories of Reading: Figural Language in Rousseau, Nietzsche, Rilke, and Proust*, de Man observes: "Making the language that denies the self into a center rescues the self linguistically at the same time that it asserts its insignificance, its emptiness as a mere figure of speech. It can only persist as self if it is displaced into the text that denies it" (1979, 111).

10. Roger Farie, *Subjectivity and Intersubjectivity in Modern Philosophy and Psychoanalysis: A Study of Sartre, Binswanger, Lacan, and Habermas* (New York: Rowman & Littlefield P, 1997), 168.

11. Jacques Lacan, *The Psychoses: Seminar of Jacques Lacan, Book III 1955-1956*, trans. Russell Grigg, ed. Jacques-Alain Miller (London: Routledge, 1993), 243.

12. . Ibid., 250.

13. Marcelle Marini, *Jacques Lacan: The French Context*, trans. Anne Tomiche (New Jersey: Rutgers UP, 1992), 105.

14. For further research of Lacan's association with the Surrealists or Surrealist moment, please refer to Elisabeth Roudinesco's *Jacques Lacan & Co: A History of Psychoanalysis in France, 1925-1985* and Marcelle Marini's *Jacques Lacan: The French Context*. Both books provide historical reviews of Lacan in the context of French cultural movements. Carolyn J. Dean in *The Self and its Pleasures: Bataille, Lacan, and the History of the Decentered subject* also notes the connection between Lacan and Surrealist art, "He began frequenting avant-garde circles in 1931 and had contributed to the surrealist periodical *Minotaure*, founded in 1933 by Georges Bataille and André Masson. His connections to surrealists such as Salvador Dali and to more shadowy avant-garde figures such as Bataille shaped his interest in madness, particularly in mad woman" (1992, 42–43).

15. Lacan, *Ecrits*, 4–5.

16. Ibid., 11.

17. Ibid., 11–12.

18. Ibid., 114.

19. Ibid., 166.

20. Kareen Ror Malone and Stephen R. Friedlander, introduction to *The Subject of Lacan: A Lacanian Reader for Psychologists (*Albany: SUNY P, 2000), 4.

21. Jacques Lacan, "Of Structure as an Immixing of an Otherness Prerequisite to Any Subject Whatever," in *Structuralist Controversy: The Languages of Criticism and the Sciences of Man*, ed. Richard Mackesy and Eugenio Donato (New Haven: Yale UP, 1970), 190.

22. Lacan, Ecrits, 29.
23. Lacan, *The Seminar of Jacques Lacan: Book II,* 72.
24. Jacques Lacan, *The Four Fundamental Concepts of Psychoanalysis*, trans. Alan Sheridan (New York: Norton, 1978), 144.
25. Lacan, *The Psychoses,* 223.
26. Lacan, *The Four Fundamental Concepts*, 185.
27. Lacan's seminars on any topics are notoriously scattered, unsystematic, repetitive, and slippery. Due to this, I would like to focus on several key seminars to explore his ideas of the imaginary, the symbolic, the phallus, etc. For instance, for the imaginary, I mostly focus on "The Mirror Stage" and "Aggressivity in Psychoanalysis"; for the symbolic, I mostly refer to "The Function and Field of Speech and Language in Psychoanalysis" and "The Agency of the Letter in the Unconscious or Reason Since Freud"; and for the phallus, I use "The Signification of the Phallus." Most of these seminars are collected in his *Ecrits*.
28. Lacan, *Ecrits*, 2–3.
29. Jacques Lacan, *The Seminar of Jacques Lacan: Book I,* trans. John Forrester, ed. Jacques-Alan Miller (Cambridge: Cambridge UP, 1988), 79.
30. Lacan, *The Four Fundamental Concepts*, 144.
31. Lacan, *Ecrits*, 4.
32. Lacan, *The Psychoses,* 240.
33. Ibid., 243.
34. Lacan, *Ecrits*, 6, 6, 18.
35. Ibid., 16.
36. Freud in "Narcissism: An Introduction" and "Mourning and Melancholy " has substantially addressed the issue of narcissism. For other interesting studies of narcissism, please see *Narcissism: Psychoanalytic Essays* by Bela Grunberger; *Narcissism and Oedipus: The Children of Psychoanalysis* by Victoria Hamilton; *The Culture of Narcissism: American Life in an Age of Diminishing Expectations* by Christopher Lasch; *Frontiers of Psychoanalysis: Between the Dream and Psychic Pain* by J. B. Pontalis; and *The Narcissistic Pursuit of Perfection* by Arnold Rothstein.
37. Lacan, *Ecrits*, 24.
38. Ibid., 19.
39. Jane Gallop, *Reading Lacan* (Ithaca: Cornell UP, 1985), 85.
40. Anthony Wilden, "Lacan and Discourse of the Other, " in Jacques Lacan, *Language of the Self: Function of Language in Psychoanalysis*, trans. Anthony Wilden (Baltimore: Johns Hopkins UP, 1986), 166.
41. Lacan, *The Psychoses*, 60.
42. Jacques Lacan, "Desire and the Interpretation of Desire in *Hamlet*," in *Literature and Psychoanalysis: The Question of Reading: Otherwise*, ed. Shoshana Felman (Baltimore: Johns Hopkins UP, 1982), 36.
43. Please see "Quentin's in *The Sound and the Fury*: Mirror, Play and Melancholy" and "The Lacanian Subject and Grotesque Desire: Between Oedipal Violation and narcissistic Closure." In these two articles, I analyzed the modern protagonists' obsession with the lost symbiosis and the lost ideal object and further explored the narcissistic desire as the grotesque impossible desire in the context of Faulkner's *The Sound and Fury* and O'Connor's *The Wise Blood.*
44. Marini, *Jacques Lacan: The French Context*, 82.
45. Lacan, *The Four Fundamental Concepts*, 188.
46. Many critics have substantially discussed the Lacanian subject's entangled relationship with language through a poststructuralist lens in generic terms. Jameson's "Imaginary and Symbolic in Lacan," one of the most lucid articles, also focuses on the subject's relation to language as a whole in an abstract category as he says: "So the subject's gradual experience of his or her own subordination to an alienating signifier is at one with the theorist's denunciation of philosophies of the subject and his Copernican attempt to assign to the subject an ex-centric position with respect to language as a whole" (Felman 1982, 369).
47. Lacan, *The Four Fundamental Concepts*, 203.
48. Ibid., 207.

49. Ibid., 218.
50. Ibid., 221.
51. Lacan, "Of Structure as an Immixing of an Otherness," 189.
52. Lacan, *Ecrits*, 42.
53. Malcolm Bower, *Lacan* (Cambridge: Harvard UP, 1991), 82.
54. Lacan, *Ecrits*, 158.
55. Ibid., 313.
56. Ibid., 287.
57. Lacan, *The Four Fundamental Concepts*, 51.
58. John P. Muller, "Language, Psychosis, and the Subject in Lacan," in *Interpreting Lacan*, ed. Joseph H. Smith and William Kerrigan (New Haven: Yale UP, 1983), 30–31.
59. Lacan, *The Seminar of Jacques Lacan: Book II*, 326.
60. Lacan, *Ecrits*, 196.
61. Jacques Lacan, "Seminar on `The Purloined Letter'," in *Literary Theories in Praxis*, ed. Shirley Staton (Philadelphia: U of Pennsylvania P, 1987), 338.
62. Lacan, *Ecrits*, 166.
63. Ibid., 263.
64. Ellie Ragland-Sullivan in *Jacques Lacan and Philosophy of Psychoanalysis* argues for a tragic ontology of the Lacanian subject: "The paradox and tragedy of being human stems from the fact that, by accepting language as a substitute for an impossible union, language itself as a symbol builds absence—Castration—into the structure of the subject and ensures that the human condition will be marked by eternal wanting (*Ecrits*, 1996, p. 319). Lacan can claim, therefore, that the structure of self or ontology comes from Real gaps (wants) in being" (1986, 172). Perhaps more than just "gaps" and "wanting" in this case. So far, desire remains to be addressed on the linguistic level, and we need to inquire further to discern that *which* other and *whose* language in the unconscious play the prominent role of the ultimate other.
65. Felman in *Jacques Lacan and the Adventure of Insight: Psychoanalysis in Contemporary Culture* observes: "The Oedipus drama mythically epitomizes the subversion of the mirroring illusion through the introduction of difference in the position of a Third: Father, Law, Language, the reality of death, all of which Lacan designates as the Other, constitutive of the unconscious (otherness to oneself) in that it is both subversive of, and radically ex-centric to, the narcissistic, specular relation of the self to other and of self to self" (1987, 105). However, we need to carefully distinguish how these others are interrelated and which other functions as *the* Other that dominates and decenters the subject. Here, the phallus is conspicuously missing. For instance, Lorenzo Chiesa in *Subjectivity and Otherness: A Philosophical Reading of Lacan* also aligns the big other with three items: the symbolic order, language, and the unconscious, without mentioning the phallus. Other critics mostly take the Other to be language. Slavoj Zizek in *Looking Awry: An Introduction to Jacques Lacan Through Popular Culture* states: "According to Lacan, the true formula of atheism is 'God is unconscious.' There is a certain fundamental belief—a belief in the Other's basic consistency—that belongs to language as well" (1991, 153). That is to say, the other in terms of the unconscious has consistently been structured by language in an abstract category.
66. Lacan, *The Four Fundamental Concepts*, 149, 126.
67. Lacan, *The Psychoses*, 41.
68. See Note 3.
69. Lacan, *The Seminar of Jacques Lacan: Book I*, 171.
70. Lacan, The *Psychoses*, 239.
71. Julia Kristeva, *The Kristeva Reader*, ed. Toril Moi (New York: Columbia UP, 1986), 252.
72. In *The Dialogic Imagination*, Bakhtin also named "the authoritative word" in terms of "the word of the fathers" (1981, 342). Bakhtin observes: "The authoritative word demands that we acknowledge it, that we make it our own; it binds us. . . . It is, so to speak, the word of the fathers" (1981, 342). Here it really sounds identical to Lacan's symbolic order that is inhabited by the words of the father.

73. Jacques Lacan, "Position of the Unconscious," in *Reading Seminar XI Lacan's Four Fundamental Concepts of Psychoanalysis,* ed. Richard Feldstein, Bruce Fink and Maire Jaanus, trans. Bruce Fink (Albany: SUNY, 1995), 272.

74. Lacan, *Ecrits*, 312.

75. Lacan, "Position of the Unconscious," 265.

76. Lacan, *The Seminar of Jacques Lacan: Book I*, 221. A good example would be Don Quixote. René Girard in *Deceit, Desire and the Novel* discusses Don Quixote in terms of "desire according to the Other." That is, Don Quixote's desire to be a knight is simulated through a symbolic identification with the absolute chivalric culture and codes which render the desire itself utterly impossible. As René Girard in *Deceit, Desire and the Novel* remarks: "He no longer chooses the objects of his own desires—Amadis must choose for him. The disciple pursues objects which are determined for him, or at least seem to be determined for him, by the model of all chivalry" (1965, 1–2).

77. Lacan, *Ecrits*, 305.

78. Ibid., 67.

79. Lacan, *The Four Fundamental Concepts*, 34. Anika Lemaire in *Jacques Lacan* also points out, "The Oedipal unconscious is homologous with all these symbolic structures. The Oedipus is the drama of a being who must become a subject and who can only do so by internalizing the social rules, by entering on an equal footing into the register of the symbolic, of Culture and of language." (1979, 91–92). That is, the oracles.

80. Lacan, *Ecrits*, 199.

81. Mark C. Taylor, *Altarity* (Chicago: U of Chicago P, 1987), 101.

82. Lacan, "Desire and the Interpretation of Desire in *Hamlet*," 12.

83. Ibid., 16.

84. Jacques Derrida, *Specters of Marx*, 7.

85. Lacan, The *Psychoses*, 87.

86. Lacan, *Ecrits*, 40.

87. Ibid., 106.

88. Ibid., 61.

89. Lacan, *The Four Fundamental Concepts*, 251.

90. Lacan, *Ecrits*, 288.

91. Lacan, "Desire and the Interpretation of Desire in *Hamlet*," 48.

92. Derrida, *Positions*, 86.

93. Luce Irigaray, *This Sex Which Is Not One*, trans. Catherine Porter (Ithaca: Cornel UP, 1985), 67.

94. Samuel Weber, *The Return to Freud: Jacques Lacan's Dislocation of Psychoanalysis.* (Cambridge: Cambridge UP, 1991), 147.

95. Lacan, *Ecrits*, 311.

96. John Brenkman, "The Other and One: Psychoanalysis, Reading, the *Symposium*" in *Literature and Psychoanalysis: The Question of Reading: Otherwise*, ed. Shoshana Felman (Baltimore: Johns Hopkins UP, 1982), 441.

97. Lacan, *Ecrits*, 288.

98. Luce Irigaray, *Sexes and Genealogies*, trans. Gillian C. Gill (New York: Columbia UP, 1993), 21.

99. Lacan, "Desire and the Interpretation of Desire in *Hamlet*," 50.

100. Weber, *The Return to Freud*, 146.

101. Simulacrum is not the mask that conceals truth; instead it masquerades nothing. The simulacrum is fabricated by a system of signs and images in a realm of representation or fantasy without any reference to the real at all. According to Baudrillard in his *Simulations*, a simulacrum is "a hyperreal, the product of an irradiating synthesis of combinatory models in a hyperspace without atmosphere" (1983, 3). Baudrillard marks the distinction between dissimulation and simulation in this way: "To dissimulate is to feign not to have what one has. To simulate is to feign to have what one hasn't. One implies a presence, the other an absence" (1983, 5). Baudrillard further exposes the nature of simulation: "It is a project of political and cultural hegemony, the fantasy of a closed mental substance" (1983, 92). This might well be a simulation study of the Lacanian phallus.

102. Franco Rella, *The Myth of the Other: Lacan, Deleuze, Foucault, Bataille*, trans. Nelson Moe (Maisonneuve P, 1994), 29.

103. Gabriele Schwab in *The Mirror and the Killer-Queen: Otherness in Literary Language* points out that Jacques Lacan has a "very different view of the subject's relation to the other/Other." Schwab states: "The most crucial difference results from the fact that Lacan tends to ontologize and universalize the subject's negative formation by the other" (1996, 27). I might as well add that Lacan tends to ontologize and universalize the Other as well. In addition, the very ontology of the Lacanian subject, negative or positive, is grounded in a hauntology by some spectral other.

104. Jacques Lacan, *Television*, trans. Denis Hollier, Rosalind Krauss, and Annette Michelson (New York: Norton, 1990), 40.

105. Lacan, Ecrits, 310–311.

106. Lorenzo Chiesa, *Subjectivity and Otherness: A Philosophical Reading of Lacan* (Cambridge: MIT P, 2007), 107.

107. Christopher Bush, "The Other of the Other?: Cultural Studies, Theory, and the Location of the Modernist Signifier," *Comparative Literature Studies* 42, no 2 (2005): 178.

108. Irigaray, *This Sex Which Is Not One*, 101.

109. Kristeva, *The Kristeva Reader*, 252.

110. Lacan, *Ecrits*, 305.

111. Irigaray, *This Sex Which Is Not One*, 98.

112. Ibid.

113. Louis Althusser, "Ideology and Ideological State Apparatuses," in *Lenin and Philosophy and Other Essays*, trans. Ben Brewster (New York: Monthly Review P, 1971), 173.

114. Ibid., 178–79.

115. Ibid., 178.

116. Ibid., 179.

117. Ibid.

118. Paul Smith, *Discerning the Subject* (Minneapolis: U of Minnesota P, 1988), 20.

119. Irigaray in *This Sex Which Is Not One*, 130, 35, 101.

120. Ibid., 132.

121. Ibid., 205.

122. Athena Athanasiou and Elena Tzelepis, "Thinking Difference as Different Thinking in Luce Irigaray's Deconstructive Genealogies," in *Rewriting Difference: Luce Irigaray and "The Greek,"* ed. Elena Tzelepis and Athena Athanasiou (Albany: SUNY P, 2010), 10.

123. Luce Irigaray, *Speculum of the Other Woman*, trans. Gillian C. Gill (Ithaca: Cornell UP, 1985), 335.

124. Ibid.

Chapter Six

From Ontology to Heterologies

A Postmodern Perspective on Otherness

In "Otherness," Tamise Van Pelt remarks: "As half of a signifying binary, the 'Other' is a term with a rich and lengthy philosophical history dating at least from Plato's Sophist, in which the Stranger participates in a dialogue on the ontological problems of being and non-being, of the One and the Other."[1] Unfortunately, this *other* half of the dialogic binary seldom signifies from its own side, and, moreover, what "the *rich* and *lengthy* philosophical history" has told us is not simply its *lack* of signification, but also its *mystification* or *repression* as if the other possesses some kind *unheimlich* (the uncanny), thus wrapped up in an alien position as a mysterious stranger. In other words, the *dialogic riddling* between Oedipus and the Sphinx in fact signifies not so much a conversation as a domination or elimination of the enigmatic other. Since Greek times, the term "other" has already gained a negative conjecture, particularly in Parmenides' philosophy that has consistently privileged a primal Oneness. In Greek, "*heteron*" indicates both *the different* and *the other*, and also means *nonidentity*. Etymologically as well as genealogically, difference/other and nonbeing are synonymous and interchangeable terms. From this perspective, the legendary encounter between Oedipus and the Sphinx in Greek myth illustrates precisely the showdown of the crucial ontological difference between being and nonbeing. If the Greek Oedipus identifies himself as a singular subject or "man" in singular form, then the alien Sphinx in contrast becomes the grotesque or monstrous other due to her "*heteron*" nature.

In his "Introduction" to *Encountering the Other(s): Studies in Literature, History and Culture,* Gisela Brinker-Gabler observes: "One of the characteristics of Western metaphysics is to deny the otherness of other/s—or if not to actually its/their otherness, then at least to appropriate it, subsuming the *other*/s dialectically within the *same* of the absolute subject."[2] Similarly, Emmanuel Levinas in "The Trace of the Other" states, "From its infancy philosophy has been struck with a horror of the other that remains other—with an insurmountable allergy."[3] Western metaphysics in general grounds itself in the ontology of the same and its most common strategy of approaching the other hinges on an imperialist mode of "suppression and possession." Therefore, typically in Western metaphysical discourse, all others have to be dialecticized into the same, differences into identity, multiplicities into singularity. In Derrida's view, "if ontology is tautology and egology, then it has always *neutralized* the other" for the sake of "the totality and unity of the same."[4] To cite a classic example set by an Enlightenment philosopher, Descartes declares, solipsistically, "I think, therefore I am." Who cares what becomes of the others!

In the wake of the demise of the central, transcendental, and singular Subject, discourses of otherness flourish in a postmodern context. A massive transition has occurred from cultural hegemony (Gramsci and Hall) to postmodern paralogy (Lyotard) and social heterologies (de Certeau). Taylor's book *Altarity* marks this transition with a sense of urgency: "The history of society and culture is, in large measure, a history of the struggle with the endless complex problems of difference and otherness. Never have the questions posed by difference and otherness been more pressing than they are today."[5] In *Deconstructive Criticism*, Vincent B. Leitch also notes the trend of transition: "Stability gives way to vertigo; identities to differences; unities to multiplicities . . . ; ontology to philosophy of language . . . ; the One to—not the Many—the Infinite."[6] Indeed, otherness has increasingly become one of the most controversial motifs that dominate contemporary intellectual debates in various terms, such as, the return of the repressed, the marginal or the hybrid, the borderland subject, the wholly other, the absolute alterity or infinite otherness, and so forth. Everyone hastens to jump over the dark shadow of the (dead) subject and embrace the other in whatever forms available. Interestingly, the recent debate about "Who comes after the subject?" is somewhat refashioned as "Who goes after the other?"

However, how *otherwise* are these others? In "Autonomy, Self-Alteration, Sexual Difference," Stathis Gourgouris cautions: "At the height of identity politics during the so-called Cultural Wars of the late 80's, the Other had already come to mean nothing, while at the same time signifying anything deemed marginal, minoritarian, oppositional, or disenfranchised."[7] In *The Illusion of the End*, Baudrillard is also concerned about the confused state of current critical debates: "We have conquered otherness with difference and, in its turn, difference has succumbed to the logic of the same and of indifference."[8] Baudrillard seems to warn us, despite the prolific re-conceptualizations of otherness, these discourses of the other tend to remain captivated within the metaphysics of the same and oftentimes entrapped within the tautological closure of singular ontology. Gourgouris argues adamantly against any kind of "singular alterity" as she alerts, "Worshipping the Absolute Other, the One (and only) Other, paralyzes the conduit of an open relation to the other . . . . This devotion to the One who is the Other makes engagement with otherness literally impossible."[9] Surprisingly, the return to the other turns out to be much more tortuous than anticipated and subsequently the field of the other turns into a controversial and carnival site where labeled, nameless, and anonymous others all vociferously voice their different positions across a broad spectrum.

In this urgent quest for otherness, many critics invoke the grotesque as a seminal trope and reconfigure it into a variety of other terms. Notably, the carnival, the abject, and the hybrid—the refashioned rhetoric of the grotesque in a postmodern perspective—play prominent part to negotiate with alterity and heterogeneity, multiplicity and difference, in a radical discourse of heterologies. In this context, the others emerge inevitably in plural forms and disparate shapes so that the *Other* in any absolute, total, or transcendental category is suspect of a return to and a repetition of the ontological myth of singular presence. Hence, this postmodern return to the grotesque initiates an array of discourses of otherness in diverse fields outside the homogeneous domain of singular ontology and consequently the others arisen in heterological spheres are irreconcilably multiple, disparate, and heterogeneous. In other words, the grotesque becomes a postmodern site for articulating differences and *riddling* of identities on behalf of the others.

I. THE DEATH OF GOD AND THE POSTMODERN TURN TOWARD THE OTHER

The Death of God and the Rise of the Other

The death of God is usually marked as a terminal event, but also in some sense an inaugural event, with linguistic, religious, and metaphysical ramifications. To some it is a ravaging ontological tragedy that, with either a "bang" or a "whimper" according to T. S. Eliot's "Hollow Men," ends the sublime illusion of the absolute subject and forecasts the catastrophic decenterment of the sovereign, autonomous, and transcendental self. That is to say, God, as the ultimate hegemonic framework that ontologizes the singular subject, elapses into a locus of void, especially for the existentialist philosophers and modernist writers alike, and, subsequently, the metaphysics of presence recedes into a haunted domain to house the ghostly subjects of absence. We still recall all the agony and despair expressed in the wake of the death of God, with ethos of absurdity and pathos of melancholia. For instance, Edvard Munch's most expressive painting, *The Scream*, has spectacularly iconized the modern subject's neurotic obsession with his wounded ego or lost self.[10] To confront this identity crisis, existentialists anchor their position decisively in the void to develop a pessimistic philosophy of despair in terms of self-loss, self-division, and self-alienation. Of course, some thinkers are quick to follow Fukuyama's eschatology and resort to an "*amort* mythology," repeating after the death of God, with the death of Man, of History, and of the Subject, (and more to follow), scandalizing the metaphysical homelessness and sensationalizing the ontological absence.[11] Whereas, others in one way or another attempt to challenge this "mythology of the end" by exploring alternative directions and uncharted fields elsewhere, adventuring beyond the hauntology of absence into other locales, such as, heterologies. The postmodernists in particular are inclined to celebrate the death of God as a prime time for change. An end always signals the occasion for a shift of paradigm, a Copernican one probably. The void left by God's disappearance that entails the subsequent ontological elision of the singular subject is radically transmuted into a new hermeneutic space to host an array of diverse discourses of heterogeneous others.

The death of the singular subject opens the door to explore and generate new discourses of diverse others. However, Walter Davis in *Inwardness and Existence* alerts: "In any case, the death of the subject is not an event that should be celebrated as merely the latest intellectual fad, nor is it an idea we have any right to place in the category of the unthinkable. It is, rather, the primary challenge of contemporary life, and as such we should welcome it as a legitimate issue for open inquiry."[12] In a postmodern context, various kinds of theoretical speculations of difference and alterity surface to challenge and displace the metaphysical framework that champions only totality and singularity. With the exit of the onto-logical singularity comes hetero-logical diversity, difference, and multiplicity. What lapses after the death of God not only leaves a void, but also unfolds a fertile heterogeneous space for alterities. In other words, to counter-narrating both against and beyond the Greek legend, the Sphinx returns in a variety of different stances and speaks in a heteroglossic language after the departure of Oedipus' capitalized "Man" in singular form.

In *The Postmodern Condition*, Lyotard projects a discourse of difference in terms of *paralogy*. Lyotard postulates that the "postmodern science" as an alternative discourse "has as its basis difference understood as paralogy."[13] The postmodern paralogy, in Lyotard's view, claims to legitimate different and heterogeneous elements after the death of the "One Master Signifier." Can we suggest that, as proposed by Lyotard, the breakdown of the metanarrative into schizophrenic "*petit récit*" to maximize difference is construed as a postmodern return to the grotesque in a new form? Jameson in his "Forward" to Lyotard's *The Postmodern Condition* seems to concur on this point: "Postmodern knowledge . . . refines our sensitivity to differences and reinforces our ability to tolerate the incommensurable. Its principle is not the expert's homology, but the inventor's paralogy."[14] Lyotard's paralogy certainly appeals to the carnival spirit of the grotesque in terms of "heterogeneity of elements" via a return to the un(re)presentable and the repressed others.

Similarly, Foucault in *Language, Counter-Memory and Practice* observes: "The death of God does not restore us to a limited and positivistic world, but to a world exposed by the experience of its limits, made and unmade by that excess which transgresses it."[15] That is, instead of being limited to the confines of the end, the death of God opens up more avenues toward potential possibilities of transgression in terms of the excessive and the heterogeneous. Foucault notes that "a void has been hollowed out in which a multiplicity of speaking subjects are joined and severed, combined and excluded."[16] Fredric Jameson, for his part in *Postmodernism*, argues for a "postmodern schizo-fragmentation as opposed to modern or modernist anxieties and hysterias."[17] For Jameson, the postmodern catchphrase is "schizophrenic," a kind of radicalization of the grotesque, and this concept certainly echoes those ideas advocated by Deleuze and Guattari in their *Anti-Oedipus* and *A Thousand Plateaus,* both subtitled *Capitalism and Schizophrenia*, i.e., the schizophrenic or "rhizomic" is valorized as a carnival form of existence. Evidently, Foucault, Jameson, Lyotard, and other postmodern thinkers all point to a heterological discourse of the grotesque to refashion different positions for alternative concepts of being.

Stefan Herbrechter in *Lawrence Durrell, Postmodernism and the Ethics of Alterity* also advocates strongly for a repositioning of postmodernism as a discourse of the other. Herbrechter remarks: "Postmodernist theory therefore attempts to erode Western metaphysics from 'within,' while inscribing itself in marginalised counter-traditions of heterology."[18] Postmodern discourse is purported to undermine the discrete ego, the autonomous individual, and the singular subject. Integrity, unity, and totality, previously taken for granted as the absolute ontological conditions and justifications for the subject, preclude any possibility for heterogeneous beings to emerge and evolve. The postmodern, with its ethics of alterity and difference, is opposed to reduction of diverse others to the same or appropriation of others into a singular shape. Instead, postmodern discourse relocates the issues of being to a different rhetorical space, i.e., heterologies, so that the other will no longer stay permanently *unheimlich* in its mystical alterity like a "stranger" as noted earlier by Tamise Van Pelt in her "Otherness."

Alterity and Heterologies: A Brief Review of Contemporary Debates

In fact, with the decease of the singular subject, there arise all kinds of discourses of otherness in various contexts and in different terms: Simone de

Beauvoir's female as the second sex in the framework of existentialism, Irigaray's woman as the other in feminism,[19] Bakhtin's heteroglossia in narrative theory, Bataille's waste in economics, Derrida's *différance* in poststructuralist theory, Levinas' infinite alterity in ethical metaphysics, Taylor's *altarity* in philosophy, Bhabha's hybridity in postcolonial studies, de Certeau's heterologies in sociology, and Anzaldúa's "*mestiza*" in ethnic studies, to name a few. Each attempts to light out for the *other* territory ahead of the rest and each tries to re-embody the Sphinx and reconfigure her riddle differently. Susan Handelman in "Facing the Other: Levinas, Perelman, Rosenzweig" notes: "Otherness, or alterity, has become a fashionable item in recent literary theory. The most problematic question, however, is defining just what and who is the 'other.'"[20] In this context, I would like to briefly trace two trajectories of the discourse of the other: one is associated with Levinas' new metaphysics of alterity, and the other, a radical discourse of heterologies across a diverse field.

Notably, Levinas' ideas, though grounded in a metaphysical tradition, have systematically employed heterogeneity, multiplicity, and alterity to negotiate with otherness. In *Time and the Other,* Levinas argues, "The other's entire being is constituted by its exteriority, or rather its alterity."[21] Beyond the ontology of singular being, Levinas conceives a different other, irreducible to the same, as the pure exterior outside the subject—pure otherness or alterity. In *An Introduction to Metaphysics*, Heidegger declares: "Over against being, the only other is nothing."[22] Levinas is not convinced at all. Being's other for Levinas is not nonbeing or nothing, but something beyond being or *otherwise than being* as he contends in *Otherwise Than Being or Beyond Essence*, "The statement of being's *other*, of the otherwise than being, claims to state a difference over and beyond that which separates being from nothingness—the very difference of the *beyond*, the difference of transcendence."[23] In *Totality and Infinity: An Essay on Exteriority*, Levinas argues for an alterity in terms of "the radical heterogeneity of the other,"[24] that is, the other arises and sustains itself in an irreducibly multiple and disparate form. Further, Levinas believes that "this radical heterogeneity, in fact indicates a mode of being."[25] In other words, this heterogeneous other signals the emergence of an alternative mode of being in terms of "otherwise than being or being otherwise," beyond the precinct of the monistic, totalized, and singular ontology. Transcending to "what is other than being," Levinas clarifies, means "passing over to being's *other*, otherwise than being. Not *to be otherwise*, but *otherwise than being.*"[26] Contrary to Hegel's "dialectics limited," Levinas in *Outside the Subject* envisions a radical "dialectic without synthesis: without repose, without totality, without closure, without conclusion."[27]

However, some of Levinas' rhetoric of the other, for instance, the total other, the infinite other, the wholly or holy other, sound more like a repeating rather than a reversing of the metaphysical tradition of the singular subject.[28] Clearly, certain notions of Levinas' otherness are not able to transcend the dead body of the spectral Holy Other or go beyond the boundary of ontological singularity. Some critics attest that Levinas ends his inquiry of the other in the same place where it has started—the locale of the absolute and transcendental ontology, thus a departure becoming a return. That is why Derrida in *Adieu to Emmanuel Levinas* critiques Levinas' tendency of positing "the Wholly Other as the Most High."[29] Despite Levinas' insistence to "use the ontological *for the same of the other*,"[30] Brian Treanor in *Aspects of Alterity: Levinas, Marcel, and the Contemporary Debate* points out that "otherness within ontology is, properly speaking, no longer otherness at all."[31] Evidently, Hegel seems to remain a spectral presence that overshadows contemporary thoughts, a kind of a ghost-father that needs to be dispelled.

Stathis Gourgouris directly challenges Levinas' infinite alterity that is defined in abstract terms and as a universal category. Gourgouris is strongly opposed to any "decontextualized uses of 'otherness' as an allegedly pure philosophical concept" that is "essentially emptied of historical content."[32] The sense of the other is always related to someone, in a specific historical context and a concrete cultural space. Gourgouris contests that "an abstracted, disembodied other lends itself seamlessly to authorizing an empty and total Other—an absolutist, indeed, totalitarian Other."[33] In this instance, Levinas' position for an ontological difference, or ethical metaphysics, only marks a start-point of departure or gesturing toward alterity, but the radical other is entirely outside and beyond metaphysics of singular or transcendent presence. Levinas ends his infinite other with God, a holy ghost, inaccessible, ineffable, universal, and metaphysical.

Apparently, the challenge that confronts us is this: can we engage the issue of the other without mythologizing it into an absolute or total other or a transcendental category of the wholly/holy other? In other words, can we rewrite the *Sphinx* stories without repeating the *Oedipus* legend and, moreover, without repeating after his transcendental and singular "Man" in another singular term? There is no doubt that in the past few decades we have witnessed extensive mythologizing of otherness across all fields. As William Desmond in *Desire, Dialectics, and Otherness* mocks that, in the discourse toward alterity, "the rhetoric is the rhetoric of difference, but the language tends to be the repetition of the same."[34] All notions of the wholly or *absolute Other* under the spell of the Holy Ghost reinstate a kind of singular alterity without differences, very much like encrypting the Sphinx's riddle in terms of Oedipus' singular "Man." Deconstructing the mythology of the singular subject does not necessarily champion a wholly or total other. Any projection of the singular other remains spellbound or haunted by an ontological ghost of the metaphysical Oneness.

Michel de Certeau's *Heterologies: Discourse of the Other* is generally marked as the seminal book that recently popularizes "heterologies" as a key concept in the discourse of the other. In his "Foreword" to de Certeau's *Heterologies*, Wlad Godzich observes, "*Heterology* is a term that has come to designate a philosophical countertradition that, in short-hand, could be described as being deeply suspicious of the Parmenidean principle of the identity of thought and being."[35] Richard Terdiman in "The Marginality of Michel de Certeau" believes that "[h]eterology then becomes a fundamental intellectual discipline for multifarious world, allowing us to relate structures of difference across the whole range of social and cultural . . . differences" for a simple reason: "Heterology deterritorializes hegemony."[36] The hegemonic or singular ontology anchors the subject in the phallocentric, logocentric or egocentric traditions and privileges the subject qua unity, singularity, and totality, i.e., an ontology qua Oneness. Whereas, the hetero-logical others signal difference, disparity, and diversity. If the onto-logic space breeds the subject of singularity, then the hetero-logic space brings out multiple heterogeneous alterities in a discursive field.

One of the earliest scholars devoted to exploring the issue of heterology is Georges Bataille. In *Visions of Excess: Selected Writings, 1927-1938*, Bataille offers his discursive discourse of the excessive, the disruptive, the heterogeneous, and the scandalous. Julian Pefanis in *Heterology and the Postmodern: Bataille, Baudrillard, and Lyotard* remarks, "Bataille takes a decidedly Nietzschean turn by linking the experience of loss of subjectivity in ecstasy and sexual rapture with the philosophical loss of sovereignty in the death of God."[37] In the spirit of Nietzsche's Dionysian principle of disruptive desire, Bataille traces the impious, transgressive, excessive, and impossible elements in terms of heterology and exposes what is expelled from the homogeneous body of religion, philosophy, or ideology. In *Visions of Excess*, Bataille defines heterology in this way: "Above all, heterology is opposed to any homogeneous representation of the world, in other words, to any philosophical system."[38] Hence, heterology is opposed to any hegemonic system or metaphysical tradition of the totalized subject and, further, the practical part of heterology "leads to an action that resolutely goes against this repression to homogeneous nature."[39] Bataille associates the homogeneous society with the totalitarian state that reduces all heterogeneous others to the identical same. He argues that "the heterogeneous world is largely comprised of the sacred world. . . . These reactions are such that the *heterogeneous* thing is assumed to be charged with an unknown and dangerous force . . . and that a certain social prohibition of contact (taboo) separates it from the *homogeneous* or ordinary world."[40] That is to say, the heterogeneous is excluded precisely due to its potential power of subversion and transgression and is henceforth "rejected by *homogeneous* society as waste or as superior transcendental value."[41] The heterogeneous other, both sacred and profane, connotes double meanings in *agio* (both soiled and holy).

According to Mark Taylor, Bataille's heterology undercuts all philosophical systems by disclosing the inevitable return of the repressed, both transgressive and excessive by nature. In *Altarity*, Taylor explains: "'Heterology' is actually an oxymoron. *Heteros* is, for Bataille, precisely what eludes the *logos*. Consequently, heterology is an *impossible* science."[42] Moreover, he traces the genealogical evolution of ideas associated with alterity and develops his own view of the other in terms of "*altarity*" with the overtone of a Derridean *différance*. Taylor writes: "'Altarity' is a slippery word whose meaning can be neither stated clearly nor fixed firmly. Though never completely decidable, the field of word 'altarity' can be approached through the network of its associations: altar, alter, alternate, alternative, alternation, alterity."[43] Further, he adds, "*Altarity* evokes dimensions of difference and aspects of otherness overlooked, excluded, or repressed by the notion of *difference*."[44] Thus, Taylor's *altarity* connotes otherness and difference as well as otherness crossed out in the name of alterity, very much like the complex genealogical transfigurations of the Sphinx.

In a postmodern context, heterologies heralds in a new hermeneutics of "*otherwise than being*" and engages the other in a broad field in terms of disparity, diversity, and heterogeneity. Instead of repeating Descartes' solipsistic motto, "I think, therefore I am," we have to do the thinking differently from the perspective of the other. Heterologies offers us an alternative to get out of the Pandora's box, possibly. Heterologies connote both alterity and heterogeneity; instead of a dialectic opposite to the singular identity in a binary structure, heterological discourse opens up a third space beyond the traditional metaphysics of total being and outside of all egocentric, logocentric, and phallocentric orders of singular ontology. In heterologies, alterity never exists in an identical Same and nor does it end in a singular Other; it neither results in the transcendental Oneness nor is it elevated to the essential Otherness. If the grotesque in the past has always been circumscribed within the metaphysics of presence and the hegemonic ontology of the singular subject, then the postmodern heterologies inaugurates a study of the grotesque in an alternative locale in terms of both heterogeneity and alterity that lie beyond the bounds of any hauntological framework of singular presence. From this perspective, I would like to situate the discourse of the other in specific social contexts with concrete embodiments as a kind of postmodern pragmatics. In other words, the spectral Sphinx arises and assumes a variety of different shapes to continue her *riddling* in the name of others.

In *The Dialogic Imagination*, Bakhtin puts forward his seminal idea of *heteroglossia*, that is, each word is inextricably interlinked with other words in various historical and cultural contexts to bring forth new or "alien words" as the result of the perpetual dialogic interactions. In Bakhtin's view, "the mixture of linguistic world views" is "pregnant with potential for new world views, with new 'internal forms' for perceiving the world in words."[45] Therefore, the term "grotesque" is recapitulated into various other rhetoric tropes in a postmodern context. For the purpose of this project, I will mainly focus on analyzing those terms that entail a dialogic translation of and negotiation with the grotesque toward a radical hermeneutics of heterologies: Bakhtin's carnival in *Rabelais and His World*, Kristeva's abject in *Powers of Horror: An Essay on Abjection*, and Anzaldúa's *mestiza* in *Borderlands/La Frontera: The New Mestiza*; each term, I argue, figures crucially in developing a heterological study of otherness in terms of alterity, heterogeneity, and disparity. Instead of perpetuating abstract speculations in generic terms, each of their respective re-visions of otherness centers on a concrete social body, in fact, a heterogeneous or grotesque body in a specific cultural space. Moreover, each distinctive embodiment of the grotesque brings forward a discrete discourse in unique terms. Bakhtin's carnival is grounded in the physical body in the folk culture, Kristeva's abjection anchors its inquiry to the female body in a maternal space, and Anzaldúa's *la mestiza* rests upon a hybrid body in ethnological borderlands. Each term negotiates with the grotesque in its specific context and develops an alternative locus toward a heterological study of the other. To a degree, their discourses return to the three distinct ways of embodying the Sphinx I discussed earlier in Chapter 3. Bakhtin invokes Nietzsche's Dionysian principle in terms of carnival, but transfers Nietzsche's Dionysian rite from a mythical terrain to a social locale of folk culture. Kristeva overhauls the Freudian maternal body, the uncanny space of horror, in terms of a semiotic Chora—an abject space of female *jouissance* and self-reproduction. Anzaldúa revisits and revamps Hegel's sphinxlike creatures at the crossroads of hybrid cultures in the name of a borderland subject. In a word, the Sphinx is invoked to assume different theoretical forms to speak for the grotesque other.

II. BAKHTIN: CARNIVALIZING THE GROTESQUE IN FOLK CULTURE

If Lacan situates and regulates the subject's coming into being through the Oedipal rites centralized by a veiled and overbearing phallus in the symbolic order, Bakhtin deploys the phallus differently in his discourse of the grotesque. By celebrating the "obscene" phallus openly and jubilantly in a public space of folk culture, Bakhtin intends to disturb and decenter all official cultures and social authorities with carnivalization of the grotesque body. In the Dionysian spirit advocated by Nietzsche, Bakhtin's carnivalesque promotes disruption and disintegration as well as embraces self-recreation and self-transcendence toward a heterodox other.

Bakhtin's monumental work *Rabelais and His World* offers a radical vision and revision of the past scholarship of the grotesque. First of all, departing from previous theoretical positions, Bakhtin develops a heterodox counter-aesthetic discourse of the grotesque grounded in the physical body in discursive social festivities and rejects all orthodox or official aesthetics from the classical era to modern times, particularly those "ideal principles" embodied by the hypothetical perfect body of classical culture and hinged upon the metaphysics of a unitary being. Secondly, Bakhtin's concept of the carnivalesque inaugurates a political discourse purported to undermine all singular subjects, subvert all dominant ideologies, and challenge all established social authorities. Thirdly, Bakhtin uses the carnivalesque to project a radical utopian vision for an "otherwise than being" in a heterological discourse of otherness.[46]

Bakhtin's "dialogic imagination" of the grotesque contains complex traces of alien voices and intricate varieties of otherness. In *The Mirror and the Killer-Queen: Otherness in Literary Language,* Gabrielle Schwab observes: "Carnivalesque texts carry within them the memory of the cultural unconscious, and of the body's Other, the grotesque body whose drama repeats the exotopy of the subject."[47] Terry Eagleton in *The Ideology of the Aesthetic* thinks that "we arrive with Mikhail Bakhtin at the revolutionary consumption of that logic, as the body's libidinal practice explodes the languages of reason, unity and identity into so many superfluous bits and pieces."[48] Further, Eagleton believes that "carnival involves both a return to the particular and a constant overriding of identity, transgressing the body's frontiers in a play of erotic solidarity with others."[49] By anchoring his inquiry of the other in concrete corporeal bodies in a particular historical locale, Bakhtin in *Rabelais and His World* returns the discourse of the grotesque to a specific social space of communal festivities that has been neglected and excluded from all official cultures as well as orthodox aesthetics in the past.

The Official Aesthetics of the Grotesque and the Counter-Aesthetics of Folk Culture: Carnivalizing the Grotesque Body

By evaluating varied meanings of the grotesque evolved in several historical periods, Bakhtin discerns a dramatic difference demarcated by the orthodox aesthetics of official schools and the discursive practice of folk culture. He argues that during the classical period "the grotesque did not die but was expelled from the sphere of official art to live and develop in certain 'low' nonclassic areas."[50] That is to say, Bakhtin's turn toward the grotesque is in effect a return to an area that is dismissed by or expelled from the official theorems of art. In regard to those grotesque images excavated in Nero's imperial palace, Bakhtin shares the Renaissance artists' excitement but not their hesitance or confusion. In his view, these ornaments are characterized distinctively by "the extremely fanciful, free, and playful treatment" and "an extreme lightness and freedom of artistic fantasy."[51] His response to and speculation of the grotesque at the primal scene is distinctly different from all those orthodox aestheticians mired with ambiguity and ambivalence. For Bakhtin, the grotesque in a fantastic combination of heterogeneous elements entertains a delightful free play of "artistic fantasy" in opposition to the classical aesthetic principles and standards that are founded upon "the completed, self-sufficient individuality of the given body."[52]

Bakhtin rejects the trajectories of the Romantic idea of the grotesque that tends to focus on, mostly, the mysterious dark inside of the subjective world as well as the modernist notion of the grotesque that centers on the absurdity and horror of the lost subject. In his opinion, the Romantic bends the grotesque toward "a terrifying world" while the modern twists it toward an absurd universe. In contrast, the medieval and Renaissance grotesque resides in communal festivities and public merriments of folk culture. In Romantic culture, the grotesque turns subjective, secretive, and cryptic, entrapped within the private interior of the individual subject. Subsequently, the grotesque loses its laughter and becomes terrifying, threatening, and alien as Bakhtin contends that "gloom is completely alien to the entire development of this world up to the romantic period."[53] It is during the Romantic period that the grotesque is perverted into "the expression of subjective, individualistic world outlook very different from the carnival folk concept of previous ages."[54] If the Romantic aesthetics of the grotesque is characterized as a discourse of the monstrous, then the folk culture of the grotesque is marked by its carnival recreation. Particularly, Bakhtin critiques Kayser's ideas of the grotesque that are engrossed in the romantic horror and the modernist alienation. Bakhtin remarks: "For Kayser the essential trait of grotesque is 'something hostile, alien, and inhuman' (*das Unheimliche, das Verfremdete und Unmenschliche*)" and his ideas are limited to the expressions of "modernist form of the grotesque."[55] To Bakhtin, Kayser's speculations of the grotesque are restricted to the modernist vision in the wake of the existentialist anxiety. Instead, Bakhtin suggests a return to the carnival tradition connected to folk culture—"the regenerating power of the laughter," rather than indulging in the gloomy and terrifying power of the unknown or the absurd.

Bakhtin argues, the idea of the grotesque that is initially associated with folk culture differs dramatically from the aesthetic concept developed in the following ages. The meanings of the grotesque change from the medieval to the Romantic era when the locus of its representation shifts from folk culture to official aesthetics, from a communal space to a subjective domain, from a comic and merry mood to macabre and morbid sentiments. Hence, Bakhtin proposes, "The problem of the grotesque and of its aesthetic nature can be correctly posed and solved only in relation to medieval folk culture and

Renaissance literature."[56] That is to say, the grotesque should be addressed "differently" by re-viewing its signification in the discursive field of folk culture prior to the onset of the standardized neoclassical aesthetics that valorizes an idealized perfect body and a totalized individual subject. Since the Romantic age, the grotesque has lost its cheerful merriment and free spirit manifested in social festivities in medieval and Renaissance carnivals. In short, Bakhtin argues for a re-vision of the grotesque by returning to folk culture and communal festivals and re-embodying the grotesque in a physical body with the carnival spirit.

Departing from the prevalent positions of all official aesthetics in the classical, Romantic and modern periods, Bakhtin relocates discourse of the grotesque to the marginalized social space, i.e., Medieval and Renaissance carnivals. Rejecting classical and Romantic aesthetic theories, he develops a counter-aesthetics in a discursive territory of the communal festivals and refreshes the grotesque body with a carnival spirit. Bakhtin observes that "the medieval and Renaissance grotesque, filled with the spirit of carnival, liberates the world from all that is dark and terrifying."[57] By shifting the focus of the grotesque discourse to the terrain of folk culture, he refashions the grotesque in an entirely different physical and social space of articulation in terms of the carnivalesque. Bakhtin rightly points out that throughout the development of philosophical aesthetics up to our times "the grotesque has not been duly understood and evaluated; there was no room for it in the system of aesthetics."[58] As a "minor art" with "no subject," not only aesthetically improper but also mimetically impossible, the grotesque requires, undoubtedly, an anti-aesthetic approach, alternative artistic principles, and a counter discourse that goes beyond the orthodox aesthetics dominated by metaphysics of singular ontology.

Bakhtin frequently juxtaposes "the carnival spirit" and "grotesque imagery" in his discourse. In effect, he intends to revive or renew the *carnival spirit* within the *grotesque body*. Hence, I propose, for Bakhtin, *the grotesque is the corporeal embodiment of the carnival spirit and the carnival is the communal festivity of the grotesque body* . In this context, the carnivalesque is put forward as a postmodern strategy of evoking, celebrating, animating or conjuring the grotesque body for specific rhetorical, political or theoretical purposes. Precisely due its ceaselessly metamorphic and transgressive nature, Bakhtin carnivalizes the grotesque, i.e. "the epitome of incompleteness," as a dynamic mode of political resistance, henceforth celebrating the freedom of self-recreation and the subversion of all restrictive social orders.

The Grotesque Body and the Heterogeneous Other

Deviating from those orthodox aestheticians, Bakhtin approaches the grotesque by focusing on the corporal or material culture instead of indulging in purely philosophical or aesthetic speculations in abstract terms. He anchors his inquiry of the grotesque in the physical body—an open, boisterous, profane, and corporeal locale, or "what is marked out as 'low,'" and "expelled as 'Other'" in the words of Stallybrass and White.[59] Though focusing on the physical terrain, his exploration of the grotesque extends far beyond corporeality, resonant with both political and social implications. That is to say, Bakhtin's discourse not only generates a "counter-aesthetics" of the grotesque body in opposition to the classical ideals, but also projects a different way of being *otherwise* than the singular ontology or the bourgeois "egology."

According to Bakhtin, the grotesque bodies are disputed as "ugly, monstrous, hideous from the point of view of 'classic' aesthetics, that is, the aesthetics of the ready-made and the completed."[60] Mary Russo in *The Female Grotesque* notes that for Bakhtin "[t]he images of the grotesque body are precisely those which are abjected from the bodily canons of classical aesthetics."[61] Evidently, the grotesque images of the material body are deemed monstrous in contrast to those idealized aesthetic images of "the finished, completed man." Bakhtin contends that the grotesque body is open to the outside world: "the open mouth, the genital organs, the breasts, the phallus, the potbelly, the nose."[62] These images of excessive physicality never cut neatly fitting figures in classical aesthetics and forever exceed the boundaries of the bourgeois individual ego. As he states, "The material bodily principle is contained not in the biological individual, not in the bourgeois ego, but in the people, a people who are continually growing and renewed."[63] Dis-located in an open, disparate, and evolving body, the grotesque transgresses and raptures the closure of the total subject, the stabilized ego, and the bourgeois individuality. In opposition to the singular subject founded upon the ideals of a complete and homogeneous body, the heterogeneous grotesque body is translated into an ontological site to refashion an incomplete, transgressive, intermixing, and excessive being, or *otherwise than being*. Bakhtin notes, instead of being in a "finished form," the grotesque shows that "the inner movement of being itself was expressed . . . in the ever incompleted character of being."[64]

Refuting the orthodox aesthetic principle dependent on the singular and coherent subject, Bakhtin evaluates the grotesque on the ground of its heterogeneous, disparate, and incomplete otherness. That is why he emphatically points out that the grotesque is "chimerical" or sphinxlike in nature by "combining heterogeneous elements."[65] "The grotesque body," states Bakhtin, "is a body in the act of becoming. It is never finished, never complete";[66] and further, it "outgrows itself, transgresses its own limit."[67] The grotesque body, in this case, consists of living mixture of varied and opposing identities. Due to its openness, the grotesque body always incorporates others with endless reformation and evolution, structurally perpetuating indeterminacy, incompleteness, and heterogeneity. In other words, the grotesque by its inherent chimeric or sphinxlike nature dissolves all stabilized identities, enclosed boundaries, fixed categories, and totalized systems.

Bakhtin notes, "This is why the essential role belongs to those parts of the grotesque body in which it outgrows its own self, transgressing its own body, in which it conceives a new, second body: the bowels and the phallus."[68] We need to be aware that though both Lacan and Bakhtin employ the phallus as the central metaphor, their respective theoretical functions mark a radical difference. For Lacan, the phallus as the mythical meta-signifier dominates, regulates, and organizes the symbolic order with sacred oracles, bending the phallus toward a transcendental position of the metaphysical Oneness whereas Bakhtin's phallus, plus bowels, means ecstatic and open material body in a Dionysian carnival rite, excessive, disruptive, and transgressive to all transcendental orders. For Lacan, the phallus is singular, sacred, hegemonic, and despotic while for Bakhtin, it is carnival, profane, chaotic, corporeal, and carnal. That is possibly why some even sneer that Bakhtin's concept of the grotesque focuses too much on "the material bodily lower stratum,"[69] and it might as well be termed "gross-tesque."

Politics of the Carnivalesque and Utopian Discourse of the Other

Bakhtin proposes that carnival, as a counter-aesthetic discourse, "belongs to the borderline between art and life," and he hastens to add: "In reality, it is life."[70] Carnival fosters open, playful, and free spirit as Bakhtin argues that during carnival time life is subject only to its own laws: "the laws of its own freedom."[71] People in festivals celebrate their diversity and embrace their transformation like a "second life," similar to the experience of undergoing Nietzsche's Dionysian rites.[72] By rejoicing the disparate open body partaking in social festivals, Bakhtin intends to carnivalize the grotesque into a political discourse of subversion to as well as disruption of social authorities, individual boundaries, and ideological confinements. As the embodiment of the other, Bakhtin's grotesque body *disembodies* the classical perfect body, the individual bourgeois ego and the totalized singular subject.

Thus, carnival is refashioned as a sort of radical play with life and a radical positioning of the political body toward social authorities and dominant ideologies. In *The Politics and Poetics of Transgression*, Peter Stallybrass and Allon White argue, "Carnival gives symbolic and ritual play, and active display, to the immixing of the subject, to the heterodox, messy, excessive and unfinished informalities of the body and social life."[73] That is to say, carnival re-territorializes and de-territorializes identity boundaries and the subjective space toward the other in terms of heterogeneity and alterity. In other words, the carnivalesque means a kind of *jouissance* of *being otherwise than being*, i.e., enjoyment of being multiple, diverse, and heterogeneous beyond all boundaries of singular identity. Embodying "the eternal incomplete unfinished nature of being" and the "flux of becoming,"[74] the carnivalesque signifies a joyful affirmation and celebration of transformation and overcoming of the individual principle or any singular ontology. Bakhtin asserts, "Carnival was the true feast of time, the feast of becoming, change, and renewal."[75] No wonder Deleuze and Guattari champion the carnivalesque in their *Anti-Oedipus* by revolutionizing carnival desire as a radical schizophrenia against all totalized systems.

The carnival spirit is marked by "its freedom, its utopian character oriented toward the future."[76] "This carnival spirit," Bakhtin projects, "offers the chance to have a new outlook on the world" and initiates "a completely new order of things."[77] The political function of carnival is, as he details for us, "to consecrate inventive freedom, to permit the combination of a variety of different elements and . . . to liberate from the prevailing point of view of the world."[78] This means that the carnivalesque opens up a fertile social space for heteroglossic discourses to emerge and enables the marginal and heterogeneous others to articulate their differences, thereby suspending and resisting the authoritative meaning or official designation. Bakhtin affirms that the carnivalesque as a political instrument "frees human consciousness, thought, and imagination for new potentialities,"[79] and, further, as he highlights, it discloses "the potentiality of an entirely different world, of another order, another way of life. It leads men out of the confines of the apparent (false) unity."[80] This indicates that the carnivalesque as a consequential trope is purported to dismantle all delusional unity of identity, phantomlike singularity of the subject, and hauntological totality of being toward a politics *of jouissance of being otherwise than being*. Kristeva rightly observes: "the carnival challenges God, authority and social law."[81]

Bakhtin's discourse of the grotesque is replete with body metaphors. Though abundant rhetoric refers to the maternal body as a deconstructive trope, Bakhtin tends to, as some feminists notice, anchor his theory of the grotesque in a neutralized or male body as the universal locus of signification despite its self-subversion and self-disruption. For example, in "The Pregnant Text: Bakhtin's Ur-Chronotope: The Womb," Ruth Ginsburg pointedly exposes the veiled maternal body in Bakhtin's discourse of the grotesque as she states, "The true meaning of the *material bodily principle* that dominates the grotesque as expressed in the carnival laughter is the *maternal bodily principle*."[82] In her view, "what is originally female—the maternal of pregnancy—becomes, so to speak, 'de-femalised' in the process of being elevated into the central site of carnival, to become part and parcel of a non-female (a-sexual?

non-gendered? male?) grotesque (pregnant) body."[83] Thus, even though words like "copulation," "pregnancy," "birth," "growth," and "dismemberment" figure as the dominate rhetorical tropes, Bakhtin is inclined to lean heavily on the phallus as the prominent symbol and the central metaphor to anchor his concept of the grotesque body. To some extent, Bakhtin's carnival eroticizes the male subject or male body, and it is Kristeva who relocates the grotesque elsewhere, to the womb, the neglected body in Bakhtin's discourse of the grotesque. In other words, the Sphinx, rather than Dionysus, moves to the center of discourse, and as the *other* body, she can speak or *riddle* in her own tongue rather than wag a male organ or a phallic wand.

III: KRISTEVA: ABJECTING THE GROTESQUE AND THE OTHER IN PROCESS

Kelly Oliver in *Reading Kristeva: Unraveling the Double-Bind* observes, "All of Kristeva's writing is concerned with various stages of identity and difference. . . . Alterity, otherness, and the stranger are always at the center of her texts."[84] In her interrogation of border, identity, and otherness, Kristeva adopts Bakhtin's dialogic method as her guiding principle as she states that "each word (text) is an intersection of word (texts) where at least one other word (text) can be read."[85] In response to Bakhtin's carnival, Kristeva creates her own "one other word," *the abject*, and simultaneously addresses what Bakhtin has overlooked or neutralized in his discourse of the grotesque body. That is, Kristeva installs the maternal body as the central metaphor and the signifying locus in her semiotic discourse of the abject; her provocative "writing back" signals both her critique of and her departure from the Lacanian symbolic order that is inscribed by the Oedipal law and centered on the phallus. In short, the Sphinx is revived to embody a radical semiotic site of *riddling*.

If Mary Russo in *The Female Grotesque* believes Julia Kristeva in *Powers of the Horror* "effects a compelling synthesis of Bakhtin's carnivalesque and Jacques Lacan's theory of subjectivity in her account of transgression and abjection,"[86] I see more "transgression" than "synthesis." What Kristeva has achieved by her return to Lacan is definitely not a repetition after him; on the contrary, she intends to expose what has been repressed—the unspeaking female other—in terms of the *un-signifiable* abject in the Lacanian symbolic order and to dispel the universal myth and sacred paternal law of Oedipal rites of castration. In a radical semiotic discourse against the Lacanian symbolic, Kristeva carnivalizes the female body through a Dionysian rite of rupture and transports her discourse of the abject outside the depressive locus of the despotic phallus to a space of alterity and heterogeneity, i.e., *the semiotic chora*, or the mystic sphinxlike body as a potent site. In addition, she refashions her concept of the abject by appropriating Bataille's heterology and Bakhtin's carnivalesque. In *Powers of Horror*, Kristeva notes that Georges Bataille remains the only one "who has linked the production of the abject to *the weakness of that prohibition* which, in other respects, necessarily constitutes each social order."[87] In her view, the abject, excluded by every system, is founded on the "logic of prohibition" precisely due to the "horror" of its transgressive power. In this instance, Kristeva evokes both Bataille and Bakhtin to develop her semiotics of the abject in order to topple Lacan's symbolic order and free the female body from its castrating circumscription. Hence, depending upon different loci of signification, this female other in terms of the abject gains entirely polarized affects as either "the ecstatic or the melancholic" through fundamentally dichotomous conditions of existence of either "sublimation or perversion."

Kristeva starts her book *Powers of Horror: An Essay on Abjection* by identifying the abject with "a massive and sudden emergence of uncanniness."[88] She deliberately positions the abject in an uncanny situation—"[t]he in-between, the ambiguous, the composite."[89] "Abjection is above all ambiguity,"[90] Kristeva states, since it can signify either the *unsignifiable* and unnamable or the joyful, ecstatic, and sublime. This "uncanniness" marks the abject as a split and slippery discourse with ambiguous meanings between two different locales of signification and two discrete languages of "body politics," so to speak. In the full semantic capacity of the term "uncanny," abject signifies both *heimlich* (home) and *unheimlich* (not home). In other words, as the uncanny other, the abject seems to slide between two signifying systems: the phallic order at the pleasure of the Holy Father or the semiotic *chora* for the *jouissance* of the *holey* mother. Therefore, for the abject females, there are two ways to being: "sublimation and perversion." Either one stays entrapped inside the symbolic system in a state of perversion or one transcends the phallic order into an alternative space in a state of sublimation. Hence, the abject signifies both pain and pleasure, related to either melancholic repression due to the primal loss of the sacred object, i.e., the phallus or ecstatic *jouissance* by enjoying the delirious self-division outside the domain of the phallic order.

Throughout *Powers of Horror*, Kristeva intentionally divides her discourse of the uncanny abject in two discrete provinces: the central phallic order of the singular subject and the ex-centric maternal body of the heterogeneous other. That is why Kristeva alerts, in order to approach the issue of being appropriately, one should inquire: "'*Where* am I?' instead of '*Who* am I?' For the space that engrosses the deject, the excluded, is never *one*, nor *homogeneous*, nor *totalizable*, but essentially divisible, foldable, and catastrophic."[91] For Kristeva, passing through the phallic rites, one is destined toward two identifications, i.e., either coming into being as the "subject of the Symbolic" or coming into nothing as the "Other of the Abject."[92]

Circumscribed within the symbolic order, the female as the unspeaking other is instituted as the abject instead of the subject. Through the Oedipal rite of passage or the symbolic register, man is symbolized *into it* as the *wholly subject* while woman is symbolized *out of it* as a *holey abject.* Kristeva clarifies: "Abjection then wavers between the *fading away* of all meaning and all humanity" and "the promised land."[93] Consequently, we see polarized outcomes for the abject: either loss of all humanity or the promise of a new land.

Abjection to the Symbolic Order: Castration, Perversion, and Melancholia

In the debut of psychoanalysis, "Father Freud" uses the word "castration" to inaugurate a sacred taboo and a violent prohibition, thereby separating the child from the mother and subordinating him to the father. The phallus or the lack thereof introduces for women terror and repression of the primal loss. Castration casts a spell, a death sentence in effect, that initiates lacking and conjures woman as the abject instead of the subject.[94] Kristeva highlights that "it is the Word that discloses the abject."[95] In this case, the Word as a sacred script from the Spectral Other or Holy Father is erected to embody the universal law of desire in the symbolic order. Under the spell of the mythical signifier, the corporeal lack is exorcised into an ontological absence and the physical body is bewitched into a metaphysical void.

Lacan's symbolic order is centered on the Oedipal theme of quest for the lost phallus. As the meta-signifier for the universal desire as well as the sacred taboo of the forbidden object, the phallus inaugurates a primal loss as well as an inherent repression for women. Ascribed by the phallic order, Kristeva notes, "The abject is the violence of mourning for an 'object' that has always already been lost."[96] Under the spell of this primordial loss, women inescapably suffer immanent abjection of essential lack and ontological decenterment, laden with "instinctive" psychotic, schizophrenic, and hysterical symptoms. The lack here means an ontological lack, or a subjectivized lack according to the schemata of the symbolic order that, in the name of castration, permanently excludes females from ever coming into whole beings. Kristeva explicates that abjection occurs "when it finds that the impossible constitutes its very *being*" and "the inaugural *loss* that laid the foundations of its own being."[97] Eventually, woman is depressed with "a weight of meaninglessness" in an eternal abject state of asymbolia in the symbolic order. The female self, as Kristeva reveals, can only feel "in-significant, 'empty,' 'null', 'devitalized', 'puppet-like.' An empty castle, haunted by unappealing ghosts—'powerless' outside, 'impossible' inside."[98] Enclosed with the phallic locus of signification, the female is perverted to personify the abject like a ghost in terms of dejection, repression, and deprivation. For woman, ontology and hauntology in the Lacanian symbolic order are synonymous terms and signify identical condition of existence.

Kristeva remarks, "I experience abjection only if . . . an Other . . . precedes and possesses me."[99] A person submits to abjection when "an Other," a ghost father in the name of Spectral Other, dispossesses one. In Kristeva's term, the singular Other in the capital form is, in effect, the Absolute Subject that dominates, subjugates, and suppresses all others. Succumbed to the Holy Other, i.e., the holy signifier of "Phallus," woman suffers abjection at the pleasure of the symbolic father. Under the hegemonic power of the spectral and specular Other, the abject occurs when the females are "no longer seen in their own right but forfeited,"[100] and when "'I' deposits it to the father's account."[101] Hence, Kristeva clarifies: "To each ego its object, to each superego its abject."[102] The Freudian superego is somewhat synonymous to Lacan's phallus, or the words and names of the father as the holy laws and sacred oracles.

In the space circumscribed by the phallus, the females turn into the abject, slipped, elided, and buried in the binary structure between the subject and the object. Further, Kristeva exposes that "it is death that most violently represents the strange state" of "a non-subject,"[103] and, therefore, "the abject is the equivalent of death."[104] Therefore, as she deplores, "'I' am in the process of becoming an other at the expense of my own death,"[105] and, moreover, the phallus as "the Other, having dwelt in me as *alter ego*, points it out to me through loathing."[106] To live by the overbearing sign of the almighty phallus and to be subordinated to the hegemonic and despotic symbolic order, woman would inevitably "anchor" herself "in the Other" and experience perversion with nausea, distaste, and horror. Passing through the Oedipal rites of the symbolic order, i.e., castration, the female body becomes a disembodied body, in fact, a dead body. Kristeva concludes, "If the Law is in the Other . . . , my fate is death."[107]

Actually, the phallus is but a phantom of a phobic object as Kristeva reveals that the phobic object is "the *hallucination of nothing*: a metaphor that is the anaphora of nothing."[108] To worship the phallus means to sublimate a phantom into an ontological locus, transform an empty word into a holy fetish, and exorcise it with both fear and desire. Kristeva points out that, regardless of its status as a metaphor or a hallucination, "the phobic object has led us, on the one hand, to the borders of psychosis and, on the other, to the strongly structuring power of symbolicity."[109] Thus, under the curse of a phallic order, woman is either pushed to the brink of madness or spellbound within the symbolic system. Via a conjuration, the phallus brands "witchmarks" on woman's body as castrated, lack, split, in short, abject. As a result, the abject constitutes "a non-assimilable alien, a monster, a tumor, a cancer."[110]

In the symbolic order, abjection initiates "a rite of defilement and pollution."[111] Undergoing the Oedipal rite of castration, the female becomes a disfigured and profane body, meaningless, incomplete, and divisive. Thus, Kristeva believes that abjection signifies "a kind of *narcissistic crisis.*"[112] Due to conjuration or mirroring by the spectral and specular Other, i.e., the phallus, woman is defiled and perverted into an absent, invisible, or defective other. Falsified specular visions in the phallic mirror initiate a self-negation, self-perversion, and self-absence for woman. What this perverse narcissistic image has generated is not at all self-love, but self-hatred and self-loathing. This specular image of the female body conjured up by the phallic mirror projects nothing else but a castrated and mutilated body that lacks meaning and being. So when the self is compelled to "contemplate itself in the Other, there is nothing either objective nor objectal to the abject. It is simply a frontier, a repulsive gift that the Other, having become *alter ego*, drops so that 'I' does not disappear in it but finds . . . a forfeited existence."[113] In short, woman is reduced to a ghost figure according to the norms of the Other and entirely dispossessed by the specular and spectral phallic mirror: identification means dispossession.

If *Powers of Horror* focuses on speculating the effect of abjection, then *Black Sun: Depression and Melancholia* further diagnoses and explores the affect of abjection in terms of melancholia. In regard to the primal loss as the love-object, Kristeva writes in *Black Sun*, "*As if her phallus were her psyche*, the loss of the erotic object breaks up and threatens to empty her whole psychical life. The outer loss is immediately and depressively experienced as an inner void."[114] Under the spell of castration, the physical loss is translated into an ontological void and the symbolic lack yields a psychological condition of melancholia. Kristeva observes: "Melancholia then ends up in asymbolia, in loss of meaning."[115] Succumbing to the rites of the phallic order, woman is to suffer the melancholic depression, loss of speech, and violent mourning for the lost sacred phallus, a primal and inaugural loss that essentializes her as the abject. Therefore, this "emptiness as living dead" is organized around this lack and the "[d]epressive behavior develops on the basis of and within such a void."[116] Eventually, as Kristeva points out, "A nothingness that is neither repression nor simply the mark of the affect but condenses into a *black hole,*"[117] and, further, "that black hole of her melancholy" perpetuates her abjection in the context of the terror of ontological absence.

In *Powers of Horror*, Kristeva states that abjection is always "at the crossroads of phobia, obsession, and perversion."[118] The abject female lapses into the psychotic and schizophrenic other as the result of the spell of a primal loss. Moreover, Kristeva notes: "*The abject would thus be the 'object' of primal repression*" and has been "always already haunted by the Other, to divide, reject, repeat."[119] The abject constitutes the *unsignifiable* that is "expelled" in the phallic order, repelled as "a threatening otherness," excluded as a taboo, and buried in the unconscious as the primal repression. In effect, what the Oedipal rite has produced is not at all the horror of parricide but a primal abhorrence of the mother.

To Kristeva, as "an otherness" or "one of those violent, dark revolts of being," the abject cannot be assimilated into the symbolic system; instead it subsists in a space "beyond the scope of the possible, the tolerable, the thinkable."[120] Hence, she suggests, "what is *abject*, on the contrary, the jettisoned object, is radically excluded and draws me toward the place where meaning collapses."[121] This *other* place of "the un-signifiable" or the *heimlich* of the uncanny for Kristeva resides precisely in an alternative locale that generates a different discourse of the abject, i.e., "the feminine body, the maternal body, in its most un-signifiable, un-symbolizable" otherness of heterogeneity and disparity.[122] Thus, the abject signifies the jettisoned, the discarded, the excluded, outside the borders and boundaries of the symbolic order; and moreover, the abject constitutes the very other that unsettles the illusion of the solipsistic singular domain of the phallic subject. In fact, the symbolic is established upon a strategic exclusion of the maternal body to ensure the closure of a narcissistic space foreclosed by patrilineal self-reflexivity between the father and the son. The only legitimate and proper name in the symbolic space is indisputably the father's name that warrants the patrilineal property of the singular identity of man alone. By probing the power of horror, Kristeva returns to this "dark continent" or "black hole" in Lacan's symbolic order, i.e., the maternal body or the Sphinx's *riddling* body.

Semiotics of Abjection in the Maternal Space: *Jouissance* of the Female Body

Elizabeth Gross in "The Body of Signification" states, "Abjection is the underside of the symbolic."[123] That is only one way, the symbolic way, to characterize the position of the abject in terms of repression. For Kristeva, the abject can also be formulated differently, beyond the perimeters circumscribed by the symbolic, instead of being placed under it. If the abject suffers asymbolia in the symbolic order as the impossible and the *unsignifiable*, Kristeva relocates her discourse of the other to an alternative locale, namely, the maternal space, to generate *jouissance* of blissful self-division and joyful heterogeneity for the abject. Instead of living by the father's words and names, i.e., repeating the same story of Oedipus, passing through the same rite of castration, and inhabiting the same phallic body, Kristeva initiates her poetics of revolution by opening up a *semiotic space of abjection* in a different locus of signification—*the chora*. In other words, to overcome its uncanny confusion, Kristeva transports the abject from the *unheimlich* or a paternal territory of the symbolic order to *heimlich* as *unheimlich*—a maternal home of *semiotic poetics*.

Kristeva positions her semiotic discourse of the abject by moving the abject outside of the symbolic order ordained by the father's sacred word and inscribed by the phallocentric culture. Judith Butler in *Bodies that Matter* explains: "The abject designates here precisely those 'unlivable' and 'uninhabitable' zones of social life which are nevertheless densely populated by those who do not enjoy the status of subject, but whose living under the sign of 'unlivable' is required to circumscribe the domain of the subject."[124] Kristeva contends, "A void that is not nothing, but indicates, within its discourse, a challenge to symbolization."[125] Put differently, the abject as the "black hole," the impossible and unsignifiable, pokes a hole in the wholeness of the Lacanian symbolic order and henceforth topples the spectral phallus and dismantles the wholly or Holy Other. Further, Kristeva notes: "Abjection is a resurrection that has gone through death (of the ego). It is an alchemy that transforms death drive into a start of life, of new signifiance [sic]."[126] In other words, the female body is rescued from depression through the radical semiotics of abjection and renovated into an "alien other," a new being, or *otherwise than being*, with the death of the singular subject. No longer anchored in or succumbing to a wholly subject or a holy other sanctioned by the phallic order, the *semiotic abject*, departing and differing from the *symbolic abject,* centers on a maternal space, a heterological locale of alterity, heterogeneity, and disparity.

As we all know, the Lacanian symbolic is governed by male genesis and genealogy and the phallus encloses the circulation of power exclusively from the father to the son. By rejecting the Oedipal rite of passage and transgressing the phallic locus of Lacan's symbolic, Kristeva wants to reinstall the maternal body as the alternative space to articulate a heterological being of heterogeneity, disparity, and multiplicity in terms of the *semiotic abject.* Kristeva's project intends to think the unthinkable and speak the unspeakable, beyond the tautologically signifying or disseminating locus of the phallus. If the female body according to the "phallic body politics" or the single sexual genealogical scripts is disfigured into an deject site of nausea, distaste, and horror, then the abject female body in a semiotic space of *the chora* radically alters its meaning and existence in terms of "joying in the truth of self-division."

Mary O'Connor in "Horror, Authors, and Heroes: Gendered Subjects and Objects in Bakhtin and Kristeva" points out that "the abject remains as . . . an abyss of no identity, no relation to the symbolic order, an abyss of absorption into the mother."[127] However, I argue against the idea, as Mary O'Connor tends to believe, that "the process of abjection, or expulsion, of the mother as a transition that prepares for the entrance into the symbolic."[128] On the contrary, the abject constitutes the excluded, the outside, permanently barred from entrance into the symbolic. Abjection is not an "unfixed subject"; instead, it is the other that unfixes the singular subject. In other words, to be the abject in a heterological sense means to disembody the subject of singularity—the very negation of all total subjects. It marks the end of the sublime ontology of singular being that is locked in a narcissistic or autistic closure of the phallic order.

In "Revolution in Poetic Language," Kristeva writes, "The mother's body . . . becomes the ordering principle of the semiotic *chora.*"[129] Kristeva institutes the maternal body as a central space to host her semiotic discourse and a signifying locus to generate a revolutionary poetics for the abject in the name of the mother. Over and beyond the symbolic sphere overpopulated by the fathers' ghosts and phallic codes, the *chora* as a radical semiotic locus of signification speaks the unspeakable in an alien tongue like Sphinx's *riddling*, i.e., heterologies. Mark Taylor in *Altarity* observes: "By evoking '*a heterogeneity of signification*,' the 'elliptical' words of the writer become the inscription of the impossible. In different terms, the impossibility of writing 'is' the writing of the impossible."[130] Thus, the very impossibility of making sense of "the *unsignifiable*" characterizes the purpose of the semiotic discourse of abjection. "Contrary to hysteria," Kristeva contends, "the subject of abjection is eminently productive of culture. Its symptom is the rejection and reconstruction of language."[131] The *re-pressive* abject is rewritten as *the re-productive* abjection in a sublime mode of self-fashioning.

Kristeva configures the *chora*, a mythical metaphor for the maternal body, as a semiotic space to invoke a carnival version of abjection. *The chora* signifies an indeterminate process, informing both separating and merging in an endless transformation and recreation. Beyond the Hegelian dialectic binaries, the abject is not pre-subject, nor post-object, but a state of flux and transformation. Here, the maternal body as a semiotic space generates a broad range of semantic significations: a biological entity, a psychological construct, a creative space, a cultural product, and a symbiotic site. The maternal space as a locale of heterologies brings forward a new being, a "carnivalized" abject, by intermixing of differences and disparities.

Kristeva's semiotic abject transgresses boundaries, disrupts closures, and challenges prohibitions and taboos, i.e., signifying "what disturbs identity, system, order."[132] In "Redefinitions of Abjection in Contemporary Performances of the Female Body," Christine Ross states, "[T]he abject never ceases to haunt the borders of identity; it constantly threatens the unity of the subject."[133] In this case, abjection not only redefines borders and dispels the phantom of the singular subject, but also entirely goes beyond the ontological category of the unitary and total subject by initiating a new locale of heterological discourse of alterity and heterogeneity. Kristeva declares joyfully: "we have lost faith in One Master Signifier."[134] As a result, we have "a hollowing out of abjection through the Crisis of the Word,"[135] or a collapsing of the hegemonic meanings of the father's words in the symbolic order and dispelling the sacred oracles or holy orders ordained by the phallus. Defined by neither the holy ghost of the father nor the transcendental signifier, the phallus, a semiotic abject other speaks an utterly different language and develops a separate identity outside the names, laws and words of the father. In a word, it is a story of Sphinx sans Oedipus or his phantom-man.

Cautiously, Kristeva does not place the mother beyond language as either pre-linguistic or post-symbolic. On the contrary, Kristeva positions the maternal body as a locus for a different language practice—an alien tongue or the (m)other tongue as a radical semiotic discourse of *riddling* outside the symbolic order. Instead of placing the mother in a supernatural territory as a spectral figure or an archaic primordial deity of mythology, Kristeva institutes a mother of social practice. In "At the limits of Discourse: Heterogeneity, Alterity, and the Maternal Body in Kristeva's Thought," Ewa Ziarek asserts that "the question of the mother will be bound up with the task of the redefinition of language as a social practice rather than being simply an escape into a prelinguistic fantasy of the maternal paradise."[136] Further, Ziarek adds: "By uncovering 'disquieting' and heterogeneous elements of signification in a variety of disciplines . . . , Kristeva is concerned with the forms of otherness and multiplicity excluded by unifying orders of discourse."[137] That is to say, Kristeva's semiotics renovates the abject, i.e., maternal body, as an alternative and heterogeneous locus of signifying practice beyond the tautology of the father's name and law—the singular ontology and the single tongue hemmed in the patrilineal tradition as exemplified by the Oedipus legend. In "Within the Microcosm of 'The Talking Cure,'" Kristeva argues strongly for "the position of the semiotic as heterogeneous" and believes that "the *semiotic chora* gives a different status to 'signifying' marks: heterogeneous, mobile, dynamic."[138] Even though "it goes by various names according to the conceptual framework of the theory," Kristeva insists that the abject always "designates something irreducible, a disquieting heterogeneousness, outside the transcendental enclosure."[139]

In this return to the mother, however, Kristeva warns against idolization of the sacrificial position of the holy mother by subordinating oneself entirely to the transcendental Holy Father, i.e., God. In "Stabat Mater," Kristeva remarks: "The Virgin assumes her feminine denial of the other sex (of man) but overcomes him by setting up a third person: *I* do not conceive with *you* but with *HIM*" and thus "being subjected to it."[140] That is to say, submitted to the absolute ideal of Virgin or the sublime image of a divine mother, woman is denied any possible identification except deprivation by the Spectral Singular Other. In fact, the phallic mother and the virgin mother are two sides of the same coin because both are subjected to, obsessed with, and haunted by the holy order of either "Phallus" or God.[141] Kristeva contends that for woman to yield to the holy Virgin is to be "a martyr" and to "dedicate her to the highest sublimation alien to her body."[142] The Virgin is established by the Holy Father as a cult figure for subjugation of woman. This certainly recalls Nietzsche's priest's obsession with and subordination to the phantom of God by practicing an ascetic ideal of self-denial. That is why Kristeva alarms: "What an inconceivable ambition it is to aspire to singularity, it is not natural, hence it is inhuman, the mania smitten with Oneness."[143] This reveals the insidious process of abjection, subjection, and alienation of the female body that Kristeva characterizes as being "impregnated by the Word."[144] The Word is, of course, the holy word, i.e., God, to quote St. John here. The virgin mother is at the pleasure of the Holy Father as her body is marked, inseminated, and inscribed by his words and his names, and henceforth her identity is violated, possessed, and forfeited by a symbolic father. Unfortunately, her role of life, as Kristeva reveals, "must be kept strictly subordinated to the rule of the Father's Name."[145]

In Kristeva's view, the concept of *jouissance* is radically different from pleasure. The pleasure means "at the pleasure" of the Spectral Other, but the *jouissance* comes from the 'schizophrenic' self. As Kristeva says, "when I *seek* (myself), l*ose* (myself), or experience *jouissance*--then 'I' is *heterogeneous*" because "the abject is edged with the sublime."[146] That is why she believes that "woman is a specialist in the unconscious, a witch, a bacchanalian, taking her *jouissance* in an anti-Apollonian Dionysian orgy."[147] The *semiotic* abject, similar to Nietzsche's Dionysian rupture, is associated with delirium—on the edge of psychosis, but not quite. Kristeva believes that "motherhood is perceived as a conspicuous sign of the *jouissance* of the female (or maternal) body" and further, the abject enjoys the "*jouissance* which breaks the symbolic chain, the taboo, the mastery."[148] By generating desire from the locus of the (m)other, Kristeva moves desire from the paternal physique of the phallus to a maternal space, the womb—the heterogeneous locale for self-recreation and self-empowerment.[149] The abject in semiotic space and phallic order yields polarized outcomes between the "orgasmic maternal body and the symbolic prohibition."[150] Jean Graybeal in "Joying in the Truth of self-Division" characterizes Kristeva's celebration of self-division as "*delighting* in the difference, the otherness, the not-self--ness of self."[151] That is to say, *jouissance* is associated with an *abject* ecstasy of delighting in disparity, otherness, and alterity. Kristeva does not see abject motherhood that different from the schizophrenic desire advocated by Deleuze and Guattari in their *Anti-Oedipus*. After all, pregnancy has always been characterized as the "institutionalized psychosis," that is: an unstable state of flux, division, and productivity.

In *Desire in Language*, Kristeva proposes that the abject must be "a questionable *subject-in-process.*"[152] Possibly it might as well be called the *other-in-process*, to be precise. For Kristeva, the abject is grounded in the position of alterity as well as heterogeneity. If Lacan focuses on how the subject comes into being, then Kristeva is interested in reviving the other, the impossible and the *unsignifiable*. In *Reading Kristeva: Unraveling the Double-Bind*, Kelly Oliver identifies an other-in-process in Kristeva's maternal space: "The maternal body itself is a primary model of the subject-in-process; its unity is called into question by the other within, an other-in-process."[153] In effect, Kristeva argues strongly for "a *heterogeneity of significance* [sic]."[154] Similar to the Sphinx's grotesque body, the maternal space as a semiotic site of the abject other hosts diverse voices and disparate positions. In Kristeva's view, the abject is "a border" and "a heterogeneous flux" beyond singular ontology because it "is never *one*, nor *homogeneous*, nor *totalizable.*"[155] As she declares, "There, I am at the border of my condition as a living being."[156] This notion of a borderland being instantly reminds us of another woman, a queer woman, to be precisely, who expresses similar position as a border woman and tries to negotiate her *mestiza* between various conflicting and contradictory borders: ethnicities, genders, and cultures. In this case, instead of probing a single border of gender, the Sphinx in Anzaldúa's discourse is refashioned as a semiotic site of difference at the crossroads that intersect various borders and territories.

IV: ANZALDÚA: HYBRIDIZING THE GROTESQUE: THE NEW MESTIZA IN ETHNOGRAPHICAL BORDERLANDS

Similar to the grotesque, hybridity—an agglomeration consisting of disparate mixtures—is always construed as the other that threatens the singularity and purity of the subject. During the past few decades, many scholars have addressed the concept of hybridity in various cultural contexts and theoretical perspectives. Due to its polemic nature, as Robert Young in *Colonial Desire* observes, "There is no single, or correct, concept of hybridity: it changes as it repeats, but it also repeats as it changes."[157] Notably, Bakhtin's *The Dialogic Imagination* extensively covers the topic of hybridization in the context of language theory while Bhabha intensively investigates the issues of hybrid positions in postcolonial studies. Currently critics respond to the debates of hybridity with all sorts of postures: some controversial and some ambiguous. For instance, Bhabha assumes somewhat an ambivalent attitude of uncertainty. In Bhabha's view, hybridity swings in an unstable condition with double edges toward either transgression or suppression.[158] Situated in a precarious position of "the in-between," hybridity can evolve into a vital political strategy for self-transformation or it can degenerate into dangerous conditions of psychological confusion and ontological contamination. Therefore, hybridity is both a contentious locale for identity to fight out differences and a fertile site to seek new subject positions.[159]

However, general theories of hybridity tend to anchor itself in a universal or neutral body, i.e., a philosophical or metaphysical body, and speculate in abstract terms without a specific locale. Departing from a generic theory of hybridity, Anzaldúa develops her own "borderland" theory of hybridity in terms of "*mestiza*" by tracking various traces of interlaced otherness written on her body—her personal experiences in a concrete multicultural environment. In *Borderlands/La Frontera: The New Mestiza,* Anzaldúa approaches the knotty issue of hybridity by exploring her specific multi-ethnic body as a borderland subject at the complex conjunctions of languages, cultures, and identities at the Mexican and American border. If Bakhtin anchors his discourse of carnival in a male or "neutral" physical body in folk festivals and Kristeva centers her semiotics of abjection on a maternal body in terms of a mythical *Chora*, then Anzaldúa positions her *personal mestiza queer* body at the crossroads of multifarious borderlands.

The Mestiza at the Borderlands: "Otherwise than Being"

In *Border Writing: The Multidimensional Text,* D. Emily Hicks writes: "The 'subject' in border writing, however, can no longer be conceived as a unified subject,"[160] mostly because the borderland subject always emerges in a highly mediated cultural network of diverse codes, languages, and histories. Further, in "Deterritorialization and Border Writing," Hicks also points out, "In border writing, the reference code of the grotesque is very important. In the border region, the notion of the 'grotesque' is linked to relations of power" since "the grotesque is . . . an anti-centering strategy."[161] In this case, the grotesque is construed as a vital discourse instrument to address the issue of the border writing and the borderland subject.[162]

Anzaldúa in *Borderland/La Frontera: The New Mestiza* effectively translated the grotesque into a new term, *la mestiza*, and has blazed a new path for ethnic studies in the context of border writings and the borderland subject. In his essay, "In Context: Gloria Anzaldúa's *Borderlands/La Frontera: The New Mestiza,*" Hector A. Torres observes that Anzaldúa's "mestiza consciousness does not totally negate the idea of identity per se but seeks instead to keep identity an open question, a possibility."[163] Suzanne Bost in *Mulattas and Mestizas: Representing Mixed Identities in the Americas* concurs, "Mestiza theory provides models for imagining identity beyond singular categories at the same time that it retains a sense of cultural specificity, politics, and resistance to hegemony."[164] Further, Bost adds, "mestizaje can present a multiplicity of possibilities and fluidity of identifications."[165] Hence, *la mestiza* for Anzaldúa possesses no single origin or singular identity; instead, it is comprised of overlapping and intersecting traces of heterogeneous others at various conjunctions of histories and cultures.

Unlike the past critics who merely speculate in terms of theoretical ambiguity or philosophical abstraction, Anzaldúa in her *Borderlands/La Frontera* goes directly into her own concrete existence located in diverse ethnographical environments. A borderland female who speaks an alien tongue and chooses to be queer somewhat characterizes where Anzaldúa stands in relation to language, culture, identity, and gender. *La mestiza*, more than merely a signifier, informs the distinct condition of her complex cultural circumstances and social existence at multiple intersections. As a lesbian female mestiza on borderlands, Anzaldúa embodies the other in various categories and cultural spaces. In other words, her mestiza situations intertwine with a whole range of otherness instead of fitting into a singular difference or alterity. To identify oneself as mestiza unveils a multitude of races, cultures, and ideologies in this context. In her "Preface" to *Borderlands/La Frontera,* Anzaldúa spells out clearly that the purpose of the book is to explore "[t]he psychological borderlands, the sexual borderlands and the spiritual borderlands."[166] As a drifting spirit of *la mestiza*, Anzaldúa attempts to articulate a new hermeneutic of the borderland subject beyond the singular category of gender, race, sexuality or culture. In short, her mestiza contests both the hegemonic One and the singular Other or any ontological position in absolute terms.

We might recall, in ancient mythology, a mystic creature of hybrid composition and ambiguous gender comes at the crossroads intersecting different cultures; she speaks an alien tongue of riddles and interrogates singular identity of man in crisis, that is, the Sphinx. Like a sphinx figure, Anzaldúa is a hybrid of Anglo, Mexican, and native composites; as a *riddling* other, she speaks a wild tongue of mixed languages; and as a "shadow beast," she casts a spell to conjure away the subject of all singular categories. Beyond the singular and more than a binary, Anzaldúa declares at the beginning of *Borderlands/La Frontera*: "I am a border woman. I grew up between two cultures."[167] Further, she explains that the condition of "living on borders and in margins," with shifting and multiple identities, "is like trying to swim in a new element, an 'alien' element" and "the 'alien' element has become familiar—never comfortable," "but home."[168] Home, both physically and metaphysically, is an uncanny hybrid space of different cultures, languages, and identities: American, Mexican, Spanish, and indigenous. This intricate multiethnic and multicultural borderland is characterized by a constant state of transition, in effect, a heterogeneous zone or an *extra-territory* fraught with alterities and replete with dynamic exchange.

Alienated from her "home culture" and inhabiting the borderlands interlacing various territories, Anzaldúa occupies a polemic position of diverse otherness as a wild, mixed, lesbian woman. She is designated as a Mexican to the dominant American society, a Chicana to Mexican patriarchal culture, and a lesbian Chicana feminist to straight Chicana women. However, she intends to unsettle the bondage of traditional Mexican culture and combat the discrimination of the Anglo culture. As Anzaldúa declares, "Being lesbian and raised Catholic, indoctrinated as straight, I *made the choice to be queer*. . . . It's an interesting path, one that continually slips in and out of the white, the Catholic, the Mexican, the indigenous, the instincts."[169] More than a slippery position, Anzaldúa's mestiza body translates into a multicultural locus that signifies multiple heterogeneous alterities in a constant flux.

That is why Anzaldúa asserts that she has to leave home in order to locate her own "intrinsic nature" buried under an alter ego that had been imposed upon her and subsequently uncovers in her a "Shadow-Beast," i.e., a rebel that refuses to take orders from social authorities and challenges those unquestionable concepts in her cultures that disfigure her hybrid existence as well as her sexual body. In "Crossing Borders: An Aesthetic Practice in Writings by Gloria Anzaldúa," Monika Kaup notes: "Anzaldúa performs an aesthetics of the grotesque, playing with the boundaries of the body, changing its shape."[170] Actually, Anzaldúa identifies her "queerness" in terms of "the embodiment of the *brieros gamos*: the coming together of opposite qualities within."[171] Put this way, the queer body is a grotesque body of irreconcilable opposites. Even though regarded as the abnormal body, Anzaldúa contests that there is "a magic aspect in abnormality" and, moreover, "abnormality was the price a person had to pay for her or his inborn extraordinary gift."[172] In this context, hybridity is regarded a gift rather than a curse. Anzaldúa elaborates:

> As a *mestiza* I have no country, my homeland cast me out; yet all countries are mine. . . . (As a lesbian I have no race, my own people disclaim me; but I am all races. . . .) I am cultureless because, as a feminist, I challenge the collective cultural/religious male derived beliefs of Indo-Hispanics and Anglos; yet I am cultured because I am participating in the creation of yet another culture, a new story to explain the world . . . , a new value system with images and symbols that connect us to each other and to the planet.[173]

Anzaldúa's borderland subject straddles and migrates across different borders of culture, nationality, sexuality, and language without resorting to any totalized identity of singular category. Tracing her mestiza genealogy to a diverse linkage of alterity, Anzaldúa claims all parts of her ex-centric otherness. Living at crossroads, inhabiting multiple personalities, and speaking different languages, she is able to transcend the singular subject in diverse excursion to an uncharted territory. Homeless, she tries to create a new culture: *una cultura mestiza* and develops a new mestiza hermeneutics to problematize identities, languages, and cultures in a discursive discourse of heterologies. Locating one's identity on the borderlines as well as crossing the lines between them, Anzaldúa is capable of negotiating with her hybrid and disparate self in a creative self-transgression. The hybrid space becomes the outpost of adventure for developing a new mestiza consciousness, a new language, and a new gendered being. Alfred Arteaga in *Chicano Poetics* argues that the "alternative third gender" brought forward by Anzaldúa "is oriented not toward reproduction of the body but toward the reproduction of culture."[174] In short, she intends to refashion herself at the conjunction of hetero-textual interactions.

The Mestiza Consciousness and the Forked Tongue

Anzaldúa writes: "Cradled in one culture, sandwiched between two cultures, straddling all three cultures and their value systems, *la mestiza* undergoes a struggle of flesh, a struggle of borders, an inner war."[175] That is why she believes that to live on borders means to exist in a state of "psychic unrest." As a nomadic traveler and "an alien" in a new territory, she represents the true spirit of "deterritorialization" in a space of perpetual transitions, shifting perspectives, and mixed personalities. To transcend the monologic frame and hegemonic paradigm, Anzaldúa advocates a new consciousness based upon a philosophy of inclusivity rather than discriminatory exclusion. She asserts that from this racial, ideological, cultural and biological conjunction, "an 'alien' consciousness is presently in the making—a new *mestiza* consciousness, *una consciencia de mujer*" or "a consciousness of the Borderlands."[176] By embracing this new consciousness, Anzaldúa contests, one is able to initiate a fundamental "change in the way we perceive reality, the way we see ourselves, and the ways we behave."[177] She further explicates that the new *mestiza* fosters "a tolerance for contradictions, a tolerance for ambiguity" so that one "learns to juggle cultures" and "operates in a pluralistic mode."[178] Moreover, she speaks a new hybrid language against all the "cultural tyrannies" of Anglo-centric and phallocentric discourses.

Bakhtin in *The Dialogic Imagination* expounds on the concept of hybridity by unfolding the dialogic nature of language.[179] Hybrid linguistic construction for Bakhtin means double voices, double accents, double languages, and double consciousnesses. Bakhtin postulates that hybridization is "a mixture of two social languages within the limits of a single utterance" and "an encounter . . . between two different linguistic consciousnesses."[180] As an alien or third term comprised of different cultural codes, a hybrid linguistic phenomenon stems from positive negotiation between and effective translation of multiple linguistic systems so that an amalgamation of new language is brought into being. Through this dialogic principle, the individual consciousness is continuously reproduced through semiotic intercourses with others and the subject is forever reinstituted by its ongoing encounters with and intermixing of others' discourses, thereby bringing together a diversity of voices, perspectives, and outlooks. That is why Bakhtin contends that hybridization of language can bring about "a fundamental liberation . . . from the hegemony of a single and unitary language" and, subsequently, "this verbal-ideological decentering will occur only when a national culture loses its sealed off and self-sufficient character."[181]

Anzaldúa's *Borderlands/La Frontera,* has accomplished exactly what Bakhtin has projected. To overcome the patriarchal tradition of the imposed silence upon woman, Anzaldúa develops a new mestiza hermeneutic to articulate her *riddling* voice as she states, "I will have my voice: Indian, Spanish, White. I will have my serpent's tongue—my woman's voice, my sexual voice, my poet's voice."[182] Her mixed voice signals that the imprisoned tongue is liberated from the confinement of the hegemonic white language and the domination of patriarchal ideology. Her language is characterized by "a patois, a forked tongue" in resistance to the monologic language as she mocks, "We are your linguistic nightmare, your linguistic aberration, your linguistic *mestizaje*, the subject of your *burla.*"[183] Her mestiza tongue with an alien accent represents those voices of the marginalized, the repressed, and the delegitimized others at the borderlands. As Alfred Arteaga in *Chicano Poetics* points out, "The language of Aztlán and the borderlands is a language of languages."[184] *La mestiza,* for Anzaldúa, is "*el lugar en medio,* the space in between, the middle ground," and a "liminal state between worlds, between realities, between systems of knowledge, between symbology systems."[185] In other words, the mestiza consciousness signifies a specific form of decentered or *grotesque* subjectivity that is produced through immersion in a complex web of social, cultural, and linguistic relations.

Growing up in a multiple-lingual society, Anzaldúa develops a sense of a new language, "the language of the Borderlands,"[186] very much like the *riddling tongue* of the Sphinx at the intersections of cultures. Moreover, her book initiates a new mode of writing, a hybrid text of both English and Spanish with rich textures interweaving autobiography, mythology, poetry, history, ethnography, and feminist theory, beyond boundaries of singular frame or single perspective. Hector A. Torres in "In Context: Gloria Anzaldúa's *Borderlands/La Frontera: The New Mestiza*" remarks, "*Borderlands* is as much a multicultural epic as an autobiography";[187] and, similarly, Monika Kaup in "Crossing Borders: An Aesthetic Practice in Writings by Gloria Anzaldúa" states: "Although written by a single author, *Borderlands* is a story told in many voices and reflecting diverse centers of consciousness."[188] That is to say, the identities and voices articulated by Anzaldúa as a single author are by no means singular or monologic. On the contrary, her narrative voices are plural and her identities are heterogeneous, affluent with diverse cultural heritages: Native American, U.S. American, Spanish, Mexican, Chicana, and so forth. Actually her book initiates a new aesthetics of border writing, a carnivalization of voices, texts, and identities. She intends to claim her mother tongue, the rich cultural heritage with which to translate all other tongues. In *Lost and Found in Translation: Contemporary Ethnic American Writing and the Politics of Language Diversity*, Martha J. Cutter argues that "[a]n effective translator can creatively mesh languages and worldviews so that the spiritual, cultural and social values of the original or parent culture are not lost as the translator moves into a new culture and language."[189] Inhabiting a multi-lingual and multicultural world, a translator is able to bring about "a plurality of interarticulated subject positions" and "a creative fusion and fission between languages and cultures that does not destroy differences but rather create something new *precisely* out of these differences."[190] What Anzaldúa has accomplished in her *Borderlands/La Frontera* exactly demonstrates her as a capable cultural translator.

In this case, Anzaldúa assumes the role of a trickster that translates and transforms languages, cultures and identities. As I mentioned earlier in Chapter 2, the Sphinx is a trickster, and so is Anzaldúa. In general, the tricksters embody difference in languages and cultures. They speak riddles in double voices and play with ambiguities, resisting the authoritative meaning and hegemonic discourse. In *Writing Tricksters: Mythical Gambols in American Ethnic Literature*, Jeanne Smith contends, "Tricksters shake things up, splinter the monologic, shatter the hierarchies" thereby "disrupting tradition and mediating change."[191] As "[i]nterpreter, storyteller, and transformer," Smith remarks, "the trickster is a master of borders and exchange, injecting multiple perspectives to challenge all that is stultifying, stratified, bland, or prescriptive."[192] Further, Smith adds, "tricksters dwell at crossroads and thresholds" and they are "free to dissolve boundaries and break taboos."[193] In *Alterity and Narrative: Stories and Negotiations of Western Identities,* Kathleen Roberts also considers "[t]rickster as an important figure for the study of alterity and intercultural ethics" because she occupies a semiotic locus to generate "rhetoric of possibility."[194] Anzaldúa in this context is an exemplary trickster who juggles cultures and translates and transforms languages.

Myth of the Other: The Sphinx and the Alternative Spirituality

To combat the dominant mythology of the West, Anzaldúa suggests, "Let's all stop importing Greek myths and the Western Cartesian split point of view and root ourselves in the mythological soil and soul of this continent."[195] Hence, to resurrect the ancient spirit of her specific cultural heritage as the locus of an alternative cosmography, Anzaldúa asserts, "*La mestiza* has gone from being the sacrificial goat to becoming the officiating priestess at the crossroads."[196] Taking the full advantage of her fertile cultural legacy, Anzaldúa envisions her new ethno-subject by invoking the mythical figures of the repressed past and constructs her new mestiza by interweaving multiple cultural traditions instead of being suspended by them.

Specifically, Anzaldúa refashions a new myth by returning to Aztlan culture and appealing to ancient specters. Anzaldúa revives the spirit of *la Víbora*, i.e., Snake Woman, as she remarks, "Like the ancient Olmecs, I know Earth is a coiled Serpent. Forty years it's taken me to enter into the Serpent."[197] The new mestiza grows out of the indigenous earth mythology of sphinxes rather than metaphysical ontology. Anzaldúa informs us, "Humans fear the supernatural, both the undivine . . . and the divine."[198] In the past, however, as she notes, "The Male-dominated Azteca-Mexica culture drove the powerful female deities underground by giving them monstrous attributes and by substituting male deities in their place, thus splitting the female Self and the female deities."[199] Demonized by the patriarchal culture, the female goddesses are all subjugated and buried underground, like the Sphinx, and forever to be haunted by all kinds of phallic specters. Anzaldúa returns to this repressed cultural legacy to claim her native power and founds an alternative locus for self-creation.

Anzaldúa observes that according to Christianity as well as most other major religions, "woman is carnal, animal, and closer to the undivine."[200] But she argues that woman is much more than that as a "shadow beast." Anzaldúa recuperates the legendary image of the serpent woman or *Coatlicue* and describes her as the Earth Mother of fertility in a grotesque image consisting of "a human skull" for a head and "a shirt of twisted serpents and taloned feet."[201] Hence, Anzaldúa adds, "As creator goddess, she was mother of the celestial deities."[202] In this context, this divine mother figure indeed looks like the Sphinx. In a sense, Anzaldúa returns to the sphinx figure as a sacred mother and a divine power of creation as she contends that *Coatlicue* is "the Earth Mother who conceived all celestial beings out of her cavernous womb" and "she is the incarnation of cosmic process."[203] Moreover, Anzaldúa postulates that *Coatlicue*, similar to the Sphinx, "is a symbol of the fusion of the opposites: the eagle and the serpent, haven and the underworld, life and death, mobility and immobility, beauty and horror."[204] Therefore, the mythical and mystical mother of heterogeneous nature is evoked to initiate new beings of the mestiza. Like Kristeva, Anzaldúa also construes the maternal space as the most potent space of cultural reproduction.

One of the most interesting figures brought forth by Anzaldúa is *La Virgen de Guadalupe*. Different from Virgin Mary of singular or pure origin, Anzaldúa contends that "*La Virgen de Guadalupe* is the single most potent religious, political, and cultural image of the Chicano/*mexicano*. . . . She is the symbol of the *mestizo* true to his or her Indian values."[205] *La Virgen de Guadalupe* exemplifies a new mode of hybrid cultural construction, a combination rather than rejection. She stands for the hybrid conglomeration of different races, religions, and languages. Anzaldúa notes, "She mediates between the Spanish and Indian cultures (or three cultures as in the case of *mexicanos* of African or other ancestry) and between Chicanos and the white world."[206] In her view, *La Virgen de Guadalupe* is the symbol of "the tolerance of ambiguity that Chicanos-*mexicanos*, people of mixed race, people who have Indian blood, people who cross cultures, by necessity possess."[207] Cultural translation or negotiation in this case yields cultural transcendence and transgression. By reclaiming and resurrecting her ancient indigenous myth and native culture from the grottoes, Anzaldúa situates her own ethnography within the multicultural textures of past cultural legacies and interweaves her stories with diverse stories of the others.

Robert Young in *Colonial Desire* suggests that we need "a historical paradigm that will acknowledge the extent to which cultures were not simply destroyed but rather layered on top of each other, giving rise to struggles that themselves only increased the imbrication of each with the other and their translation into increasingly uncertain patchwork of identities."[208] Yes, all identities are covered in layers and in palimpsest: multiple and heterogeneous, infinitely interlinked with others and otherness. Young alerts us, without the knowledge of past linkages, we will "remain unaware of how much that otherness both formed and still secretly informs our present."[209] Stuart Hall in ""Cultural Identity and Diaspora" concurs that cultural identity is "a matter of 'becoming' as well as 'being.' It belongs to the future as much as to the past."[210] "Far from being grounded in mere 'recovery' of the past," Hall continues, "identities are the names we give to the different ways we are positioned by, and position ourselves within, the narratives of the past,"[211] so that we are able to reproduce ourselves anew through self-transformation and mixing with otherness and difference. Hybrid cultures and identities are inescapably interlaced with disparate alterities of all kinds, conscious or unconscious, stable or diaspora. Anzaldúa's new mestiza of the *Borderlands/La Frontera* is evidently a case in point.

NOTES

1. Tamise Van Pelt, "Otherness," *Postmodern Culture* 10, no. 2 (2000): 1.

2. Gisela Brinker-Gabler, introduction to *Encountering the Other(s): Studies in Literature, History, and Culture,* ed. Gisela Brinker-Gabler (Albany: SUNY P, 1995), 1.

3. Emmanuel Levinas, "The Trace of the Other," in *Deconstruction in Context: Literature and Philosophy,* ed. Mark Taylor (Chicago: U of Chicago P, 1986), 346.

4. Jacques Derrida, *Writing and Difference*, trans. Alan Bass (Chicago: U of Chicago, 1978), 96, 98.

5. Mark C. Taylor, *Altarity* (Chicago: U of Chicago P, 1987), xxi.

6. Vincent B. Leitch, *Deconstructive Criticism: An Advanced Introduction* (New York: Columbia UP, 1982), 240.

7. Stathis Gourgouris, "Autonomy, Self-Alteration, Sexual Difference," in *Rewriting Difference: Luce Irigaray and "The Greek,"* ed. Elena Tzelepis and Athena Athanasiou (Albany: SUNY P, 2010), 139.

8. Jean Baudrillard, *The Illusion of the End*, trans. Chris Turner (Stanford: Stanford UP, 1994), 109.

9. Gourgouris, "Autonomy, Self-Alteration, Sexual Difference," 144.

10. The central motif of modernism, in Jameson's view, can be summarized by one of Edvard Munch's iconic paintings of a ghastly figure. In *Postmodernism*, Jameson states: "Edward Munch's painting *The Scream* is, of course, a canonical expression of the great modernist thematics of alienation, anomie, solitude, social fragmentation, and isolation, a virtually programmatic emblem of what used to be called the age of anxiety" (1991, 11). Munch himself in his diary indicates that this painting originates from his own experience on a bridge, a kind of metaphor between life and death, where he feels the utmost loneliness and total loss. Further, I

believe, the painting epitomizes a narcissistic wound over the loss of the center. Frederick B. Deknatel in *Edvard Munch* notes: "The people in his paintings seem under a spell as if they were possessed by something so completely that no power of individual will or decision remains" (1950, 26). That is, they are haunted by some spectral others. For further analysis of Edvard Munch's paintings, please see Ragna Stang's *Edvard Munch: The Man and His Art*, Jean Selz's *Edvard Munch*, and Reinhold Heller's *Munch: His Life and Work*.

11. Please refer to Alan Friedman's book on modernism *Fictional Death and Modernist Enterprise* where he comprehensively analyzes the modernists' obsession with death. Several critics also point out the haunting effect of modernism. For instance, Jean-Michel Rabaté in *The Ghosts of Modernity* inquires: "Has modernity, then, always been haunted? Yes, since a refutation of specters has always served as the very background for its formation" (1996, 216). Numerous ghosts haunt modernity, and among them, the most powerful one is associated with the death of God that transforms ontology into hauntology and the subject of presence into a ghost figure. In short, a spectral *Other* is haunting at the center of modern culture; the existentialists have substantively elaborated on this point.

12. Walter A. Davis, *Inwardness and Existence: Subjectivity in/and Hegel, Heidegger, Marx and Freud* (Madison: U of Wisconsin P, 1989), 7.

13. Jean-François Lyotard, *The Postmodern Condition: A Report on Knowledge*, trans. Geoff Bennington and Brian Massumi (Minneapolis: U of Minnesota P, 1988), 60.

14. Fredric Jameson, foreword to *The Postmodern Condition: A Report on Knowledge*, by Jean-François Lyotard (Minneapolis: U of Minnesota P, 1988), xxx.

15. Michel Foucault, *Language, Counter-Memory, Practice*, ed. Donald F. Bouchard, trans. Donald E. Bouchard and Sherry Simon (Ithaca: Cornell UP, 1977), 32.

16. Ibid., 42.

17. Fredric Jameson, *Postmodernism or The Cultural Logic of Late Capitalism* (Durham: Duke UP, 1991), 372.

18. Stefan Herbrechter, *Lawrence Durrell, Postmodernism and the Ethics of Alterity*, (Atlanta: Rodopi, 1999), 3.

19. Historically, many feminists have engaged the issue of the other in a binary structure between man and woman. For the purpose of clarification, I provide a few examples here. Simone de Beauvoir in *The Second Sex* argues, "Otherness is a fundamental category of human thought" (1980, xxiii), and she engages the issue of the female as the other in relation to the "male sovereignty" from an existentialist perspective. De Beauvoir writes, "she is the incidental, the inessential as opposed to the essential. He is the Subject, he is the Absolute—she is the Other" (1980, xxii). Woman, according to de Beauvoir, can only find "herself living in a world where men compel her to assume the status of the Other" (1980, xxxv), thus women have been living an inessential and inauthentic existence without autonomy or agency. Similarly, in *This Sex Which is Not One*, Luce Irigaray argues that woman poses as a separate other from the centric Other in the symbolic order, a different other beyond the Lacanian Other. Irigaray notes, woman is "indefinitely other in herself" (1985, 28) and therefore a "black continent, hole in the symbolic, breach in discourse" (1985, 176). Because she is not One, she is "counted as none" (1985, 26).

20. Susan Handelman, "Facing the Other: Levinas, Perelman, Rosenzweig," in *Divine Aporia: Postmodern Conversation about the Other*, ed. John C. Hawley (Lewisburg: Bucknell UP, 2000), 263.

21. Emmanuel Levinas, *Time and the Other*, trans. Richard A. Cohen (Pittsburgh: Duquesne UP, 1978), 75–76.

22. Martin Heidegger, *An Introduction to Metaphysics*, trans. Ralph Manheim (New Haven: Yale UP, 1987), 79.

23. Emmanuel Levinas, *Otherwise than Being or Beyond Essence*, trans. Alphonso Lingis (The Hague, 1981), 3.

24. Emmanuel Levinas, *Totality and Infinity: An Essay on Exteriority*, trans. Alphonso Lingis (Pittsburg: Duquesne UP, 1969), 36.

25. Ibid., 294.

26. Levinas, *Otherwise than Being*, 3.

27. Emmanuel Levinas, *Outside the Subject*, trans. Michael B. Smith (Stanford: Stanford UP, 1994), 74.

28. Levinas' thoughts cover a huge field of diverse interests, contradictory to say the least. Some of his ideas, especially his notions like the infinite other, the absolute other, or the total other, clearly reflect the haunting effects of the spectral presence of a wholly or Holy Other in universal and abstract terms whereas some of his other ideas demonstrate his struggle with and combat against singular beings. For instance, Levinas in "Ethics of the Infinite" exposes that in Greek ontology, "the last word is unity, the many becoming one, the truth as synthesis" (Kearney 1984, 58) and the ontological approach to the other is always marked by "suppression and possession." Further, in "Philosophy and the Idea of the Infinite," Levinas exposes that the Western philosophy always seems to "encompass every Other in the Same, and proclaim the philosophical birthright of autonomy" (Peperzak 1993, 93). All these contestations are evidently targeted at Heidegger. In *Basic Concepts,* Heidegger argues that Being is singular in terms of self-identical totality as he states: "Rather, being, as the unique, is always the Same," and "this Same is being itself" in spite of "being in their multiplicities" or "discord" (60, 103, 44).However, part of Levinas' discourse of the other is trapped in the metaphysical tradition and haunted by the holy ghost of Hegel due to his essentializing and totalizing tendency. Therefore, the Other that Levinas projects is an onto-theological other as he postulates in "Ethics of the Infinite": "The heteronomy of our response to the human other, or to God as the absolute Other, precedes the autonomy of our subjective freedom" (Kearney 1984, 63). When Levinas invokes God as the infinite and singular Other, he remains captive of the theo-ontological tradition.

Many critics have raised serious issues with Levinas' other, particularly Derrida and Irigaray, from either a poststructuralist or a feminist perspective. In "Violence and Metaphysics: An Essay on the Thought of Emmanuel Levinas" collected in *Writing and Difference*, Derrida offers his most comprehensive critique of Levinas' idea of "the infinite other" and exposes the inherent contradiction and inevitable hauntology of Levinas' Other: "The infinitely other, the infinity of the other, is not the other *as* a positive infinity, as God, or as resemblance with God. . . . The positive Infinity (God)—if these words are meaningful—cannot be infinitely Other" (114). Also, Derrida in *The Gift of Death* uncovers God in Levinas' theory as the "completely other," "infinitely other," and "wholly other" (77) and hence Derrida concludes, "His ethics is already a religious one" (84). In "Questions to Emmanuel Levinas: On the Divinity of Love," Luce Irigaray interrogates Levinas' claim to both ethics and metaphysics as she discloses the phallocentric center as the anchorage for his heteronomy. As she points out, for Levinas, "the other is always situated within the realm of the father, of the father-son, man-God relation, and that it is there only there that ethics may be established" (Bernasconi 1991, 113). Further, Irigaray uncovers Levinas' neglected area: "The feminine other is left without her own specific face. On this point, his philosophy falls radically short of ethics" (Bernasconi 1991, 113). Hence, Irigaray concludes: "Thus, unlike Heidegger, he writes that Being is the other or he points to the other as Being" (Bernasconi 1991, 114). Clearly, instead of being apart from Heidegger as Levinas claims, Irigaray unveils the complicity between them because both are locked in the metaphysical tradition, be it either the singular subject or the infinite other. For Irigaray, Levinas is still perpetuating the same Oedipal rite of the male subject in a holy family based upon a male genealogy and a phallocentric tradition. Consequently, the trinity of father-son-ghost constitutes a family of the male conspiracy that excludes the female. Ironically, in Levinas' very discourse of the other, the *other others* are excluded, that is, those who have never made it to the circle of the holy family. His entire project of ethical metaphysics seems to fall short of ethics.

29. Jacques Derrida, *Adieu to Emmanuel Levinas*, trans. Pascale-Ann Brault and Michael Nass (Stanford UP, 1999), 54.

30. Emmanuel Levinas, "Ethics of the Infinite," in *Dialogues with Contemporary Continental Thinkers: The Phenomenological Heritage*, ed. Richard Kearney (Manchester: Manchester UP, 1984), 64.

31. Brian Treanor, *Aspects of Alterity: Levinas, Marcel, and the Contemporary Debate* (New York: Fordham UP, 2006), 14.

32. Gourgouris, "Autonomy, Self-Alteration, Sexual Difference," 139.

33. Ibid.

34. William Desmond, *Desire, Dialectics, and Otherness: An Essay on Origins* (New Haven: Yale UP, 1987), ix.

35. Wlad Godzich, foreword to *Heterologies: Discourse on the Other*, by Michel de Certeau, trans. Brian Massumi (Minneapolis: U of Minnesota P, 1986), vii.

36. Richard Terdiman, "The Marginality of Michel de Certeau," *The South Atlantic Quarterly* 100, no. 2 (2001): 407, 408.

37. Julian Pefanis, *Heterology and the Postmodern: Bataille, Baudrillard, and Lyotard* (Durham: Duke UP, 1991), 45.

38. Georges Bataille, *Visions of Excess: Selected Writings, 1927-1938,* ed. Allan Stoekl, trans. Allan Stoekl, Carl R. Lovitt, and Donald M. Leslie Jr. (Minneapolis: U of Minnesota P, 1985), 97.

39. Ibid., 98.

40. Ibid., 142.

41. Ibid.

42. Taylor, *Altarity*, 133.

43. Ibid., xxviii.

44. Ibid., xxix

45. Mikhail Bakhtin, *The Dialogical Imagination: Four Essays*, ed. Michael Holquist, trans. Caryl Emerson and Michael Holquist (Austin: U of Texas P, 1981), 360.

46. Critics in the past primarily focused on discussing the similarities between carnival and the grotesque but few explored their differences. For instance, Katerina Clark and Michael Holquist in *Mikhail Bakhtin* observe: "Carnival and the grotesque both have the effect of plunging certainly into ambivalence and uncertainty, as a result of their emphasis on contradictions and relativity of all classificatory systems" (1984, 304). I think their difference needs to be addressed as well.

47. Gabriele Schwab, *The Mirror and the Killer-Queen: Otherness in Literary Language* (Bloomington: Indiana UP, 1996), 22.

48. Terry Eagleton, *The Ideology of the Aesthetic* (Malden: Blackwell P, 1990), 337.

49. Ibid.

50. Mikhail Bakhtin, *Rabelais and His World*, trans. Helene Iswolsky (Bloomington: Indiana UP, 1984), 31.

51. Ibid., 32.

52. Ibid., 29.

53. Ibid., 47.

54. Ibid., 36.

55. Ibid., 47, 48.

56. Ibid., 51.

57. Ibid., 47.

58. Ibid., 45.

59. Peter Stallybrass and Allon White, *The Politics and Poetics of Transgression* (Ithaca: Cornell UP, 1986), 191.

60. Bakhtin, *Rabelais and His World*, 25

61. Mary Russo, *The Female Grotesque: Risk, Excess and Modernity* (New York: Routledge, 1994), 8.

62. Bakhtin, *Rabelais and His World*, 26.

63. Ibid., 19.

64. Ibid., 32.

65. Ibid., 35.

66. Ibid., 317.

67. Ibid., 26.

68. Ibid., 317.

69. Ibid., 82.

70. Ibid., 7.

71. Ibid., 7.

72. If Nietzsche returns to the mythical figures like Dionysus and mythical rituals, then Bakhtin returns to folklore culture and communal festivals. In a sense, Nietzsche's Dionysian

ritual is a kind of mythical grotesque whereas Bakhtin's carnival is a sort of folk grotesque; and each aims to liberate oneself from the confines of the dominant, official, singular, and unitary subject.

73. Peter Stallybrass and Allon White, *The Politics and Poetics of Transgression*, 183.
74. Bakhtin, *Rabelais and His World*, 52, 53.
75. Ibid., 10.
76. Ibid., 33.
77. Ibid., 34.
78. Ibid.
79. Ibid., 49.
80. Ibid., 48.
81. Julia Kristeva, *The Kristeva Reader*, ed. Toril Moi (New York: Columbia UP, 1986), 49.
82. Ruth Ginsburg, "The Pregnant Text: Bakhtin's Ur-Chronotope: The Womb," in *Bakhtin: Carnival and Other Subjects,* ed. David Shepherd (Amsterdam: Rodopi, 1993), 173.
83. Ibid., 168.
84. Kelly Oliver, *Reading Kristeva: Unraveling the Double-Bind* (Bloomington: Indiana UP, 1993), 12.
85. Kristeva, *The Kristeva Reader*, 37.
86. Russo, *The Female Grotesque*, 10.
87. Julia Kristeva, *Powers of Horror: An Essay on Abjection*, trans. Leon S. Roudiez (New York: Columbia UP, 1989), 64.
88. Ibid., 2.
89. Ibid., 4.
90. Ibid., 9.
91. Ibid., 8.
92. Ibid., 112.
93. Ibid., 18.
94. Kristeva clarifies, "Castration puts the finished touches on the process of separation that posits the subject as signifiable. . . . The discovery of castration, however, detaches the subject from his dependence on the mother, and the perception of this lack [*manqué*] makes the phallic function a symbolic function—*the* symbolic function. This is a decisive moment fraught with consequences: the subject, finding his identity in the symbolic, *separates* from his fusion with the mother, *confines* his *jouissance* to the genital and transfers semiotic motility on to the symbolic order" (1986, 101).
95. Kristeva, *Powers of Horror*, 23.
96. Ibid., 15.
97. Ibid., 5.
98. Ibid., 49.
99. Ibid., 10.
100. Ibid., 5.
101. Ibid., 2.
102. Ibid.
103. Ibid., 25.
104. Ibid., 26.
105. Ibid., 2.
106. Ibid., 10.
107. Ibid., 87.
108. Ibid., 42.
109. Ibid., 46.
110. Ibid.,11.
111. Ibid., 17.
112. Ibid., 14.
113. Ibid., 9.
114. Julia Kristeva, *Black Sun: Depression And Melancholia*, trans. Leon S. Roudiez (New York: Columbia UP, 1982), 82.
115. Ibid., 42.

116. Ibid., 82.
117. Ibid., 87.
118. Kristeva, *Powers of Horror*, 45.
119. Ibid., 12.
120. Ibid., 1.
121. Ibid., 2.
122. Ibid., 20.
123. Elizabeth Gross, "The Body of Signification," in *Abjection, Melancholy and Love: The Work of Julia Kristeva*, ed. John Fletcher and Andrew Benjamin (London: Routledge, 1990), 89.
124. Judith Butler, *Bodies That Matter: On the Discursive Limits of Sex* (New York: Routledge, 1993), 3.
125. Kristeva, *Powers of Horror*, 51.
126. Ibid., 15.
127. Mary O'Connor, "Horror, Authors, and Heroes: Gendered Subjects and Objects in Bakhtin and Kristeva," in *Bakhtin: Carnival and Other Subjects*, ed. David Shepherd (Amsterdam: Rodopi, 1993), 251–52.
128. Ibid., 251.
129. Kristeva, *The Kristeva Reader*, 95.
130. Taylor, *Altarity*, 179.
131. Kristeva, *Powers of Horror*, 45.
132. Ibid., 4.
133. Christine Ross, "Redefinitions of Abjection in Contemporary Performances of the Female Body," in *Modern Art and the Grotesque*, ed. Frances S. Connelly (Cambridge: Cambridge UP, 2003), 281–82.
134. Kristeva, *Powers of Horror*, 209.
135. Ibid., 208.
136. Ewa Ziarek, "At the Limits of Discourse: Heterogeneity, Alterity, and the Maternal Body in Kristeva's Thought," *Hypatia* 7, no. 2 (1992): 93.
137. Ibid.
138. Julia Kristeva, "Within the Microcosm of 'The Talking Cure,'" in *Interpreting Lacan*, ed. Joseph H. Smith and William Kerrigan (New Haven: Yale UP, 1983), 36, 37.
139. Ibid. 40–41.
140. Kristeva, *The Kristeva Reader*, 180.
141. The phallic mother for Kristeva is not empowered by or is possession of the penis. On the contrary, it indicates the mother has been dispossessed like a ghost, split like a schizophrenic, and disfigured into a grotesque figure by the phallus. In *Desire in Language*, Kristeva has this to say about the phallic mother, "Any subject posits himself in relation to the phallus—that much everyone understands. That the phallus could be the mother is something often said, but here we are all stopped short by this 'truth': the hysteric, the obsessed, the fetishist, and the schizoid" (1980, 191). That is to say, being a phallic mother signifies nothing else but a dispossessed subject.
142. Kristeva, *The Kristeva Reader*, 181.
143. Ibid., 182.
144. Ibid., 147.
145. Ibid., 138.
146. Kristeva, *Powers of Horror*, 10, 11.
147. Kristeva, *The Kristeva Reader*, 154.
148. Ibid., 138, 154.
149. Many feminist scholars have explored the maternal body in terms of multiplicity, disparity, and heterogeneity. Notably, Lucy Irigaray, Helen Cixous, and Gilbert and Gubar all suggest a return to the female body, specifically to the womb as the unconscious locus of signification to recuperate woman's identity differently. For further readings, please see Irigaray's *The Sex Which is Not One* and *Speculum of the Other Woman*, Cixous' "Laugh of Medusa," and *The Mad Woman in the Attic* by Sandra M. Gilbert and Susan Gubar.
150. Kristeva, *The Kristeva Reader*, 147.

151. Jean Graybeal, "Joying in the Truth of Self-Division," in *Body/Text in Julia Kristeva: Religion, Women and Psychoanalysis,* ed. David R. Crownfield (Albany: SUNY P, 1992), 132–33.

152. Julia Kristeva, *Desire in Language: A Semiotic Approach to Literature and Art,* ed. Leon S. Roudiez, trans. Thomas Gora, Alice Jardine, and Leon S. Roudiez (New York: Columbia UP, 1980), 135.

153. Oliver, *Reading Kristeva,* 13.

154. Kristeva, *Powers of Horror,* 51.

155. Ibid., 8.

156. Ibid., 3.

157. Robert C. Young, *Colonial Desire: Hybridity in Theory, Culture and Race,* London: Routledge, 1995), 27.

158. For instance, in "Signs Taken for Wonders," Bhabha expounds on the negative outcome of hybridity, a process involving and informing deformation, displacement, and domination by the colonial power that forbids emergence of agency or possibility of self-transcendence. Bhabha observes: "Hybridity represents that ambivalent 'turn' of the discriminated subject into the terrifying, exorbitant object of paranoia classification" (Gates 1985, 174). Whereas, in other contexts, hybridity can initiate transaction and negotiation as Bhabha argues in *The Location of Culture* that the power of hybridization resides in its "transformational value of change" and "in the rearticulation, or translation" (1994, 28). In this case, hybridity becomes a positive process of self-reformation and translation. In "Cultural Diversity and Cultural Difference," Bhabha posits the idea that hybridity generates an intertextual space so that "they are now free to negotiate and translate their cultural identities in a discontinuous intertextual temporality of cultural difference" (Ervin 1999, 271). Further, in *The Location of Culture,* Bhabha states, "These 'in-between' spaces provide the terrain for elaborating strategies of selfhood—singular or communal—that initiate new signs of identity" (1994, 1) and "open[s] up the possibility of a cultural hybridity that entertains difference without an assumed or imposed hierarchy" (1994, 4). In other words, this "in-between" terrain constitutes a potential space of self-recreation and self-transfiguration; and it is instrumental to "'remarking the boundaries, exposing the limits of any claim to a singular or autonomous sign of difference" (1994, 219).

159. Hybridity is a contentious and ambiguous concept and critics of both past and present have acknowledged its complex nature. For further reference, please see the following sources that have addressed this issue comprehensively. Monika Fludernick's "The Constitution of Hybridity: Postcolonial Interventions"; *Cultural Hybridity* by Peter Burke; *Multicultural Hybridity: Transforming American Literary Scholarship & Pedagogy* by Laurie Grobman; and *Reconstructing Hybridity: Post-Colonial Studies in Transition* co-edited by Joel Kuortti and Jopi Nyman. They all lean on Bhabha to develop their different theoretical positions to hybridity. In addition, there are a lot of focused studies on the mestiza. Please see Tanja Reiffenrath's *At Borders and Crossroads: Conceptualizing the New Mestiza in Chicana*; Edwina Barvosa's *Wealth of Selves: Multiple Identities, Mestiza Consciousness, and the Subject of Politics;* Alfred Arteaga's *Chicano Poetics: Heterotexts and Hybridities*; and *Reconstructing Hybridity: Post-Colonial Studies in Transition* edited by Joel Kuortti and Jopi Nyman.

160. D. Emily Hicks, *Border Writing: The Multidimensional Text* (Minneapolis: U of Minnesota P, 1991), 14–15.

161. D. Emily Hicks, "Deterritorialization and Border Writing," in *Ethics and Aesthetics: Post-modern Positions,* ed. Robert Merrill (DC: Maisonneuve P, 1988), 50, 51.

162. Some critics, such as Paula Uruburu in *The Gruesome Doorway: An Analysis of the American Grotesque* and Van O'Connor in *The Grotesque: An American Genre and Other Essays,* already noted the unique position the grotesque occupies in representing American literature and society because America as a nation consists of diverse people from all races, cultures, religions, and languages. Paula Uruburu remarks, "America has, from its very beginning, been an incomplete nation, inhabited by displaced people in search of an identity and writers looking for a literary voice that would reflect that fragmented national character" (1987, 16). Leonard Cassuto in *The Inhuman Race: The Racial Grotesque in American Literature and Culture* argues that "the American literature of race is, on the most basic and fundamental level, a continuing story of the encounter with the grotesque" (1996, 28). In fact, most American

literature is about the encounter with the other, thus a continued story of the grotesque in the course of its history. James Goodwin in *Modern American Grotesque: Literature and Photography* also observes, "In the early decades of nineteenth-century American literature the grotesque is commonly invoked through the presence of strange, misshapen, or intimidating forms, and there in turn often reflect anxiety over an encounter with 'foreign' or 'alien' elements" (2009, 18). Indeed, America emerges with continued immigration that shapes and reshapes the nation in an ongoing flux of diverse people all over the world. Mae M. Ngai in "Transnationalism and the Transformation of the 'Other': Response to the President Address" also observes that America is not exactly a static state with stable population, but a transnational nation in a constant flow of immigration and migration, a perpetual reproduction of itself in terms of exchanges between people, texts, and cultures, and a constant reconfiguration of identities and otherness. Thus, critics, past and present, traditional or ethnic, all identify something "grotesque" about America as a nation due to the mixed nature of its people all over the world, a kind of hybrid or grotesque nationhood which consists of, instead of any singular genesis, multiple genealogical flows across nations, cultures and continents. When St. John de Crèvecoeur in his *Letters from an American Farmer* inquires "What then is the American, this new man?" he is already struck by "that strange mixtures of blood which you will find in no other country" (1905, 54), despite his limited focus on mixture of people from only Europe. Recently, many new immigrants reconceive themselves as the border subject, straddling cultures, languages, countries, and societies, and negotiating various kinds of borders: psychological, social, religious, linguistics, cultural, and national. The border subject becomes a new semiotic site of contention and poetic reconstitution. Thus, the American culture is unique in its grotesqueness and the United States as a nation is comprised of diverse people that subvert the mythology of singular identity.

163. Hector A Torres, "In Context: Gloria Anzaldúa's *Borderlands/La Frontera: The New Mestiza*," in *US Latino Literature: A Critical Guide for Students and Teachers*, ed. Harold Augenbraum and Margarite Fernández Olmas (Westport: Greenwood P, 2000), 128.

164. Susie Bost, *Mulattas and Mestiza: Representation of Mixed Identities in the Americas* (Athens and London: U of Georgia P, 2003), 9.

165. Ibid.

166. Gloria E. Anzaldúa, *Borderlands/La Frontera: The New Mestiza* (San Francisco: Aunt Lute Books, 1999), 19.

167. Ibid.

168. Ibid.

169. Ibid., 41.

170. Monika Kaup, "Crossing Borders: An Aesthetic Practice in Writings by Gloria Anzaldúa," in *Hispanic-American Writers*, ed. Harold Bloom (Philadelphia: Chelsea House P, 1998), 201–202.

171. Anzaldúa, *Borderlands/La Frontera*, 41.

172. Ibid., 41.

173. Ibid., 102.

174. Alfred Arteaga, *Chicano Poetics: Heterotexts and Hybridities* (New York: Cambridge UP, 1997), 35.

175. Anzaldúa, *Borderlands/La Frontera*, 100.

176. Ibid., 99.

177. Ibid., 102.

178. Ibid., 101.

179. Tventan Todorov in his *Mikhail Bakhtin: The Dialogical Principle* offered to correct some of the mis-translations of Bakhtin's key concepts and provided his own translation to some key concepts such as discourse, utterance, heterology, and exotopy. In the section on "Heterology," Todorov observes: "To name the irreducible diversity of discursive types, Bakhtin introduces a neologism, *raznorečie*, which I translate (literally, but with the aid of a Greek root) by heterology, a term that inserts itself between two other parallel coinages, *raznojazyčie*, heteroglossia or diversity of languages, and *raznogolosie*, heterophony of diversity of (individual) voices" (1984, 56). Here Todorov presents a more accurate and more relevant definition to my project. Todorov continues: "Heterology is, in a way, natural to society; it arises spontane-

ously from social diversity. But just as the latter is constrained by the rules imposed by the single State, the diversity of discourses is fought against by the aspiration, correlative to all power, to institute a common language (or rather a speech)" (1984, 57). For Bakhtin, "a common language" is based upon linguistic unification and centralization, opposed to heterology.

180. Bakhtin, *The Dialogical Imagination*, 358.
181. Ibid., 367, 379.
182. Anzaldúa, *Borderlands/La Frontera*, 81.
183. Ibid., 80.
184. Arteaga, *Chicano Poetics*, 16.
185. Gloria E. Anzaldúa, *Interviews/Entrevista*, ed. AnaLouise Keating (New York: Routledge, 2000), 268.
186. Anzaldúa, *Borderlands/La Frontera*, 20.
187. Torres, "In Context: Gloria Anzaldúa's *Borderlands/La Frontera,*" 127.
188. Kaup, "Crossing Borders," 199.
189. Martha J. Cutter, *Lost and Found in Translation: Contemporary Ethnic American Writing and the Politics of Language Diversity* (Chapel Hill: U of North Carolina P, 2005), 2.
190. Ibid., 6, 30.
191. Jeanne Rosier Smith, *Writing Tricksters: Mythical Gambols in American Ethnic Literature* (Berkley: U of California P, 1997), xii.
192. Ibid., xiii.
193. Ibid., 7.
194. Kathleen Glenister Roberts, *Alterity and Narrative: Stories and the Negotiation of Western Identities* (Albany: SUNY P, 2007), 172, 173.
195. Anzaldúa, *Borderlands/La Frontera*, 90.
196. Ibid., 102.
197. Ibid., 48.
198. Ibid., 39.
199. Ibid., 49.
200. Ibid., 39.
201. Ibid., 49.
202. Ibid., 49.
203. Ibid., 68.
204. Ibid., 69.
205. Ibid., 52.
206. Ibid.
207. Ibid.
208. Young, *Colonial Desire*, 173–74.
209. Ibid., 179.
210. Stuart Hall, "Cultural Identity and Diaspora," in *Colonial Discourse and Postcolonial Theory,* ed. Patrick Williams and Laura Christma (New York: Columbia UP, 1994), 394.
211. Ibid.

Afterword

The Cyborg: A Post-human Return to the Grotesque

The end of the grotesque? Not exactly. We all know the implication of Samuel Beckett's *Endgame*, especially in the context of Freud's "masterplot" of repetition, that any end will unavoidably provoke another round of language game. In fact, it is hardly possible for an "afterword" to conjure up an ending for the grotesque since, as I discussed earlier, an "afterword" always suggests an invocation from or a return of some spectral other. At the end, I would like to reiterate: the grotesque still haunts us in a variety of forms, frequently taking possession of a different body to repeat itself because a specter, as Derrida said numerous times in his *Specters of Marx*, cannot be easily exorcized away. The afterword of a book seems certainly not an appropriate juncture to open another can of worms; however, any attempts to end the grotesque would inevitably bring up other round of debates in *other* terms. Hence, this "Afterword" to the grotesque is, in some sense, very much a foreword to another grotesque turn, or a post-human return to the grotesque in this case.

If the cyborg can be construed, arguably, the central metaphor of *post-human* discourses, then Donna Haraway's "A Manifesto for Cyborgs" would be a prime example of launching and developing a new rhetoric, a new theory, and a new cultural territory beyond humanism. Despite her radical ventures into a novel realm, Haraway's theory for cyborgs, more or less, renews, continues, and expands the discussion of the grotesque in the spirit of Bakhtin's carnival and in terms of hybridity: organic and inorganic, science fiction and social reality, human and machine, biotech and informatics. It appears, so far, post-humanistic theories have been restating a lot of the same rhetoric, same stories, and same theories of the grotesque studies, and perpetuating largely the same *riddling* game between the Sphinx and Oedipus, or, to borrow Peter Brook's words, by binding one textual moment to another. For instance, Haraway remarks, in "our time, a mythical time, we are all chimeras . . . ; we are all cyborgs."[1] Further, Haraway might as well evoke the Sphinx herself when she states, "The cyborg appears in myth precisely where the boundary between human and animal is transgressed."[2] The new myth of the cyborg returns to and recapitulates, to a great degree, the old myth of the Sphinx, fraught with "potent fusions, and dangerous possibilities,"[3] and moreover, as Haraway points out, "the most promising monsters in cyborg worlds are embodied in non-Oedipal narratives,"[4] a kind of resurrection of sphinxes beyond the framework of the *Oedipus* legend. In this case, Haraway targets the same egocentric and "phallogocentric origin stories,"[5] the founding myth of Oedipus, in both Hegel's philosophy of history and Freud's civilization of man. In particular, she highlights the importance of "how not to be Man, the embodiment of Western logos,"[6] that is, refusing to reinstate the same logocentric, Eurocentric, and phallogocentric order epitomized by Apollo and declining to reincarnate the same phantom of singular identity embodied by Oedipus. The story of the cyborgs disputes the fairy tale of the tragic fall of man anchored in the phallic mythology, or the apocalyptic fall of the whole man of Western ontology because "man," from the post-human point of view, is never wholly or holy, but a ghost conjured up by solipsistic philosophers of the past humanistic tradition.

The cyborg, a post-human Sphinx in a sense, starts another *riddling* game between identity and difference by relocating its locus from metaphysics to informatics and biotech—a kind of postmodern condition in Lyotard's words, or some sort of grotesque condition in a post-human and post-metaphysical world. Nevertheless, none of these "posts" in current theories implies the end of the grotesque or signals a passage into a post-grotesque era; on the contrary, the cyborg emerges as a renovated grotesque figure in the post-human era. In this context, it did seem to have taken humanism a long time to arrive at its "post" position, i.e., the grotesque, not so much a journey toward the end as a return trip to the beginning. Hence, post-humanism informs not exactly a radical break from, but instead, a continuation of, the grotesque in a different form; and henceforth, a provocative departure lapses into another evocative return to the grotesque. Post-humanism, in this sense, constitutes a return to the myth of the Sphinx or a refashioning of the grotesque prior to the illusion of the sublime totality of man projected by Oedipus. Instead of repeating Descartes' motto, "I think, therefore I am," we have to do the thinking differently from some "other" perspectives.

In *Specters of Marx,* Derrida envisions that, after the fall of the subject, the "*other man*" or "man *as the other,*" i.e., "*the pure humanity of man*" (italic added),[7] will come, but most likely in a time framed in the same Oedipal calendar or the Hegelian history. Surprisingly, when this "other" did show up, according to post-humanists, he was not exactly human, but grotesque, in the true sense of the word. Consequently, post-humanism, for one, projects a different other with an alternative calendar, no longer grounded in a being of totality and singularity and no longer confined to the time of the Hegelian subject. The other that comes after the subject, from the post-humanist point of view, is not at all related to any ideas of totality and purity, but a cyborg instead of a replica of the singular being. That is why Francis Fukuyama in *Our Posthuman Future* revised his previous prediction presented in *The End of History and the Last Man* and anticipated the beginning of an *altered* man to the final form of the humanist history. As a result, instead of rehearsing another apocalyptic drama of the death of man, or being continuously obsessed with the same specter of singular ontology, we found ourselves to be inherently grotesque (post-human or not), *other* to all the ontological phantoms that haunt us. Like Nietzsche, in *Ecce Homo*, who would "prefer to be even a satyr than being a saint,"[8] Haraway declares, similarly, at the end of her manifesto for post-humanism: "I would rather be a cyborg than a goddess."[9] In short, the grotesque is a preferred state of being while the posture of divinity is simply a sublime illusion to be dispelled.

This project of the grotesque, in the main, entertains no excursion into post-humanist studies of the grotesque and thus leaves a huge space for future evolution of the grotesque along this trajectory. That is to say, the post-humanistic discourses will, one more time, probe the *riddling* game between Oedipus and the Sphinx, the ontology of unity and totality and heterologies of disparity and hybridity. So the *riddling* continues.

NOTES

1. Donna Haraway, "A Manifesto for Cyborgs: Science, Technology, and Socialist Feminism in the 1980's," in *Feminism/Postmodernisms*, ed. Linda J. Nicholson (New York, Routledge, 1990), 191.
2. Ibid., 193.
3. Ibid., 196.
4. Ibid., 192.
5. Ibid., 217.
6. Ibid., 215.
7. Jacques Derrida, *Specters of Marx: The State of the Debt, the Work of Mourning, and the New International*, trans. Peggy Kamuf (New York: Routledge, 1994), 74.
8. Friedrich Nietzsche, *On the Genealogy of Morals and Ecce Homo*, trans. Walter Kaufman (New York: Vintage, 1967), 217.
9. Haraway, "Manifesto," 223.

Bibliography

Abraham, Nicolas, and Maria Torok. *The Wolf Man's Magic Word: A Cryptonymy*. Translated by Nicholas Rand. Minneapolis: U of Minnesota P, 1986.

Adams, James Luther, and Wilson Yates. eds. *The Grotesque in Art and Literature: Theological Reflections*. Michigan: William B. Eerdmans P, 1997.

Adorno, Theodor. *Aesthetic Theory*. Translated by Robert Hullot-Kentor. Minneapolis: U of Minnesota P, 1997.

Althusser, Louis. "Ideology and Ideological State Apparatuses." In *Lenin and Philosophy and Other Essays*, 127–188. Translated by Ben Brewster, New York: Monthly Review P, 1971.

Anderson, Sherwood. "*Winesburg, Ohio": Text and Criticism*. Edited by John H. Perres. New York: Penguin Books, 1977.

Anzaldúa, Gloria E. *Borderlands/La Frontera: The New Mestiza*. San Francisco: Aunt Lute Books, 1999.

———. *Interviews/Entrevista*. Edited by AnaLouise Keating. New York: Routledge, 2000.

Arteaga, Alfred. *Chicano Poetics: Heterotexts and Hybridities*. New York: Cambridge UP, 1997.

Athanasiou, Athena, and Elena Tzelepis. "Thinking Difference as Different Thinking in Luce Irigaray's Deconstructive Genealogies." In *Rewriting Difference: Luce Irigaray and "The Greek,"* 1–14. Edited by Elena Tzelepis and Athena Athanasiou. Albany: SUNY P, 2010.

Augenbraum, Harold, and Margarite Fernández Olmas. eds. *US Latino Literature: A Critical Guide for Students and Teachers*. Westport: Greenwood P, 2000.

Bakhtin, Mikhail. *The Dialogical Imagination: Four Essays*. Edited by Michael Holquist. Translated by Caryl Emerson and Michael Holquist. Austin: U of Texas P, 1981.

———. *Rabelais and His World*. Translated by Helene Iswolsky. Bloomington: Indiana UP, 1984.

Barasch, Frances. *The Grotesque: A Study in Meaning*. The Hague: Mouton, 1971.

Barthes, Roland. *The Pleasure of the Text*. Translated by Richard Miller. New York: Hill and Wang, 1975.

Barvosa, Edwina. *Wealth of Selves: Multiple Identities, Mestiza Consciousness, and the Subject of Politics*. College Station: Texas A & M UP, 2008.

Bataille, Georges. *Visions of Excess: Selected Writings, 1927-1938*. Edited by Allan Stoekl. Translated by Allan Stoekl, Carl R. Lovitt, and Donald M. Leslie Jr. Minneapolis: U of Minnesota P, 1985.

Baudrillard, Jean. *The Illusion of the End*. Translated by Chris Turner. Stanford: Stanford UP, 1994.

———. *Simulations*. Translated by Paul Foss, Paul Patton, and Philip Beitchman. Cambridge: MIT P, 1983.

Benardete, Seth. "Sophocles' *Oedipus Tyrannus*." In *Sophocles: A Collection of Critical Essays*, 105–121. Edited by Thomas Woodard, New Jersey: Prentice-Hall, 1966.

Bernasconi, Robert, and Simon Critchley. eds. *Re-reading Levinas*. Bloomington: Indiana UP, 1991.

Bernstein, Michael Andre. *Bitter Carnival: Ressentiment and the Abject Hero*. Princeton: Princeton UP, 1992.

Bhabha, Homi K. "Cultural Diversity and Cultural Difference." In *African American Literary Criticism, 1773-2000*, 268–272. Edited by Hazel Arnett Ervin. New York: Twayne P, 1999.

———. *The Location of Culture*. London: Routledge, 1994.

———. "Signs Taken for Wonders: Questions of Ambivalence and Authority under a Tree Outside Delhi, May 1817." In *"Race," Writing and Difference*, 163–184. Edited by Henry Louis Gates Jr. Chicago: U of Chicago U, 1985.

Blanchot, Maurice. "Our Clandestine Companion." In *Face to Face with Levinas*, 41–52. Edited by Richard A. Cohen. Albany: SUNY P, 1986.

Bloom, Harold. ed. *Hispanic-American Writers*. Philadelphia: Chelsea House P, 1998.

Bost, Susie. *Mulattas and Mestiza: Representation of Mixed Identities in the Americas*. Athens and London: U of Georgia P, 2003.

Bower, Malcolm. *Lacan*. Cambridge: Harvard UP, 1991.

Bowie, Andrew. *Aesthetics and Subjectivity: From Kant to Nietzsche*. Manchester: Manchester UP, 1990.

Bozal, Valeriano, et al. *The Grotesque Factor*. Museo Picasso Málaga, 2013.

Brenkman, John. "The Other and the One: Psychoanalysis, Reading and the Symposium." In *Literature and Psychoanalysis: The Question of Reading: Otherwise*, 396–456. Edited by Shoshana Felman. Baltimore: Johns Hopkins UP, 1982.

Brinker-Gabler, Gisela. ed. *Encountering the Other(s): Studies in Literature, History, and Culture*. Albany: SUNY P, 1995.

Brogan, Kathleen. *Cultural Haunting: Ghosts and Ethnicity in Recent American Literature*. Charlottesville: U of Virginia P, 1998.

Brombert, Victor. *In Praise of Antiheroes: Figures and Themes in Modern European Literature: 1830-1980*. Chicago: U of Chicago P, 1999.

Brooks, Peter. "Freud's Masterplot." In *The Critical Tradition: Classical Texts and Contemporary Trends*, 2nd ed., 1033–1044. Edited by David Richter. New York: St. Martin's Press, 1998.

Burke, Janine. *The Sphinx on the Table: Sigmund Freud's Art Collection and the Development of Psychoanalysis*. New York: Walker & Co, 2006.

Burke, Peter. *Cultural Hybridity*. Cambridge: Polilty P, 2009.

Buse, Peter, and Andrew Stott. eds. *Ghosts: Deconstruction, Psychoanalysis, History*. London: Macmillan P, 1999.

Bush, Christopher. "The Other of the Other?: Cultural Studies, Theory, and the Location of the Modernist Signifier." *Comparative Literature Studies* 42, no. 2 (2005): 162–80.

Butler, Judith. *Bodies That Matter: On the Discursive Limits of Sex*. New York: Routledge, 1993.

———. *Gender Trouble: Feminism and the Subversion of Identity*. New York: Routledge, 1990.

———. *Subjects of Desire: Hegelian Reflections in Twentieth-Century France*. New York: Columbia UP, 1987.

Cadava, Eduardo, Peter Connor, and Jean-Luc Nancy. eds. *Who Comes After the Subject?* New York: Routledge, 1991.

Caputo, John D. "God is Wholly Other—Almost: Difference and the Hyperbolic Alterity of God." In *The Otherness of God*, 190–205. Edited by Orrin F. Summerell. Charlottesville: UP of Virginia, 1998.

Cassuto, Leonard. *The Inhuman Race: The Racial Grotesque in American Literature and Culture*. New York: Columbia UP, 1996.

Castricano, Jodey. *Cryptomimesis: The Gothic and Jacques Derrida's Ghost Writing*. Montreal: McGill-Queen's UP, 2001.

Chase, Cynthia. "Oedipal Textuality: Reading Freud's Reading of Oedipus." *Diacritics* 9 (1979): 54–68.

Chiesa, Lorenzo. *Subjectivity and Otherness: A Philosophical Reading of Lacan*. Cambridge: MIT P, 2007.

Cixous, Hélène. "Fiction and Its Phantoms: A Reading of Freud's 'Das Unheimliche' (The 'Uncanny')." *New Literary History* 7, no. 3 (1976): 525–48.

———. "The Laugh of the Medusa." In *The Critical Tradition: Classical Texts and Contemporary Trends*, 2nd ed., 1454–66. Edited by David Richter. New York: St. Martin's Press, 1998.

Clark, Katerina and Michael Holquist. *Mikhail Bakhtin*. Cambridge: Harvard UP, 1984.

Clark, John. *The Modern Satirical Grotesque and Its Tradition*. Lexington: Lexington UP, 1991.

Clayborough, Arthur. *The Grotesque in English Literature*. Oxford: Clarendon P, 1965.

Cohen, Richard A. ed. *Face to Face with Levinas*. Albany: SUNY P, 1986.

Connelly, Frances S. *The Grotesque in Western Art and Culture: Image at Play*. New York: Cambridge UP, 2012.

———. Introduction to *Modern Art and the Grotesque*, 1–19. Edited by Frances Connelly. Cambridge: Cambridge UP, 2003.

———. ed. *Modern Art and the Grotesque*. Cambridge: Cambridge UP, 2003.

Coronato, Rocco. *Jonson versus Bakhtin: Carnival and the Grotesque*. New York: Rodopi, 2003.

Critchley, Simon. "Prolegomena to Any Post-Deconstructive Subjectivity." In *Deconstructive Subjectivities*, 13–46. Edited by Simon Critchley and Peter Dews. New York: SUNY P, 1996.

Critchley, Simon, and Peter Dews. eds. *Deconstructive Subjectivities*. New York: SUNY P, 1996.

Crownfield, David R. ed. *Body/Text in Julia Kristeva: Religion, Women and Psychoanalysis*. Albany: SUNY P, 1992.

Cuddon, J. A. ed. *A Dictionary of Literary Terms and Literary Theory*. Cambridge: Blackwell, 1991.

Cutter, Martha J. *Lost and Found in Translation: Contemporary Ethnic American Writing and the Politics of Language Diversity*. Chapel Hill: U of North Carolina P, 2005.

Davis, Colin. *Haunted Subject: Deconstruction, Psychoanalysis and the Return of the Dead*. New York: Palgrave Macmillan, 2007.

Davis, Walter A. *Inwardness and Existence: Subjectivity in/and Hegel, Heidegger, Marx and Freud*. Madison: U of Wisconsin P, 1989.

Dean, Carolyn. *The Self and Its Pleasures: Bataille, Lacan, and the History of the Decentered Subject*. Ithaca: Cornell UP, 1992.

De Beauvoir, Simone. *The Second Sex*. Translated by H. M. Parshley. New York: Vintage Books, 1980.

De Certeau, Michel. *Heterologies: Discourse on the Other*. Translated by Brian Massumi. Minneapolis: U of Minnesota P, 1986.

———. *The Practice of Everyday Life*. Translated by Steven Rendall. Berkley: U of California P, 1984.

De Crévecoeur, St. John. *Letters from an American Farmer, 1782*. London: Chatto & Windus, 1905.

Deknatel, Frederick B. *Edvard Munch*. New York: Chanticleer Press, 1950.

Deleuze, Gilles. *Nietzsche and Philosophy*. Translated by Hugh Tomlinson. New York: Columbia UP, 1983.

Deleuze, Gilles, and Felix Guattari. *Anti-Oedipus: Capitalism and Schizophrenia*. Translated by Robert Hurley, Mark Semm, and Helen R. Lane. Minneapolis: U of Minnesota P, 1987.

———. *A Thousand Plateaus: Capitalism and Schizophrenia*. Trans. Brian Massumi. Minneapolis: U of Minnesota P, 1983.

De Man, Paul. *Allegories of Reading: Figural Language in Rousseau, Nietzsche, Rilke, and Proust*. New Haven: Yale UP, 1979.

———. *Blindness and Insight: Essays in the Rhetoric of Contemporary Criticism*. Minneapolis: U of Minnesota P, 1971.

Derrida, Jacques. *Adieu to Emmanuel Levinas*. Translated by Pascale-Ann Brault and Michael Nass. Stanford: Stanford UP, 1999.

———. *The Ear of the Other: Otobiography, Transference, Translation*. Translated by Peggy Kamuf. Edited by Christie McDonald. Lincoln: U of Nebraska P, 1988.

———. "'Eating Well,' or the Calculation of the Subject: An Interview with Jacques Derrida." In *Who Comes After the Subject*, 96 –119. Edited by Educardo Cadava. New York: Routledge, 1991.

———. "Fors: The Anglish Words of Nicolas Abraham and Maria Torok." In *The Wolf Man's Magic Word: A Cryptonymy*, xi-xlviii. Translated by Barbara Johnson. Edited by Nicolas Abraham and Maria Torok. Minneapolis: U of Minnesota P, 1986.

———. *The Gift of Death*. Translated by David Wills. Chicago: U of Chicago P, 1995.

———. *Of Spirit: Heidegger and the Question*. Translated by Geoffrey Bennington and Rachel Bowlby. Chicago: U of Chicago P, 1989.

———. *On the Name*. Translated by Thomas Dutoit. Stanford: Stanford UP, 1993.

———. *Positions*. Translated by Alan Bass. Chicago: U Chicago P, 1972.

———. *Specters of Marx: The State of the Debt, the Work of Mourning, and the New International*. Translated by Peggy Kamuf. New York: Routledge, 1994.

———. *Writing and Difference*. Translated by Alan Bass. Chicago: U of Chicago, 1978.

Desmond, William. *Desire, Dialectics, and Otherness: An Essay on Origins*. New Haven: Yale UP, 1987.

Doty, Robert. *Human Concern/Personal Torment: The Grotesque in American Art*. New York: Praeger Publishers, 1969.

Dunne, Robert. *A New Book of the Grotesques: Contemporary Approaches to Sherwood Anderson's Early Fiction*. Ohio: Kent UP, 2005.

Eagleton, Terry. *The Ideology of the Aesthetic*. Malden: Blackwell P, 1990.

Edmunds, Lowell. *Oedipus: The Ancient Legend and Its Later Analogues*. Baltimore: Johns Hopkins U, 1986.

———. "The Sphinx in the Oedipus Legend." In *Oedipus: A Folklore Casebook*, 147–73. Edited by Lowell Edmunds and Alan Dundes. New York: Garland P, 1983.

Edmunds, Lowell, and Alan Dundes. eds. *Oedipus: A Folklore Casebook*. New York: Garland P, 1983.

Edwards, Justin D, and Rune Graulund. *Grotesque*. New York: Routledge, 2013.

Ervin, Hazel Arnett. ed. *African American Literary Criticism, 1773-2000*. New York: Twayne P, 1999.

Feldstein, Richard, Bruce Fink, and Maire Jaanus. eds. *Reading Seminar XI Lacan's "Four Fundamental Concepts of Psychoanalysis."* Albany: SUNY P, 1995.

Felman, Shoshana. *Jacques Lacan and the Adventure of Insight: Psychoanalysis in Contemporary Culture*. Cambridge: Harvard UP, 1987.

———. ed. *Literature and Psychoanalysis: The Question of Reading: Otherwise*. Baltimore: Johns Hopkins UP, 1982.

Fletcher, John, and Andrew Benjamin. eds. *Abjection, Melancholy, and Love: The Works of Julia Kristeva*. London: Routledge, 1990.

Fludernik, Monika. "The Constitution of Hybridity: Postcolonial Intervention." In *Hybridity and Postcolonialism: Twentieth Century Indian Literature*, 19–54. Edited by Monika Fludernik. Stauffenburg Verlag, 1998.

———. ed. *Hybridity and Postcolonialism: Twentieth Century Indian Literature*. Stauffenburg Verlag, 1998.

———. Introduction to *Hybridity and Postcolonialism: Twentieth Century Indian Literature*, 9 –18. Edited by Monika Fludernik. Stauffenburg Verlag, 1998.

Foucault, Michel. *Language, Counter-Memory, Practice*. Edited by Donald F. Bouchard. Translated by Donald E. Bouchard and Sherry Simon. Ithaca: Cornell UP, 1977.

———. *The Order of Things: An Archaeology of the Human Sciences*. New York: Random, 1970.

Fowler, Roger. ed. *A Dictionary of Modern Critical Terms.* New York: Routledge & Kegan Paul, 1987.

Freud, Sigmund. *Civilization and Its Discontents.* Translated by James Strachey. New York: Norton, 1961.

———. *The Future of an Illusion.* Translated by James Strachey. New York: Norton, 1961

———. *The Interpretation of Dreams.* Translated by James Strachey. New York: Avon Books, 1965.

———. "On narcissism: An Introduction." In *The Standard Edition of the Complete Psychological Works of Sigmund Freud,* vol. 14, 73 –102. Translated by James Strachey. London: Hogarth P, 1955.

———. "The 'Uncanny.'" In *The Standard Edition of the Complete Psychological Works of Sigmund Freud,* vol. 17, 219–56. Translated by James Strachey. London: Hogarth P, 1955.

Frie, Roger. *Subjectivity and Intersubjectivity in Modern Philosophy and Psychoanalysis: A Study of Sartre, Binswanger, Lacan, and Habermas.* New York: Rowman & Littlefield P, 1997.

Friedman, Alan W. *Fictional Death and the Modernist Enterprise.* New York: Cambridge UP, 1995.

Fukuyama, Francis. *The End of History and the Last Man.* New York: Free P, 2006.

Gallop, Jane. *Reading Lacan.* Ithaca: Cornell UP, 1985.

Gasché, Rodolphe. *The Tain of the Mirror: Derrida and the Philosophy of Reflection.* Cambridge: Harvard UP, 1986.

Gates Jr., Henry Louis. ed. *"Race," Writing, and Difference.* Chicago: U of Chicago U, 1985.

Ginsburg, Ruth. "A Primal Scene of Reading: Freud and Hoffman." *Literature and Psychology* 38, no. 2 (1992): 24-46.

Ginsburg, Ruth. "The Pregnant Text: Bakhtin's Ur-Chronotope: The Womb." In *Bakhtin: Carnival and Other Subjects,* 165–76. Edited by David Shepherd. Amsterdam: Rodopi, 1993.

Girard, René. *Deceit, Desire and the Novel: Self and the Other in Literary Structure.* Translated by Y. Freccero. Baltimore: Johns Hopkins UP, 1965.

———. *Violence and the Sacred.* Translated by Patrick Gregory. Baltimore: Johns Hopkins UP, 1979.

Godzich, Wlad. Foreword to *Heterologies: Discourse on the Other,* by Michel de Certeau (vii-xxi). Minneapolis: U of Minnesota P, 1986.

Gombrich, E.H. *The Sense of Order: A Study in the Psychology of Decoration Art.* Ithaca: Cornel UP, 1979.

Goodwin, James. *Modern American Grotesque: Literature and Photography.* Columbus: Ohio State UP, 2009.

Gourgouris, Stathis. "Autonomy, Self-Alteration, Sexual Difference." In *Rewriting Difference: Luce Irigaray and "The Greek,"* 135–48. Edited by Elena Tzelepis and Athena Athanasious. Albany: SUNY P, 2010.

Goux, Jean-Joseph. *Oedipus, Philosopher.* Translated by Catherine Porter. Stanford: Stanford UP, 1993.

Graybeal, Jean. "Joying in the Truth of Self-Division." In *Body/Text in Julia Kristeva: Religion, Women and Psychoanalysis,* 129–38. Edited by David R. Crownfield. Albany: SUNY P, 1992.

Grobman, Laurie. *Multicultural Hybridity: Transforming American Literary Scholarship & Pedagogy.* Urbana: National Council of Teachers of English, 2007.

Gross Elizabeth. "The Body of Signification." In *Abjection, Melancholy and Love: The Work of Julia Kristeva,* 80–103. Edited by John Fletcher and Andrew Benjamin. London: Routledge, 1990.

Haar, Maria. *The Phenomenon of the Grotesque in Modern Southern Fiction: Some Aspects of its Form and Function.* Stockholm: Alquist and Wiksel International, 1983.

Habermas, Jűrgen. *The Philosophical Discourse of Modernity: Twelve Lectures.* Translated by Fredrick Lawrence. Cambridge: MIT Press, 1996.

Hall, Stuart. "Cultural Identity and Diaspora." In *Colonial Discourse and Postcolonial Theory,* 392–403. Edited by Patrick Williams and Laura Christma. New York: Columbia UP, 1994.

Hamilton, Victoria. *Narcissism and Oedipus: The Children of Psychoanalysis*. London: Routledge and Kegan Paul, 1982.

Hand, Sean. Introduction to *The Levinas Reader*, by Emmanuel Levinas, 1-8. Cambridge: Blackwell P, 1989.

Handelman, Susan. "Facing the Other: Levinas, Perelman, Rosenzweig." In *Divine Aporia: Postmodern Conversation about the Other*, 263 –87. Edited by John C. Hawley. Lewisburg: Bucknell UP, 2000.

Haraway, Donna. "A Manifesto for Cyborgs: Science, Technology, and Socialist Feminism in the 1980's," 190–233. In *Feminism/Postmodernism*. Ed. Linda J. Nicholson. New York: Routledge, 1990.

Hardt, Michael. Foreword to *Nietzsche and Philosophy*, by Gilles Deleuze, ix-xx. New York: Columbia UP, 1983.

Harmon, William, and Hugh Holman. eds. *A Handbook to Literature*. New Jersey: Pearson Prentice Hall, 2009.

Harpham, Geoffrey Galt. *On the Grotesque: Strategies of Contradiction in Art and Literature*. Princeton: Princeton UP, 1982.

———. "The Grotesque: The First Principle." *Journal of Aesthetics and Art Criticism* 34, no. 4 (1976): 461–68.

Hawley, John C. ed. *Divine Aporia: Postmodern Conversation about the Other*. Lewisburg: Bucknell UP, 2000.

Hegel, Georg Wilhelm Friedrich. *Aesthetics: Lectures on Fine Art*. Translated by T. M. Knox. Oxford: Clarendon P, 1975.

———. "Introduction to the Philosophy of Art." In *The Critical Tradition: Classical Texts and Contemporary Trends*, 2nd ed., 345–56. Edited by David Richter. New York: St. Martin's Press, 1998.

———. *Phenomenology of Spirit*. Translated by A. V. Miller. Oxford: Oxford UP, 1977.

———. *The Philosophy of History*. Translated by J. Sibree. New York: Dover, 1956.

Heidegger, Martin. *Basic Concepts*. Translated by Gary E. Aylesworth. Bloomington: Indiana UP, 1993.

———. *An Introduction to Metaphysics*. Translated by Ralph Manheim. New Haven: Yale UP, 1987.

Helbling, Robert E. *The Power of Negative Thinking: The Grotesque in Modern World*. Salt Lake City: Reynolds Association, 1982.

Heller, Reinhold. *Munch: His Life and Work*. Chicago: U of Chicago P, 1984.

Herbrechter, Stefan. *Lawrence Durrell, Postmodernism and the Ethnics of Alterity*. Atlanta: Rodopi, 1999.

Hicks, D. Emily. *Border Writing: The Multidimensional Text*. Minneapolis: U of Minnesota P, 1991.

———. "Deterritorialization and Border Writing." In *Ethics and Aesthetics: Post-modern Positions*, 47–58. Edited by Robert Merrill. DC: Maisonneuve P, 1988.

Holland, Nancy J. "The Death of the Other/Father: A Feminist Reading of Derrida's Hauntology." *Hypatia* 16, no. 1 (2001): 64-71.

Horkheimer, Max, and Theodor W. Adorno. *Dialectic of Enlightenment*. Translated by John Cumming. New York: Continuum, 1998.

Irigaray, Luce. "Questions to Emmanuel Levinas: On the Divinity of Love." Translated by Margaret Whitford. In *Re-reading Levinas*, 109–118. Edited by Robert Bernasconi and Simon Critchley. Bloomington: Indiana UP, 1991.

———. *Sexes and Genealogies*. Translated by Gillian C. Gill. New York: Columbia UP, 1993.

———. *Speculum of the Other Woman*. Translated by Gillian C. Gill. Ithaca: Cornell UP, 1985.

———. *This Sex Which Is Not One*. Translated by Catherine Porter. Ithaca: Cornel UP, 1985.

Jameson, Fredric. Foreword to *The Postmodern Condition: A Report on Knowledge*, by Jean-François Lyotard, vii-xxi. Minneapolis: U of Minnesota P, 1988.

———. "Imaginary and Symbolic in Lacan: Marxism, Psychoanalytic Criticism and the Problem of the Subject." In *Literature and Psychoanalysis: The Question of Reading: Otherwise*, 338–95. Edited by Shoshana Felman. Baltimore: Johns Hopkins UP, 1982.

———. *Postmodernism or The Cultural Logic of Late Capitalism.* Durham: Duke UP, 1991.

Jaurretch, Collen. ed. *European Joyce Studies Annual: Beckett, Joyce and the Art of the Negative.* New York: Rodopi, 2005.

Johnson, Samuel. "From *Preface to Shakespeare.*" In *The Critical Tradition: Classical Texts and Contemporary Trends*, 2nd ed., 224–239. Edited by David Richter. New York: St. Martin's Press, 1998.

Jonte-Pace, Diane. *Speaking the Unspeakable: Religion, Misogyny, and the Uncanny Mother in Freud's Cultural Texts.* Berkeley: U of California P, 2001

Kant, Immanuel. "From *Critique of Judgment.*" In *The Critical Tradition: Classical Texts and Contemporary Trends*, 2nd ed., 353–80. Edited by David Richter. New York: St. Martin's Press, 1998.

Kaup, Monika. "Crossing Borders: An Aesthetic Practice in Writings by Gloria Anzaldúa." In *Hispanic-American Writers*, 195–204. Edited by Harold Bloom. Philadelphia: Chelsea House P, 1998.

Kayser, Wolfgang J. *The Grotesque in Art and Literature.* Translated by Ulrich Weisstein. Bloomington: Indiana UP, 1963.

Kearney, Richard. ed. *Dialogues with Contemporary Continental Thinkers: The Phenomenological Heritage.* Manchester: Manchester UP, 1984.

Kovel, Joel. "Schizophrenic Being and Technocratic Society." In *Pathologies of the Modern Self: Postmodern Studies on Narcissism, Schizophrenia, and Depression*, 330-47. Edited by David Michael Levin. New York: New York UP, 1987.

Kristeva, Julia. *Black Sun: Depression And Melancholia.* Translated by Leon S. Roudiez. New York: Columbia UP, 1982.

———. *Desire in Language: A Semiotic Approach to Literature and Art.* Edited by Leon S. Roudiez. Translated by Thomas Gora, Alice Jardine, and Leon S. Roudiez. New York: Columbia UP, 1980.

———. *The Kristeva Reader.* Edited by Toril Moi. New York: Columbia UP, 1986.

———. *Powers of Horror: An Essay on Abjection.* Translated by Leon S. Roudiez. New York: Columbia UP, 1989.

———. *Strangers to Ourselves.* Translated by Leon S. Roudiez. New York: Columbia UP, 1991.

———. "Within the Microcosm of 'The Talking Cure.'" In *Interpreting Lacan,* 33–48. Edited by Joseph H. Smith and William Kerrigan. New Haven: Yale UP, 1983.

Kuortti, Joel, and Jopi Nyman. eds. *Reconstructing Hybridity: Post-Colonial Studies in Transition.* New York: Rodopi, 2007.

Lacan, Jacques. "Desire and the Interpretation of Desire in *Hamlet.*" In *Literature and Psychoanalysis: The Question of Reading: Otherwise*, 11–52. Edited by Shoshana Felman. Baltimore: Johns Hopkins UP, 1982.

———. *Ecrits: A Selection.* Translated by Alan Sheridan. New York: Norton, 1977.

———. *The Four Fundamental Concepts of Psychoanalysis.* Translated by Alan Sheridan. New York: Norton, 1978.

———. *Language of the Self: Function of Language in Psychoanalysis.* Translated by Anthony Wilden. Baltimore: Johns Hopkins UP, 1968.

———. "The Neurotic's Individual Myth." *Psychoanalytic Quarterly* 48 (1974): 405-422.

———. "Of Structure as an Immixing of an Otherness Prerequisite to Any Subject Whatever." In *Structuralist Controversy: The Languages of Criticism and the Sciences of Man*, 186–200. Edited by Richard Mackesy and Eugenio Donato. New Haven: Yale UP, 1970.

———. "Position of the Unconscious." In *Reading Seminar XI Lacan's "Four Fundamental Concepts of Psychoanalysis,*" 259–83. Edited by Richard Feldstein, Bruce Fink, and Maire Jaanus. Trans. Bruce Fink. Albany: SUNY P, 1995.

———. *The Psychoses: Seminar of Jacques Lacan, Book III 1955-1956.* Translated by Russell Grigg. Edited by Jacques-Alain Miller. London: Routledge, 1993.

———. *The Seminar of Jacques Lacan: Book I.* Translated by John Forrester. Edited by Jacques-Alan Miller. Cambridge: Cambridge UP, 1988.

———. *The Seminar of Jacques Lacan: Book II.* Translated by Sylbvana Tomaselli. Edited by Jacques-Alan Miller. Cambridge: Cambridge UP, 1988.

———. "Seminar on 'The Purloined Letter'." In *Literary Theories in Praxis*, 320–48. Edited by Shirley Staton. Philadelphia: U of Pennsylvania P, 1987.

———. *Television*. Translated by Denis Hollier, Rosalind Krauss, and Annette Michelson. New York: Norton. 1990.

Lachmann, Renate. "Bakhtin and Carnival: Culture as Counter-Culture." *Cultural Critique* 11 (1989-1990): 115-152.

Lakeland, Paul. "Is the Holy Wholly Other, and is the Wholly Other Really Holy? Reflections of the Postmodern Doctrine of God." In *Divine Aporia: Postmodern Conversation about the Other*, 57–69. Edited by John C. Hawley. Lewisburg: Bucknell UP, 2000.

Lasch, Christopher. *The Culture of Narcissism: American Life in an Age of Diminishing Expectations*. London: W. W. Norton, 1991.

Leitch, Vincent B. *Deconstructive Criticism: An Advanced Introduction*. New York: Columbia UP, 1982.

Lemaire, Anika. *Jacques Lacan*. Translated by David Macey. London: Routledge & Kegan Paul, 1979.

Levin, David Michael. ed. *Pathologies of the Modern Self: Postmodern Studies on Narcissism, Schizophrenia, and Depression*. New York: New York UP, 1987.

———. "Psychopathology in the Epoch of Nihilism." In *Pathologies of the Modern Self: Postmodern Studies on Narcissism, Schizophrenia, and Depression*, 21–83. Edited by David Michael Levin. New York: New York UP, 1987.

Levinas, Emmanuel. *Alterity and Transcendence*. Translated by Michael B Smith. New York: Columbia UP, 1999.

———. "Ethics of the Infinite." In *Dialogues with Contemporary Continental Thinkers: The Phenomenological Heritage*, 47 –70. Edited by Richard Kearney. Manchester: Manchester UP, 1984.

———. *The Levinas Reader*. Edited by Sean Hand. Cambridge: Blackwell P, 1989.

———. *Otherwise than Being or Beyond Essence*. Translated by Alphonso Lingis. The Hague, 1981.

———. *Outside the Subject*. Translated by Michael B. Smith. Stanford: Stanford UP, 1994.

———. "Philosophy and the Idea of the Infinite." Translated by Alfanso Lingis. In *To the Other: An Introduction to the Philosophy of Emmanuel Levinas*, 88 –119. Edited by Adriaan Peperzak. West Lafayette: Purdue UP, 1993

———. *Time and the Other*. Translated by Richard A. Cohen. Pittsburgh: Duquesne UP, 1978.

———. *Totality and Infinity: An Essay on Exteriority*. Translated by Alphonso Lingis. Pittsburg: Duquesne UP, 1969.

———. "The Trace of the Other." In *Deconstruction in Context: Literature and Philosophy*, 345–59. Edited by Mark Taylor. Chicago: U of Chicago P, 1986.

Lukács, George. "The Ideology of Modernism." In *The Critical Tradition: Classical Texts and Contemporary Trends*, 2nd ed., 1127–41. Edited by David Richter. New York: St. Martin's Press, 1998.

Lyotard, Jean-François. "Levinas' Logic." In *Face to Face with Levinas*, 117–58. Edited by Richard A. Cohen. Albany: SUNY P, 1986.

———. *The Postmodern Condition: A Report on Knowledge*. Translated by Geoff Bennington and Brian Massumi. Minneapolis: U of Minnesota P, 1988.

Lydenberg, Robin. "Freud's Uncanny Narrative." *PMLA* 12, no. 5 (1997): 1072-1086.

Mackesy, Richard, and Eugenio Donato. eds. *Structuralist Controversy: The Languages of Criticism and the Sciences of Man*. New Haven: Yale UP, 1970.

Mahony, Patriack J. *Cries of the Wolf Man*. New York: International UP, 1984

———. *Freud and the Rat Man*. New Haven: Yale UP, 1986.

Malone, Kareen Ror, and Stephen R. Friedlander. eds. *The Subject of Lacan: A Lacanian Reader for Psychologists*. Albany: SUNY P, 2000.

Man, Thomas. "Conrad's Secret Agent." In *The Art of Joseph Conrad: A Critical Symposium*, 227–34. Edited by R. W. Stallman: East Lansing: Michigan UP, 1960.

Marini, Marcelle. *Jacques Lacan: The French Context*. Translated by Anne Tomiche. New Jersey: Rutgers UP, 1992.

Marion, Jean-Luc. *God Without Being*. Translated by Thomas A. Carlson. Chicago: U of Chicago P, 1991.

Markaryk, Irena R. ed. *Encyclopedia of Contemporary Literary Theory: Approaches, Scholars, Terms*. U Toronto P, 1993.

McElroy, Bernard. *Fiction of the Modern Grotesque*. Basingstoke: Macmillan, 1989.

Meindl, Dieter. *American Fiction and the Metaphysics of the Grotesque*. Columbia: U of Missouri P, 1996.

Merrill, Robert. ed. *Ethics and Aesthetics: Post-Modern Positions*. DC: Maisonneuve P, 1988.

Meyer, Michael. ed. *Literature and the Grotesque*. Amsterdam: Rodopi, 1995.

———. Introduction to *Literature and the Grotesque*, by Michael Meyer, i–iii. Amsterdam: Rodopi, 1995.

Montag, Warren. "Spirits Armed and Unarmed: Derrida's *Specters of Marx*." In *Ghostly Demarcations: A Symposium on Jacques Derrida's Specters of Marx*, 68–82. Edited by Michael Sprinker. London: Verso, 1999.

Muller, John P. "Language, Psychosis, and the Subject in Lacan." In *Interpreting Lacan*, 21–32. Edited by Joseph H. Smith and William Kerrigan. New Haven: Yale UP, 1983.

Murfin, Ross, and Supryia M Ray. eds. *The Bedford Glossary of Critical and Literary Terms*. Boston: Bedford Books, 1997.

Nelson, Linda. ed. *Feminism/Postmodernism*. New York: Routledge, 1990.

Ngai, Mae M. "Transnationalism and the Transformation of the 'Other': Response to the President Address." *American Quarterly* 57, no.1 (2005): 59-65.

Nietzsche, Friedrich. *The Birth of Tragedy and the Genealogy of Morals*. Translated by Francis Golffing. New York: Doubleday, 1956.

———. *The Gay Science*. Edited by Bernard Williams. Translated by Josephine Nauckhoff. Cambridge: Cambridge UP, 2001.

———. *On the Genealogy of Morals and Ecce Homo*. Translated by Walter Kaufman. New York: Vintage, 1967.

———. *Twilight of the Idols, Or, How to Philosophize with the Hammer*. Translated by Richard Polt. Indianapolis: Hackett P, 1997.

———. *Twilight of the Idols and The Anti-Christ*. Translated by R. J. Hollindale. London: Penguin, 2003.

———. *The Will to Power*. Translated by Walter Kaufmann and R. J. Hollingdale. New York: Vintage, 1968.

O'Connor, Mary. "Horror, Authors, and Heroes: Gendered Subjects and Objects in Bakhtin and Kristeva." In *Bakhtin: Carnival and Other Subjects*, 242–58. Edited by David Shepherd. Amsterdam: Rodopi, 1993.

O'Connor, William Van. *The Grotesque: An American Genre and Other Essays*. Carbondale: Southern Illinois UP, 1962.

Oliver, Kelly. *Reading Kristeva: Unraveling the Double-Bind*. Bloomington: Indiana UP, 1993.

Pefanis, Julian. *Heterology and the Postmodern: Bataille, Baudrillard, and Lyotard*. Durham: Duke UP, 1991.

Peperzak, Adriaan. *To the Other: An Introduction to the Philosophy of Emmanuel Levinas*. West Lafayette: Purdue UP, 1993.

Pontalis, J. B. *Frontiers in Psychoanalysis: Between the Dream and Psychic Pain*. Translated by Catherine Cullen and Philip Cullen. New York: International UP, 1981.

Pucci, Pietro. *Oedipus and the Fabrication of the Father*. Baltimore: Johns Hopkins UP, 1992.

Puelles, Luis. "Nothing Under One's Feet: Approaches to an Aesthetic of the Grotesque." In *The Grotesque Factor*, by Valeriano Bozal et al, 19 -58. Museo Picasso Málaga, 2013.

Ragland-Sullivan, Ellie. *Jacques Lacan and Philosophy of Psychoanalysis*. Chicago: U of Illinois P, 1986.

Rabaté, Jean-Michel. *The Ghosts of Modernity*. Gainesville: UP of Florida, 1996.

Regier, Willis Goth. *Book of the Sphinx*. Lincoln: U of Nebraska P, 2004

Reiffenrath, Tanja. *At Borders and Crossroads: Conceptualizing the New Mestiza in Chicana*. Műnchen: AVM, 2008.

Reik, Theodor. *Dogma and Compulsion: Psychoanalytic Studies of Religion and Myths*. Westport: Greenwood P, 1951.

Rella, Franco. *The Myth of the Other: Lacan, Deleuze, Foucault, Bataille*. Translated by Nelson Moe. Maisonneuve P, 1994.

Richter, David. ed. *The Critical Tradition: Classical Texts and Contemporary Trends*, 2rd ed. New York: St. Martin's Press, 1998.

Roberts, Kathleen Glenister. *Alterity and Narrative: Stories and the Negotiation of Western Identities*. Albany: SUNY P, 2007.

Róheim, Géza. *The Riddle of the Sphinx or Human Origins*. Translated by R. Money-Kyrle. London: Hogarth P, 1934.

Ross, Christine. "Redefinitions of Abjection in Contemporary Performances of the Female Body." In *Modern Art and the Grotesque*, 281–290. Ed. Frances S. Connelly. Cambridge: Cambridge UP, 2003.

Rothstein, Arnold. *The Narcissistic Pursuit of Perfection*. New York: International UP, 1984.

Roudinesco, Elisabeth. *Jacques Lacan & Co: A History of Psychoanalysis in France: 1925-1985*. Translated by Jeffrey Mehlman. Chicago: U of Chicago P, 1986.

Rudnytsky, Peter. *Freud and Oedipus*. New York: Columbia UP, 1987.

Ruskin, John. *The Stones of Venice*, vol. 3. London: Dent, 1907.

Russo, Mary. *The Female Grotesque: Risk, Excess and Modernity*. New York: Routledge, 1994.

Schiesari, Julianna. *The Gendering of Melancholia: Feminism, Psychoanalysis, and the Symbolics of Loss in Renaissance Literature*. Ithaca: Cornell UP, 1992.

Schneiderman, Stuart. *Rat Man*. New York: New York UP, 1977.

Schwab, Gabriele. *The Mirror and the Killer-Queen: Otherness in Literary Language*. Bloomington: Indiana UP, 1996.

Segal, Charles. *Oedipus Tyrannus: Tragic Heroism and the Limits of Knowledge*. New York: Twayne P, 1993.

Seigneuret, Jean-Charles. ed. *Dictionary of Literary Terms and Motifs*. New York: Greenwood P, 1988.

Selz, Jean. *Edvard Munch*. New York: Crown P, 1974.

Shakespeare, William. *The Tragedy of Hamlet, Prince of Denmark*. New York: Pocket Books, 1992.

Shepherd, David. ed. *Bakhtin: Carnival and the Other Subjects*. Amsterdam: Rodopi, 1993.

Smith, Jeanne Rosier. *Writing Tricksters: Mythical Gambols in American Ethnic Literature*. Berkley: U of California P, 1997.

Smith, Joseph H, and William Kerrigan. eds. *Interpreting Lacan*. New Haven: Yale UP, 1983.

Smith, Paul. *Discerning the Subject*. Minneapolis: U of Minnesota P, 1988.

Smith, William. ed. *A Dictionary of Greek and Roman Biography and Mythology*, vol. 3. Boston: Little Brown & Co, 1867.

Spiegel, Alan. "A Theory of the Grotesque in Southern Fiction." *Georgia Review* 26 (1977): 426–27.

Sprengnether, Madelon. *The Spectral Mother: Freud, Feminism, and Psychoanalysis*. Ithaca: Cornell UP, 1990

Sprinker, Michael. ed. *Ghostly Demarcations: A Symposium on Jacques Derrida's Specters of Marx*. London: Verso, 1999.

Stallman, R. W. ed. *The Art of Joseph Conrad: A Critical Symposium*. East Lansing: Michigan UP, 1960.

Stallybrass, Peter, and Allon White. *The Politics and Poetics of Transgression*. Ithaca: Cornell UP, 1986.

Stang, Ragna. *Edvard Munch: The Man and His Art*. Translated by Geoffrey Culverwell. New York: Abbeville P, 1986.

Staton, Shirley. ed. *Literary Theories in Praxis*. Philadelphia: U of Pennsylvania P, 1987.

Strandberg, Victor. "The Crisis of Belief in Modern Literature." *The English Journal* 53, no.7 (1964): 465–54.

Summerell, Orrin F. ed. *The Otherness of God*. Charlottesville: UP of Virginia, 1998.

Swain, Virginia. *Grotesque Figures: Baudelaire, Rousseau, and the Aesthetics of modernity*. Baltimore: Johns Hopkins UP, 2004.

Taylor, Mark C. *Altarity*. Chicago: U of Chicago P, 1987.

———. ed. *Deconstruction in Context: Literature and Philosophy*. Chicago: U of Chicago P, 1986.

———. Introduction to *Deconstruction in Context: Literature and Philosophy*, 1–34. Edited by Mark Taylor. Chicago: U of Chicago P, 1986.

Terdiman, Richard "The Marginality of Michel de Certeau." *The South Atlantic Quarterly* 100, no.2 (2001): 399–421.

Thomson, Philip John. *The Grotesque*. London: Methuen, 1972.

Tod, Jane. "The Veiled Woman in Freud's 'Das Unheimliche'." *Signs: Journal of Women in Culture and Society* 12, no.3 (1986): 519–26.

Todorov, Tventan. *Mikhail Bakhtin: The Dialogic Principle*. Translated by Wlad Godzich. Minneapolis: U of Minnesota P, 1984.

Torres, Hector A. "In Context: Gloria Anzaldúa's *Borderlands/La Frontera: The New Mestiza*." In *US Latino Literature: A Critical Guide for Students and Teachers*, 123 –34. Edited by Harold Augenbraum and Margarite Fernández Olmas. Westport: Greenwood P, 2000.

Treanor, Brian. *Aspects of Alterity: Levinas, Marcel, and the Contemporary Debate*. New York: Fordham UP, 2006.

Tzelepis, Elena, and Athena Athanasiou. eds. *Rewriting Difference: Luce Irigaray and "The Greek."* Albany: SUNY P, 2010.

Uruburu, Paula. *The Gruesome Doorway: An Analysis of the American Grotesque*. New York: Peter Lang, 1987.

Van Pelt, Tamise. "Otherness." *Postmodern Culture* 10 no. 2 (2000): 1–47.

Vernant, Jean-Pierre, and Pierre Vidal-Naquet. *Tragedy and Myth in Ancient Greece*. Translated by Janet Lloyd. Brighton: The Harvester Press Limited, 1981.

Vitruvius, Marcus. *De Architectura*. Translated by Frank Granger, New York, 1934.

Weber, Samuel. *The Return to Freud: Jacques Lacan's Dislocation of Psychoanalysis*. Cambridge: Cambridge UP, 1991.

Wilden, Anthony. "Lacan and Discourse of the Other." In *Language of the Self: Function of Language in Psychoanalysis*, by Jacques Lacan, 159–311. Baltimore: Johns Hopkins UP, 1968

Williams, Patrick, and Laura Christma. eds. *Colonial Discourse and Postcolonial Theory*. New York: Columbia UP, 1994.

Woodard, Thomas. ed. *Sophocles: A Collection of Critical Essays*. New Jersey: Prentice-Hall, 1966.

Yates, Wilson. "An Introduction to the Grotesque: Theoretical and Theological consideration." In *The Grotesque in Art and Literature: Theological Reflections*, 1–68. Edited by James Luther Adams and Wilson Yates. Michigan: William B. Eerdmans P, 1997.

Young, Julian. *Nietzsche's Philosophy of Art*. Cambridge: Cambridge UP, 1992.

Young, Robert C. *Colonial Desire: Hybridity in Theory, Culture and Race*. London: Routledge, 1995.

Yuan, Yuan. "From Ideology of Loss to Aesthetics of Absence: The Endgame in Beckett's *The Lost Ones*." In *European Joyce Studies Annual: Beckett, Joyce and the Art of the Negative*," 235–46. Edited by Collen Jaurretch. New York: Rodopi, 2005.

———. "The Lacanian Subject and Grotesque Desires: Between Oedipal Violation and Narcissistic Closure." *The American Journal of Psychoanalysis* 56, no. 1 (1996): 35–47.

———. "Narcissism of Quentin in *The Sound and the Fury*: Mirror, Play and Melancholy." *Studies of Psychoanalytic Theories* 1, no.1 (1992): 69–86.

Zamperini, Alessandra. *Ornament and the Grotesque: Fantastic Decoration from Antiquity to Art Nouveau*. Translated by Peter Spring. London: Thames & Hudson, 2008.

Zandstra, Dianne Marie. *Embodying Resistance: Griselda Gambaro and the Grotesque*. Lewisburg: Bucknell UP, 2007.

Ziarek, Ewa. "At the Limits of Discourse: Heterogeneity, Alterity, and the Maternal Body in Kristeva's Thought." *Hypatia* 7, no. 2 (1992): 92–108.

Zizek, Slavoj. *Looking Awry: An Introduction to Jacques Lacan Through Popular Culture*. Cambridge: MIT, 1991.

Index

www.ingramcontent.com/pod-product-compliance
Lightning Source LLC
LaVergne TN
LVHW101446200926
848483LV00001B/65